# MORE
## STORY
### S-T-R-E-T-C-H-E-R-S

# MORE STORY S-T-R-E-T-C-H-E-R-S

## More Activities to Expand Children's Favorite Books

Shirley C. Raines and Robert J. Canady

gryphon house

Mt. Rainier, Maryland

# ACKNOWLEDGMENTS

**CHAPTER 1**

Jacket illustration from **I LIKE ME!** by Nancy Carlson. Copyright © 1988 by Nancy Carlson. Reprinted by permission of Viking Kestrel, a division of Penguin USA.

Jacket illustration from **QUICK AS A CRICKET** by Audrey Wood, illustrated by Don Wood. Copyright © 1982 by M. Twinn. Reprinted by permission of Child's Play (International) Ltd.

Jacket illustration from **SILLY FRED** by Karen Wagner, illustrated by Normand Chartier. Text copyright © 1989 by Karen Wagner. Illustrations copyright © 1989 by Normand Chartier. Reprinted by permission of Macmillan Publishing Company, a division of Macmillan, Inc.

Jacket illustration from **SOMETHING TO CROW ABOUT** by Megan Halsey Lane. Copyright © 1990 by Megan Halsey Lane. Reprinted by permission of Dial Books for Young Readers, a division of Penguin USA.

Jacket illustration from **TACKY THE PENGUIN** by Helen Lester, illustrated by Lynn Munsinger. Text copyright © 1988 by Helen Lester. Illustrations copyright © 1988 by Lynn Munsinger. Reprinted by permission of Houghton Mifflin Company.

Library of Congress Catalog Number: 91–71105

Design: Graves Fowler Associates
Cover Photo: Lauri M. Bridgeforth

**Publisher's Cataloging in Publication**
*(Prepared by Quality Books Inc.)*

Raines, Shirley C.
    More story stretchers : more activities to expand children's favorite books / Shirley C. Raines and Robert J. Canady.—
    p. cm.
    Includes bibliographical references and index.
    ISBN 0-87659-153-5

    1. Early childhood education—Activity programs—Handbooks, manuals, etc. 2. Children's literature—Bibliography. 3. Teaching—Aids and devices—Handbooks, manuals, etc. 4. Children—Books and reading—Handbooks, manuals, etc. I. Canady, Robert J. II. Title.

LB1139.35.A37          372.6'4'044
                         QBI91-547

**CHAPTER 2**

Jacket illustration from **ARTHUR'S BABY** by Marc Brown. Copyright © 1987 by Marc Brown. Reprinted by permission of Little, Brown and Company.

Jacket illustration from **DADDY MAKES THE BEST SPAGHETTI** by Anna Grossnickle Hines. Copyright © 1986 by Anna Grossnickle Hines. Reprinted by permission of Clarion Books.

Jacket illustration from **LOVING** by Ann Morris, photographs by Ken Heyman. Text copyright © 1990 by Ann Morris. Photographs copyright © 1990 by Ken Heyman. Reprinted by permission of Greenwillow Books, a division of William Morrow and Company, Inc.

Jacket illustration from **MY GREAT GRANDPA** by Martin Waddell, illustrated by Dom Mansell. Text copyright © 1990 by Martin Waddell. Illustrations copyright © 1990 by Dom Mansell. Reprinted by permission of G.P. Putnam's Sons, a division of The Putnam & Grosset Group.

Jacket illustration from **A WALK IN THE RAIN** by Ursel Scheffler, illustrated by Ulises Wensell. Copyright © 1984 by Otto Maier Verlag. English translation copyright © 1986 by G.P. Putnam's Sons. Reprinted by permission of G.P. Putnam's Sons, a division of The Putnam & Grosset Group.

**CHAPTER 3**

Jacket illustration from **A HOME** by Nola Malone. Copyright © 1988 by Nola Langner Malone. Reprinted by permission of Bradbury Press, an affiliate of Macmillan, Inc.

Jacket illustration from **IRA SLEEPS OVER** by Bernard Waber. Copyright © 1972 by Bernard Waber. Reprinted by permission of Houghton Mifflin Company.

Jacket illustration from **JESSICA** by Kevin Henkes. Copyright © 1989 by Kevin Henkes. Reprinted by permission of Greenwillow Books, a division of William Morrow & Company, Inc.

Jacket illustration from **MY FRIEND LESLIE: The Story of a Handicapped Child** by Maxine B. Rosenberg, photographs by George Ancona. Text copyright © 1983 by Maxine B. Rosenberg. Photographs copyright © 1983 by George Ancona. Reprinted by permission of Lothrop, Lee and Shepard, a division of William Morrow & Company, Inc.

Jacket illustration from **WE ARE BEST FRIENDS** by Aliki. Copyright © 1982 by Aliki Brandenberg. Reprinted by permission of Greenwillow Books, a division of William Morrow and Company, Inc.

**CHAPTER 4**

Jacket illustration from **AARON'S SHIRT** by Deborah Gould, illustrated by Cheryl Harness. Text copyright © 1989 by Deborah Gould. Illustrations copyright © by Cheryl Harness. Reprinted by permission of Bradbury Press, an affiliate of Macmillan, Inc.

Jacket illustration from **FEELINGS** by Joanne Brisson Murphy, illustrated by Heather Collins. Text copyright © 1985 by Joanne Brisson Murphy. Illustrations copyright © 1985 by Heather Collins. Reprinted by permission of Black Moss Press.

Jacket illustration from **SLOPPY KISSES** by Elizabeth Winthrop, illustrated by Anne Burgess. Text copyright © 1980 by Elizabeth Winthrop Mahony. Illustrations copyright © 1980 by Anne Burgess Ashley. Reprinted by permission of Puffin Books, a division of Penguin USA.

Jacket illustration from **THE TEMPER TANTRUM BOOK** by Edna Mitchell Preston, illustrated by Rainey Bennet. Text copyright © 1969 by Edna Mitchell Preston. Illustrations copyright © 1969 by Rainey Bennett. Reprinted by permission of Puffin Books, a division of Penguin USA.

*To Bill Martin, Jr.*
*who helped us hear the "music in the language"*
*— Canady & Raines*


*To the memory of*
*Mrs. Elizabeth Jackson,*
*affectionately known as "Miss Elizabeth"*
*who said you can "teach and write"*
*— Raines*

# PREFACE

THIS IS THE SECOND BOOK IN WHAT WE hope will become a series of books on a literature-based curriculum for early childhood education. Our first book from Gryphon House was STORY S-T-R-E-T-C-H-E-R-S: ACTIVITIES TO EXPAND CHILDREN'S FAVORITE BOOKS. Aptly named, this second book is a collection of "more story s-t-r-e-t-c-h-e-r-s." We followed the same format and design of the first book because you, as teachers, librarians and parents who purchased the book and talked with us at conferences, workshops and autograph parties around the country, told us you wanted the same format and design. However, we also listened to you and made some changes. We added three new thematic units you requested. The three new themes are "I Am Me, I Am Special, Look What I Can Do," "Animals, Real and Fanciful" and "Plants — I Like Growing Things."

For this second book, we selected 90 books different than those found in the first STORY S-T-R-E-T-C-H-E-R-S and also provided different books for the additional references listed at the end of the chapter. In addition to the storyline descriptions and suggestions for 90 circle time presentations of the featured books, there are five extension suggestions per book or 450 story s-t-r-e-t-c-h-e-r-s to integrate the stories across the curriculum.

The idea of a literature-based early childhood curriculum is one which has been simmering in our minds for many years. We, like many of you, used children's books as an integral part of the curriculum, but always felt there were many more possibilities for connecting the books to other areas. When we were teachers and center directors, we used many of the ideas in this book with young children. But as wonderful new books came on the market and as heightened interest grew in providing a "print-rich and literature-rich" environment for young children, it seemed the right time to collect our ideas, organize them and place them in the hands of teachers, librarians and parents.

You may wonder why some of your children's favorite books were not selected. There are many excellent children's books which cannot be stretched easily or extended into activities for other areas of the curriculum. To extend the book somehow takes away from the "essence" of the story. Some of these books have a particularly powerful theme, as THE TENTH GOOD THING ABOUT BARNEY (Viorst, 1971), or FRIDAY NIGHT IS PAPA NIGHT (Sonneborn, 1987) or KNOTS ON A COUNTING ROPE (Martin & Archambault, 1987). While these books with their sensitive themes or keenly edged plots are wonderful selections for reading aloud and for discussion, somehow it trivializes the theme or the plot to stretch the book to other areas of the curriculum. However, these read aloud books become even more potent when paired with other books which can be stretched and the main ideas studied in the units on "Pets," or "Families" or "I Am Me, I Am Special, Look What I Can Do."

We wrote both the story s-t-r-e-t-c-h-e-r books as a way to support teachers who develop environments where young children grow to love books, poems, jokes, riddles, songs — the stories of our culture. As professors and consultants, we study language development and emerging literacy, and we observe children becoming interested in literature. We know that the books and the story s-t-r-e-t-c-h-e-r-s support teachers in their quest for well-developed literate environments for young children while retaining the concept development and resources which also support a sound curriculum.

We are indebted to the students and teachers enrolled in classes at George Mason University in Fairfax, Virginia, and Marymount University in Arlington, Virginia, who field-tested many of the ideas with the children they teach. We also appreciate the early childhood educators from a creative teaching course at Northeastern State University in Tahlequah, Oklahoma. It was their inspiration that caused us to write our ideas for other teachers to use. You will find teachers' names mentioned throughout the book when we adapted ideas from their classrooms. We would be remiss, however, if we did not thank three of our best consultants for our first book, Michelle, Damien and Tina Roberts, our grandchildren. Even as they have gotten older, they are good critics and continue to connect us to some of the new books which young children will enjoy. Finally, our loving thoughts go to Irene and Athel Raines and to the memory of Polly and Bob Canady because they loved us when we were children and taught us to love a good story.

We have been fortunate to work with the fine professionals at Gryphon House. Leah Curry-Rood, with her vast knowledge of children's literature, has a keen eye for stories which will delight and intrigue young children. She introduced us to many new books and was right on target regarding children's appreciation of the stories when the books were read aloud. Sarabeth Goodwin produced and formatted the book, making it one of the most attractive and usable resource books available to teachers. Kathy Charner edited the manuscript and helped us stay true to our goal of keeping active learning at center stage. We also must thank Larry Rood for guiding us in this writing project and for seeing the "possibilities" when we first came to him with the idea of a different kind of curriculum book.

Over the years when we spoke about a literature-based early childhood curriculum, teachers often asked if we had a book of these teaching ideas. Finally, we can say, "Yes, two books —STORY S-T-R-E-T-C-H-E-R-S: ACTIVITIES TO EXPAND CHILDREN'S FAVORITE BOOKS and now a second book, MORE STORY S-T-R-E-T-C-H-E-R-S: ACTIVITIES TO EXPAND CHILDREN'S FAVORITE BOOKS."

Shirley C. Raines, Ed.D., Associate Professor, George Mason University, Fairfax, Virginia

Robert J. Canady, Ed.D., Professor, Marymount University, Arlington, Virginia

## References From The Preface

Martin, Bill, Jr., & Archambault, John. (1987). **KNOTS ON A COUNTING ROPE.** New York: Henry Holt.

Sonneborn, Ruth. (1987). Illustrated by Emily McCully. **FRIDAY NIGHT IS PAPA NIGHT.** New York: Penguin.

Viorst, Judith. (1971). Illustrated by Eric Blegvad. **THE TENTH GOOD THING ABOUT BARNEY.** New York: Atheneum.

# INTRODUCTION

"READ IT AGAIN!" IS THE PLEA WHEN CHILD and story connect. A good teacher knows by the giggles, the sighs, the absolute stillness and by the way the children inch closer that a book is a "read-it-again" story. The love of a good story, the classic ones, the humorous ones, the sad tales, the tall tales, the chants and rhymes that get stuck in our heads, the bold graphics, the weepy watercolors, the muted charcoals, the funny cartoons— the reasons children shout, "Read it again!" are as varied and rich as the authors' and illustrators' imaginations.

Knowing young children's love of good stories, we devised "story s-t-r-e-t-c-h-e-r-s" as a means to extend that enthusiasm and better connect children's books and teaching ideas with other areas of the curriculum. This book, the second in a series, is a literature-based approach to planning circle time, centers and activities organized around themes often found in the early childhood curriculum.

As former teachers and center directors and now as teacher educators, we know the importance of reading to children every day. After hearing that message over and over in the methods classes we teach at our universities, we tell our students a little story which they all remember. We tell them we are going to stand on the graduation platform beside the president of the university and before the president can give the students their diplomas, they must repeat, "I do solemnly swear that I will read to my children every day." And while we've never stood beside the president of the university and included that vow in the graduation ceremony, when they see us afterward, they always say, "I do, I will, I promise, I'll read to my children every day."

Over the years, as teachers read to their children every day, they find favorite stories which children request and favorite books which the teachers themselves enjoy. As in the first story s-t-r-e-t-c-h-e-r-s book, we selected some old favorites, classics, which have stood the test of time, and we included some new favorites which teachers, librarians and children called to our attention. From the hundreds of new children's books on the market, we also chose new ones which bookstore owners recommended, and then we asked teachers to read them to their classes and tell us the children's responses. We also verified that the books we selected are currently in print and readily available.

From our research on emerging literacy behaviors and from our experiences in the classroom, we know that children who have an environment at home and at school where they are read to and where they interact with adults about books usually become good readers. Therefore, we encourage you to use story s-t-r-e-t-c-h-e-r-s not only for their importance in promoting children's interest in books and the payoff that they are more likely to become good readers in later schooling, but also because the activities have immediate value. The children and the teachers enjoy the story s-t-r-e-t-c-h-e-r-s because they are inherently interesting and appealing.

The first story s-t-r-e-t-c-h-e-r-s book was written for classrooms with young children, three, four and five year-olds. However, we heard from bookstore owners and librarians that first and second grade teachers were also purchasing the book. We are delighted with this response because the active hands-on learning which connects "child and story and curriculum" is key at whatever the grade level. MORE STORY S-T-R-E-T-C-H-E-R-S: MORE ACTIVITIES TO EXPAND CHILDREN'S FAVORITE BOOKS was also written as an active learning resource book to connect child and story and curriculum. We continue to focus on young children, but for us, early childhood includes first and second grade, and we are convinced that primary teachers will find this book appropriate and adaptable for them as well. They, like all creative teachers, will modify our suggestions to fit their children.

## About The Format Of The Book

As in our first story s-t-r-e-t-c-h-e-r-s book, we acknowledge that early childhood teachers plan the curriculum around "themes." Therefore, we organized each of the eighteen chapters around a common theme or unit taught in early childhood classrooms. For example, there are chapters on the themes of feelings, the different seasons, pets, transportation and friendship. Five books have been selected for each of the eighteen themes, 90 books in all. Each of the books has a suggested way to present the book during circle time, followed by five extension activities: 90 circle time presentations and 450 active learning ideas which have children's literature as their foundation. Story s-t-r-e-t-c-h-e-r-s, then, are teaching ideas for active learning based on the stories in children's favorite books.

In each chapter, the books selected for the theme are stretched into different centers or activities which usually take place in a well-planned early childhood classroom. We have story s-t-r-e-t-c-h-e-r-s for art activities, the block building center, creative dramatics, cooking and snack time, the housekeeping and dress-up corner, the library corner including the writing center, the mathematics and manipulatives center, music and movement, the sand table, science and nature, the water table and the woodworking bench. Each book is stretched into the five activities or centers which best fit that book.

A photograph of the cover of the book and a description of the storyline and illustrations introduces each book in the chapter. A brief example of ways to stretch the story during circle time follows the storyline description. The circle time book then will have story s-t-r-e-t-c-h-e-r-s for five activities or centers which

best connect that book and the curriculum. For each story s-t-r-e-t-c-h-e-r, we listed "what the children will learn," "materials needed," "what to do" and in the "something to think about" section we added pointers about the topic or about guiding children's behavior. A list of additional children's books related to the theme is provided at the end of each chapter. Teachers can read these books at other group times and provide them in the class library for individual children or small groups to explore on their own.

The schedule for story s-t-r-e-t-c-h-e-r-s fits the schedule most effective teachers of young children already follow. Children participate in a large group circle time activity, and then they are free to choose the centers and activities they want during a large block of time called free play or center time. Many early childhood teachers have a short circle time which is teacher-directed followed by a long free play time for children to choose their activities. This pattern follows throughout the day of alternating brief, teacher-directed times with long, child-choice times.

None of the story s-t-r-e-t-c-h-e-r activities for the centers must be done by each child; they are available, if the child chooses to participate. While we have listed ways the teachers can interact with the children during the center activities, often the teacher need only begin the activity and children can continue on their own because the learning materials and resources are organized for hands-on, manipulative, active learning. Many of the cooking, creative dramatics and the music and movement activities can be used with small groups or the entire class.

Classrooms for young children are most often divided into learning centers or areas where the same type of activity occurs each day. For example, easels, a table, paintbrushes, a variety of paints and paper, scissors, tape and staplers are all collected in an area designed for art activity. In addition to the art center, other areas found in many classes include block building area, housekeeping and dress-up corner, library corner, an area for puzzles and small blocks — which we call the mathematics and manipulatives center—and a science table for nature displays. Often classrooms are equipped with a sand table, water table and work bench. Multi-use tables serve as both the center for cooking activities and for serving snacks. Usually, a large circle time rug is the place to gather children for group story reading, creative dramatics, music and movement.

We have expanded the use of several of the centers. For example, we suggest you also use the library corner as a writing center for children to scribble, invent spellings and write on their own at whatever their abilities. In the library corner, the children also can tell stories for the teacher to record or write down through dictation or on experience charts. We recommend many story retelling activities for young children to develop a sense of story structure and simply to savor the story again. Retelling a favorite story using the flannel board or making a tape for the listening station can be a small group or individual language activity.

The materials we recommend are, for the most part, readily available in early childhood classrooms. We suggest inviting parents to contribute "old" dress-up clothes and unusual display items. Most of the field trips we recommend are walking expeditions on the center or school grounds or into the neighborhood.

For each book, the centers and follow-up activities are listed in alphabetical order for easy reference. The index provides a quick cross-reference for activities, titles of books and authors' and illustrators' names. In addition, the appendix, includes tips on book binding, making rebus charts and a recipe for playdough.

## How To Use The Book

We suggest you use MORE STORY S-T-R-E-T-C-H -E-R-S: ACTIVITIES TO EXPAND CHILDREN'S FAVORITE BOOKS as a resource and begin to devise story s-t-r-e-t-c-h-e-r-s for your children which best meet their needs. Some teachers select a different book for each day of the week and include all the story s-t-r-e-t-c-h-e-r-s as a base for their curriculum plan for the unit. In some half-day programs, teachers select a book from the five recommended, read the featured book on Monday at the first group time of the day, complete one story s-t-r-e-t-c-h-e-r for each day of the week and read the other recommended books throughout the unit.

Connecting the child, the story and the curriculum builds a greater interest in books because the books are translated into and associated with the very active learning children enjoy in centers and daily activities. One teacher commented, "I knew the children connected the books and the story s-t-r-e-t-c-h-e-r ideas when Michael said, 'Let's make a tape of this book, I want to hear it about fifty times'" (THE LITTLE MOUSE, THE RED RIPE STRAWBERRY, AND THE BIG HUNGRY BEAR, Wood, 1989). Latrice was overheard in the housekeeping area teaching the dolls "Chick-a-boom-chick-a-boom," then stopping to go get the book from the library corner to make sure she was "getting it right" (CHICKA CHICKA BOOM! BOOM!, Martin & Archambault, 1989). Brian flew his model plane down to the airport and picked up a little boy who was scared to fly and paused for him to get his "bear friend" on board (FIRST FLIGHT, McPhail, 1990).

A cooperating teacher gave her student teacher a copy of our first story s-t-r-e-t-c-h-e-r-s book and reported it was a "confidence builder" for the new teacher. She used the story s-t-r-e-t-c-h-e-r-s model to plan her lessons and organize activities around a theme. Some child care center directors tell us that when they hire a new employee part of the employment package is a copy of our story s-t-r-e-t-c-h-e-r-s book. We are pleased that our writing has been of assistance to beginning teachers and new employees, but we are especially gratified when seasoned veteran teachers tell us that the story s-t-r-e-t-c-h-e-r-s sparked their imaginations, as well. As a continuing in-service project, some program directors have created story s-t-r-e-t-c-h-e-r files and scheduled training sessions for teachers to share their inventive variations for other books we did not feature in our writing.

Now that we have heard about many of the creative ways new teachers, veteran teachers and program directors used the first story s-t-r-e-t-c-h-e-r-s book, we are eager to hear success stories based on MORE STORY S-T-R-E-T-C-H-E-R-S: ACTIVITIES TO EXPAND CHILDREN'S FAVORITE BOOKS. We encourage you to stretch other books which are your children's favorites, modify the activities we suggest, expand them even further and, most importantly, make them your own.

## References From The Introduction

Martin, Bill, Jr., & Archambault, John. (1989). Illustrated by Lois Ehlert. **CHICKA CHICKA BOOM! BOOM!** New York: Simon and Schuster Books for Young Readers.

McPhail, David. (1987). **FIRST FLIGHT**. Boston: Little, Brown and Company.

Wood, Don, & Wood, Audrey. (1989). **THE LITTLE MOUSE, THE RED RIPE STRAWBERRY, AND THE BIG HUNGRY BEAR.** London: Child's Play.

# Contents

# I AM ME,
# I AM SPECIAL,
# LOOK WHAT I CAN DO!

*I Like Me !*
*Tacky the Penguin*
*Silly Fred*
*Quick as a Cricket*
*Something to Crow About*

# I AM ME,
## I AM SPECIAL
## LOOK WHAT
## I CAN DO!

## I LIKE ME !

*By Nancy Carlson*

*A delightful and cheerful pig introduces the reader to her best friend when she says, "That best friend is me!" The pig goes on to tell all the things she likes to do such as draw beautiful pictures and read good books; the ways she takes care of herself, by exercising and brushing her teeth; the things she likes about herself such as her curly tail, round tummy and tiny feet. The best friend pig goes on to say what she does to cheer herself up, how she tries again when she makes mistakes, and finally, that she will always be, "Me, and I like that!" The illustrations are just as bright, cheerful and delightful as the text.*

## Circle Time Presentation

Begin circle time by saying, "I am me, I am special and here are some of the things I like to do." Go on to tell some of the things you enjoy. Ask several children what they enjoy. Have them begin by repeating the "I am me, I am special" phrase. Read I LIKE ME! After reading the book, repeat "I am me, I am special and here are the ways I take care of myself." Give some examples before going on to ask some of the children how they take care of themselves. After a few children contribute to the discussion say, "I am me, I am special and here is what I do to cheer myself up." Then ask several children to talk about how they cheer themselves up. Have each child repeat the phrase "I am me, I am special" at the beginning of their comments. End the circle time with everyone repeating together, "I am me, I am special, I like me!"

### STORY STRETCHER
## For Art: "I Like Me!" Cards

**What the children will learn—**
To express in drawing some of their special characteristics

**Materials you will need—**
Variety of crayons, markers or colored pencils and manilla paper or construction paper

**What to do—**
1. Ask the children to fold their papers like a greeting card. On the outside, ask them to draw a self-portrait using any of the art supplies.

2. On the left inside of the folded paper, ask them to draw a picture of things they like to do.

3. On the right inside of the folded paper, have the children draw pictures of how they take care of themselves.

4. On the back of the card, ask the children to draw pictures of how they cheer themselves up.

**Something to think about—**
Place these cards in the library corner to inspire the children's writing.

### STORY STRETCHER
## For Housekeeping And Dress-up Corner: Exercise Clothing

**What the children will learn—**
To practice dressing themselves and to play roles

**Materials you will need—**
Loose fitting shirts, shorts, warm-up pants and shirts, skating outfits, wristbands, headbands, gym bag or tote bag

**What to do—**
1. With the small group of children who choose the housekeeping and dress-up corner, look through the illustrations in I LIKE ME! for all of the different exercise outfits that "pig" wears.

2. Ask the children to separate the clothing which could be exercise clothing for aerobics classes or for special activities such as skating, aerobics classes, soccer and rowing, as seen in the book I LIKE ME!

3. Encourage the children to dress up in the clothing.

**Something to think about—**
When young children dress up in costumes, they pretend the roles associated with the pieces of clothing. Play encourages socialization, a wider vocabulary usage and a complex set of interactions around a theme which the children decide among themselves. For example, while three girls sorted

through the clothing, one decided to become the aerobics instructor and two others were her students. They negotiated among themselves what to wear, how they would carpool to class, the specific exercises and who would take care of the baby while the mommies worked out. (Adapted from Vera Peter's classroom.)

## For Library Corner: Writing About Me

**What the children will learn—**
To express positive thoughts about themselves

**Materials you will need—**
Lined and unlined paper, pens or pencils

**What to do—**
1. Encourage the children who are interested to bring their "I Like Me!" cards from the art activity to the writing table to discuss them.

2. As a part of the discussion, ask specific questions to extend the comments. For example, if a child says, "I am me, I am special because I ride my bicycle fast," then ask her to tell you more about when she learned to ride a bicycle.

3. After the discussion, encourage the children to write about themselves, what they like to do, the things they are good at, how they care for themselves and cheer themselves up. They can write in general or write about specific instances they recall.

**Something to think about—**
Older children may want to write a collection of stories to bind into an "I Am Me, I Am Special, Look What I Can Do Book." See binding instructions in the appendix. Younger children can use their "I Like Me!" cards from the art activity as a source of inspiration to re-

call specifics they would like to include in a story. They may prefer to write their own captions for each of the four sections of the card or dictate a sentence for you to write.

## For Mathematics And Manipulatives: Wallpaper Patterns

**What the children will learn—**
To sort and match by patterns

**Materials you will need—**
Wallpaper books, scissors, pencils or crayons, ruler, clear plastic bags, storage box

**What to do—**
1. Have the children look through I LIKE ME! and notice all the different wallpaper patterns.

2. Ask a wallpaper store for old pattern books. Show the children the books and leave them intact for the children to explore on their own for a few days.

3. Let the children select wallpaper patterns they like and cut them out from the book.

4. Have the children use a ruler and draw four squares on the back of the paper and cut it in squares.

5. Mix up the squares, and then have the children re-sort them and store them in a large clear plastic bag. Store about 20 pieces together.

6. As other groups of children come to the area, let them make more wallpaper pattern sorting sets.

**Something to think about—**
It may be necessary for you to cut the wallpaper squares for younger children who may not be able to handle the cutting of heavy wallpaper. Ask a parent or a grandparent to come to the classroom and wall-

paper a large cardboard box so the children can see how it is done.

## For Music And Movement: "Row, Row, Row Your Boat"

**What the children will learn—**
To sing the round, "Row, Row, Row Your Boat"

**Materials you will need—**
Chart tablet or posterboard, marker

**What to do—**
1. Show the children the illustration of Pig rowing down the river. Tell the children that when you saw the picture, it reminded you of a song.

2. Print the words to the traditional round of "Row, Row, Row Your Boat" on chart tablet or on posterboard.

3. On the first day, teach the round to the children as if it is a song, rather than a round.

4. On the second day, with the assistance of an aide or a child who sings in a children's choir, sing the song in rounds.

**Something to think about—**
A chart tablet filled with the words to different tunes is actually a "Big Book." When you sing the songs in the class's Big Book of Music, move your hands under the words in a sweeping motion so that the children read the words as fluently as they sing them.

## 1
## I AM ME,
## I AM SPECIAL,
## LOOK WHAT
## I CAN DO!

## TACKY THE PENGUIN

*By Helen Lester*

*Illustrated by Lynn Munsinger*

*Tacky is an eccentric penguin who enjoys zany antics like marching in a most "unpenguinly" way, doing cannonball dives and singing goofy songs. His companions, Goodly, Lovely, Angel, Neatly and Perfect do everything like good little penguins, not like Tacky. One day, when the hunters came to trap some of the perfect penguins, Tacky performed for them in his goofy ways and they left the island to go in search of perfect penguins, not ones like Tacky. Munsinger's comical illustrations of Tacky in his flowery shirt with a purple and white checked bow tie and the drawings of his goofy antics endear him to the reader.*

## Circle Time Presentation

Wear a flowery blouse or shirt and a patterned scarf or tie that clashes with the rest of your outfit. Tell the children that sometimes you like to dress goofy. Read TACKY THE PENGUIN. Discuss with the children how the other penguins' opinions of Tacky changed and how they came to appreciated him. Discuss with the children some things they like to do that other people may think are funny or goofy. Ask the children to talk about the funny scenes from the book. If time permits, ask several children to help retell the story. Let them take turns and retell the story while looking at the illustrations. Announce that today is Tacky Dress Day in honor of TACKY THE PENGUIN. Have the children go to the housekeeping and dress-up corner to make their selections of Tacky clothing.

STORY STRETCHER

## For Art: Icebergs With Thumb Print Penguins

**What the children will learn—**
To shade chalk for water scenes

**Materials you will need—**
White construction paper, blue chalk, inked stamp pad, paper towels, colored pens

**What to do—**
1. Show the children in the art center Lynn Munsinger's illustrations in TACKY THE PENGUIN. Call attention to the whiteness of the icebergs and the blue of the sky and water.

2. Demonstrate how to use chalk on its side and rub it on the white construction paper to create the blue of sky and water.

3. Let the children experiment with the shading technique.

4. Practice making penguins by letting the children place their thumbs in ink and pressing them onto scraps of paper. After they have practiced, they can make their own Tacky and his penguin friends.

5. Add details with the colored pens.

6. Display the "Icebergs with Thumb Print Penguins" near the library corner and the book jacket of TACKY THE PENGUIN.

**Something to think about—**
Teachers often worry that if they show children specific art techniques, as how to shade using chalk or how to print with ink, that they will interfere with the child's creativity. The opposite is true. The more techniques, variety of materials and diversity of art experiences the child has in her or his repertoire, the more creative possibilities exist for the child.

STORY STRETCHER

## For Housekeeping And Dress-up Corner: Tacky Shirts And Funny Bow Ties

**What the children will learn—**
To enjoy patterns and to tie scarves and ties

**Materials you will need—**
Hawaiian or flowery shirts and blouses, a variety of scarves and tacky ties, full length mirror

**What to do—**
1. At the end of circle time, assist the children in finding a funny shirt and tie to wear for the morning.

2. Have them look in the mirror and put together costumes that look like they do not go together. Remind them that Tacky the Penguin wore a flowery shirt and a purple and white checked bow tie.

3. Use words which describe the patterns in the clothing, such as plaid, paisley, checked, stripes, flowers, prints. Also emphasize the colors.

**Something to think about—**
In a parent newsletter, ask parents to donate old Hawaiian shirts, flowery blouses and funny looking ties and scarves.

## For Library Corner: Writing Another Tacky Adventure

**What the children will learn—**
To write a story in keeping with the character

**Materials you will need—**
Paper, pencils, crayons, drawing paper

**What to do—**
1. Discuss with the children what Tacky the Penguin was like. Tell them they are characterizing Tacky.

2. Brainstorm with the children what might happen the next day as Tacky and the other penguins played on the iceberg.

3. Invite the children to write their own stories about Tacky using one of the brainstormed ideas, or write something entirely different.

**Something to think about—**
Children enjoy the sense of community that arises when they write about the same topic; however, this should always be a matter of choice. Notice the word "invite" was used. Some children may be involved in writing another story and will not be interested in writing about Tacky the Penguin today. If the writing area is a permanent fixture in the library corner, then children are more likely to become writers as a natural ex-

pansion of the books they are enjoying in the library.

## For Music And Movement: Marching To A Tacky Tune

**What the children will learn—**
To improvise a march like Tacky's

**Materials you will need—**
Instrumental march music

**What to do—**
1. During the second circle time of the day, show the children how Tacky's friends marched. Then have them look at Tacky's march.

2. Ask a child who enjoys movement activities to show how Tacky's march might look if we did it. Be prepared to demonstrate Tacky's march yourself, if the child cannot improvise on the spot.

3. Tell the children to march like Tacky's friends marched while the music is playing, but when the music stops to march like Tacky.

4. Vary the activity by having the children march like Tacky's friends while the music is playing, then when you stop the music, put a flowery shirt on one child and let him or her pretend to be Tacky.

**Something to think about—**
Teachers often use one circle time of the day for group music and movement activities. We recommend having some music, fingerplay or movement activity at each group meeting. After children have been sitting quietly and passively listening, then insert a music or movement task. Alternating passive and active times is a good pattern for circle time and for the entire daily schedule.

## For Water Table: Cannonball Splashes

**What the children will learn—**
To design a water slide

**Materials you will need—**
Water table, bits of plastic tubing or plastic track from a car racing set or connections of plastic blocks, plastic animals

**What to do—**
1. Move the water table outside for Tacky the Penguin cannonball dives.

2. Ask the children to design a water slide for Tacky's cannonball dives. Have them look around the classroom for possible plastic pieces that could be used for a slide.

3. Collect an assortment of plastic tubing, plastic track from race car sets or plastic blocks which can be connected.

4. Let three or four children work together to create the water slide and later become the first ones to have small plastic animals slide down for cannonball splashes.

**Something to think about—**
Have a "Tacky the Penguin Pool Party." If it is warm enough and there is a swimming pool near the school or center, plan a field trip. The pool at the home of one of the children or a grandparent is often a better choice for young children than large club pools which seem overwhelming. Of course, plan for many extra adults to assist on pool party day.

## 1

## I AM ME,
## I AM SPECIAL,
## LOOK WHAT
## I CAN DO!

## SILLY FRED

*By Karen Wagner*

*Illustrated by Normand Chartier*

*Fred's mother called him "Silly Fred" because he liked to sing silly songs and turn silly somersaults. She often said to Father Pig, "I wonder what makes Fred so silly?" Father and Mother Pig enjoyed their Silly Fred, and Fred enjoyed himself until he met Beaver, who was a serious fellow and did not enjoy Fred's silly antics. Fred was hurt by Beaver's remarks and quit being silly. He wandered through the forest in its fall colors and moped around. His parents thought he was sick and took him to the clinic to see Doctor Rabbit. Fred stayed sad for weeks until he observed Beaver for a whole day, washing dishes, reading, cleaning and cooking. He noticed that Beaver was not a happy beaver. Silly Fred decided he wanted to be happy and silly and be himself.*

## Circle Time Presentation

Ask the children if their parents ever call them "silly." Have the children tell some of the things their parents call them, such as "Silly Willy," "Monkey," "You silly boy" or "You silly girl." Turn to the title page where the pig is marching through the forest covered with fall leaves and introduce the children to Silly Fred. Read SILLY FRED and let the children repeat Fred's silly songs. Have a few children volunteer to retell the story as you turn the pages. Accept their interpretations and variations as long as they are true to the storyline.

STORY STRETCHER
## For Art: Silly Fred Leaf Necklaces

**What the children will learn—**
To draw leaf shapes, to practice cutting and to create a pattern

**Materials you will need—**
Leaves, pencils, yellow, orange, red and brown construction paper, yarn, hole punchers, masking tape

**What to do—**
1. Take a walk with the children and collect fall leaves.

2. Let the children place their leaves on different fall colored construction paper. Tape it in place. trace around the leaves.

3. Trace around the leaves and cut out the leaf shapes.

4. Place a small piece of masking tape near the top of the back of each leaf to reinforce it.

5. Punch a hole through the masking tape and construction paper leaf.

6. String the leaves onto yarn to make Silly Fred leaf necklaces.

**Something to think about—**
Do not be concerned if the children are not able to trace exactly or to cut out the forms exactly. Avoid tracing and cutting for them. It is important that we accept the children at whatever their ability levels in art and craft activities, as well as in all other areas of the curriculum.

ANOTHER STORY STRETCHER
## For Art: Talking Mural

**What the children will learn—**
To interpret their words and observations into drawings

**Materials you will need—**
Large sheet of butcher paper, crayons

**What to do—**
1. Place a large sheet of butcher paper on the table in the art center. Divide the butcher paper into sections, leaving enough room for each child to draw a picture. The divisions can be folds or actual lines for younger children.

2. Draw large bubbles, like the ones in newspaper cartoons, and print the children's comments in the bubbles.

3. Share with the children the comments the parents wrote down while walking with them in the woods. (See the Science And Nature Story S-t-r-e-t-c-h-e-r listed below.)

4. Ask the children to draw themselves making these comments to create the "talking mural."

**Something to think about—**
If you are not able to take the walk in the woods, let the children develop a talking mural recalling when they have walked in the forest. This activity could be considered an art activity, a writing

activity for the library corner or a science and nature activity.

## For Library Corner: Silly Fred Flannel Board Story

**What the children will learn—**
To select flannel board pieces to represent the story

**Materials you will need—**
Flannel board, construction paper, scissors, glue, clear contact paper or laminating film, small pieces of sandpaper

**What to do—**
1. With the children who select the library during choice time, make flannel board pieces by sketching and cutting out of construction paper the following — Fred, his mother and father, Beaver, Doctor Rabbit, leaves, dishes, book, dust cloth, saucepan.

2. Cover with clear contact paper or laminating film.

3. Glue small pieces of sandpaper onto the backs of the pieces so they will adhere to the flannel on the board.

4. After the pieces are made, retell the story.

**Something to think about—**
Encourage active children who may show less interest in books than others to retell stories using flannel board pieces. Manipulating the pieces is often an enticement which helps the child become more interested in stories. Also, the fact that the children helped to make the flannel board pieces gives them a sense of ownership.

## For Music And Movement: Silly Fred Somersaults

**What the children will learn—**
To do a somersault

**Materials you will need—**
Tumbling mats or napping mats

**What to do—**
1. Ask one of the children who can turn a somersault to demonstrate.

2. Describe the child's actions, as "Marcie leans forward, putting her head between her legs, then rolls on over."

3. Have the children practice their somersaults on tumbling mats, napping mats or on the carpeted area if it is soft enough.

**Something to think about—**
If you have the appropriate equipment in your center or school, invite older children who are in gymnastics classes to give a demonstration of somersaults, cartwheels and other acrobatic moves.

## For Science And Nature: A Fall Walk In The Woods

**What the children will learn—**
To observe the changes in the leaves

**Materials you will need—**
Note pads and pencils, paper grocery bags, parent and grandparent volunteers

**What to do—**
1. Ask parents and grandparents to serve as volunteers for the walk in the woods.

2. Have a volunteer who knows a great deal about trees instruct the others on the identity of common trees.

3. Divide the children into groups, three or four per volunteer. Give each child a grocery bag for their leaf collecting.

4. Ask the children to select some pretty leaves for the science and nature display table.

5. Have the volunteers jot down some of the comments the children make about the trees and the experience of collecting the leaves while walking in the woods. For example, Brian said, "I have a tree just like this one in my front yard." Michelle said, "Look, there are black beetles under these leaves."

6. Upon returning, let the children each select five leaves for the science and nature display table.

7. Collect the children's comments from the volunteers and use them to create a talking mural. (See the instructions under Another Story S-t-r-e-t-c-h-e-r for Art.)

**Something to think about—**
The SILLY FRED book is about a positive self-concept, but an underlying theme is Fred's enjoyment of the fall as he walked through the woods, collecting leaves and making leaf necklaces.

# I AM ME,
# I AM SPECIAL,
# LOOK WHAT
# I CAN DO

by Audrey Wood · illustrated by Don Wood
Child's Play

## QUICK AS A CRICKET

*By Audrey Wood*

*Illustrated by Don Wood*

*A little boy uses many different phrases, "Quick as a cricket, strong as an ox, loud as a lion," and puts them all together to describe himself. The full-page illustrations are cheerful, bright, detailed and imaginative with exuberant expressions. As the child describes himself, he is like the animal. For example, when the text reads, "as large as a whale," the boy is shown swimming beside a large whale and he and the whale are the same size. At the end of the book, a little boy stands in front of the bulletin board in his bedroom and looks at all the pictures of the animals he has posted there. The reader is shown the source of the boy's imaginings.*

## Circle Time Presentation

Ask the children to show you what "quiet as a mouse" means. Also, ask if anyone has said to them, "You swim like a fish," or "You run like a deer." Have the children look at the cover of QUICK AS A CRICKET and think of a saying for the little boy. Help them to come up with, "Quick as a cricket." Read the book pausing for the children to savor the pictures. Pause longer at the illustration showing the little boy looking at all the animal pictures on his bulletin board. Reread the book and discuss with the children the phrases which they think describe themselves.

STORY STRETCHER

## For Art: Animal Bulletin Boards

**What the children will learn—**
To plan a joint art project

**Materials you will need—**
Variety of art media, variety of shapes and colors of paper, scissors

**What to do—**
1. Ask the children to look at the illustration of the boy staring at his bulletin board. Tell them you would like to have an animal bulletin board that shows all the animals they are like. Also, call attention to the variety of shapes of pictures.

2. Have the children decide what they are like, as "loud as a lion" or "nice as a bunny." Then ask them to draw and color or paint pictures of the animals they are like for a bulletin board display.

3. Cut sheets of construction or manilla paper into a variety of shapes: pennant, post card size, small circles like badges, large circles, small and large rectangles and squares.

**Something to think about—**
For the first art session of the QUICK AS A CRICKET day or days, the children will probably choose the animal and phrase they like most. On another day, emphasize a new phrase, "Sometimes I am as sad as a basset," or "sometimes I am as lazy as a lizard." Instead of emphasizing individuals, you might use the phrase, "Sometimes we are as weak as kittens," or "we are as shy as shrimps."

STORY STRETCHER

## For Library Corner: Writing, Describing Myself

**What the children will learn—**
To use descriptive phrases

**Materials you will need—**
Writing supplies — lined and unlined paper, pens, pencils

**What to do—**
1. Reread QUICK AS A CRICKET.

2. Help the children think about the phrases which best describe themselves. It may be helpful to use the word "sometimes" to get the discussion started.

3. Talk about the "sometimes," the instances when the children could describe themselves with the phrases. For example, in the book, the phrases "hot as a fox" and "cold as a toad" are used. Have the children recall when those phrases might have fit them.

4. Encourage the children to dictate or write the phrases or longer stories that illustrate the times when they felt like the phrase.

**Something to think about—**
Older children might like to write a collection of opposites, with stories to illustrate each feeling, cold

or hot, strong or weak, loud or quiet. Younger children could draw opposite pictures and dictate captions. Remember that young children who are in the emergent literacy stage may scribble their writing or some may use letters they know how to form, even if they do not yet know sound/symbol relationships or are not able to spell correctly. As with their drawings, they may not yet be able to draw pictures that we recognize, but we encourage them to draw anyway. The same is true for writing. They may not yet be able to write in letter forms that we can read, but we encourage them to write anyway.

## For Mathematics And Manipulatives : Classifying And Counting

**What the children will learn—**
To classify and count insects, sea life and animals

**Materials you will need—**
Chart tablet and marker or chalkboard and chalk

**What to do—**
1. With the children who come to the mathematics and manipulatives center during choice time, go through the book and name all the insects, sea life and animals which are featured. Print them on a list.

2. Have the children look at the list and think of names which could be grouped together — insects, sea life and animals.

3. Reprint the list with the three headings.

4. Then ask the children to recall whether there was one, a few or many of the insects, sea life or animals.

**Something to think about—**
If you teach this unit after your study of animal life, the children could classify the animals as mammals or not mammals. Older children might group the animals in more than one category, as the whale is a mammal and it also is sea life.

## For Music And Movement: Quick As A Cricket, Slow As A Snail

**What the children will learn—**
To improvise movements to illustrate descriptive phrases

**Materials you will need—**
None needed

**What to do—**
1. With the children seated in a circle, ask individuals to improvise movements that illustrate the phrases "quick as a cricket" or "tough as a rhino."

2. Tell the children you will clap your hands and at that signal they can move. When you clap again they need to freeze.

3. Select phrases in order at first, then at random.

**Something to think about—**
Some descriptive phrases are more difficult to illustrate, as "large as a whale" or "small as an ant." Have the children brainstorm as a group for the possible movements.

## For Science And Nature: Cricket Terrarium

**What the children will learn—**
To construct a cricket habitat and observe cricket behaviors

**Materials you will need—**
Large terrarium, soil, plants, crickets, small water dishes, resource books on insects and terrariums, chart tablet, marker

**What to do—**
1. Announce to the children that this science and nature activity will take several days to arrange.

2. Read about crickets and terrariums in a resource book. Select pertinent passages to read to the children, which describe the needs a cricket has for food, water and hiding places from the light, as well as how to construct a terrarium.

3. Write on the chart tablet the key phrases that will help the children remember what the crickets need. Also, list all the supplies that will be needed.

4. Collect the supplies over the next few days and as children and parents bring them in, check them off the chart tablet list.

5. Construct the habitat.

6. Begin the observations, charting what is seen, when crickets chirp, how big they are, where they hide and other behaviors.

**Something to think about—**
Ask the children and parents to volunteer for some of the supplies. For example, a parent who enjoys plants may have soil he can contribute, or a child may recall that her mother has an empty terrarium in the basement.

# 1
## I AM ME, I AM SPECIAL, LOOK WHAT I CAN DO

## SOMETHING TO CROW ABOUT

*By Megan Halsey Lane*

*Randall is jealous of all the things that Cassie, another young chick, can do better. She can cheep better, find worms better and even lay eggs. It is not until Randall "cock-a-doodle-dos" that he finds something which Cassie wishes she could do. The illustrations of the two chicks are large enough for a circle time sharing of the book. The chicks' expressions depict the feelings of jealousy, pride and then mutual respect. The colors used are warm — soft yellows, oranges and rosy browns. The end paper pages at the front of the book are of Cassie and Randall as baby chicks and the end paper pages at the back of the book show them as grown hen and rooster.*

## Circle Time Presentation

Introduce the book by having the children notice that on the title page there are some eggs with tiny cracks in them, then turn the page to the dedication page and there are two nests with eggs with larger cracks and a bit of yellow fluff and a beak. Have the children tell you what is happening. On the first page of the story, we meet Cassie and Randall. Randall still has a bit of shell on his head, tail and wing. Then read the story, pausing at the page that shows Randall imagining himself doing a lot of things better than Cassie. Have the children tell what each part of the large bubble over Randall's head means. They can finish the sentence, "Randall wishes he could _____."

"Randall wishes he could scratch better than Cassie."

"Randall wishes he could strut better than Cassie."

"Randall wishes he could cheep better than Cassie."

"Randall wishes he could find worms better than Cassie."

If the children vary the phrases, accept their answers. Continue reading the story. Discuss how Randall wanted to be able to lay an egg, but he couldn't. Discuss how Cassie wanted to "cock-a-doodle-do," but she couldn't. In the end, they learned to respect their different abilities. Ask the children to tell some things they wish they could do that a brother or sister or a friend does well. Ask the children to tell some things they each do well. Announce that this week is Differences Week. Throughout the week you will be pointing out many things the children do well, and how we can enjoy each other's differences.

## For Art: I Wish I Could Drawings

**What the children will learn—** To express their feelings through drawings

**Materials you will need—** Manilla paper, crayons or colored pencils

**What to do—**

1. Turn to the page in SOMETHING TO CROW ABOUT which shows Randall imagining himself doing things better than Cassie. Point out how the illustrator of the book made a large bubble over Randall's head and drew smaller pictures of Randall imagining himself doing all those things.

2. Ask the children to draw a picture of themselves on the lower left-hand corner of the paper, then make a large bubble extending over their heads and covering most of the space on the paper.

3. Discuss with them some things they would like to be able to do better, such as ride a bicycle, play a computer game, read a book, play soccer or bake a cake.

4. Ask them to draw themselves doing these activities or use symbols of these activities, such as a bike, computer, book, soccer ball or cake to be placed in the balloon over their heads.

**Something to think about—** Younger children may draw themselves doing one thing they wish they could do better. Older children may want to create two pictures: one showing what they do well and another showing what they would like to do better.

## For Creative Dramatics: Cassie's And Randall's Story

**What the children will learn—**
To move like baby chicks and hens and roosters

**Materials you will need—**
Book

**What to do—**
1. After reading the story once, tell the children that this time you are going to read the story and ask the girls to be Cassies and the boys to be Randalls. They act out the story when you pause and give them directions.

2. Establish a hand motion to let the actors know when to stop and listen to the story again.

3. Read the story and pause for the children to pretend pecking out of the egg. Then let the Cassies scratch the ground, strut, cheep and find worms.

4. At the scene of Randall imagining he can do these things better than Cassie, ask the Randalls to act out scratching the ground, strutting, cheeping and finding worms.

5. As the story progresses, let the Cassies sit on their nests and pretend to lay an egg. Have the Randalls sit on their nests, then make a loud "cock-a-doodle-do."

6. Have the Cassies pretend to "cock-a-doodle-do" but help them remember that Cassies only peep.

7. End the story by having the Cassies and Randalls face each other and say together, "Being different is really something to crow about."

**Something to think about—**
If some children do not feel comfortable participating, let them be the audience for the day. At the end of the drama session, ask the audience members to tell which parts of the story they liked best. This gives them a sense of participating without being involved in the drama.

## For Library Corner: Cassie And Randall Flannel Board Story

**What the children will learn—**
To sequence the events in the story

**Materials you will need—**
Construction paper, crayons, scissors, emery board or sandpaper, glue, flannel board

**What to do—**
1. With the children's assistance, make the flannel board pieces for SOMETHING TO CROW ABOUT. Look through the book and assign the pictures they are to draw.

2. Emphasize that outlines are all that are necessary.

3. After the children draw, color and cut out their Cassies and Randalls, write on the back of each piece what it represents, as "Cassie cheeping better."

4. Cut small pieces of emery board or sandpaper and glue them onto the backs of the cutouts of Cassie and Randall.

5. Let the children help you retell the story by placing their cutouts onto the flannel board in sequence.

**Something to think about—**
For younger children, make the flannel board pieces and have them help you retell the story. Older children can make individual sets of a baby chick Cassie and Randall and a hen and rooster of Cassie and Randall. They can retell the story by moving the pieces without having to have Cassies and Randalls for every scene.

## For Library Corner: Writing About What I Do Well

**What the children will learn—**
To write about themselves

**Materials you will need—**
Paper, pencils or markers

**What to do—**
1. With a small group of children, discuss how Randall and Cassie compared themselves to each other, but in the end of the story, they realized that each could do something well.

2. Compliment each child in the group on something she or he does well in the classroom, as telling flannel board stories, using the work bench, counting, sculpting with clay, drawing pictures, making up stories to act out in the drama center, sharing the bristle blocks or helping with snacks.

3. Then ask each child to tell something he or she likes to do and does well in the classroom.

4. After the discussion, ask the children to either draw about or write and draw about themselves and all the things they do well at school.

**Something to think about—**
Children are usually able to write about a topic after they have talked about it. Younger children often want to draw before writing. As they become more experienced writers, youngsters will write and then draw to illustrate their stories.

## For Mathematics And Manipulatives: Forward And Backward, Reversible Patterns

**What the children will learn—**
To replicate a pattern and then reverse it

**Materials you will need—**
Construction paper, scissors, pencils, markers

**What to do—**

1. Ask the children to look at the front end paper pages of the book. There they will see side view pictures of Cassie and Randall when they were baby chicks. We can tell them apart by the different bows around their necks.

2. Have the children draw a picture of Cassie as a chick and Randall as a chick.

3. Let the children cut out their pictures, then draw around them to create a pattern and make two more sets of chicks.

4. Decorate both sides of the construction paper chicks so that the chicks can be turned forward or backward.

5. Ask the children to look at the end paper pages again and create the same pattern as on the end papers. First a Cassie chick, then a Randall, then a Cassie, next a Randall, then a Cassie.

6. Next ask the children to create the pattern by having the chicks face forward, then backward, then make up several random patterns for them to replicate. After making the pattern, reverse it in order or by the direction the chicks heads are pointing.

**Something to think about—**
For younger children, you may want to cut out the chick patterns and let them decorate the bows to tell the chicks apart. For older children, let them draw the chicks in a variety of positions, as scratching, strutting, pulling up worms, sitting on nests "cock-a-doodle-doing." They can then use the chicks for creating more elaborate patterns.

## REFERENCES

Carlson, Nancy. (1988). **I LIKE ME!** New York: Viking Kestrel.

Lane, Megan Halsey. (1990). **SOMETHING TO CROW ABOUT**. New York: Dial Books for Young Readers.

Lester, Helen. (1988). Illustrated by Lynn Munsinger. **TACKY THE PENGUIN.** Boston: Houghton Mifflin Company.

Wagner, Karen. (1989). Illustrated by Normand Chartier. **SILLY FRED.** New York: Macmillan Publishing Company.

Wood, Audrey. (1982). Illustrated by Don Wood. **QUICK AS A CRICKET.** London: Child's Play.

### Additional References For I Am Me, I Am Special, Look What I Can Do!

Asch, Frank. (1985). **BEAR'S BARGAIN.** New York: Simon and Schuster. *Bear and Little Bird try to help each other achieve some impossible tasks.*

Carlson, Nancy. (1990). **ARNIE AND THE NEW KID.** New York: Viking. *Arnie teases Phillip, who is in a wheelchair, then when misfortune puts Arnie on crutches temporarily, he discovers that you can be different and still be a lot alike.*

Kraus, Robert. (1974). Illustrated by José Aruego and Ariane Dewey. **HERMAN THE HELPER.** New York: Simon and Schuster. *Herman the helper octopus is always willing to assist anyone who needs his help — old or young, friend or enemy.*

Little, Lessie Jones, & Greenfield, Eloise. (1978). Illustrated by Carole Byard. **I CAN DO IT MYSELF.** New York: Thomas Y. Crowell. *Donny is determined to buy his mother's birthday present all by himself, but he meets a scary challenge on the way home.*

McPhail, David. (1988). **SOMETHING SPECIAL.** Boston: Little Brown and Company. *Surrounded by parents and siblings with remarkable talents, Sam Raccoon yearns to be good at something himself, and finds his own special niche when he discovers the pleasures of painting.*

# FAMILIES

*Arthur's Baby*
*Daddy Makes the Best Spaghetti*
*A Walk in the Rain*
*My Great Grandpa*
*Loving*

## ARTHUR'S BABY

*By Marc Brown*

*Arthur's parents announce that he and D.W. will have a new brother or sister in about six months. After Arthur's friends tell him all the problems with having a baby in the house, he is not too sure he wants the new arrival, while his little sister is excited and helps with all the preparations. When the new baby, Kate, arrives, an unexpected event changes Arthur's mind about babies. Marc Brown's Arthur series has become a favorite among young children and beginning readers. This book, the fourteenth in the Arthur series, is illustrated in Brown's familiar style which makes it instantly recognizable to young readers. His illustrations are rich enough in detail that children enjoy returning to them often.*

## Circle Time Presentation

If the children are familiar with the Arthur series, have them recall the main characters — Arthur, Arthur's sister, D.W., and his friends, Binky, Francine, Buster and Muffy. Begin by asking the children what happens when there is a new baby in a family. Let the children who have baby sisters or brothers contribute to the discussion. Read ARTHUR'S BABY and then recall all the things that Arthur's friends told him would happen when a new baby comes. Discuss how Arthur's mother interested him in babies by showing the photo album of when he and D.W. were babies. Ask the children what happened to make Arthur change his mind about Kate, the baby.

STORY STRETCHER

### For Art: Then And Now Pictures

**What the children will learn—**
To make pictures that represent themselves as babies and how they look now

**Materials you will need—**
Manilla or white paper, crayons, markers or colored pens

**What to do—**
1. For the small group who come to the art center during free choice time, show the illustrations of Arthur and D.W. when they were babies.

2. Let the children talk about any cute pictures they may have at home of themselves when they were babies.

3. Have the children fold their papers down the middle and on one side draw a picture of themselves as babies, and on the other side draw a picture of themselves as they are now.

**Something to think about—**
Teachers often ask children to bring in pictures of themselves when they were babies. Make this request only if you are certain the families have pictures of the children as infants. In some communities with poor families and immigrant children, they may have few or no family photos. Whenever possible, take pictures of the children and distribute them at parent meetings. They are a real incentive to attend the meetings. Local photography clubs or college photography classes may be willing to take pictures, with parental permission of course.

STORY STRETCHER

### For Housekeeping And Dress-up Corner: Setting Up A Nursery

**What the children will learn—**
To recall the special arrangements babies need

**Materials you will need—**
Baby clothes, bottles, diapers, blankets, cribs, bath tubs, baby toys, baby books, diaper bags, car seats, as many other baby items as you can collect

**What to do—**
1. With the small group of children who selected the housekeeping and dress-up corner for free play, look through ARTHUR'S BABY and spot all the items included in the illustrations that are there for the baby.

2. Have the children look around the room and collect as many items as they can find which a baby could use.

3. Bring the items to the house-keeping and dress-up corner and ask the children to set up a nursery.

4. After the nursery is set up, have the children list some items they could bring from home which would make the nursery more complete.

5. Ask the children to leave the nursery set up for at least a week so they can role play families with new babies.

**Something to think about—**
Try to include the children in this activity who have new babies at home or whose families expect a baby soon. Tell the child you need his or her help to set up a good nursery.

S T O R Y   S T R E T C H E R

## For Library Corner: Author's Chair For Arthur's Baby Stories

**What the children will learn—**
To express their feelings, prior experiences and concerns about a new baby in the household by writing or drawing about them

**Materials you will need—**
Assortment of writing paper, pencils, pens or markers

**What to do—**
1. Let a small group of children talk about their experiences with babies. Try to have at least one child in the group who currently has a baby at home. Encourage them to talk about all the ways they help take care of the baby.

2. Ask the children to write or draw about babies.

3. Display the writings and drawings in the library area near the book shelves where a copy of ARTHUR'S BABY can be found on the shelves.

4. Let the authors and artists share their stories with the class during "Author's Chair" at circle time.

**Something to think about—**
For young writers, the cycle of talking, drawing and writing is a natural one. They often move back and forth between the processes as they create compositions.

S T O R Y   S T R E T C H E R

## For Music And Movement: "A Baby, A Baby, A Baby Sister Kate"

**What the children will learn—**
To add motions to a song

**Materials you will need—**
Chart tablet, marker

**What to do—**
1. Print the song on chart tablet, leaving a wide margin to the left to add symbols for motions.

2. Talk with the children about Arthur's friends' reactions to the news that Arthur's parents were going to have a baby.

3. Add drawings or rebus symbols to the chart for the motions.

4. Sing,
*A ba-by, a ba-by, Arthur's family's having a ba-by*
*Will she cry? Oh yes, she'll cry!*
*A ba-by, a ba-by, Arthur's family's having a ba-by*
*Will she want a bot-tle? Oh yes, she'll need a bot-tle!*
*A ba-by, a ba-by, Arthur's family's having a ba-by*
*Will she wet? Oh yes, she'll wet!*
*A ba-by, a ba-by, Arthur's family's having a ba-by*
*Will Arthur have to babysit? Oh yes, Arthur'll have to babysit!*
*A ba-by, a ba-by, Arthur's family's having a ba-by*
*Will Arthur love to babysit? Oh yes, Arthur'll love to take care of the ba-by!*

*My sister, Kate, my sister Kate,*
*Arthur's family has a ba-by, a ba-by,*
*a ba-by sis-ter, Kate. (Raines, 1991).*

**Something to think about—**
Teachers who are not musically inclined can read the song as a poem or chant the song in a "sing-song" rhythm.

S T O R Y   S T R E T C H E R

## For Water Table: Bathing Baby Dolls

**What the children will learn—**
To handle the dolls carefully and to role play caring for a baby

**Materials you will need—**
Water table or baby bath tubs, dolls, wash cloths, towels, mild soap, baby clothes

**What to do—**
1. Demonstrate how to hold a baby and give the baby a bath.

2. Have some of the children pretend the babies are infants who cannot sit alone yet, while others can pretend their babies are active and can sit up.

3. Ask a child who has a baby at home to assist with the demonstration.

**Something to think about—**
If possible, ask the parent who brings the baby to give the baby a bath. Let the children watch. Have the brother or sister from the class become the special assistant who tells what the mother is doing. Be prepared that bathing babies, whether dolls or real ones, often produces some discussion of body parts. Use the proper names for the body parts and answer children's questions without over-emphasizing genitals and always being sensitive to caring for the baby.

## FAMILIES

## DADDY MAKES THE BEST SPAGHETTI

*By Anna Grossnickle Hines*

*The book covers an afternoon and evening when Corey and his Dad cook spaghetti for his Mom for dinner. They shop for ingredients, cook, enjoy the meal and clean up the kitchen. Dad's antics after dinner and the clever transition to bath, bedtime reading and good-night kisses displays the warmth, imagination and sheer delight the family feels for each other. The children will giggle at Hines's illustrations of Corey's bath and will enjoy the simple but expressive drawings of family life.*

## Circle Time Presentation

Show the children the cover of Corey and Dad marching and making music with pots and pans. Ask the children to predict what they think the story is about. After reading the title, DADDY MAKES THE BEST SPAGHETTI, ask if anyone wants to change their minds about what will happen in the story. Read DADDY MAKES THE BEST SPAGHETTI and pause for the children to giggle at Dad's impersonations of "Bathman" and the delightful suspense as Corey tries to find Dad while almost losing his bath towel. At the end of the reading, several children probably will volunteer some descriptions of funny games their parents play. Encourage them to also talk about cooking with their dads.

STORY STRETCHER

## For Cooking And Snack Time: Making The Best Spaghetti

**What the children will learn—**
To assist in making spaghetti

**Materials you will need—**
Prepared sauce or ingredients for your own sauce, range or hot plate, spaghetti, water, salt, butter, one large saucepan and one large pot, wooden spoons, colander, plates, silverware, brightly colored napkins and tablecloths

**What to do—**
1. Divide the children into four groups of chef's assistants. Discuss with each group what their task will include.

2. Make a rebus chart, a combination of words and symbols, for each group's instructions and the spaghetti recipe. (See the appendix for a sample rebus chart.) Post the chart and refer to it throughout the cooking experience.

3. If possible, have a parent come to the classroom and prepare his or her favorite spaghetti sauce with the help of a small group of children acting as chef's assistants. If this is not possible, let this group help warm up the sauce in a large saucepan or place sauce in a microwave to heat.

4. Let another small group of children cook the spaghetti by boiling water, adding salt and butter, cooking the noodles and, finally, draining them in a colander.

5. Have the third group of children set the table with brightly colored napkins and tablecloth.

6. Ask the fourth group of chef's assistants to serve the spaghetti to the rest of the class and parents.

**Something to think about—**
While cooking hot foods with young children takes extra preparation and caution, the pride of accomplishment the children feel and the valuable learning experiences are worth the extra efforts.

ANOTHER STORY STRETCHER

## For Cooking And Snack Time: Families Setting The Table And Eating Together

**What the children will learn—**
To pretend to be families during snack time and how to set the table

**Materials you will need—**
If possible, real silverware, dishes, glassware, napkins and placemats or tablecloths

**What to do—**
1. Look again at the illustration of the family eating together in the book.

2. Ask the children to sit at the snack tables; then at random ask children to pretend to be the father, mother, grandfather, grandmother

and children. At some tables there might not be a mother and at others there might not be a father. Discuss that we are still families even if one of our parents is not present.

3. Have these children sit together as families throughout the week during snack time.

4. Let different members of the family take turns setting the table.

**Something to think about—**
With older children, encourage table conversations with each person maintaining their role. With younger children, since snack time is not usually a pretending time, a teacher, aide or volunteer may need to sit at the table to encourage conversation.

STORY STRETCHER

## For Housekeeping And Dress-up Corner: Grocery Store

**What the children will learn—**
To set up the area, improvise props, play the roles involved

**Materials you will need—**
Canned and boxed foods, grocery bags, aprons, cash register, cents-off coupons, newspaper ads, scratch pads, pencils, posterboard, markers, optional — grocery carts

**What to do—**

1. In the parent newsletter, announce the grocery store center and ask for empty cans and boxes.

2. After the cans and boxes have arrived, collect cents-off coupons and newspaper ads which correspond to the containers.

3. Give the players in the area the coupons, ads, scratch pads, pencils, posterboard and markers. Ask them what they can do with these materials to make the area look like a real grocery store.

Expect to see them make posters guiding the shoppers to the food displays and matching the cents-off coupons to the food. Eventually, as they shop expect them to use the scratch pads to write checks for their groceries.

4. After the grocery store is set up, let the arrangers become the first customers, cashiers, produce managers and baggers.

**Something to think about—**
A grocery store is a wonderfully rich center for learning about community helpers, emergent literacy, nutrition, mathematics and social studies as the children play the roles.

STORY STRETCHER

## For Library Corner: Our Favorite Bedtime Books

**What the children will learn—**
To select a favorite bedtime book

**Materials you will need—**
Collection of books about bedtime, naptime, nighttime or family experiences

**What to do—**

1. Show the illustration from DADDY MAKES THE BEST SPAGHETTI where the little boy and his father are listening to his mother read a bedtime story.

2. Read one of your favorite bedtime or naptime books in a lowered, calm voice. Talk with the children about how it makes you relax when you read the book.

3. Ask the children to bring a copy of a book from home, one of their favorite books that helps them relax and go to sleep.

4. During the week, select bedtime books to read aloud in the library corner and at times during the day when a relaxing mood is needed.

**Something to think about—**
If some of your children have few books at home, let these children go with you to the school or city library and check out books for the rest of the class.

STORY STRETCHER

## For Music And Movement: Pots And Pans For Our Kitchen Band

**What the children will learn—**
To march and keep the beat on their kitchen utensils and pots and pans

**Materials you will need—**
Large cardboard box, pots and pans, lids, coffee cans, large metal and wooden serving spoons, tablespoons, cassette recording of march music, tape player

**What to do—**

1. Collect all the instruments, pots and pans and utensils for the kitchen band and place them in a large cardboard box.

2. During a second circle time of the day, play some march music and let the children parade around the edge of the circle time rug, marching and clapping their hands.

3. Have the children sit on the circle time rug again and at random, call out the names of children to come up and select an instrument for the kitchen band.

4. March around the room, leading the kitchen band as they keep time with the march music.

**Something to think about—**
Banging around on pots and pans and coffee cans certainly is not real music; however, the improvised pretend band can enjoy the movement of the activity.

## 2
## FAMILIES

## A WALK IN THE RAIN

*By Ursel Scheffler*

*Illustrated by Ulises Wensell*

*Translated by Andrea Mernan*

*The book is the story of an afternoon walk in the rain which Josh and his grandmother enjoy. Dressed in his new yellow rain slicker, Josh makes many discoveries during their walk through city streets and out into the forest. He finds out where ladybugs and birds go when it rains. The adventure heightens when Barney the dog temporarily disappears. The story ends with Barney, Josh and Grandmother back home listening to Grandfather read a book. Wensell's watercolor illustrations capture the warmth and the suspense Josh and his grandmother share.*

## Circle Time Presentation

If possible, read this book on a rainy day. Place a rain hat on your head or wear a rain slicker for today's circle time. Ask the children where they think ladybugs and birds go when it rains. After a few guesses, read A WALK IN THE RAIN. Help the children recall all the things Josh and his grandmother enjoyed and discovered on their walk. Show the illustrations of Josh removing some leaves which had created a dam above a storm drain, of Josh watching twigs in the swirling stream, of the two of them pretending to be tightrope walkers, of their search for Barney and of the mushrooms growing. Conclude the circle time by having children talk about the special feelings Josh and Grandmother shared when they walked in the rain. Ask a few children to mention activities they like to do with their grandmothers.

S T O R Y   S T R E T C H E R

## For Art: Watercolors And Rain

**What the children will learn—**
To diffuse colors by using watercolors

**Materials you will need—**
Watercolors, paper, brushes, margarine tubs filled with water, sponges, salt and shakers

**What to do—**

1. Continue the discussion of favorite activities children do with their grandmothers or other family members.

2. Look at Wensell's illustrations and help the children see that the watercolors are soft and diffused, rather than having sharp lines and edges.

3. Demonstrate how to load a watercolor brush with paint and how to dry the brush on a damp sponge. Let the children experiment on scrap paper.

4. Have the children paint their pictures and after they have completed their watercolors, show them how to sprinkle salt onto the picture, let it set for a minute, then turn the painting upside down and shake off excess salt. The salt absorbs some of the moisture and makes it look like raindrops.

**Something to think about—**
Young children will enjoy the process and probably will not paint an actual picture. Older children also need to experiment with the process, but will move more quickly into illustrating favorite scenes with grandmothers.

S T O R Y   S T R E T C H E R

## For Creative Dramatics: Walking In The Rain

**What the children will learn—**
To pantomime Josh's and Grandmother's rainy day walk

**Materials you will need—**
None needed

**What to do—**

1. Look at the illustrations in A WALK IN THE RAIN and pause after each scene for the children to brainstorm how they could pantomime Josh's actions. Some children can demonstrate their movements.

2. Read the story and let the children pretend to be Josh.

3. At a later date, let some of the children pretend to be Grandmother while others are Josh.

**Something to think about—**
Younger children may need to follow or mimic the teacher's motions. Older children can pantomime different scenes and let the audience guess what scenes they are dramatizing.

## For Housekeeping And Dress-up Corner: Yellow Rain Slickers And Other Rain Wear

**What the children will learn—**
To dress themselves in rain wear and to improvise "walking in the rain" play episodes

**Materials you will need—**
Four or five sets of rain wear, as slickers, raincoats, rain hats, boots, umbrellas

**What to do—**
1. Ask parents to send in umbrellas, boots, extra raincoats and slickers that older children have outgrown, including some adult sizes that can be cut off.

2. Place the rain gear in the housekeeping and dress-up corner. Remind children of how to play safely with umbrellas.

3. Begin the play session by pretending to be Josh's grandmother who loves to walk in the rain.

4. After a brief time, leave the children to play on their own.

**Something to think about—**
The props, such as the rain slickers, serve as a stimulus for the children to role play activities associated with them and with the book. You only need four or five sets of rainwear, not enough for each child in the class, because only four or five children are in the housekeeping and dress-up corner at one time.

## For Sand Table: Making A Dam

**What the children will learn—**
To build and test dam constructions

**Materials you will need—**
Sand table, sand, water and watering can, small pieces of wood or long plastic blocks, piece of plastic wrap

**What to do—**
1. Show the illustrations of Josh playing with the leaf dam that blocked the storm drain.

2. Demonstrate how to moisten the sand and form a small dam by compacting sand together.

3. Have a child pour some water, a cup or so at a time, pausing to ask the children if the dam will hold.

4. Let the children experiment with reinforcing their compacted sand dams with various objects and test them to see which will hold back the water.

5. After the children have played and experimented with the dam building, ask them to state their observations by answering questions. What happened? What worked? What would they recommend to other dam builders?

**Something to think about—**
Young children will enjoy the sensorimotor experiences of building the dam. Older children can see the significance of having dams to control flood waters from too much rain.

## For Science And Nature: Ladybugs In A Terrarium

**What the children will learn—**
To observe ladybugs

**Materials you will need—**
Terrarium with soil and plants, ladybugs, magnifying glasses

**What to do—**
1. With the children's help, fill the terrarium with soil and add small plants. Allow the plants a few days to get well established.

2. Add a few ladybugs, 5-10, to the terrarium.

3. Help the children observe the ladybugs and also guide the children in using the magnifying glasses.

4. Discuss how ladybugs help gardeners by eating aphids which destroy vegetables and other plants.

5. After a few days, release the ladybugs into the outdoors.

**Something to think about—**
Plant nurseries will often provide a few ladybugs from a large order they have for gardeners. Some school supply stores will order ladybugs for you. Old aquariums make good terrariums. Make a top by covering with plastic wrap.

## MY GREAT GRANDPA

*By Martin Waddell*

*Illustrated by Dom Mansell*

*A little girl tells about what she and Great Grandpa do when she takes him for a ride in his wheelchair. They go down familiar streets and he watches her play in the park. When they stop to look at the house where he used to live, he tells her stories about her great grandmother. They visit Ted's shop and buy berries. One day Great Grandpa gets overheated and has to spend several days in bed resting. Granny and the little girl take good care of him. Munsell's charming illustrations are bright and extend across the pages, surrounding the print. The characters' facial expressions are easily interpreted.*

## Circle Time Presentation

Show the children the first scene where Great Grandpa and the little girl are sneaking out of the house. Ask the children to tell you what is happening in the illustration and what they think will happen next. Then read MY GREAT GRANDPA. Read the book again and pause at the scenes of their ride-walk through town and let the children tell some of the things they notice about the pictures, which are filled with busy people doing many activities. At the illustrations of Great Grandpa's old house, ask the children to describe what they see, windows boarded up, door dangling from one hinge, broken shingles and an overgrown lawn. At the next scene where Grandpa is remembering what it looked like, let other children describe the beautiful house. Continue reading and pausing for the children to describe details of the different scenes. If you know an older person who uses a wheelchair, ask the person to come to class and show the children how it operates.

STORY STRETCHER

## For Block Building: Two-story Houses

**What the children will learn—**
To construct two-story houses

**Materials you will need—**
Legos or other plastic connecting blocks, optional — scraps of construction paper, tape, plastic straws

**What to do—**
1. Have the block builders look at all the houses in the book, MY GREAT GRANDPA, and ask how the houses are alike.

2. Ask the children to build some two-story houses which can be placed on the snack tables as centerpieces.

3. After the houses are used one day on the snack tables, let the children proceed to build the whole street and park where the little girl took her great grandfather. The children can improvise ways to build swings with plastic straws, tape and construction paper.

**Something to think about—**
After Great Grandpa's village is built, leave it on a card table as a display for the library corner.

STORY STRETCHER

## For Cooking And Snack Time: Our Favorite Berries

**What the children will learn—**
To taste and select a favorite variety of berries

**Materials you will need—**
Blueberries, blackberries, raspberries, as many or as few types of berries that are available, colander, bowls, serving spoons, napkins, small plates, markers, construction paper, chart tablet or posterboard

**What to do—**
1. With a few helpers, wash and drain the berries, then place in serving bowls for each snack table.

2. Let the children serve themselves a few of each variety of berries.

3. Have the children taste the different berries and decide which ones they like best.

4. Make a simple graph of the children's preferences by asking the children to raise their hands when you call the name of their favorite berry.

5. Give each child a small square piece of construction paper which corresponds to the color of the berry they like best. For example,

blue for blueberries, black for blackberries, red for raspberries.

**6.** Let each child tape his square onto the graph, stacking them up to make a vertical column.

**7.** Have the whole class count the number of squares. Write the numeral under each column of berry squares.

**Something to think about—**
If you do not have fresh berries, taste different varieties of unsweetened frozen berries. Another type of simple graph can be made by having the children draw horizontal lines with colored markers which correspond to the color of berries they like.

## For Housekeeping And Dress-up Corner: Decorating Grandpa's Room

**What the children will learn—**
To consider what people confined to bed need to make them comfortable

**Materials you will need—**
Afghan or quilt, pillow, doll, thermometer, tray, books, magazines, games, portable radio, picture album

**What to do—**
**1.** Read again the section of MY GREAT GRANDPA where Granny and the little girl take care of Great Grandpa.

**2.** Brainstorm with the children what could be done in the housekeeping corner that would make it a good place to rest for a few days. If needed, pretend that one of the dolls is sick.

**3.** Arrange the bedroom of the housekeeping corner like Great Grandpa's room.

**4.** The children will naturally begin pretending to be Great Grandpa, Granny and the little girl.

**Something to think about—**
Helping young children to consider the needs of sick family members or to recall what made them feel better when they were sick is a way to develop empathy.

## For Library Corner: Grandparents' Storytelling

**What the children will learn—**
To listen to grandparents tell stories

**Materials you will need—**
Grandparents, optional — tape recorder and cassette tapes

**What to do—**
**1.** Invite grandparents and great grandparents to come to the classroom and to bring pictures of themselves and their families when they were young.

**2.** Have the grandparents share the pictures and tell about games and activities they enjoyed when they were children.

**3.** If some grandparents are particularly adept at storytelling, invite them to tell a favorite story they enjoyed when they were children.

**Something to think about—**
If possible, include older adults in your classroom regularly as volunteers for the library corner. Encourage children who may not be read to often at home to spend some special time listening to the grandparent read.

## For Mathematics And Manipulatives: Weighing Produce From Ted's Shop

**What the children will learn—**
To measure equivalent amounts and to handle fruits and vegetables gently

**Materials you will need—**
Balance, fruits and vegetables, apron, optional — produce scale

**What to do—**
**1.** Ask food service personnel to provide produce for the activity and then use the fruits and vegetables for snacks that the children will help to prepare during the week.

**2.** With a group of children who choose the mathematics and manipulatives area, set up the balance or produce scale and the fruit and vegetable displays.

**3.** Select a "Ted," name of the produce stand owner in MY GREAT GRANDPA, and have that person wear an apron and serve customers.

**4.** When the customers select their produce, let them place their choice in one side of the balance and let Ted try to find an equivalent amount so that the balance "balances."

**Something to think about—**
Older children can write equations. Tina's one apple equals Ted's orange and five strawberries. They can also write fruits and vegetable equations. Michelle's one grapefruit equals Ted's one squash and one cucumber. For younger children place a consistent weight in one size, as a grapefruit, and let the children find a variety of combinations which balance.

## LOVING

*By Ann Morris*

*Photographs by Ken Heyman*

*Ann Morris captures in simple eloquent text what Ken Heyman photographs eloquently — the security of warm, loving families. Families from many cultures from around the world in both city and country life are shown eating together, bathing their children, dressing, walking, talking, reading, playing and expressing their affections for each other. The index at the end of the book is a small snapshot of each large photograph with details about where the picture is made and information about the location or the family. Also at the end is a map of the world to answer, "Where in the world were these photographs taken?"*

## Circle Time Presentation

Show the children the cover of the book and tell them this book about families has a very simple title, LOVING, and you want them to listen and decide if this is a good title for the book. Read LOVING through once, then go back through, pausing for the children to talk about the pictures. Some of the pictures will cause the children to ask questions, as what is the red dot on the little girl's and the mother's head, and how can the boy make an airplane with that kind of arm, an artificial limb. Other photos will prompt the children to talk about shows they have seen on television and about the families' pets. Announce that LOVING will be in the library corner because it is one of those books that they will want to look at many times.

S T O R Y   S T R E T C H E R
## For Art: Our Gallery Of Family Photographs

**What the children will learn—**
To display photographs in unusual ways

**Materials you will need—**
Posterboard, track computer paper, variety of colors of construction paper, scissors, glue, string or yarn, coat hangers

**What to do—**
1. Ask the children to bring in photographs of themselves and their families doing a variety of activities.

2. Spread the photographs out on the table in the art center.

3. Let the children group photographs which seem to go together, such as vacation pictures, at Grandma's pictures, baby photos, etc.

4. Glue the largest group of pictures on a continuous track of computer paper and display horizontally across a chalkboard tray.

5. Attach another group of photos onto squares, rectangles, circles, and triangles of posterboard and hang from a clothes hanger with yarn or twine to create a mobile.

6. Glue another group of photos onto colorful mats of construction paper using contrasting colors.

**Something to think about—**
If possible, take the children to an art gallery for a photography show. Help children appreciate the beauty of black and white photographs by displaying them in gallery style. Also, ask a professional or talented amateur photographer to display his or her pictures alongside the children's.

S T O R Y   S T R E T C H E R
## For Housekeeping And Dress-up Corner: Costumes From Other Lands

**What the children will learn—**
To dress in clothing from different cultures and countries

**Materials you will need—**
Variety of costumes for both boys and girls, full-length mirror

**What to do—**
1. Survey your children's families for any native costumes they may have from other countries. Ask them to let the children dress up in the clothing, reminding them that it needs to be sturdy.

2. Display the costumes during a circle time during the week before moving them over to the housekeeping and dress-up corner.

3. Provide a full-length mirror and assist the children in dressing

until they can see how the clothing is supposed to be worn.

**4.** Let the children model their different costumes during one of the circle times for the day.

**Something to think about—**
Be sure to include clothing for both boys and girls. Invite parents from the different cultures to bring in the clothing and help with the fashion show from different cultures. Also ask them to bring in photographs of children from their cultures dressed in native apparel.

STORY STRETCHER

## For Library Corner: Our Book Of Families

**What the children will learn—**
To use photographs and write a text which tells about families

**Materials you will need—**
Old magazines, scissors, rubber cement or glue, typing paper, pencils or pens, cardboard, masking tape, contact paper

**What to do—**
**1.** As one of the table top activities when the children first arrive in the morning and as one of the free play choices for the library, have children cut out pictures from magazines of families. Remind the children that families can be just two people.

**2.** Let the children select at least one picture they would like to write about. Have them discuss their picture with the group or with a writing partner.

**3.** Provide typing paper for them to glue their magazine photos onto and for their writing. Draw a one-inch margin down the right hand side of one sheet of paper. Let the children write their text on this sheet.

**4.** On another sheet of paper, which will become the facing page, draw a one-inch margin down the left hand side of the paper. Let the children glue their photographs on this page. Show the children how to lay out the facing pages.

**5.** Have the children write their text by writing on their own or by dictating to you. Encourage children to write even if they are at the scribble stage or are just beginning to form letters.

**6.** Follow the simple directions in the appendix and bind the children's photographs and writings by using cardboard, masking tape and contact paper.

**Something to think about—**
Continue to add to the family book collection by checking out from the library the books listed under "Additional References for Families" found at the end of this chapter. Also continue binding children's stories about families into other books to add to the class collection. Some titles children might write or draw about include "Families Cooking and Eating," "Families Playing Together," "Families Working Together" and "Family Holidays and Celebrations.

STORY STRETCHER

## For Mathematics And Manipulatives: Wooden Bead Abacus

**What the children will learn—**
To manipulate an abacus and count

**Materials you will need—**
Abacus, wooden beads, shoelaces, cardboard, clothespin

**What to do—**
**1.** Show the children the photograph in LOVING of the Chinese-American girl whose father is teaching her to count on an abacus.

**2.** Use an abacus and demonstrate how to move the beads to count.

**3.** Let the children tell each other numbers to show on the abacus.

**4.** Tie knots in one end of the shoelaces and have the children make a simple abacus by stringing ten wooden beads.

**5.** Tie knots in the other ends of the shoelaces to keep the beads on, leaving enough space to move the beads.

**6.** Support the beads and shoelaces by cutting a one-inch slash in the edge of the top and bottom of a sheet of cardboard and pulling the end of the shoelace through to hold them in place.

**7.** Have the children use the clothespins to count the number of beads, then clip the clothespin onto the shoelace to hold the beads together which represent that number.

**Something to think about—**
Give the children interesting objects to count such as sea shells, toy cars, dishes from the housekeeping corner. Then have the children move a bead on the abacus as each object is counted.

STORY STRETCHER

## For Science And Nature: Caring For Our Pet In Loving Ways

**What the children will learn—**
To show affection and care for a classroom pet

**Materials you will need—**
Gerbil, hamster or guinea pig, cage and habitat supplies, feed, water

**What to do—**

**1.** Look back through the pictures in LOVING and find all of the pictures of family pets.

**2.** Discuss how pets are a part of families and that they need taking care of just like parents take care of us.

**3.** Talk about the classroom pet and how we take care of our pet.

**4.** Gently remove the animal from the cage and show the children how to hold and gently stroke the animal. Pass the animal to a calm child, and as the child holds the animal, talk about how well the child is doing at holding the animal.

**5.** Each day let a few children take turns holding the class pet. Also talk about providing other necessities to take care of the animal, as a clean cage, food, water, privacy.

**Something to think about—**

If you do not have a classroom pet, have the children take turns bringing in their animals and let each child talk about how they and their family members care for the pet.

# REFERENCES

Brown, Marc. (1987). **ARTHUR'S BABY.** New York: Joy Street Books

Hines, Anna Grossnickle. (1986). **DADDY MAKES THE BEST SPAGHETTI.** New York: Clarion Books.

Morris, Ann. (1990). Photographs by Ken Heyman. **LOVING.** New York: Lothrop, Lee & Shepard Books.

Scheffler, Ursel. (1986). Illustrated by Ulises Wensell, translated by Andrea Mernan. **A WALK IN THE RAIN.** New York: G. P. Putnam's Sons.

Waddell, Martin. (1990). Illustrated by Dom Mansell. **MY GREAT GRANDPA.** New York: G. P. Putnam's Sons.

## Additional References For Families

Bogart, Jo Ellen. (1990). Illustrated by Janet Wilson. **DANIEL'S DOG.** New York: Scholastic. *A young boy adjusts to the arrival of his new baby sister with the help of his imaginary dog, Lucy.*

Bunting, Eve. (1989). Illustrated by Susan Meddaugh. **NO NAP.** New York: Clarion Books. *Dad tries various activities to get Susie tired enough to take her nap, but they only exhaust him.*

Hessell, Jenny. (1989). Illustrated by Jenny Williams. **STAYING AT SAM'S.** New York: Lippincott. *Two boys who are friends compare differences in their families, such as at Sam's where there's all that kissing.*

Yolen, Jane. (1978). Illustrated by Nancy Winslow Parker. **NO BATH TO-NIGHT.** New York: Harper & Row. *A small boy refuses to take a bath until his grandmother shows him how to make kid tea.*

Zolotow, Charlotte. (1966). Illustrated by Martha Alexander. **BIG SIS-TER, LITTLE SISTER.** New York: Harper & Row. *Big Sister and Little Sister enjoy each other's company until Little Sister gets tired of being told what to do and runs away.*

# 3

# FRIENDS

*Jessica*

*We Are Best Friends*

*A Home*

*My Friend Leslie: The Story of a Handicapped Child*

*Ira Sleeps Over*

## 3
## FRIENDS

## JESSICA

*By Kevin Henkes*

*Ruthie had an imaginary friend named Jessica, but her parents keep saying to her again and again, "There is no Jessica." Ruthie, however, continued to play with Jessica on the playground and at Grandma's on the weekend. Jessica also ate with her, read books with Ruthie, built blocks with her, and even had the same feelings. When Ruthie was mad, so was Jessica. When Ruthie was sad or glad, Jessica was too. When Ruthie had a birthday party, so did Jessica. Ruthie's parents continued to insist there was no Jessica, and that Ruthie would make new friends at school and that Jessica should stay home. But Jessica went anyway and Ruthie felt better when she imagined Jessica was with her. Then, guess who Ruthie met at school, a real girl, a new friend, named Jessica. Henke's illustrations are brightly colored and the arrangement of the print adds to the expressiveness of the story.*

## Circle Time Presentation

If you had an imaginary friend when you were a child, talk about your friend. If you did not, tell about someone's imaginary play-mate they had. Ask the children if they like to pretend that they have a friend playing with them when they are home playing alone. Read JESSICA, saying the stern words of the parents in an emphatic voice, "There is no Jessica!" This is one of those stories which the children will want you to read again. Reread it and pause for the children to say the part about there is no Jessica. At the end of the book, have the children line up two by two and ask, "Can I be your partner?" just as Ruthie and Jessica found each other as partners. Be certain to pair the children yourself, so no one is left out, rather than having the students make the selections. Then dismiss the partners, by twos, to choose whatever center or activity they would like for free play.

STORY STRETCHER

## For Art: Sharing Paintbrushes To Make One Picture

**What the children will learn—**
To take turns and to respond to each other's painting

**Materials you will need—**
Easels, paper, tempera paint, brushes

**What to do—**
1. With four children in the art center, pair them to paint together, one pair on each side of the easel.
2. Show them the picture in JESSICA where Ruthie painted with her imaginary friend by sharing the paintbrush. Ask the children to share the paintbrush with each other and make a picture together.

3. Have the children brainstorm how they might work together, as one paints a stroke and then gives the brush to the other, or one paints one side of the paper and the other paints the other side.
4. Stay nearby without hovering over the painters and encourage co-operation.

**Something to think about—**
Younger children may have difficulty painting together by alternating brush strokes, but they can share the space on the paper. Older children may enjoy writing about their painting and how they decided what to paint by talking with their friend.

ANOTHER STORY STRETCHER

## For Art: Crayon Resist Of Favorite Designs

**What the children will learn—**
To make a painting using crayon and paints

**Materials you will need—**
Crayons, manilla paper or construction paper, tempera or watercolor paints, brushes, clean-up supplies

**What to do—**
1. Show the children the end paper pages of JESSICA and talk about how the artists decorated the pages with the flower designs.
2. Ask the children what some of their favorite designs are, such as birds flying, sunbursts, stars, bows, balloons.
3. Have the children draw a page of their designs using very heavy markings of the wax crayons. Go over the designs twice if needed.
4. Demonstrate how to wet the paintbrush with tempera paint or watercolors and paint over the designs. The paint will not be ab-

sorbed by the paper where the crayon designs are colored.

**5.** Allow the paints to dry overnight, then display them near a copy of the book open to the end paper pages.

**Something to think about—**
Always plan to have art activities available for several days. Children need to experiment with the techniques and explore the possibilities of the media, and then they can go on to create some of their original designs.

STORY STRETCHER

## For Library Corner: Our Class Poster, Who We Are

**What the children will learn—**
To recall the names of their classmates

**Materials you will need—**
Instant print camera and film, posterboard, name tags, markers

**What to do—**
**1.** Take a picture of the children during circle time, or if the photo will be too crowded, take several snapshots of the children playing throughout the room.

**2.** In a second circle time of the day or in the library corner during free play, show the children the illustration from JESSICA in which all the children are pictured. Around the picture, the names of the children are printed at random.

**3.** Glue the photo of the class in the center of the poster.

**4.** Have the children recall the names of their classmates and print each person's name on the poster. Then print the name on a name tag for the child to wear.

**Something to think about—**
For younger children, already have the name tags printed and spread out on a table. After you print

each child's name on the poster, the children can find their own names. For older children, let the children dictate sentences about each other. For example, Chris might say, "I like Darla's tennis shoes with red stripes." Print the sentences under the snapshot on the poster.

STORY STRETCHER

## For Mathematics And Manipulatives: Building Ruthie's And Jessica's Towers

**What the children will learn—**
To build a name tower and count the letters needed

**Materials you will need—**
Alphabet blocks, optional — counting blocks, small Post-it notes

**What to do—**
**1.** Show the children who come to the center the illustration of the name towers which Ruthie built.

**2.** Have the children count the number of blocks needed to build a tower of each child's name, Jessica (7 blocks) and Ruthie (6 blocks).

**3.** Then ask the children how many blocks it would take to build their name towers.

**4.** Ask them to build name towers using the alphabet blocks. If there is not enough of one letter, stick a Post-it note with the letter printed on it on a counting block as an alternative.

**Something to think about—**
For younger children, it will be easier for them to line up the blocks like trains. To help them, print their names in large block letters about the same size as the wooden blocks, then the child can match letter to block. Older children may enjoy building their friends' name towers or making a

train of all the girls' names or boys' names and counting how many letter blocks are needed.

STORY STRETCHER

## For Music And Movement: Crawling Through Tunnels

**What the children will learn—**
To realize how much space their bodies occupy

**Materials you will need—**
Collapsible fabric indoor tunnel, or small boxes open at both ends, cassette player and lively recording of favorite song

**What to do—**
**1.** Talk about Ruthie's feelings when she was crawling through the tunnel in JESSICA. She was afraid she might get lost.

**2.** Start to crawl through a tunnel and ask the children if there is enough space for you.

**3.** Some child will volunteer that she is not too big for the tunnel. Encourage her crawl through.

**4.** Have the children try out the tunnels, and while they are inside, ask them to reach over their heads and see how far they can reach, as well as how far their arms can stretch.

**5.** Add music and have the children crawl through the tunnel. When the music stops no one should be in the tunnel. Do not use the music as an elimination game. It is exciting enough just trying to get through the tunnel before the music stops.

**Something to think about—**
As a relaxation technique to prepare for nap time, ask the children to lie down flat and stretch out as far as they can stretch. Then, have them make their bodies small enough to crawl through the tunnel. Repeat several times to relax.

## 3
## FRIENDS

## WE ARE BEST FRIENDS

*By Aliki*

*Robert is devastated by the news that Peter, his best friend, is moving away. Robert thinks he will never find another friend like Peter, and he hopes that Peter will miss him too. Eventually after many days of longing, both boys find new friends, but remain best friends and keep their friendship alive by drawing pictures and writing letters. Bright fluid marker illustrations in appealing Aliki artistic style make this a visually appealing book.*

## Circle Time Presentation

Show the children the cover of the book and tell them the boys are Robert and Peter, who are best friends. On the cover, the boys are swinging together. Discuss other things that friends like to do together. Read WE ARE BEST FRIENDS. At the end, several children who have had the experience of friends moving away will identify with Robert and the feeling of being left behind. Let two or three children share their stories before talking about how each child can make new friends in the classroom.

STORY STRETCHER

## For Art: Picture Letter For A Friend

**What the children will learn—**
To communicate with a friend through a sketch

**Materials you will need—**
Paper, pencils, magic markers, long business-size envelopes

**What to do—**

1.   Call attention to Aliki's illustrations and have the children notice how brightly colored they are. Ask the children how they think Aliki made those bright colors. Someone will mention magic markers.

2.   Ask the children to sketch first with the pencils and then add color with the magic markers.

3.   Mention that Robert and Peter sent pictures back and forth in the mail as a way to tell each other what they were doing.

4.   Assign each child a partner so that each person has a special friend at school for whom to draw and write a picture letter.

5.   After the children have finished their pictures, let them write

a few sentences on their own, or assist them in writing a message by letting them dictate and you write for them.

6.   Demonstrate how to fold the pictures so that they will fit into a long envelope.

**Something to think about—**
Pairing children, rather than letting them choose, protects the new child who may not yet have friends.

STORY STRETCHER

## For Cooking And Snack Time: A Birthday Party For Robert

**What the children will learn—**
To prepare a birthday cake

**Materials you will need—**
Cake mix, two eggs, milk or water depending on the recipe, cake pan, microwave or toaster oven, measuring cups and spoons, mixing bowl, spatula, canned frosting, knives, candles, napkins, plates, forks, glasses, milk

**What to do—**

1.   Remind the children that one of Robert's concerns was that Peter was moving away before Robert's birthday and would miss his party. Tell the children that you are going to have a party for Robert and bake a birthday cake for him.

2.   On the day of the cake baking, divide the children into groups of mixers, decorators, cleaners, servers.

3.   Follow the package directions for baking in a microwave or toaster oven.

4.   When the cake has baked and cooled, let the decorators spread the frosting and add the candles. Dipping a knife or spatula in water and then into the frosting helps to spread the frosting more easily.

5. Have the servers set the table with napkins, plates, forks and glasses for milk.

6. Light the candles and sing "Happy Birthday to You" to Robert.

7. With your assistance, let each child cut his or her own piece of cake.

8. Have the cleaners clear the snack tables and help them wash the baking and serving utensils.

**Something to think about—**

When you have birthday parties for real children, plan carefully with parents so that they do not bring too many sweets. Also, if some parents cannot afford birthday cakes or cupcakes, ask the parents' permission for a group of "bakery helpers" from the school to provide the cake.

STORY STRETCHER

## For Library Corner: Book Of Messages To Our Friend

**What the children will learn—**
To compose a message and illustrate it, telling what their friend would like to know

**Materials you will need—**
Typing paper, pencils, pens, fineline markers, colored pencils or crayons

**What to do—**
1. When a classmate moves away, it is difficult for the child who moves, but it is also puzzling for the children who are left behind. Discuss their feelings and what they remember about their friend "David" who moved recently.

2. Tell the children that you have been thinking about "David" and how he must be wondering what is happening in the class since he left. Brainstorm some ideas which

the children think "David" would like to hear about.

3. Let each child dictate a sentence or two about how "David" is missed or tell him some class news. Leaving a one-inch margin on the left, print their sentences on the bottom of sheets of typing paper.

4. Ask each child to draw a picture which illustrates their message to "David."

5. When the children have finished their illustrations, staple the pages together, add a cover sheet and bind into a book. See the appendix for the steps in binding a book.

6. Mail the message book to "David."

**Something to think about—**
Ask "David" to write and draw a letter about his new home, friends and school. Some children whose families have video cameras may send a video tape instead of a letter and drawing.

STORY STRETCHER

## For Mathematics And Manipulatives: Replicating Patterns With Blocks

**What the children will learn—**
To observe and replicate a friend's building structure

**Materials you will need—**
Small wooden blocks or plastic connecting blocks, toy cars and trucks

**What to do—**
1. Show the illustrations from WE ARE BEST FRIENDS of the boys building block structures and playing with the toy cars and trucks.

2. Build a simple structure with blocks and ask a child to build another one just like it.

3. Pairs of children can build structures, with one child as builder the second as replicator. Then they can switch roles.

**Something to think about—**
Younger children will place blocks end on end to create a train and other linear structures, while older children may use a variety of ways to replicate their friend's work, adding a block at a time or completing a structure.

STORY STRETCHER

## For Science And Nature: Finding Greenies, Looking For Frogs

**What the children will learn—**
To look for frogs in cool, wet places

**Materials you will need—**
Parents and other volunteers, parent permission slips, transportation

1. If possible, take the children on a field trip to a pond to look for frogs. If the field trip is not possible, ask a parent who lives in an area where frogs can be found to bring in a frog.

2. Have the children look for frogs, which Will called "Greenies" in WE ARE BEST FRIENDS. Show them how to look along the pond bank and in cool, shaded, damp places. Demonstrate how to gently push back the lower branches of weeds and grasses and look near the cool wet earth.

**Something to think about—**
If you have access to tadpoles, bring some in for the children to observe how they grow. Call them "Inkywiggles," as Peter did in the book WE ARE BEST FRIENDS.

## 3
## FRIENDS

## A HOME

*By Nola Langner Malone*

*The book opens with scenes of Molly saying good-bye to her old house and her favorite places to play. At the new house, nothing seems right until she meets one of her neighbors, Miranda Marie, a girl her age. They play throughout the day, "pigs in the mud," "fish in the water," "caterpillars dancing," until it is dark outside, and they end the day with a fight over who sees the first star. Lonely and upset, Molly returns to the new house feeling dejected, until she looks out the window and sees Miranda Marie looking out her window directly across from her. They wave to each other and declare they will play again tomorrow. Malone's line drawings washed with cheerful colors are wonderfully complementary to the various moods in the story. The shadows in the day scenes and the layers of dark blue with twinkling stars for the evening are especially effective. Malone's depictions of Molly and Miranda Marie and their expressive faces heighten the interest in the story of the new friendship.*

## Circle Time Presentation

Ask the children how many of them have ever moved. Talk about the experience of saying good-bye to the old house and then how strangely the new house felt. Tell them sometimes girls and boys feel lonely because they have not made any new friends in their new neighborhoods. After reading A HOME, ask a few children to help you retell the story by looking at the pictures. Allow time for any comments the children may want to share about their moving experiences or their arguments and making up with friends.

STORY STRETCHER
## For Art: Starry Nights

**What the children will learn—**
To control dark watercolors

**Materials you will need—**
Dark blue watercolor paints, small brushes, paper, margarine tubs with water, newspapers or paper towels, salt in a large shaker, manilla paper, crayons, scissors

**What to do—**
1. Show a small group of children in the art center the night scenes from A HOME and explain the dark blue is watercolor.

2. Demonstrate how to wet the paper with water, load the watercolor brush with blue paint and how to dry the brush by dabbing it onto old newspaper or paper towels.

3. Let the children experiment with making dark blue night skies. Allow the paint to almost dry, then shake salt onto the painting. It will crystalize and look like stars.

4. While the watercolor skies are drying, ask the children to draw and color either Molly and Miranda Marie or themselves with a friend.

5. Have the children cut out the friends and paste them onto the starry night background.

**Something to think about—**
Demonstrate painting techniques on your own paper but avoid painting for the children. Also, if the children are not able to cut out their drawings well, avoid cutting for them. Accept whatever level of skill the child brings to the task.

STORY STRETCHER
## For Blocks: Building Ranch Houses, Two-story Houses, Apartments

**What the children will learn—**
To build a variety of houses

**Materials you will need—**
Preferably large hollow blocks, smaller wooden blocks, large index cards or construction paper, markers

**What to do—**
1. With a small group of block builders, discuss how Molly moved from a one-story ranch-type house to a two-story house.

2. Ask them to build some houses like Molly's old one and her new one. Be sure to emphasize placing Miranda Marie's and Molly's house close enough together that they can see each other from their windows.

3. Make signs for Miranda Marie's and Molly's houses using large index cards or construction paper and markers.

4. Leave the houses set up in the block corner throughout the day. If the blocks are a heavy usage center, have the two model houses built on a table.

**Something to think about—**
If you have a number of children who have moved recently, have them build models of their old and new apartment buildings or houses. Label the exhibits and allow time during the second circle time of the day for the children to talk about their buildings.

STORY STRETCHER

## For Housekeeping And Dress-up Corner: Moving Day

**What the children will learn—**
To pack and label boxes

**Materials you will need—**
Board or chart tablet, packing boxes, newspaper, wagons, labels, markers

**What to do—**
1. At circle time, discuss that today is moving day. Today, we will move the housekeeping corner to another area of the room. There will be packing to do, labeling boxes, loading the van (wagons), unloading, unpacking and deciding where everything goes in the new house area.

2. Ask the children to volunteer for jobs for each stage of moving, packing and labeling, loading and unloading, unpacking and arranging the new house area. Write the volunteers' names on the board or a chart tablet under their job.

3. Have the packers come to the housekeeping and dress-up corner first and help them assemble the boxes and begin wrapping each item individually for moving. Let the packers decide how to label the boxes. They may want to draw pictures, as a cup and saucer to label the box of dishes, or write the words for the contents.

4. Continue with minimal supervision for each stage, calling the next group of workers for loading, hauling and unloading. Have the unpackers and arrangers finish the move.

5. At each stage of the moving process, emphasize how everyone is working together.

**Something to think about—**
Everyone will want to be involved in the move. Usually, moving one center or area of the classroom necessitates another move.

(Idea adapted from one discussed with Sharon Winstead.)

STORY STRETCHER

## For Library Corner: Talking About Moving And New Friends

**What the children will learn—**
To participate in a discussion of feelings

**Materials you will need—**
None needed

**What to do—**
1. Ask the small group of children who have moved recently to come to the library corner with you.

2. Reread A HOME and then select one child and ask if it would be all right if you made up a story about his or her move.

3. Using A HOME as the model, retell the story using the child's name. For example, "One hot day in August, Eric moved to a new apartment. He said good-bye to the swings in his old playground. Good-bye to James who lived next door."

4. When you get to the part of the story where Eric meets a new friend, if he hasn't met anyone in the neighborhood yet, then tell the story of Eric's coming to school for the first day and making a new friend.

5. If Eric hasn't had an argument with a friend, end the story with the friends planning to see each other the next day.

**Something to think about—**
For young children moving to a new neighborhood in the same town or moving to a new school can be as traumatic as moving across the country. Story retelling will help the new student deal with the mixed feelings of excitement and anxiety that often accompany the first moves the children can remember.

STORY STRETCHER

## For Music And Movement: Caterpillars Dancing

**What the children will learn—**
To move like caterpillars wiggling out of a cocoon

**Materials you will need—**
Large pieces of old fabric or sheeting or rolls of paper toweling

**What to do—**
1. Show the children the scene from A HOME where Molly and Miranda Marie are wrapped up in towels and are wiggling, bouncing and leaping up and down as they pretend to be caterpillars.

2. Have a few children do the caterpillar dance by wrapping them up and letting them wiggle out of their fabric or towel cocoons. Do not make the wrapping too constraining.

3. Add music on a second day and continue the caterpillar dances throughout the week.

**Something to think about—**
Often parents or grandparents who sew have many pieces of fabric which they can donate to make the cocoons.

## MY FRIEND LESLIE:
## The Story Of A
## Handicapped Child

*By Maxine B. Rosenberg*

*Photographs by George Ancona*

*Leslie and Karin are best friends in kindergarten. The text which accompanies the black and white photographs is Karin's story about her friend Leslie who has multiple handicaps. Seen through a child's eyes, Leslie is accepted as a real friend to enjoy, a capable friend whose ways of acting and means of getting things done are different. Karin tells about Leslie's behaviors, her special hearing aids and ways the teachers and other children help Leslie. A pleasingly honest book which tells Leslie's capabilities and limitations. The photographs capture the girls' friendship and tell the story even without the text.*

## Circle Time Presentation

Talk about someone you know who is handicapped. Speak positively about the person complimenting her or him on all the things he or she knows how to do. If some of the children in the class are handicapped or have a brother or sister who has disabilities, let the children talk about their friends or family members, again in the positive tone you have modeled. Show the cover photograph of the book and ask the children if these two girls are friends. Read MY FRIEND LESLIE: THE STORY OF A HANDICAPPED CHILD. At the end of the story, discuss with the children all the ways Leslie did things differently but still did them, as putting the book up very close to her face to see the pictures, taking more time to walk down the hall and dressing up to play ballerina. Let them discuss how Karin helped Leslie and recall what they enjoyed doing together. Emphasize their friendship, more than Leslie's handicaps.

STORY STRETCHER
## For Art: Painting Large Leslie Flowers

**What the children will learn—**
To paint in a large size so that their paintings can be easily seen

**Materials you will need—**
Easel, paper, brushes, paints, clothespins, clothes line

**What to do—**
1. Talk with the children who come to the art center about Leslie's having difficulty seeing small flowers, so she paints large ones. Ask the children to paint large flowers that almost fill the paper.

2. Display the flowers along a chalkboard or hang them on a line with clothespins. Intersperse among the paintings some earlier ones the children have done where they painted in normal size.

3. After there is a collection of "Large Leslie Flowers," have the children stand all the way across the room and notice how much easier it is to see the large proportions of the flowers than to see the smaller objects in other paintings.

**Something to think about—**
For several days after reading MY FRIEND LESLIE: THE STORY OF A HANDICAPPED CHILD, when the children paint or draw something large, say, "Oh, that would be a good tree for Leslie to see, it nearly fills up the paper."

STORY STRETCHER
## For Cooking And Snack Time: Crunchy Veggies

**What the children will learn—**
To wash, peel and cut vegetables for a snack

**Materials you will need—**
Carrots, celery, zucchini, cucumbers, broccoli, vegetable peelers, vegetable brush, paring knives, cutting boards, serving tray, napkins

**What to do—**
1. Demonstrate for the cooking and snack helpers, how to wash the vegetables, including using the vegetable brush.

2. When they have finished washing the vegetables, demonstrate how to use the vegetable peelers and knives.

3. Peel and cut the vegetables.

4. Let the children arrange the vegetables in a nice arrangement on a serving tray.

5. Serve the vegetables at snack time and discuss how Leslie and

Karin liked peeling carrots when their class was preparing a stew.

**Something to think about—**
Some teachers are reluctant to let young children have real paring knives. If you have the snack helpers sit at a table with you and show them how to place the vegetable down on a cutting board and how to hold the knife, they are quite capable of remembering the safety precautions.

STORY STRETCHER

## For Creative Dramatics: Dramatizing Our Friends' Favorite Stories

**What the children will learn—**
To consider their friends' favorite stories and to pantomime actions or say lines from the stories

**Materials you will need—**
None needed

**What to do—**
1. Show the photographs of Leslie reading her favorite story, "Little Red Riding Hood," and acting out the parts.

2. Select at least two children who will go to two other children and ask their favorite stories.

3. The children who are asked will whisper their favorite stories and the children who are actors will have to think of an action or a line which will dramatize the story. For example, if one child said her favorite story was "The Gingerbread Boy," then the actor might run across the floor and say, "Run, run, as fast as you can. You can't catch me I'm the _____."
4. Continue with the favorite story pairs.

**Something to think about—**
Have younger children whisper their favorite stories to you and help them think of an action or a line from the story which they could give as a clue. Older children can form more elaborate productions and dramatize entire tales.

STORY STRETCHER

## For Library Corner: Tape Of "My Friend Leslie"

**What the children will learn—**
To follow directions

**Materials you will need—**
Tape recorder, cassette tape, listening station, headphones

**What to do—**
1. Invite the children who choose to come to the library corner during center time or free play to help you make a tape recording of MY FRIEND LESLIE.

2. Let the children help you decide what a good page turning signal might be, as a stapler clicking, a tap of a spoon or fork against a glass, a tiny bell or a word the children all want to say together at your cue. They might say, "friends," and when the listeners hear several children's voices at once saying "friends," then it is time to turn the page.

3. Ask one child to speak into the microphone and record instructions, telling the children who will be listening to the tape what their page-turning signal will be.

4. Practice reading the book and having the children make the page turning signal on cue.

5. Tape record the book.

6. Let the tape recorders be the first children to have a turn hearing the book.

**Something to think about—**
Discuss the volume control at the listening station. If you have a child who wears a hearing aid, let the child experiment with a variety of sound levels so he or she can enjoy the tapes.

STORY STRETCHER

## For Science And Nature: Hearing Aids

**What the children will learn—**
To examine a variety of types of hearing aids

**Materials you will need—**
An audiologist or therapist, model or enlarged cut-away drawing of an ear, hearing aids

**What to do—**
1. Invite an audiologist or medical supplier to come to the classroom and show the children some different kinds of hearing aids. Be certain to have one like Leslie's which is worn like a headband.

2. Discuss with the speaker ahead of time that the children will want to handle these hearing aids and try them on.

3. If possible, have the hearing aids, any models of the ear and safety tips for good hearing remain in the classroom for the children to examine over the course of the week.

**Something to think about—**
Select a speaker who either has children this age or who understands how to interact with young children. Guest speakers are often disappointed with young children's lack of interest in a topic; however, often it is because the speaker has forgotten that young children learn best by active learning, not passive listening.

## 3
## FRIENDS

## IRA SLEEPS OVER

*By Bernard Waber*

*IRA SLEEPS OVER is the story of a little boy's dilemma about whether or not to take his teddy bear to his friend's house for his first time ever to sleep away from home. His sister taunted Ira, telling him he wouldn't be able to sleep without Tah Tah and that Reggie would laugh at him. When the fateful night came, after a round of ghost stories, Reggie got out his teddy bear. Ira went next door, found Tah Tah, marched past his family and went to Reggie's to find him fast asleep with his teddy bear in his arms. Bold black line drawings with reds, yellows, pinks and greens provide the background for Waber's comic, but near realistic illustrations.*

## Circle Time Presentation

IRA SLEEPS OVER is a selection for the unit on friendship, but it could be used for the "feelings" unit or the "teddy bears and other bears" theme. Hold a teddy bear on your lap and tell what you like about this bear. If it belongs to you, tell where you got it, how long you've had it, his or her name, and where your teddy bear sleeps. Ask the children if any of them sleep with a teddy bear. Have a few volunteers tell about their stuffed animals. Show the cover of the book and introduce them to Ira. Read IRA SLEEPS OVER while cuddling your teddy bear. Discuss that Ira was afraid his friend would tease him, and Reggie was afraid too because he hid his teddy bear. Let the children talk about what the two friends enjoyed doing together, such as looking at Reggie's junk collection, pillow fights, looking through a magnifying glass and just being together. End by showing the children the front of the book again and let someone tell what Ira is doing and when this scene happened in IRA SLEEPS OVER.

STORY STRETCHER

## For Art: Friends Together

**What the children will learn—**
To depict friends enjoying each other's company

**Materials you will need—**
Choice of art media, paints, easel, brushes, paper, crayons, markers, charcoals, colored pencils

**What to do—**
1. With the children who come to the art area during free play or center time, discuss some of the activities they like to do with their friends at school or when visiting each other.

2. Ask the children to make a picture of themselves playing with a friend.

3. When the drawings or paintings are finished, add captions that the children dictate.

4. Display their artwork on a "friends together" bulletin board.

**Something to think about—**
Be sure to include some of the less popular children in the discussions. If you have children who have no friends at school, in a private discussion try to find out if they have playmates in their neighborhoods. Begin a "friend for the day" arrangement and pair children to sit together during circle and snack time. Often friendships will bud when they get to know each other more.

STORY STRETCHER

## For Housekeeping And Dress-up Corner: Sleeping Over

**What the children will learn—**
To role play sleeping over

**Materials you will need—**
Suitcase or backpack, stuffed animals, house shoes, pajamas or doll clothes sleepers, crib, blankets

**What to do—**
1. Provide any extra props that you think might help the children relate to IRA SLEEPS OVER. For example, Ira walks around with a blanket over his shoulders.

2. Place a blanket over your shoulders and pretend to be Ira going home to get his teddy bear.

3. After a few minutes of playing with the children, place the blanket around a child's shoulder and let that child become Ira.

**Something to think about—**
Teachers are often reluctant to interject themselves into young children's play. A good rule of thumb is that if the play is already in progress, then wait for a natural break. The blanket and Ira interactions above are a good stimulus for play; however, often the teacher's presence will not be needed. Simply providing the props will be suggestive enough that the children will pretend their own sleepover adventures.

STORY STRETCHER

## For Library Corner: What I Like About My Friend For The Day

**What the children will learn—**
To plan the kinds of compliments they will give and say them into a microphone

**Materials you will need—**
Tape recorder, cassette tape

**What to do—**
1. Select several of the "friendship pairs" who are not normally playmates and have them come to the library area for a special activity.

2. Compliment two children, a boy and a girl. You might say, " I like the way Rebecca paints," and go on by telling an example you recall from her artwork. You could say, "I like the way Jorge sings and plays the rhythm instruments. He likes music."

3. Ask one of the very verbal children to compliment his or her "friend for the day."

4. After everyone has made some nice comments, tell the children that they did so well that you want to tape record their compliments so they can keep them and listen whenever they choose.

5. Begin each tape by having the children greet the listener and then introduce their special friend by giving their friend a compliment. Continue the tape by asking the introducer what the two friends have done together today.

6. After the children have finished speaking about their friends, label the tapes and let the children listen to them.

7. Later, tape compliments you notice about the children, how one helps take care of the plants, enjoys housekeeping and dress-up, shares materials easily with friends, eagerly helps take playground equipment outside, pretends to read or really reads, tells good stories, writes using whatever letters they know, sings joyfully, builds skillfully with blocks.

**Something to think about—**
If possible, send the tapes home with the children. Many parents of less popular children are very concerned about their child's social acceptance.

STORY STRETCHER

## For Mathematics And Manipulatives: Sorting Daytime And Nighttime Pictures

**What the children will learn—**
To classify activities by when they take place, daytime or nighttime

**Materials you will need—**
Magazine pictures, scissors, yarn

**What to do—**
1. Let the children look through magazines and catalogs and find pictures of items that represent different activities which take place in the daytime or nighttime. A box of cereal might represent breakfast, daytime, and a picture of a child in pajamas might represent nighttime.

2. After the children have cut out their pictures, place two large circles of yarn on the table. Let the children sort their pictures into daytime or nighttime.

3. When they begin sorting, there will be problems. Some pictures of items will represent activities that could be daytime or nighttime. For example, a tube of toothpaste might represent brushing one's teeth in the morning or in the evening. Ask the children what to do to solve the problem.

4. Accept their solutions and let them continue sorting.

**Something to think about—**
One way young children solve the problem is by discarding pictures which are not definitely daytime or nighttime. Another solution young children often come up with is simply to let the child who cut out the picture decide whether to place it in the daytime circle or the nighttime circle. Older children will place the pictures which can go either place in a separate stack. When asked what the extra stack of pictures outside the circles is for, the discussion may lead to the decision to have the circles overlap in the middle as a place for the pictures which represent both daytime and nighttime activities.

STORY STRETCHER

## For Science And Nature: That's Not Junk, That's My Science Collection

**What the children will learn—**
To describe their collection of objects from nature

**Materials you will need—**
Sea shells, index cards or Post-it notes, marker

**What to do—**

1. Turn to the pages in IRA SLEEPS OVER where Reggie is showing IRA his junk collection.

2. Let volunteers tell what they have in their special collections.

3. Tell the children that you or a young friend of yours like to collect sea shells. Discuss that the sea shells you have placed on the science table are part of a nature collection.

4. Have the children think of other things they collect that come from nature, such as rocks, bird feathers, butterfly wings.

5. Discuss that some collections are not real objects from nature like those already mentioned, but are collections of pictures of animals, birds, butterflies or flowers. Ask if anyone collects pictures of things found in nature.

6. Request that the children take turns bringing in their collections. Ask three children who participated in the discussion to bring in their collections the next day.

7. Display the collections on the science and nature table. Place an index card and quotes from the children about the items in their boxes.

**Something to think about—**

In a newsletter, alert the parents about your request for the nature collections and explain that what they think of as children's junk collections often have a variety of natural items. Also consider letting the children tape record information about their collections and leave the tapes inside their collection box. Anyone who wants to hear about the collection can listen. Taping often promotes better listening than a show and tell exercise.

# REFERENCES

Aliki. (1982). **WE ARE BEST FRIENDS**. New York: Mulberry Books.

Henkes, Kevin. (1989). **JESSICA**. New York: Greenwillow Books.

Malone, Nola Langner. (1988). **A HOME**. New York: Bradbury Press.

Rosenberg, Maxine B. (1983). Photographs by George Ancona. **MY FRIEND LESLIE: The Story Of A Handicapped Child**. New York: Lothrop, Lee & Shepard.

Waber, Bernard. (1972). **IRA SLEEPS OVER**. Boston: Houghton Mifflin Company

## Additional References For Friends

Bunting, Eve. (1988). Illustrated by Jan Brett. **HAPPY BIRTHDAY, DEAR DUCK**. New York: Clarion Books. *Duck's birthday gifts from his animal friends are wonderful but cannot be used away from water, a problem solved by the last gift.*

Delacre, Lulu. (1986). **NATHAN AND NICHOLAS ALEXANDER**. New York: Scholastic. *The story of how a mouse and an elephant make friends and share a room.*

Havill, Juanita. (1986). Illustrated by Anne Sibley O'Brien. **JAMAICA'S FIND**. Boston: Houghton Mifflin Company. *A little girl finds a stuffed dog at the park and takes it home with her, later deciding to take it to the lost and found at the park office. The next day she meets the child who lost the toy and finds a new friend.*

Lillie, Patricia. (1989). **JAKE AND ROSIE**. New York: Greenwillow Books. *Jake is upset not to find his best friend at home, but Rosie soon returns and shows Jake a nice surprise of new shoes just like his.*

Zolotow, Charlotte. (1969). Illustrated by Ben Shecter. **THE HATING BOOK**. New York: Harper & Row. *After a name calling episode, two girls who were once friends think things will never be right again, but in the end they make up.*

# 4

# FEELINGS

*Feelings*
*The Temper Tantrum Book*
*Sloppy Kisses*
*Aaron's Shirt*
*There's a Nightmare in My Closet*

# FEELINGS

*By Joanne Brisson Murphy*

*Illustrated by Heather Collins*

*Written in poetry form, a little boy expresses his good and bad feelings throughout the day and in many different situations. He tells how he feels when he makes his own breakfast, ties his shoes, waits for the circus, daydreams, wrestles with dad, is scared in bed, fights with friends, watches the rain, cuddles with mom, plays in the bath, gets a present and is tired at the end of the day. Heather Collins' illustrations are filled with background details of modern houses and family life. The child's facial expressions and the lighting in each scene capture the many moods.*

## Circle Time Presentation

Leaf through FEELINGS and select five different illustrations. Ask the children what they think the little boy is feeling and why. Read FEELINGS and then ask the children to tell you when the boy felt a sense of accomplishment, surprised, happy, cozy, angry and afraid. Help the children use the words as labels for their feelings by asking when they feel surprised, happy and other feelings. Ask when they feel a sense of accomplishment at school. Announce several of the "feelings" activities for today which will give them a sense of accomplishment.

STORY STRETCHER

## For Art: Collage Of Feelings

**What the children will learn—**
To select pictures which express a variety of feelings

**Materials you will need—**
Old magazines, scissors, construction or manilla paper, glue

**What to do—**
1. As a table top activity in the morning when the children first arrive, have the supplies for this art activity already assembled.

2. With the children who arrive first, leaf through several magazines and help them find pictures which show different feelings.

3. Let the children cut out the pictures and paste them onto paper in an overlapping arrangement to create a collage of feelings.

**Something to think about—**
Many teachers have the easel available everyday as a choice for an art activity and then try to have at least one special art activity to accompany the theme of the unit. Older children may choose magazine pictures which are symbols to represent feelings, as sunshine to represent happy, rather than people showing these feelings through facial expressions and body movements.

STORY STRETCHER

## For Cooking And Snack Time: Making Juice And Toast

**What the children will learn—**
To prepare their own snacks

**Materials you will need—**
Toaster, bread, knives, jam or jelly, napkins, glasses, pitcher, juice

**What to do—**
1. During free play or choice time, let a few children come to the snack area and make their own toast and jam and pour their own juice.

2. While the children are working, remind them of the little boy in FEELINGS who felt a sense of accomplishment when he made his own breakfast.

**Something to think about—**
In our hurried modern world, many parents do for their children what the children are capable of doing on their own. In a newsletter, encourage parents to spend extra time on the weekend showing children how to take care of themselves and allowing more time for breakfast, getting dressed and helping with everyday household chores.

STORY STRETCHER

## For Creative Dramatics: Show This Feeling With Your Face

**What the children will learn—**
To imitate or improvise facial expressions to show a variety of emotions

**Materials you will need—**
Mirrors, if available

**What to do—**

1. At a second circle time of the day, read FEELINGS again and pause after each scene for the children to imitate the little boy's facial expressions and body movements.

2. After each scene ask the children to name the emotions the little boy and they were expressing.

3. Pair up the children to watch each other's faces.

4. After the reading name some emotions at random, and let the children try to show each other these feelings. Expect a lot of giggles. Mention a sense of accomplishment (pride), happy, mad, cozy (secure), frustrated, surprised (excited).

**Something to think about—**
Young children will be able to make the facial expressions better if they have mirrors. Older children might enjoy making the expressions and letting their partners try to figure out what emotion they are expressing. If the partner has difficulty guessing, then as additional clues, let the "expressor" tell a situation where this emotion might happen.

STORY STRETCHER

## For Library Corner: Writing A Book About Our Feelings

**What the children will learn—**
To use the names of emotions and feelings in their own writing

**Materials you will need—**
Variety of sizes and shapes of paper, as well as variety of writing instruments, crayons or markers, chalk, chalkboard

**What to do—**

1. Brainstorm a list of emotions and write them on the chalkboard.

Leaf through FEELINGS and add any to the list which were not mentioned.

2. Ask the children to select some emotions and write or draw about situations when they had these feelings.

3. Interact with the writers or the artists when you notice they may be needing assistance. Ask questions, such as, "Read to me or tell me what you have done so far." "Tell me what you were thinking about." "What happened next?"

4. Allow several days for the children to write and draw, and to return to their work to add more information.

5. When some children have finished, select compositions or drawings expressing different emotions and let the children sit in an "Author's Chair" while they "read" to the class. Continue the "Author's Chair" throughout the week.

**Something to think about—**
Younger children may prefer to draw their pictures and write a few words or even scribble a few lines. Accept this writing as their attempts and encourage them to try more on their own. These authors can share their stories through illustrations.

STORY STRETCHER

## For Mathematics And Manipulatives: Lacing And Tying Shoes

**What the children will learn—**
To practice lacing and tying shoes

**Materials you will need—**
Variety of bigger-sized, old shoes

**What to do—**

1. Let the children put the big shoes on over their own shoes.

2. Unlace and untie the shoes.

3. Sit on the floor with the child and let her sit beside you. Demonstrate how to lace and each step in the tying.

4. Praise the child and let her continue working with different shoes.

**Something to think about—**
Young children are often frustrated by lacing and tying shoes. Do not place so much emphasis on the task that the child feels like a failure. Tell the children that lacing and tying shoes is just like working a puzzle. Have them recall difficult puzzles they have now learned to work. Also, if you have children who seem to lack the manual dexterity to lace and tie, make other fine motor activities available for them, as stringing beads, placing clothespins on cards, cutting and pasting.

## THE TEMPER TANTRUM BOOK

*By Edna Mitchell Preston*

*Illustrated by Rainey Bennett*

*A number of baby animals are having temper tantrums. Each one is upset and creating quite an uproar. Preston describes each animal's outrageous actions by asking four questions. Then, the baby lion, elephant, pig, turtle, kangaroo, otter, tiger and hippopotamus tell why they hate what is happening to them. For instance, the baby lion is having a temper tantrum because he doesn't like getting his mane combed when it is all tangled. Rainey Bennett's illustrations, simple line drawings with washes of watercolors, are humorous and most expressive.*

## Circle Time Presentation

Ask the children if they have ever seen someone have a temper tantrum and have the ones who answer describe what the person was doing. Read THE TEMPER TANTRUM BOOK. Be prepared for a few giggles and a few confessions of what the children "hate" to have happen to them. They will identify with being told no they can't play outside like baby turtle wanted to do and getting soap in their eyes like elephant or not being able to sit still like kangaroo. Ask the children to tell you some things which make them want to have a temper tantrum. If a child has had tantrums and wants to discuss it, encourage the child to share some thoughts about what he does instead of having a tantrum. The book ends with Henrietta Hippopotamus saying what she loves when her mother tells her "yes" she can play in the mud. End the circle time with examples of some "yeses" which the children love to hear from their parents.

STORY STRETCHER

## For Art: Spatter Painting

**What the children will learn—**
To use spatter painting to add texture to drawings

**Materials you will need—**
Old toothbrushes, at least three colors of tempera paints, newspaper, paint shirts, wet sponge, scrap paper, construction paper

**What to do—**
1. Have the children look at Rainey Bennett's effective use of spattering to add texture to the illustrations.

2. Cover tables with newspaper and have children put on paint shirts.

3. Demonstrate how to load tempera paints onto toothbrushes, then turn the toothbrush bristles-side down and run a thumb across the bristles, spattering paint onto paper.

4. Let the children practice with scrap paper, then go on to use layers of different colors of spatters.

5. Leave the spatter painting out for several days and ask the children to add texture to their paintings and drawings they make for the feelings unit.

**Something to think about—**
Younger children will enjoy watching the results of their layers of spatter painting. Older children can make a line drawing and try the light spattering for texture. Watercolors are also appropriate extensions of this story because the illustrator combines watercolors and spatters of paint for texturing.

STORY STRETCHER

## For Library Corner: Reading With Verbal Cloze

**What the children will learn—**
To complete the phrases when the teacher pauses

**Materials you will need—**
None needed

**What to do—**
1. Read THE TEMPER TANTRUM BOOK again without stopping.

2. Tell the children that this time when you pause you want them to finish the sentence or phrase.

3. The questions about the animals' temper tantrums are written in rhyming couplets. Pause for the children to fill in the second rhyming word.

4. Also pause for the children to complete the sentence which tells what each baby animal hates.

**5.** At a later reading, leave out more of the phrases until the children are able to read the book with very little prompting on their own.

**Something to think about—**
At the end of each reading session, give the book to a child and encourage her to read it to someone else using whatever she can recall at the time. Let the children know that they do not have to know all the words to understand the meaning of the story.

ANOTHER STORY STRETCHER

## For Library Corner: The Reverse Temper Tantrum Book

**What the children will learn—**
To compose a story expressing their feelings

**Materials you will need—**
Heavy typing paper, colored pens, ruler, pencil, bookbinding materials (See the appendix for an example of how to bind a book.)

**What to do—**
**1.** Have the children draw a one-inch margin along the right side of one sheet of paper and along the left side of the other sheet. Place the pages side by side so that the margins are in the middle. This is where the staples will go when the book is bound together. Have them draw on one page and write on the other.

**2.** Discuss THE TEMPER TANTRUM BOOK, and ask the children who come to the writing area of the library corner what the opposite or reverse of a temper tantrum would be. What could Lionel Lion have said or done when his mane was all tangled? Continue and discuss alternatives for each of the animals.

**3.** After the discussion, let each child choose an animal to draw and write about "having a reverse temper tantrum." For example,

*When Lionel Lion was a little cub,*
*He used to kick and scream,*
*But now when Lionel has a tangled*
*  mane*
*He just asks for conditioning cream.*

Younger children may dictate a sentence about what the animal could do instead of having a temper tantrum.

**4.** Bind the groups' stories into a book for the class library.

**Something to think about—**
Older children can add more animals to the story using Preston's structure of asking four questions in poetry form.

STORY STRETCHER

## For Music And Movement: Temper Tantrum Dance

**What the children will learn—**
To move as the words direct them

**Materials you will need—**
None needed

**What to do—**
**1.** Read THE TEMPER TANTRUM BOOK and act like Lionel Lion.

**2.** Ask the children to make his hopping, roaring, raging, stomping movements with you.

**3.** Continue reading, then stop to act out the action words. Have the children join you for each scene.

**Something to think about—**
Add some fast paced instrumental violin or guitar music to the background. End the session with a relaxing piece of music so the children can unwind.

STORY STRETCHER

## For Sand And Water Table: Henrietta Hippo's Mud Delight

**What the children will learn—**
To enjoy the sensorimotor experience of making things with mud

**Materials you will need—**
Soil or sand, water, old shirts, optional — plastic trays

**What to do—**
**1.** Have the children put on old shirts which will cover their clothing. Let them help you set up the sand and water table and fill it with soil or a mixture of soil and sand.

**2.** Let them mix the soil and water to make mud and talk about how it feels and how much Henrietta Hippo liked the feeling. Talk with the children about how some people feel relaxed when they do things with their hands.

**3.** Show the children how to shape mud pies.

**4.** After they begin shaping some things they want to keep, place them out on plastic trays to dry.

**Something to think about—**
In the parent newsletter, ask parents to send in additional old shirts for this "messy, muddy" activity.

## 4
## FEELINGS

## SLOPPY KISSES

*By Elizabeth Winthrop*

*Illustrated by Anne Burgess*

*Sometimes parents embarrass their children by kissing them in public. Emmy Lou Pig was not embarrassed until Rosemary told her that kissing is for babies. Emmy Lou declared to her family that she would not kiss Papa good-bye when he dropped her off at school and there would be no more kisses at home. In the end, Emmy Lou missed her family's affectionate goodnights and good-byes, even Papa's sloppy kisses. The illustrations are warm watercolors surrounded by large white space margins.*

## Circle Time Presentation

Recall an incident where children were embarrassed by their parents. For example, once a little boy was playing soccer and his mother yelled, "Run, honey, run." The little boy told his mother never to call him "honey" again. He was embarrassed. Ask the children to listen to what embarrassed Emmy Lou Pig. Read SLOPPY KISSES. Have the children tell what they would have done if they had been Emmy Lou. Also, discuss that families show affection in different ways. Some kiss, others hug, some smile and laugh a lot together. Others do these things when they say goodnight in their homes, but they do not hug and kiss in public.

STORY STRETCHER

## For Art: Affectionate Expressions Pictures

**What the children will learn—**
To read facial expressions and body language

**Materials you will need—**
Old magazines, scissors, glue, paper

**What to do—**

1. On a table in the art center, place a stack of old magazines and the collage supplies.

2. Ask the children to leaf through the magazines, find and cut out pictures of people who like each other or love each other.

3. When they find a few pictures, have the children tell how they know these people like each other or love each other.

4. Let the children glue their "affectionate expression pictures" onto paper to create a collage. Show the children how to overlap the edges.

**Something to think about—**
Help the children appreciate how illustrators show their characters' feelings by looking at the artwork in several books in the classroom collection.

STORY STRETCHER

## For Housekeeping And Dress-up Corner: Putting Children To Bed

**What the children will learn—**
To arrange the housekeeping corner for the bedtime activities which take place in a family

**Materials you will need—**
Dolls, stuffed animals, bedroom furniture, blankets, pillows, kitchen appliances, table, utensils

**What to do—**

1. Show the pictures in SLOPPY KISSES of the family eating together and then of the children being tucked in and saying "goodnight."

2. Ask the children about the routines of their family from dinner time through going to bed.

3. Have one child show his family routine by putting a doll or stuffed animal to bed. Ask what happens first, second, next. If the child's parent reads a book, have the child read or pretend to read a book. If the child's parent sings a lullaby, ask the child to sing the lullaby.

4. Let other children tell more about what their families do, then ask the players to pretend they are a family and it is bedtime for the children.

5. Leave the players to change and improvise the roles on their own.

**Something to think about—**
The play in this area should not be directed or even suggested for the entire free play or choice time.

STORY STRETCHER

## For Library Corner: "Sloppy Kisses Tape"

**What the children will learn—**
To listen and follow the story by turning the page at the signal

**Materials you will need—**
Cassette tape, tape recorder and player, headphones

**What to do—**
1. Record yourself reading SLOPPY KISSES. Use a gentle rap of the knuckle on a wooden table as the page turning signal.

2. Announce the sound the children should listen for as the page-turning signal.

3. Tell the listener to turn to the picture with one girl pig kissing the mother pig, the other girl pig with a bunch of flowers and Papa Pig riding a bicycle. Also mention that the first word on the page begins with a big red "E."

**Something to think about—**
Books which have natural page turning breaks, such as repeated phrases or obvious scene changes, are good selections for group listening at a listening station. SLOPPY KISSES and other stories with a more continuous flow are best for individual listening tapes.

ANOTHER STORY STRETCHER

## For Library Corner: Writing—How My Family Expresses Affection

**What the children will learn—**
To express words and actions which show affection

**Materials you will need—**
Lined and unlined paper, pencils, pens

**What to do—**
1. With the children who come to the writing area of the library corner, discuss SLOPPY KISSES and how Emmy Lou's family expressed their affection.

2. Have the children talk about how their families express affection.

3. Ask the children to write about their families' expressions of affection. Younger children can draw pictures and dictate a caption or sentences to write about their drawings.

**Something to think about—**
Older children may choose to tell about how their family expresses affection differently than other families they know.

STORY STRETCHER

## For Music And Movement: "We Are Loved!"

**What the children will learn—**
To read together and sing together

**Materials you will need—**
Chart tablet or posterboard, pointer

**What to do—**
1. Say the words to the first four lines together.

2. Teach the next three verses one verse at a time. Have the words printed in the Big Book of Music (chart tablet). With a pointer or your hands, sing the words emphasizing which notes to hold by holding the pointer in place.

3. Sing the three verses to the tune of "Some-where o-ver the rain-bow, blue birds fly. Some-where o-ver the rainbow, once in a lull-a-by."

(Read together)

*Sometimes when Mama says, "Now honey don't be late,"*
*My friends will later say, "Honey's not your name."*
*Sometimes when Daddy says, "Love-ya, Swee-tie,"*
*My friends will later say, "Sweetie's not your name."*

(Sing)

*My fam-i-ly says "hon-ey,"*
*With a big kiss*
*My fam-i-ly gives bear hugs,*
*Yo-ur fam-i-ly doesn't.*

*Your fam-i-ly loves gig-gles,*
*Mine does-n't.*
*Your fam-i-ly laughs and teases,*
*My fam-i-ly doesn't.*

*I like m-y fam-i-ly*
*Your family too!*
*What we like is knowing that*
*WE ARE LOVED!*
*(Raines, 1991)*

**Something to think about—**
If you are not comfortable singing the words, use the song as an action poem and have the children point to themselves when they say "I" or "my" and point to you when they say "your." Have the children say the word giggles with laughter in their voices and hug themselves at the end for "we are loved."

## AARON'S SHIRT

*By Deborah Gould*

*Illustrated by Cheryl Harness*

*On the first day Aaron wears his new short-sleeved red and white shirt he wins a teddy bear at the fair. On the second day he makes a new friend. The red and white shirt quickly becomes his favorite shirt. He wants to wear it all the time. He has a hard time putting it away for the winter. Aaron has a problem when he outgrows the shirt, but finds a surprising way to keep it near him. The bright watercolor illustrations provide realistic glimpses into a modern department store, house, school and family activities.*

## Circle Time Presentation

Wear a favorite piece of clothing and tell the children why you like it so much. Ask several children what they like to wear most. Sing the song, "Mary wore her red dress, red dress, red dress. Mary wore her favorite dress all day long," and use the children's names and their favorite piece of clothing (see the Music and Movement Story S-t-r-e-t-c-h-e-r below). Show the cover of AARON'S SHIRT and ask the children why the illustrator made the red and white shirt so big. Read AARON'S SHIRT.

STORY STRETCHER

## For Art: Painting Favorite Shirts

**What the children will learn—**
To paint a pattern onto a precut form

**Materials you will need—**
Large sheets of manilla or construction paper, scissors, easel, clothespins, tempera paint, brushes, catalogs showing children's clothing, optional — clothesline

**What to do—**
1. Cut a shape of a short-sleeved shirt from a large sheet of manilla or construction paper. Make enough for all of the children to have one.

2. Attach the paper shirt to the easel by clipping clothespins onto the shoulders.

3. Let the children look at the catalogs and describe the different colors and patterns they see. Some have pictures on the front of shirts. Others have writing. Some may have checks or stripes or plaids. Remind them that Aaron

saw shirts with dinosaurs and shirts with writing on them.

4. Ask the children to paint their favorite shirt, or one they would like to have, using the paper shape of a shirt.

5. Display the favorite shirts across the bottom of a chalkboard or on a clothesline stretched from the art area to the library corner where the copy of AARON'S SHIRT is on the shelf.

**Something to think about—**
For older children, cut one large tagboard shirt shape and have the students cut out their own forms.

STORY STRETCHER

## For Housekeeping And Dress-up Corner: Department Store Shopping

**What the children will learn—**
To rearrange the housekeeping and dress-up corner to simulate a department store

**Materials you will need—**
Boxes, clothes rack, hangers, price tags and shopping bags, cash register, sales flyers, note pads, pencils

**What to do—**
1. Have the children who often play in the housekeeping and dress-up corner brainstorm with you what changes would be needed to turn the area into a department store.

2. Give the children the additional items, shopping bags, etc. and let them set up the area.

3. Pretend to be Aaron shopping for a new shirt.

4. After the play has begun, leave the shoppers to role play on their own.

**Something to think about—**
Also encourage the use of the transportation toys to make deliver-

ies to the area. Place large boxes in wagons and wheelbarrows.

STORY STRETCHER

## For Library Corner: Story Sequence Cards

**What the children will learn—**
To retell the story using main events

**Materials you will need—**
Tagboard or posterboard, pencil, ruler, colored markers or pencils, scissors

**What to do—**
1.   Divide a large sheet of tagboard or posterboard into eight sections. Have the children think of the first scene which happened in the story, buying the shirt in the department store.

2.   Cut one section off the tagboard and ask a child to draw something about buying the shirt at the department store.

3.   Continue listing the scenes and cutting off sections for the children to draw pictures which remind them of that scene. A list of the scenes which could be shown on the eight blocks are
   * department store,
   * good things which happened when he wore the shirt — won teddy bear and made a new friend,
   * waiting for the shirt at washing machine,
   * summer activities,
   * packing the shirt away for winter,
   * tearing the shirt and sewing it up,
   * too small shirt and Mom placing it in "give-away" box, and
   * Aaron putting the shirt on teddy bear.

4.   When the cards are finished, mix them up and let the children sequence them in the correct order to retell the story.

**Something to think about—**
Younger children can draw pictures of the main scenes and older children can draw symbols. For

example, the first scene in the department store could be represented by a price tag.

STORY STRETCHER

## For Mathematics And Manipulatives: How Many Is Seventy-nine?

**What the children will learn—**
To group ten objects and count the number of groups.

**Materials you will need—**
Strings, wooden beads, clothespins

**What to do—**
1.   Show the children the illustration in AARON'S SHIRT where his mother and he are discussing how often he has worn the shirt. Read the sentence about Aaron's having worn the shirt seventy-nine times. Ask the children how much seventy-nine is. Is it more than twenty? Is it more than one hundred?

2.   Let the children count wooden beads into groups of tens and string them onto the strings.

3.   When you have eight strings of ten beads, count the beads together. When you get to seventy-nine, pause and say, "How many times did Aaron's mother say he had worn the shirt?"

4.   Tie the strings of beads together and let the children hold them, stretching the long line across the floor.

5.   Have the bead stringers go and get friends from other areas of the classroom and bring them over to show them how many beads seventy-nine beads are.

**Something to think about—**
For younger children, the purpose of the lesson is to have them begin associating counting large quantities, even if they cannot yet count that far. Older children can count

the days on a calendar. Begin with today's day and count backwards or forwards to see how many days, weeks and months are involved.

STORY STRETCHER

## For Music And Movement: "Aaron Wore His Favorite Shirt"

**What the children will learn—**
To sing a familiar song and change the words to fit the class and the story

**Materials you will need—**
None needed

**What to do—**
1.   Have the children sing "Mary wore a red dress, red dress, red dress. Mary wore a red dress, all day long."

2.   Then sing, "Aaron wore a red and white shirt, red and white shirt, red and white shirt, all day long."

3.   Change the words again and add, "Aaron wore his favorite shirt, favorite shirt, favorite shirt. Aaron wore his favorite shirt, all day long."

4.   Sing about what individual children are wearing, describing their clothes by color or pattern, then sing the second verse substituting their names such as, "Damien wore his favorite pants, favorite pants, favorite pants. Damien wore his favorite pants, all day long."

5.   End by holding up the book, AARON'S SHIRT, and singing again about Aaron.

**Something to think about—**
Choose children to sing about first who may hesitate to ask you to sing about them.

## 4
## FEELINGS

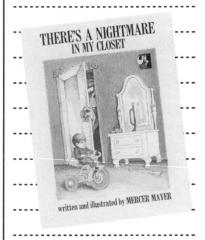

## THERE'S A NIGHTMARE IN MY CLOSET

*By Mercer Mayer*

*Suspenseful, yet humorous, Mayer expresses a child's nightmares and lets the child heroically invite the nightmare to share his bed. This 1968 book with a simple text has become a best seller and a childhood favorite. Mayer's appreciation of children's feelings and his sensitivity can be seen in both words and illustrations. Characteristic of many Mayer tales, the scary monster turns into a friendly, slightly adorable companion. This Mayer book is also available in big book form.*

## Circle Time Presentation

Without showing the book, ask the children what they do when they are scared at night. Discuss what they can do to make themselves less frightened, turn on a night light, think of something happy that happened that day, snuggle into their favorite blanket, remember Mom and Dad are close by. Show the children the cover of THERE'S A NIGHTMARE IN MY CLOSET. Instantly, many children will tell you that they have this book or have heard it read to them. Ask them to listen for the part where the little boy was frightened and when his feelings changed. When you finish, the children will request that you read the story again. Announce that the book will be available in the library corner with a tape recording.

STORY STRETCHER

## For Art: Playdough Nightmare Monsters

**What the children will learn—**
To sculpt their own imaginary nightmares

**Materials you will need—**
Playdough in a variety of colors, plastic knives

**What to do—**
1. Show the children the two nightmares in THERE'S A NIGHTMARE IN MY CLOSET. Ask the children to think of some scary-looking nightmare they could create.

2. Leave the children to improvise on their own.

3. Make a display of nightmare monsters and place them near the listening station in the library corner.

**Something to think about—**
Whenever possible, use real potter's clay instead of playdough. Sculpting is a very different experience with clay.

ANOTHER STORY STRETCHER

## For Art: What's In The Closet Pictures

**What the children will learn—**
To make pictures with something behind the door

**Materials you will need—**
Sheets of construction paper, scraps of construction paper, scissors, glue or stapler, crayons, colored pens, pencils, markers

**What to do—**
1. Show the children the illustrations in THERE'S A NIGHTMARE IN MY CLOSET where the closet door is opening. Ask the children to make pictures which include a door opening and a surprise behind it.

2. Have the children cut a door from a scrap of construction paper, make a little hinge by folding over a narrow edge along one side, then glue it onto their papers.

3. Let the children finish their pictures with something behind the closet door. Provide a variety of drawing materials.

**Something to think about—**
Older children may make a whole house looking like the back of a doll house and have a closet door for each room. Younger children may not be able to draw realistic pictures yet.

## For Creative Dramatics: Inviting A Nightmare To My Bed

**What the children will learn—**
To role play the scenes, expressing feelings with facial expressions and body positions

**Materials you will need—**
None needed

**What to do—**
1. Tell the children you will read the story and be the nightmare and that they should be the little boy.

2. Read the book and after each scene let the children think of ways to express the little boy's actions and feelings.

3. Read the book again and let the children act like the little boy.

4. If you have some children who are hesitant to role play, let them be the little boy's voice and repeat the few lines of dialogue.

**Something to think about—**
Role playing helps young children conquer fears.

## For Library Corner: Tape Of "There's A Nightmare In My Closet"

**What the children will learn—**
To make sound effects

**Materials you will need—**
A squeaky door, stapler, glue, cassette tape and recorder

**What to do—**
1. When other children are outside of the classroom, make a tape with a group who selected the library corner during choice time or free play.

2. Move tape recorder, tape, stapler, near the squeaky door.

3. Tell the children the plan for making the tape. One child will click the stapler as a page-turning signal, another child will squeak the door, and the other children will repeat the dialogue the little boy said to the nightmare.

4. Practice the taping session once and then record the tape.

5. Place the tape in the library corner listening station.

**Something to think about—**
After the children have learned the song, "All A-Round My Lit-tle Bed," in the Music And Movement Story S-t-r-e-t-c-h-e-r, record the song on the opposite side of the tape. Glue the words to the song in the back of THERE'S A NIGHTMARE IN MY CLOSET.

## For Music And Movement: "All A-round My Lit-tle Bed"

**What the children will learn—**
To sing a new song to an old tune

**Materials you will need—**
Posterboard or chart tablet and marker, optional — pointer

**What to do—**
1. Print the words to the song on a large posterboard or add it to the chart tablet collection of songs, the class's Big Book of Music.

2. Sing the song through once, then read the song with the children repeating the phrases and run a pointer or your hand under the phrases in a fluid motion. Sing it again with the children joining in.

3. Sing to the tune of "Pop, Goes the Weasel." Clap hands at the "Oops."

*All a-round my lit-tle bed,*
*the dark is com-ing near-er,*
*All around my lit-tle bed,*
*Oops, I think I'll cover my head!*

*Here I am, snug in bed,*
*I thi-nk I hear a squeak in the floor,*
*Here I am, snug in my bed,*
*Oops, I think I'll cover my head!*

*Here I am, snug in my bed,*
*I thi-nk I hear a scratch at the door,*
*Here I am, snug in my bed,*
*Oops, I think I need a night light!*

*Here I am, snug in my bed,*
*I thi-nk I hear something coming in,*
*Here I am, snug in my bed,*
*Oops, I think I'll scream in my bed!*

*Here I am, scared in my bed,*
*I thi-nk it's going to get me,*
*Here I am, snug in my bed,*
*Meow, Meow?*
*It's Henry, my cat!*

*Meow, meow, meow, meow,*
*Meow! It's Henry, my cat! (Raines,*
*1991).*

**Something to think about—**
Let the children compose additional verses and decide on appropriate motions.

# REFERENCES

Gould, Deborah. (1989). Illustrated by Cheryl Harness. **AARON'S SHIRT.** New York: Bradbury Press.

Mayer, Mercer. (1968). **THERE'S A NIGHTMARE IN MY CLOSET.** New York: Dial Books for Young Readers.

Murphy, Joanne Brisson. (1985). Illustrated by Heather Collins. **FEELINGS.** Windsor, Ontario: Black Moss Press.

Preston, Edna Mitchell. (1976). Illustrated by Rainey Bennett. **THE TEMPER TANTRUM BOOK.** New York: Puffin Books.

Winthrop, Elizabeth. (1980). Illustrated by Anne Burgess. **SLOPPY KISSES**. New York: Puffin Books.

## Additional References For Feelings

Cooney, Nancy Evans. (1981). Illustrated by Diane Dawson. **THE BLANKET THAT HAD TO GO.** New York: G. P. Putnam's Sons. *Attached to the blanket she carries everywhere, Susie must decide what to do with it on her first day in kindergarten.*

Goode, Diane. (1988). **I HEAR A NOISE**. New York: E. P. Dutton. *A little boy, hearing noises at the window at bedtime, calls for his mother. His worst fears are realized, but he learns that monsters have mothers too.*

Kachenmeister, Cherryl. (1989). Photographs by Tom Berthiaume. **ON MONDAY WHEN IT RAINED.** Boston: Houghton Mifflin. *A young boy describes, in text and photographs of his facial expressions, the different emotions he feels each day.*

Mayer, Mercer. (1988). **THERE'S SOMETHING IN MY ATTIC.** New York: Dial Books for Young Readers. *Convinced there is something making noise in the attic at night, a brave little girl sneaks up the stairs, lasso in hand, to capture whatever it is.*

Viorst, Judith. (1988). Illustrated by Kay Chorao. **THE GOOD-BYE BOOK.** New York: Atheneum. *A child, on the verge of being left behind by parents who are going out, comes up with a variety of pleas and excuses about why they should not go.*

# ANIMALS, REAL AND FANCIFUL

*Big Red Barn*
*Animals Born Alive and Well*
*Is Your Mama a Llama?*
*Pretend You're a Cat*
*Baby Animals*

---

## BIG RED BARN

---

*By Margaret Wise Brown*

---

*Illustrated by Felicia Bond*

---

*Margaret Wise Brown's story, told in verse, is about the farm animals who live in and around the big red barn and what they do on a day when the children are away. This classic book is a reissue of a 1956 version with new colorful illustrations by Felicia Bond. The story follows the animals through the day from waking in the morning, to eating and ending with nightfall. Bond's full-page illustrations in strong colors are large enough to make the book a good one for a whole class presentation, yet there also is enough detail that children will enjoy browsing through the book on their own.*

## Circle Time Presentation

Ask the children to think of animals that live on a farm. List the names on a chalk board or a chart tablet. Then look at the cover of BIG RED BARN and see how many of the animals the children named are shown on the cover. Tell the children there are some other animals in the book which are not on the cover. Read BIG RED BARN and pause for the children to imitate the sounds of the animals. After reading the book, have the children recall other farm animals mentioned in the book to add to their list. Also have them think of the one character in the book which was not a farm animal, the scarecrow.

STORY STRETCHER

## For Art: The Big Red Barn Door Opens

**What the children will learn—**
To construct an art project that is three dimensional

**Materials you will need—**
Red construction paper, scraps of manilla and construction paper, tape, scissors, pencils, crayons, glue

**What to do—**
1.   Cut the shape of the big barn out of red construction paper. Make it as large as possible. See the scene of the barn near the end of the book and draw the outline from that picture.

2.   Have the children cut a large door in the middle of the barn, leaving the paper attached on one side.

3.   Demonstrate how to reinforce the barn door on the inside by placing a piece of tape along the edge where it opens and along the hinge where it connects to the rest of the paper.

4.   Have each child draw, color and cut out an animal which can fit inside the barn door.

5.   Cut a scrap of construction paper, fold it in accordion style and glue one side of it to the back of the barn door and the other side to the back of the cutout of the animal. When the barn door is opened, out pops the animal.

**Something to think about—**
Older students can cut out windows and have horses or cows poking their heads out of the barn windows. The activity can also be extended by gluing the entire barn onto a large sheet of green posterboard and adding animals all around the barn.

STORY STRETCHER

## For Blocks: Building Barns And Farm Houses

**What the children will learn—**
To construct forms which look like farm buildings

**Materials you will need—**
Large hollow blocks or smaller building blocks, plastic farm animals, tractors, trucks, optional — farm equipment toys

**What to do—**
1.   Have the block builders look through the illustrations in BIG RED BARN and other books about farms for ideas.

2.   Add the tractors, trucks and any farm equipment toys you may have. Discuss how some barns are now used to park tractors and farm equipment so they have open sides, like garages with no doors.

3.   Ask the children to build at least three different types of barns or storage buildings. Leave the buildings set up after the children

finish playing so that the other students can see them during the second group time of the day.

**Something to think about—**
If yours is a farming community, the shapes and forms of barns and farm buildings will be familiar to the children. A good beginning for these children might include comparing how the barns look in the book to the ones they know. Children who are not familiar with farms will need many pictures to inspire their buildings.

## For Library Corner: Listening Tape With Sound Effects

**What the children will learn—**
To make the sounds of the farm animals on cue

**Materials you will need—**
Cassette tape recorder, tape, glass, fork

**What to do—**
1. Have a small group of children record the sound effects for a cassette recording of BIG RED BARN. You will read the book, and they will make the sounds at the appropriate times.

2. Decide on a signal you will give them to know when to make their sounds. For example, tell them when you point to the picture of the rooster, they are to crow, "cock-a-doodle-doooo!" Have them practice the sounds for each picture before beginning the tape recording.

3. Ask one child to make the page-turning signal by gently tapping a fork onto the side of a glass.

**Something to think about—**
At the end of the tape, tell the names of the children who helped with the recording. Include children in the taping group who are very verbal and those who are sometimes hesitant to speak.

## For Music And Movement: The Scarecrow Wakes Up In The Morning

**What the children will learn—**
To relax and move with their muscles limp

**Materials you will need—**
None needed

**What to do—**
1. Show the pictures of the scarecrow near the beginning of the book and at the end. Discuss how he is made by filling old clothes with straw.

2. Then stand and hold your arms out, but let your lower arms and hands dangle, put your knees together and tell the children the scarecrow is going to wake up. Put your chin down on your chest and have your head over to one side.

3. Pretend a minute or two of waking movements, using limp and disjointed motions.

4. Have the children stand and pretend to be scarecrows who are asleep, and then have them wake up. Narrate their waking by saying phrases such as, "The scarecrow is feeling the sun on the back of his neck, he rolls his head from side to side, then he opens his eyes."

5. Continue until the scarecrow is moving limply around the room and greeting all the animals who live near the BIG RED BARN.

**Something to think about—**
After the children are comfortable with their movements as scarecrows, add slow waltz music and let them move on their own without the narration.

## For Science And Nature: Weather Vanes

**What the children will learn—**
To construct a weather vane which will show the direction the wind is blowing

**Materials you will need—**
Paper towel or toilet tissue rolls, scraps of posterboard or any light weight cardboard which has layers, scissors, straight pins or long needles, thimble, tape

**What to do—**
1. Cut a demonstration arrow from a piece of posterboard or cardboard which is about two inches long and an inch wide.

2. Let each child cut an arrow shape. Do not be concerned if the arrow is not exact.

3. With a thimble, press a straight pin through the arrow and into the top of the paper towel or toilet tissue roll, leaving it loose enough to turn.

4. Show the children how to blow on their weather vanes. Ask them which direction the arrow is pointing when it stops. It always points toward the source of the wind, the child.

5. To send the weather vanes home, take off the arrow and pin and tape them onto the side of the roll, covering the pin entirely with tape.

**Something to think about—**
Ask a parent or grandparent who is a gardener to bring in a garden pinwheel or weather vane. Some are often shaped like a bird with wings that rotate or like a flower with petals that rotate.

# 5
## ANIMALS, REAL AND FANCIFUL

## ANIMALS BORN ALIVE AND WELL

*By Ruth Heller*

*Ruth Heller's book is beautifully illustrated, contains key scientific concepts and includes so much inherently interesting information that children enjoy reading it many times and poring over the illustrations to identify the common and unfamiliar animals. She begins with wild mammals, inserts a few tame pets, mentions humans, and even prehistoric mammals, before leaving the reader with a new term, "viviparous," which means born alive. The colors, shading, animal movements and even the composition of each page enhance the text which is written in rhyme. The illustrations are large enough for a whole class reading, but the children will want to look through it individually and with an adult nearby to pronounce the names of uncommon animals.*

## Circle Time Presentation

Tell the children that for the animal unit, they have learned the names of the farm animals in BIG RED BARN, the names of the baby animals from the book by the same title, BABY ANIMALS, and now there are many other animals' names they can learn from this book, ANIMALS BORN ALIVE AND WELL. Explain that mammals are animals with fur or hair that get nourishment from their mothers and that breathe fresh air. Read ANIMALS BORN ALIVE AND WELL without pausing to point out all the different animals. Read it a second time, and this time pause to point out all the animals and emphasize their names.

STORY STRETCHER
## For Art: Colorful Sea, Jungle, Desert Or Plain

**What the children will learn—**
To represent a variety of habitats where mammals live

**Materials you will need—**
Assorted colors of construction paper, white typing paper or manilla paper, crayons, markers, chalk or colored pens

**What to do—**
1. With the group of children who choose the art center during free play or choice time, look again at Ruth Heller's illustrations. Talk about what she has added to the pictures that let us know where the animal lives, as branches from trees for the jungle, sprigs of grass for the plain, blue and green backgrounds for the sea and a tan color for the desert.

2. Ask the children to select a mammal they would like to draw and to decide what they will add to their illustrations to let the people looking at their drawings know

where the mammal lives. Brainstorm a few ideas.

3. Assist the children in getting started, then leave them to work on their own.

4. Display the "Colorful Sea, Desert, Jungle or Plain" pictures in the science and nature center.

**Something to think about—**
When young children have experienced a variety of materials, such as crayons, markers, chalks or colored pens, they will begin to select the media which best fits their needs as artists.

STORY STRETCHER
## For Library Corner: Learning About Mammals By Listening And Looking

**What the children will learn—**
To coordinate what they are hearing with illustrations they are seeing

**Materials you will need—**
Cassette tape and recorder

**What to do—**
1. Make a tape of yourself reading ANIMALS BORN ALIVE AND WELL.

2. Give directions by describing what the child should be seeing on the page. For example, say, "Open the cover and you will see two pages filled with pictures of snowshoe hares. Turn the page and you will see a house mouse with four little babies. This is the title page and you can see printed in large letters, ANIMALS BORN ALIVE AND WELL by Ruth Heller. Now turn the page again and you should see some long green leaves and two strange animals at the bottom of the page."

3. Continue the pattern of telling the listeners what they should be

seeing on each page and then reading the text.

**Something to think about—**
Try to create a variety of listening experiences for the library corner. Include some group listening station tapes, some tapes of music with accompanying lyrics the child can follow, commercial tapes and those with a variety of different page-turning cues.

STORY STRETCHER

## For Mathematics And Manipulatives: How Many Mammals?

**What the children will learn—**
To count the number of mammals on each set of pages

**Materials you will need—**
Posterboard or chart tablet, markers

**What to do—**
1. With a small group of children in the mathematics and manipulatives area of the classroom, look again at the pictures in ANIMALS BORN ALIVE AND WELL.

2. Tell the children that as they look through the book, you want to make a list of how many animals are in the illustrations. Begin with the end paper pages where there is an illustration of how the snowshoe hare changes his coat for winter, spring, summer and fall. Count the number of hares. Count the number in each row, then the number of rows. Then count to see how many there are all together (20).

3. On the chart tablet or posterboard, write 20 snowshoe hares, 4 house mice, 1 spiny anteater, 1 duckbill platypus, 8 African elephants.

4. Continue counting the number of animals on each page. Group

some of the animals, as mammals with scales or spikes.

**Something to think about—**
Let younger children touch each picture as they count. Older children may make groups of mammals to count, as marsupials, pets that are mammals, mammals with stripes, mammals with spots, underwater mammals or mammals that fly.

STORY STRETCHER

## For Music And Movement: Lumber Like An Elephant

**What the children will learn—**
To move like different animals

**Materials you will need—**
None needed

**What to do—**
1. At the second group time of the day, let the children look through the book and select some mammals whose movements they can imitate. For example, they may lumber along like the elephant, run on all fours with little short steps like a Pekingese, gallop like a zebra, hop like a kangaroo, run fast like a deer.

2. Decide on a signal, such as a clap of hands, which you will use to tell the children when to start and stop the movement.

3. Let the children practice their moves as a group. Then, divide them into smaller groups representing different animals and let them all move at your signal. You might have a group of lumbering elephants, hopping kangaroos, running deer and flying bats, who must all look out for each other.

**Something to think about—**
As an extension, ask the children to predict how they think an animal might move even if they have never seen one. For example, an

okapi looks like a cross between a deer and a zebra, so it probably runs and gallops fast.

STORY STRETCHER

## For Science And Nature: Grouping Mammals By Habitats

**What the children will learn—**
To classify mammals by where they live

**Materials you will need—**
Posterboard, magnetic tape, index card, sturdy paper, crayons, scissors, glue, optional — clear contact paper or laminating film

**What to do—**
1. Divide a large sheet of posterboard into four columns.

2. Place a long strip of magnetic tape onto the posterboard, extending the length of each column.

3. At the top of each column, place a symbol to represent each habitat, such as land, trees, underwater and houses. Print the name of the habitat under the symbol.

4. Construct illustrations of mammals from each habitat by letting the children draw and color pictures of mammals on sturdy paper. Cut out the pictures. Cover with clear contact paper or laminating film, if available. Attach a small strip of magnetic tape to the back of the pictures.

5. Mix up all the pictures and have the children sort them by attaching a picture under the column which represents that animal's habitat.

**Something to think about—**
If you teach younger children whose drawing skills are not up to the task of making illustrations which others can recognize easily, then make the sketches yourself or trace them.

# 5

# ANIMALS, REAL AND FANCIFUL

## IS YOUR MAMA A LLAMA?

*By Deborah Guarino*

*Illustrated by Steven Kellogg*

*Lloyd, the llama, asks a bat, a swan, a calf, a seal, a kangaroo and another llama about their mamas. Each responds with a riddle written as a rhyme telling about their mamas. Young children will enjoy guessing the answers from the clues. Steven Kellogg's illustrations have a marvelous golden glow with shadows and shading adding texture. There are full-page illustrations of the animals' mothers, while the illustrations on the riddle and clue pages are smaller and enclosed in a border. The animals' expressions are endearing to young children.*

## Circle Time Presentation

Tell the children that today you are going to read a book which has "story puzzles." A story puzzle is a riddle hidden in a story. There are clues given in the story to help the listener or the reader solve the puzzle. Read IS YOUR MAMA A LLAMA? and pause before turning the pages where the answers are found. When you pause, ask the children to "predict" what they think the answer might be. After completing the book, go back through it and let the children tell you which clues helped them solve the riddle. Eventually a child will mention that the answers rhyme with the last clue. Reread the book and during this reading, pause and let the children fill in the rhyming clues.

STORY STRETCHER

## For Art: Golden Glow Pictures

**What the children will learn—**
To make illustrations which have a golden glow

**Materials you will need—**
Light yellow or light orange construction paper, pastel chalks, water, sponge, margarine tubs

**What to do—**
1. At the art table set up work stations with sponges, construction paper and water in margarine tubs.

2. Demonstrate for the children how to wet the sponge and gently go over the surface of the construction paper so that it is damp. Use the pastel chalks for drawing on the light yellow or light orange construction paper.

3. Leave the materials out several days for the children to experiment with letting the yellow background glow through like golden sunlight.

**Something to think about—**
More experienced pastel artists can use the paper dry and when completed lightly spray it with hair spray to keep the chalk from flaking off. Younger children can practice their pastel drawings by wetting a brown paper towel, squeezing the water out, spreading the towel out flat, then drawing their illustrations on it.

STORY STRETCHER

## For Library Corner: Story Puzzle Clues About Animal Mamas

**What the children will learn—**
To listen for clues to solve riddles about animals

**Materials you will need—**
Cassette tape, recorder, magazine or calendar pictures of animals, scissors, large envelope or clear plastic bag

**What to do—**
1. Cut out pictures of animals from magazines or calendars.

2. With a small group of children in the library corner, have them think of three or four clues which would help the other children figure out which animal is being described on tape.

3. Write notes from the children's discussion and decide on three or four clues. For example, my animal has babies born in litters, likes to play with a ball and has a name which rhymes with "hog."

4. Let each child in the group tape record the clues for her or his animal.

5. After all the animal clues have been given, record the answers at the end of the tape.

6. Store the pictures and cassette recording in a large envelope or clear plastic bag.

**Something to think about—**
Add an animal a day for two weeks. Let a second group make a tape using the same animal pictures but different clues. For younger children use fewer animals. For older children, include more difficult clues, such as I am a mammal who lives in Australia.

## For Mathematics And Manipulatives: Making A Match — Water Or Land Or Both

**What the children will learn—**
To classify the animals by where they live in the water, on the land or on both

**Materials you will need—**
Long strings of yarn, table, pictures of animals or index cards

**What to do—**
1. Make two large circles with the yarn and overlap each circle so that a third circle is created between the two.

2. Distribute the cards to the children with either pictures of the animals on them or index cards with the animals' names on them.

3. Tell the children that the first circle represents land and to place their card in the first circle if their animal lives on the land. Have the second circle represent the water.

4. There will be some animals, the swan and the seal, which live on both. Help the children to see that these cards need to go in the overlapping circle.

**Something to think about—**
Explore the children's ideas. Ask them why they made their choices. Often their ideas are quite reason-

able. For example, a child said to one of the authors, "The bat cannot go on this table because he doesn't live on the land or in the water. He said a cave is 'in' the land, not 'on' the land."

## For Music And Movement: Movement Clues To Solve Riddles

**What the children will learn—**
To interpret the clues of physical movement to solve a riddle

**Materials you will need—**
None needed

**What to do—**
1. With a small group of children in the library corner, recall all the animals Lloyd, the llama, met in the book IS YOUR MAMA A LLAMA?

2. Have them think of the ways that each animal would move or behave. For example, the bat flies, the swan swims, the cow grazes on grass, the seal swims, the kangaroo hops and the llamas graze, too.

3. After they have decided on the motions, practice them, then have another group of children come over and guess which animals the children are pretending to be by their movement clues.

**Something to think about—**
If the audience has difficulty deciding on which animal the child is pretending to be, let the child give a clue from the book, such as "My mama lives in a cave."

## For Science And Nature: Animals' Homes Are Habitats

**What the children will learn—**
To match animals with their habitats

**Materials you will need—**
Chart tablet or posterboard, Post-it notes or large index cards with tape on the back, marker

**What to do—**
1. Look at the pictures of the animals in IS YOUR MAMA A LLAMA? Show the picture on the dedication page of the duck and newly hatched baby duck. Ask the children where these ducks live — the seashore.

2. Draw a line down the middle of the chart tablet or posterboard to form two large columns. At the top of the left column, print "animals." At the top of the right column, print "habitats."

3. Begin classifying the animals by looking at the animals as they appear in the book. The first picture on the dedication page is of ducks. Write ducks in the left column. Then on a large Post-it note or index card with tape on it, write seashore in blue marker.

4. Continue the process of looking at all the animals in the pictures and writing their names on one side of the chart and where they live on the index card or Post-it note. The next picture is of the bat. Write bat on one side and with a black marker write cave on the index card or Post-it note.

5. After the chart is completed, let the children mix up the habitats and try to match them again.

**Something to think about—**
For younger children, combine words, rebus symbols or real pictures. For older children, instead of writing the name of the habitat have them write clues, such as "frogs also live in this habitat," meaning the "lake."

## 5
## ANIMALS, REAL AND FANCIFUL

## PRETEND YOU'RE A CAT

*By Jean Marzollo*

*Illustrated by Jerry Pinkney*

*The rhyming verses ask the children to pretend they are different animals. Each line of the verse gives another action of the animal and each verse ends with "What else can you do like a _____?" The children are invited to move like a cat, dog, fish, bee, chick, bird, squirrel, pig, cow, horse, seal, snake and a bear. The pencil, watercolor and colored pencil illustrations of the children's movements are wonderfully appealing and rich with patterns. The text is printed on one page with a boxed illustration and faced with a full-page illustration. At the beginning of the book, the animals the children are imitating are in the boxes, but after the middle of the book, the remainder of the illustrations are large ones of the animals and smaller ones of the children. The layout and beautiful illustrations contribute enormously to the children's enjoyment of this book.*

## Circle Time Presentation

Begin the circle time by telling the children that you want to show them some beautiful pictures in a book. Ask them to look at the illustrations and guess what the children are doing. Leaf through the book, pausing at each set of pictures for the children's guesses. Read the book and after the verse where the author says, "What else can you do like a cat?" have the children think of other actions. Continue reading, pausing after each verse for additional comments. After reading the book, tell the children that throughout the day, they can refer to the book for their face painting, for the horse masks, for their animal dances and in the library corner.

STORY STRETCHER

## For Art: Face Painting

**What the children will learn—**
To paint faces

**Materials you will need—**
Clown make-up from a children's toy store, cleansing cream, hand mirrors

**What to do—**
1. Let the classroom aide paint your face or you paint the aide's face.

2. Ask some parent volunteers or older children to paint the children's faces like animals.

3. Provide hand mirrors for the children to check the progress of their make-up.

**Something to think about—**
Tell parents about the face painting day in the parent newsletter. If some children do not want their faces painted, let them make up a doll's face which can be washed easily.

ANOTHER STORY STRETCHER

## For Art: Horse Masks

**What the children will learn—**
To follow directions to make a mask and then decorate it with their own designs

**Materials you will need—**
Brown paper bags, yarn, stapler, hole puncher, scissors, crayons

**What to do—**
1. Show the children the picture of the horse mask in PRETEND YOU'RE A CAT.

2. Cut the shape of the mask by cutting down the seam of the grocery bag until it lies flat. Then sketch the outline of a horse face on the bag as it appears in the book. Let the children cut around the shape.

3. Have an adult cut holes for the eyes.

4. Ask the children to draw the markings on the horses' faces. They can look at the beautiful horses in the book for inspiration.

5. Show the children how to cut lengths of yarn and staple it along the top for the horse's mane.

6. Have the children punch holes in the back to thread the yarn through to hold the mask in place.

**Something to think about—**
Some teachers, eager for their children to have attractive art or craft projects, complete too much of the project for the child. Leave as much as possible to each child's own design and creativity.

STORY STRETCHER

## For Library Corner: Writing More Animal Rhymes

**What the children will learn—**
To write rhymes using the pattern in PRETEND YOU'RE A CAT

**Materials you will need—**
Chart tablet and markers or chalkboard and chalk

**What to do—**

1. With a few children together at the writing table in the library corner, reread several of the animal riddle rhymes. Focus on the pattern the author uses of asking questions to structure the rhyme. Read the cat and squirrel rhymes.

2. Let the children decide on three animals they would like to add to the book, such as a monkey, a goat and a deer.

3. Brainstorm some behaviors and movements of these animals, such as monkeys swing from trees, scurry around, climbing up high, eat bananas, hold their babies, chatter, play and tease.

4. From the brainstormed list, use the pattern and write some additional rhymes. The one for the monkey might read:

> *Can you climb*
> *Up high?*
> *Nearly touching*
> *The sky?*
> *Can you swing*
> *From the trees?*
> *Can you chatter,*
> *Play and tease?*
> *What else can you do like a monkey?*
> *(Raines, 1991)*

**Something to think about—**
Young children can brainstorm the ideas for you to write the animal rhymes. Older children can pair up and write them together. For art work, cut pages the same size as the book and add the children's rhymes to the end of the book. For another group time, read the book including the children's additions.

## For Music And Movement: Animal Dances, Pretend You Are ...

**What the children will learn—**
To stretch, twirl and move like the animals they are pretending to be

**Materials you will need—**
Chalk board and chalk

**What to do—**

1. Have the children recall all the animals in PRETEND YOU'RE A CAT.

2. Show the illustration of the little girl in dance costume, pretending to be a bird. Ask the children to fly around as if they were "dance flying."

3. Continue the dance flying for the bee, but change the movements to shorter, quicker steps and faster arm movements.

4. Then have the children get down on all fours and pretend to be a cat, stretching their arms out, purring gently, then hissing before scatting off quickly.

5. Continue the instructions with descriptions of the movements, but ask the children to continue the animal dance, by always moving and changing their movements to show the actions you describe.

**Something to think about—**
Teachers need to participate with their children in the movements. When children see adults and the other students moving, they are less inhibited. Enjoy the experience with the children.

## For Science And Nature: What Sounds Do We Make?

**What the children will learn—**
To make the sounds associated with the animals in PRETEND YOU'RE A CAT

**Materials you will need—**
Pictures of the animals from PRETEND YOU'RE A CAT, cassette tape and recorder

**What to do—**

1. Show the illustrations and ask the children who come to the science and nature center to make the sounds the animals in the pictures might make.

2. Encourage the children to think of more than one sound. A cat meows, purrs and hisses. A dog barks different ways and whines for attention. For some of the animals the children may not be able to come up with more than one sound.

3. After a practice session, tape record the sounds. Instruct the listeners by saying, "Listen to the animal sounds on this tape. Here is sound number one. (Sound) Now turn off the tape recorder and find the picture of the animal which makes this sound. When you find the picture, turn the tape recorder on again."

**Something to think about—**
Try to include activities which have a range of participation possibilities. For example, listening to the tape and selecting the pictures can be an activity for individuals, partners or a small group.

## BABY ANIMALS

*By Margaret Wise Brown*

*Illustrated by Susan Jeffers*

*BABY ANIMALS is another classic Margaret Wise Brown book which was originally published in 1941 and released again in 1989 with lovely new illustrations by Susan Jeffers. A little girl awakens on the farm and all around her the birds and animals are waking as well. As the child notices the different birds and animals, they are being fed or finding food for themselves. The story continues to show the animals falling asleep at the end of the day and the little girl's parents saying, "Good night, sweet dreams." The richly detailed illustrations are pen and ink drawings with washes of watercolor. The illustrations are beautiful with realistic animal movements, swaying grasses in the meadow scenes, and tender family feelings conveyed with warm expressions and pastel colors.*

## Circle Time Presentation

BABY ANIMALS will become one of the children's favorite books because it can be enjoyed equally for the story and for the richness of the illustrations. The large book format makes it particularly appealing for a circle time presentation, but the details in the illustrations make it one children will enjoy browsing through many times on their own. Have the children recall all the animals they saw in the book BIG RED BARN. There were no people in BIG RED BARN. Then, tell them this is a book which does have people in it. It is about a little girl who lives on a farm. Read BABY ANIMALS, then ask the children if there are any pictures they would like to see again. Invariably, they will want to see all the illustrations one more time. Let different children tell why they like each picture. Select a child who usually shows little interest in books and ask her to take the copy of BABY ANIMALS over to the library center and place it on the book shelf.

STORY STRETCHER

## For Art: Pen Drawings With Watercolor Washes

**What the children will learn—**
To create pictures with two art media

**Materials you will need—**
Black ball point pens or pencils, crayons or watercolors, brushes, margarine tubs with water, manilla paper scraps and whole sheets, paper towels

**What to do—**
1. Tell the children that you would like to make a bulletin board of baby animal pictures. They may choose any baby farm animals they would like to draw.

2. Show them Susan Jeffers illustrations and explain that she made them by first drawing with a pen and then coloring over her drawings with watercolors. They may use watercolors or crayons to add the color after they have drawn with the pens or pencils.

3. For the children who choose watercolors, demonstrate how to load the watercolor paints onto the brushes, and how to dry the brush on the towels when they have too much water.

4. Provide scraps of paper for the children to experiment mixing the art media.

**Something to think about—**
Many teachers are hesitant to request that children draw something specific, and while children should always be given a choice of what they would like to paint or draw for art, they also enjoy contributing to a group project on the same theme, such as the bulletin board of BABY ANIMALS.

STORY STRETCHER

## For Creative Dramatics: Animal Antics

**What the children will learn—**
To make movements and sounds to accompany scenes from BABY ANIMALS

**Materials you will need—**
None needed

**What to do—**
1. Highlight some of the animal and bird movements from the book by rereading several pages.

2. Ask the children to make the movements and sounds which they think of when they hear the words. For instance, they can flutter and flap their wings, open their beaks and make a chirp like the birds waking up. Or they might roll on

their backs like the little pigs and oink and squeal for their breakfast.

**3.** After they have practiced their movements, reread the book and pause after each scene for the children to act out the motions and sounds.

**Something to think about—**
Younger children will want to act out each scene with animal movements and sounds. Older children can volunteer for different scenes. Several children can do each scene so that everyone in the class participates.

STORY STRETCHER

## For Library Corner: Flannel Board Match Of Sights And Sounds Of Animals

**What the children will learn—**
To associate the pictures of the animals with the sounds

**Materials you will need—**
Flannel board pieces of birds, horse and colt, pig and piglet, sheep and lamb, cat and kitten, dog and puppies, little girl and parents picture, posterboard, glue, emery board, cassette tape and tape recorder

**What to do—**
**1.** Make felt animal shapes by tracing around pictures of the animals or birds. You do not have to add details, the outline of the shape is sufficient.

**2.** Construct the little girl and parents flannel board pieces by cutting out a picture of a child and parents from a magazine or catalog. Glue the picture onto posterboard, then glue on a piece of old emery board which will make the pictures stick onto the flannel board.

**3.** Record yourself reading BABY ANIMALS and let a small group of children provide the sound effects. Be sure to include a page-turning signal. Simply say in a lowered tone of voice, "Please turn the page."

**4.** During one of the circle times for the day, demonstrate how to place the pieces onto the flannel board as they are introduced in the book, then remove the pieces as each animal goes to sleep.

**5.** Place the flannel board and tape recording in the library center for the children to enjoy on their own.

**Something to think about—**
Young children can match the baby animal to its mother without listening to the recording of the book. Older children can make the animal flannel board pictures by drawing their own animal pictures, cutting them out and gluing them onto posterboard.

STORY STRETCHER

## For Science And Nature: Our Visit To The Farm

**What the children will learn—**
To recall specific information about the farm animals

**Materials you will need—**
Camera, film, chart tablet, marker, construction paper or posterboard, glue, pen or pencil

**What to do—**
**1.** Arrange for a field trip to a working animal farm, if possible.

**2.** Take photographs of the animals and of the children.

**3.** After returning from the field trip, let the children draw some of their favorite animals or experiences from the day, add captions, then display them in the science and nature center.

**4.** Attach one photograph to a large sheet of construction paper or posterboard. Let the children who are in the picture dictate sentences about what they learned about the animals. For example, a child might say, "The sheep's wool was tight and not so soft on his back. Then, when it was cut off it felt softer."

**Something to think about—**
Many farms today do not have the variety of animals which are seen in the book BABY ANIMALS. Some zoos and community projects now include working farms. Try to visit a place which has a variety of animal life. Avoid the petting zoos where animals may not be treated respectfully.

ANOTHER STORY STRETCHER

## For Science And Nature: Whose Baby Am I?

**What the children will learn—**
To associate baby animals with their parents

**Materials you will need—**
Pictures of baby animals and their parents, posterboard, magnetic tape, glue, optional — clear contact paper or laminating film

**What to do—**
**1.** Let the children cut out pictures of baby animals and their parents from old magazines, calendars or coloring books.

**2.** Cover the pictures with clear contact paper or laminating film.

**3.** Attach a piece of magnetic tape to each animal picture.

**4.** Make a poster with two columns, one marked babies and the second marked parents.

**5.** Place a strip of the magnetic tape down each column.

**6.** Let the children match the baby animals to their parents.

**Something to think about—**
Have more babies than adults. Mix the types of pictures so that there may be two colts, one from a calendar picture and one from a coloring book, but include only one parent. Also use different breeds of cats, dogs and other animals to make the task more challenging.

## REFERENCES

Brown, Margaret Wise. (1989). Illustrated by Felicia Bond. **BIG RED BARN.** New York: Harper & Row.

Brown, Margaret Wise. (1989). Illustrated by Susan Jeffers. **BABY ANIMALS.** New York: Random House.

Guarino, Deborah. (1989). Illustrated by Steven Kellogg. **IS YOUR MAMA A LLAMA?** New York: Scholastic, Inc.

Heller, Ruth. (1982). **ANIMALS BORN ALIVE AND WELL.** New York: Grosset & Dunlap.

Marzollo, Jean. (1990). Illustrated by Jerry Pinkney. **PRETEND YOU'RE A CAT**. New York: Dial Books for Young Readers.

### Additional References For Animals, Real And Fanciful

Cowcher, Helen. (1990). **ANTARCTICA.** New York: Farrar, Straus and Giroux. *The story of animal life in Antarctica and the uncertainty of what changes the arrival of people will bring.*

Ehlert, Lois. (1990). **FEATHERS FOR LUNCH.** San Diego: Harcourt Brace Jovanovich. *The cat goes out and almost catches different birds, but never gets more than a mouth full of feathers.*

Goennel, Heidi. (1989). **IF I WERE A PENGUIN.** Boston: Little, Brown and Company. *A child imagines the fun of being different animals, such as an eagle, a camel and a giraffe, as well as a penguin.*

Pizer, Abigail. (1990). **IT'S A PERFECT DAY.** New York: J.B. Lippincott. *A repetitive text with barnyard animal sounds.*

Ryder, Joanne. (1989). Illustrated by Cheryl Harness. **UNDER THE MOON.** New York: Random House. *Mama Mouse teaches her little mouse how to tell where home is by reminding her of its special smells, sounds and textures.*

# PLANTS—I LIKE GROWING THINGS

*This Year's Garden*
*Planting a Rainbow*
*Plants That Never Ever Bloom*
*The Empty Pot*
*The Mouse and the Potato*

## THIS YEAR'S GARDEN

*By Cynthia Rylant*

*Illustrated by Mary Szilagyi*

*The warm and interesting story of a family working together to plant, care for and harvest the produce from a garden. The book highlights the growing cycle of year and the enjoyment of the company of others while one works. Szilagyi's illustrations have a warm glow with yellow and orange tones bringing to life realistically colored drawings.*

## Circle Time Presentation

Discuss what the weather is like outside and what season of the year it is. Ask the children what season they usually think about when they think of a garden. Read THIS YEAR'S GARDEN. After you have read it, lead the children in a discussion of what the family did each season that had to do with the garden. Let the children say the kinds of vegetables they would like to grow if they had a garden. End the discussion by talking about how all the family members worked together to plan the garden, to plant it, to weed it and to harvest the produce, as well as to enjoy the fruits and vegetables.

### STORY STRETCHER
## For Art: Glowing Warm Prints

**What the children will learn—**
To use background color to create a mood

**Materials you will need—**
Sheets of yellow, orange and brown construction paper, paper scraps, colored pencils, crayons

**What to do—**
1. Show the children Mary Szilagyi's illustrations in THIS YEAR'S GARDEN. Let them discuss what they like about the pictures. Help them notice how she uses yellows and oranges in muted tones to create a warm feeling, and the browns to show the earth and evening approaching.

2. On scraps of paper, let the children experiment with coloring lightly over the different colors of paper and seeing what effects they can create.

3. Ask the children to draw a picture where they use the colored backgrounds to create a mood.

**Something to think about—**
Young children will be more interested in experimenting with layering the crayons over the color of the paper than trying to create a certain mood; however, it is still appropriate to talk with young children about how artists create certain effects.

### STORY STRETCHER
## For Housekeeping And Dress-up Corner: Gardening Clothes

**What the children will learn—**
To dress in clothing which they are not used to wearing

**Materials you will need—**
Jeans, shirts, straw hats, caps, gloves, seed catalogs, seed packages, home canned foods, watering can

**What to do—**
1. Collect the clothing, catalogs and home canned foods from supplies in the classroom, your household and donations from parents.

2. Help the children begin to sort and arrange their farm house to get ready for the gardening season.

3. Start the play by pretending to be Granny who is looking at the seed catalog and says she doesn't want to plant so many beans this year because she is tired of canning.

4. After the play is underway, quietly leave the group to their own play themes.

**Something to think about—**
Dramatic play is a marvelous time for children to try on new roles, and with each new role comes an opportunity to try on new vocabulary, to say words they have never said before, such as "canning," "raking," "hoeing," "catalogs."

## For Library Corner: Seed And Gardening Catalogs

**What the children will learn—**
To select favorite pictures of fruits, vegetables, flowers, trees, and shrubs, and to use descriptive words

**Materials you will need—**
Variety of seed and plant catalogs

**What to do—**

**1.** Place the catalogs on the library shelves alongside the books on plants and gardening which you have selected for this unit.

**2.** Interact with the children, telling them some of your favorite fruits, as "granny apples," "big-boy tomatoes," "purple dwarf iris," "camellia shrubs" and "silver maple trees."

**3.** Encourage the children to select fruits, vegetables, flowers, shrubs and trees they like. As they read and look at the pictures, take time to read aloud some of the descriptions.

**4.** After a few days of the children looking at and reading the catalogs, let them begin to predict what the text might say to describe the plant. They can think of descriptive words by looking at the pictures.

**Something to think about—**
Make the covers of the catalogs more durable by covering them with clear contact paper and taping over the places where the staples hold the pages together. For younger children roll a strip of clear tape along the edge of each page and they can grasp them to turn pages more easily.

## For Mathematics And Manipulatives: Recycling Catalogs Into Puzzles

**What the children will learn—**
To make their own puzzles

**Materials you will need—**
Catalogs, scissors, posterboard or construction paper, rubber cement, pencils, envelopes

**What to do—**

**1.** Let the children look through the flower and seed catalogs and select pictures they like.

**2.** Have them cut out the pictures and adhere them to a piece of posterboard or construction paper with rubber cement.

**3.** Turn the puzzle over on the back and draw random puzzle-shaped pieces.

**4.** Cut out the pieces and place them in an envelope with the child's name on the outside.

**Something to think about—**
Talk with the children about how you are recycling the old catalogs by using them in other ways. Discuss other kinds of pictures which could be used, such as calendar pictures and magazine pictures.

## For Science And Nature: Raking And Hoeing

**What the children will learn—**
To use a rake and a hoe

**Materials you will need—**
Garden plot, spades, rakes, hoes, water hose, watering can

**What to do—**

**1.** Collect old gardening tools from parents.

**2.** Ask a parent to make the rake and hoe easier for young children to use by shortening the handles.

**3.** Visit a neighbor near the school or center who has a garden plot. Let the children watch the gardener till the soil with a tractor or a rototiller. Allow them to watch as much of the process as possible.

**4.** After the soil has been tilled, let the children use the rakes and hoes to help build the beds for the plants.

**5.** If possible, let the children plant a row of vegetables.

**Something to think about—**
This is an excellent activity in which to involve grandparents and community volunteers. Explore your neighborhood for mini-field trips that have maximum learning possibilities.

## PLANTING A RAINBOW

*By Lois Ehlert*

*In boldly colored graphic prints, Ehlert illustrates a simple text loaded with key concepts about growing things. We see colored bulbs, bright the seed packages, bold early blossoms, a wagon filled with an array of seedlings, and finally the wide variety of flowers blooming in the garden. The book ends with layers of pages from narrow to wide, each showing flowers the same color as the edge of that particular page. For example, on a narrow page we see an orange tulip, orange zinnia, orange tiger lily and orange poppy, and at the end of the page is a one-inch stripe of orange. The next page is a bit wider with a collection of yellow flowers and a wide yellow stripe. Throughout the book each flower is labeled.*

## Circle Time Presentation

Show the children the cover of PLANTING A RAINBOW by Lois Ehlert and THIS YEAR'S GARDEN by Cynthia Rylant and pictures by Mary Szilagyi. Have the children recall some scenes they remember from THIS YEAR'S GARDEN and ask who the gardeners were. Read PLANTING A RAINBOW and at the end ask who the gardeners are. We are not told if the gardener is a boy or a girl working with the mother. Ask children to tell you their favorite flowers, encourage them to say the color of the flower. Tell the children that this will be a colorful gardening day.

STORY STRETCHER

## For Art: Collage Flowers

**What the children will learn—**
To use shapes and bold colors to make collages

**Materials you will need—**
White construction paper or computer paper, scissors, scraps of brightly colored construction paper, gluesticks, optional — markers

**What to do—**
1.   With the children who come to the art center during free play or center time, look again at Lois Ehlert's PLANTING A RAINBOW.

2.   Let the children brainstorm about how the pictures could have been made.

3.   Provide the art materials and let the children experiment with the forms to make the flowers.

**Something to think about—**
Because Ehlert's graphics look so simple, young children often think a child did them. Encourage them to make real or imaginary flowers..

STORY STRETCHER

## For Creative Dramatics: Gardening

**What the children will learn—**
To pantomime the actions of gardening

**Materials you will need—**
None needed

**What to do—**
1.   During a second group time of the day, pantomime down on your knees, digging in the dirt. Wipe your brow with back of your hand or pretend to take a handkerchief from your pocket. Have the children guess what you are doing.

2.   Let volunteers pantomime different actions. First, have the child whisper in your ear what action she is going to pantomime, Have her do it for the children so that they can guess what her motions mean.

3.   Ask pairs of children to do some actions together for the group to guess.

**Something to think about—**
Having the child whisper in your ear allows you to be able to assist her if she can't think of what to do. If the child freezes, you can say, "Would you like me to do it with you?" Then the child can imitate you. Younger children may need props to pantomime or may need to rehearse their movements in front of a mirror before doing them for the entire group.

STORY STRETCHER

## For Mathematics And Manipulatives: Grouping By Color

**What the children will learn—**
To form sets of flowers by their colors

**Materials you will need—**
Pictures of flowers from catalogs, calendars or seed packages, scissors, cardboard or old file folders, rubber cement, sheets of construction paper

**What to do—**
1.  Let the children help you construct flower picture cards.

2.  Cut pictures of flowers from catalogs, old calendars or seed packages.

3.  With rubber cement, glue the pictures onto cardboard or old file folders cut the same size as the flower picture.

4.  When the flower picture cards are finished, place sheets of construction paper of the primary and secondary colors on the table.

5.  Let the children sort the flower cards by colors.

6.  Count the number of flowers of each color.

7.  Fold the construction paper into fourths and store with the flower picture cards in a large plastic bag.

**Something to think about—**
Teachers often do too much work for the children, pre-cutting, shaping and constructing elaborate materials. Often simple materials that children help to produce themselves will get the most use and it lets the children know that they are capable people.

STORY STRETCHER

## For Library Corner: Our Rainbow Of Flowers Book

**What the children will learn—**
To compose a text with other children

**Materials you will need—**
Typing paper, construction paper, cardboard, clear contact paper, scissors, markers, glue

**What to do—**
1.  Let the children use the flower collages they made in art or make a second one.

2.  When the flower collages are completed, place them face down on another sheet of paper and staple the sheets together along the left edge. Then open them and they will look like the facing pages of a book. Ask the children what they would like to say about their flower collages for the "Rainbow of Flowers Books."

3.  Either take dictation from the children or let them write on their own. Accept whatever their level of writing is from scribbles to mock writing or to using some letters to represent words.

4.  Staple the pages of collages and text together and bind according to the directions in the appendix. The contact paper and cardboard binding makes an attractive "real" book.

**Something to think about—**
If the children construct elaborate collage pictures, slip them into plastic photograph pages, place in a loose leaf notebook and make a "Notebook of Our Rainbow of Flowers."

STORY STRETCHER

## For Science And Nature: Planting Bulbs, Seeds, Seedlings

**What the children will learn—**
To observe the differences in appearance of bulbs, seeds and seedlings and the differences in growth patterns

**Materials you will need—**
Bulbs, seeds, seedlings, potting soil, dishes, clear plastic glasses, pots, spades, watering cans, tongue depressors, permanent markers, stapler, seed packages

**What to do—**
1.  On one day plant bulbs, on another seeds and on another seedlings.

2.  Use the sand and water table to hold the soil and the science table for the pots and other equipment.

3.  Plant bulbs in the soil and force some in low flat dishes.

4.  Plant seeds in clear plastic glasses so the children can see the root systems developing.

5.  Plant seedlings in clay pots.

6.  Mark each bulb, the seeds and seedlings by printing the name on a tongue depressor or popsicle stick and placing it in the soil. For the seeds, you can also staple the seed package to a tongue depressor and place it in the soil. Later the children can compare their plants to the ones pictured on the package.

7.  Group the plants on the science table by whether they are bulbs, seeds or seedlings.

8.  Help the children become systematic observers by assigning different children to each group, then having the groups rotate.

9.  Each day have the observers look at the plants and tell you something they notice which is different today. Write their observations in a notebook with entries for each date.

**Something to think about—**
Spread this activity out over several days. For younger children, choose quick growing seeds which will germinate rapidly and seedlings which are about ready to add leaves.

# 6
# PLANTS—I LIKE GROWING THINGS

## PLANTS THAT NEVER EVER BLOOM

*By Ruth Heller*

*Teachers have come to depend on Ruth Heller's science books for their sound concept development, lyrical prose and beautiful illustrations. Children will return to the book again and again to look at the richly detailed feast of rich colors and marvelous, but natural shapes. The bold colors and rhyming text, characteristic of Ruth Heller books, make it especially appropriate for reading to a group at circle time.*

## Circle Time Presentation

Leave the book lying flat on your lap. Begin the group time by encouraging the children to talk about some of their favorite plants and telling why they like them. Many will like flowers because of their beautiful blossoms. Ask the children if they like plants which do not bloom. Before you start reading, tell the children that you will read the book through once without stopping, then you will read it again and pause for them to look more closely at the illustrations. Read PLANTS THAT NEVER EVER BLOOM. Expect "oohs" and "aahs" over the beautiful pictures and some children coming up to the pictures and pointing while asking, "What's that?" At the end of the second reading, have the children practice saying, "Gym-no-sperms," which is the scientific name for "plants that never ever bloom."

STORY STRETCHER
## For Art: Brightly Colored Backgrounds

**What the children will learn—**
To construct an art project which take two days

**Materials you will need—**
Easels, tempera paints, butcher paper, brushes, index card, marker, tape

**What to do—**
1.  Ask every child in the class to participate in this art activity.
2.  For the first day, have the children use brightly colored tempera paints and paint a solid color background.
3.  On the second day, on their brightly colored background, ask them to paint any plant they would like that never ever blooms.

4.  When the paintings are finished, let them dry by hanging them on a clothesline with clothespins.
5.  On an index card, write whatever title the child wants you to write. Attach the title card to the painting.

**Something to think about—**
To avoid the edges of the paper curling, place a strip of masking tape on the back of the paper along all four edges.

STORY STRETCHER
## For Cooking And Snack Time: Tasting Mushrooms

**What the children will learn—**
To compare the tastes of raw and cooked mushrooms

**Materials you will need—**
Fresh mushrooms, knives, cutting board, canned mushrooms, salad greens, colander, large salad bowl, smaller salad bowls, apple juice, saltines, forks, glasses, napkins

**What to do—**
1.  Ask the cooking and snack time helpers to assist you and prepare the salad greens.
2.  Wash the lettuce and other vegetables and place them in a colander to drain.
3.  Help the children set the table by setting one place setting and let them make duplicates of yours.
4.  Place a small serving of salad in each child's bowl.
5.  In the center of the snack tables, place a cutting board with a knife and some fresh mushrooms, as well as a bowl of cooked mushrooms.
6.  Talk with the children about foods they have eaten which have mushrooms in them, such as salads, soups and pizza.

7. Suggest each child cut off a small slice of mushroom and taste it and decide if you or the aid should add more mushrooms to their salad.

8. Discuss that mushrooms look different when they are cooked and have the children notice how the canned mushrooms look. They are like the ones we see in soup and on pizza.

9. Encourage the children to compare the tastes of the raw mushroom and the canned mushrooms. Discuss that mushrooms are one of the plants you read about in PLANTS THAT NEVER EVER BLOOM.

**Something to think about—**
Having children slice off their own bite of mushroom encourages them to try it on their own. Avoid forcing or even overly encouraging children to try foods which they are reluctant to eat.

## For Library Corner: Listening Station, Tape Of "Plants That Never Ever Bloom"

**What the children will learn—**
To say their lines on cue

**Materials you will need—**
Cassette tape and recorder, stapler, listening station, headphones

**What to do—**
1. With a small group of children who choose the library corner during free play or center time, make a tape of PLANTS THAT NEVER EVER BLOOM.

2. Read the book again and this time pause and insert a questioning refrain. For example, where the text says, "A mushroom doesn't ever bloom," let the children say with a question in their voice, "Never, ever, doesn't ever bloom?"

3. Continue with this pattern and say "Never, ever, doesn't ever bloom?" after the opening line about the seaweed, and the opening line about the lichen.

4. At the end of the book have the children say, "Yes, there are many plants that never ever bloom."

5. Practice the lines and cues. Assign one child to make the page-turning signal by clicking a stapler next to the microphone.

6. Make the tape and let the recorders be the first children to hear the tape at the listening station.

**Something to think about—**
With young children, simply let them say, "NO?" in a questioning voice each time you point to them, which is their cue.

## For Science And Nature: Plants That Grow In Aquariums

**What the children will learn—**
To identify plants, and types of algae that grow in the sea

**Materials you will need—**
Aquarium, plants

**What to do—**
1. If you do not have an aquarium, invite someone who does to bring his or hers to school or go visit one which is already at the school.

2. The aquarium owner may know the names of the plants in their fish tank, but if they do not, visit a pet store that specializes in fish and bring back samples of some of the usual plants people place in their aquariums.

3. Look at the pictures in Ruth Heller's PLANTS THAT NEVER EVER BLOOM and see if the plants in the aquarium look like those in the book.

4. Talk with the children about how the fish use the plants for camouflage.

**Something to think about—**
If you are not particularly good at remembering the names of plants, print the names in permanent ink on a Post-it note and stick it on the glass of the aquarium to identify the plants.

## For Science And Nature: Looking For Lichen

**What the children will learn—**
To look for lichen on logs, trees and rocks

**Materials you will need—**
Parent or community volunteers, magnifying glasses

**What to do—**
1. If you have a woods nearby, take a walk there. If not, arrange for a short field trip to a nearby woods or nature center.

2. Before leaving, look again at Ruth Heller's illustrations of lichen.

3. Ask the parents or volunteers to help the children see the lichen growing.

4. If possible, bring back a sample from three places, a log, a piece of bark and a rock.

5. Display the lichen on the science table. Place the hand-held magnifying glass on the table for the children to examine the lichen more closely.

**Something to think about—**
If you have a parent who is a good photographer, ask the parent to take pictures of the children as they discover various lichen.

# 6
## PLANTS—I LIKE
## GROWING THINGS

## THE EMPTY POT
### By Demi

*A folktale set in China where the emperor uses an ingenious plan to choose his successor. Ping, a boy who loved flowers, seemed to have a magic touch. Every plant he touched seemed to grow well. One day the emperor called all the children in the land to his palace and gave them some special seeds, telling the children that whoever does his best in a year's time can become the new emperor. Ping planted his seeds carefully and took good care of them, but nothing grew. On the last day of the year, he had to go to the emperor with an "empty pot," while all the other children came with beautiful plants. The emperor chose Ping because Ping did his best and was honest. The seeds had been cooked and none of them could grow. The book has lovely fine-line, watercolor illustrations to accompany this powerful moral and memorable folktale form.*

## Circle Time Presentation

Show the children all the featured books on plants that you have read to them. Let them decide which books are real or could have happened and those which are imaginary. All the books are based on fact, except the one you are going to read today. Show the children the cover of THE EMPTY POT. Place a lovely ceramic flower pot on the floor near you and read THE EMPTY POT through without stopping. At the end, when the suspense is building, lower your voice almost to a whisper. Look through the book a second time, turning the pages slowly for the children to look at the beautiful illustrations. Ask a child who usually does not go to the library corner to take the book there and wait for you so the two of you can look at the book together. Dismiss the children to the centers by asking them to name one of their favorite flowers.

STORY STRETCHER
## For Art: Appreciating Oriental Art

**What the children will learn—**
To associate fine-line watercolors with oriental art

**Materials you will need—**
Oriental art prints

**What to do—**
1. Invite an artist who knows and appreciates oriental art, particularly Chinese art, to come to the class and bring some prints.

2. Help the children see the traditional characteristics of oriental art, such as water scenes with bamboo branches in the foreground, waterfowl and traditional robes.

3. Allow the children enough time to really admire the prints, and if possible, leave some of them in the classroom for the children to return to again.

4. After the visitor has left, look again at Demi's watercolor illustrations of THE EMPTY POT and compare them to the fine art prints.

**Something to think about—**
If you have a family among your children who is Chinese, ask them if they have any artwork they would like to share with the class.

ANOTHER STORY STRETCHER
## For Art: Watercolor Prints

**What the children will learn—**
To use fine-line watercolor brushes

**Materials you will need—**
Construction paper or heavy paper, scissors, watercolors, fine-line watercolor brushes, margarine tubs with warm water, paper towels or newspaper, glue

**What to do—**
1. Talk about the fine-line oriental prints your guest brought for the children to see. Discuss that many were long pieces of paper rolled up like scrolls.

2. Look at the Demi's illustrations in THE EMPTY POT. Have the children notice the circular shape, instead of the long rectangular shape of the fine art prints.

3. Ask the children which shape they would like to paint.

4. Cut the paper in whichever shape they desire.

5. Demonstrate how to load the watercolor paints onto the brushes and how to dry them on paper towels or newspaper if they have too much paint or too much water.

6. When the paintings are dried, mount the circular prints onto sheets of construction paper.

7. Display the children's artwork on a bulletin board.

**Something to think about—**
Many teachers believe that young children should only have long handled thick brushes, but after observing many children, we think it is appropriate to have a wide variety of sizes and shapes of brushes.

STORY STRETCHER

## For Mathematics And Manipulatives: Sorting Seeds

**What the children will learn—**
To sort seeds which are alike

**Materials you will need—**
A variety of seeds, clear plastic glasses, envelopes, tray

**What to do—**
1. Pour many different variety of seeds together into a glass jar or clear plastic container.

2. Let the children sort the seeds which are alike and place them into the plastic glasses.

3. To make the seeds easier to handle, pour the seeds out onto a tray. Do not pour all the seeds out at once or the task becomes overwhelming.

**Something to think about—**
When the seeds are all sorted, the children could make a display of layers of seeds by filling the plastic glasses. For example, have the children pour yellow corn seeds in the bottom, add a layer of black watermelon seeds, a layer of white lima bean seeds, and continue the pattern until the glass is filled. Top with a piece of plastic wrap held in place with a rubber band. If you want a functional use for this activity, begin by placing a candle in the middle of the plastic glass and layer the seeds around it. The candle can be used for a table

decoration. It is particularly appropriate for Thanksgiving.

(Idea adapted from one shared by Jane Kolakowski.)

STORY STRETCHER

## For Music And Movement: Musical Proclamation

**What the children will learn—**
To hear the differences between oriental musical instruments and the music to which they are accustomed

**Materials you will need—**
If possible, a real oriental musician with instruments, or a recording of Chinese music, tape or record player

**What to do—**
1. If you are able to arrange for someone who plays an oriental instrument to come to the class, ask the musician to play something very gentle which would sound like Ping planting his tiny seed.

2. Proceed with the story, asking the musician to play chords which would express the emotions or activities of the story.

3. When the story is over, ask the musician to play something cheerful and exciting where all the children are dancing through the streets, bringing their beautiful flowers to the emperor.

4. Let the children pretend to be holding their flowers and dancing around in tune to the music.

5. Then have them put their flowers down and pretend to be Ping cautiously bringing his empty pot.

6. Next, let them pretend to be the new emperor marching through the streets and celebrating. Let the children move as the music inspires them.

**Something to think about—**
Help the children appreciate the different sounds of music from many cultures, including first the varieties among the cultures represented in your classroom.

STORY STRETCHER

## For Science And Nature: Which Seeds Are Cooked?

**What the children will learn—**
To conduct an experiment comparing uncooked seeds with cooked seeds

**Materials you will need—**
Seeds, potting soil, pot

**What to do—**
1. Cook some lima bean seeds and leave some uncooked.

2. Bring the seeds to class and let the children plant them. Do not tell them which seeds are cooked and which are not.

3. Number the pots and let them predict whether or not the seeds will germinate and grow.

4. Have the children make daily observations for two weeks.

**Something to think about—**
Usually when we have children plant seeds we give everyone some seeds; however, since some of these seeds will not come up, number the pots instead of letting each child claim one.

# PLANTS—I LIKE GROWING THINGS

## THE MOUSE AND THE POTATO

*Retold by Thomas Berger*

*Illustrated by Carla Grillis*

*A farmer grows an enormous potato, but he can't get it out of the ground. He pulls and he pulls, but the enormous potato does not budge. In this cumulative tale, the farmer's wife, the farm hand, the milk maid, Maggie the daughter, the dog and the cat, and finally a little mouse pull on the potato until it explodes from the ground leaving the whole line of "pullers" topsy turvy. The farmer's wife cooks a huge plate of potato scones for the hungry family and their helpers. The book is a good one for circle time because of the large format and the bright, humorous illustrations.*

## Circle Time Presentations

Show the children the cover of THE MOUSE AND THE POTATO. Ask them to predict what the mouse has to do with the potato. Read THE MOUSE AND THE POTATO and pause after the farmer has pulled and pulled on the potato and cannot get it out of the ground. Solicit suggestions from the children about what the farmer could do. Read on and pause after the farmer gets the dog and cat to help and ask who else might join their "tugging line." Finish the story. Let the children recall the parts of the story where the writer surprised them, as when the dog joined the line and when the farmer's wife cooked potato scones from the enormous potato.

STORY STRETCHER

## For Cooking And Snack Time: Peeling Potatoes For Potato Soup

**What the children will learn—**
To peel potatoes and to follow recipe directions

**Materials you will need—**
Potatoes, water, milk, salt, pepper, vegetable peelers, paring knives, measuring cup, mixing bowl, crock pot, soup bowls, soup spoons, chart tablet or posterboard, marker, optional — crackers and cheese

**What to do—**
1. Print a recipe for potato soup on a chart tablet or posterboard. Use rebus symbols for the potatoes, measuring cup, mixing bowls, paring knife, crock pot.

2. With the children who choose the cooking and snack area during center time, demonstrate how to peel potatoes with the vegetable peeler and the paring knives.

3. When the children have peeled enough potatoes for the soup, cut them up and place in the water, milk, salt and pepper mixture and cook slowly in the crock pot.

4. Serve hot soup with crackers and cheese.

5. Demonstrate for the children how to use a soup spoon.

**Something to think about—**
Make a Big Book of Class Recipes. The children can read the recipes as a way to recall their cooking experiences. For one of the parent meetings, distribute copies of the rebus recipes the children have made in class and encourage parents to prepare the dishes at home with their children's help.

STORY STRETCHER

## For Library Corner: Flannel Board Story Of "The Mouse And The Potato"

**What the children will learn—**
To sequence the characters and events in the story

**Materials you will need—**
Flannel board, plastic bag, clothespin, construction paper or felt pieces for characters, potato, stove

**What to do—**
1. Construct the felt pieces for the characters, the potato and the stove, which represents the potato scones.

2. Retell the story using the flannel board pieces.

3. Distribute the character pieces among the listeners in the library corner.

4. As you retell the story, let the children add their pieces to the flannel board.

5. Store the flannel board pieces in a large plastic bag and clip the

bag onto the book with a large clothespin.

**6.** Place the featured story in a prominent place in the library corner.

**7.** Let the children who helped with the flannel board story retell it at a second group time of the day.

**Something to think about—**
As a variation, ask some children to make small puppets of the characters, the potato and the stove. Suggest the children make them about the size of their hand. They can draw the puppets on construction paper, color them or glue on scraps of brightly colored paper for the clothing. Attach the construction paper puppets to tongue depressors or to folded and stapled wands of construction paper to use as holders.

STORY STRETCHER

## For Mathematics And Manipulatives: "One Potato, Two Potato, Three Potato, Four"

**What the children will learn—**
To say the counting rhyme and to use it for deciding turns

**Materials you will need—**
Variety of puzzles, chart tablet or posterboard, marker

**What to do—**

**1.** Print the rhyme on a chart tablet or posterboard.

**2.** Teach the children the "One Potato, Two Potato" rhyme used to decide turns.

*One potato, two potato,*
*Three potato, four,*
*Five potato, six potato,*
*Seven potato, more.*

**3.** Show the children how to make a potato of their fists and then with a partner to stack them as they say the rhyme. The child

with his fist on the top when the rhyme ends with "more" is the winner and gets to select the first puzzle.

**4.** Discuss with the children that this rhyme is one their parents probably know and used when they were children to decide who goes first.

**Something to think about—**
Older children can play the elimination hand rhyme with several children.

STORY STRETCHER

## For Music And Movement: "The Farmer In The Dell"

**What the children will learn—**
To vary a familiar song to match the story

**Materials you will need—**
None needed

**What to do—**

**1.** If your children do not know "The Farmer in the Dell," teach it to them, or have them recall it.

**2.** Teach the children a variation of "The Farmer in the Dell" to match the story of THE MOUSE AND THE POTATO.

**3.** Have the children recall the characters in the story: the farmer, farmer's wife, the farm hand, milk maid, Maggie, dog, cat, mouse.

**4.** Print the following words on a chart tablet or posterboard for the class' Big Book of Music. Teach the children the new words to the song.

*The farmer grows potatoes,*
*The farmer grows potatoes,*
*Hi-ho, the garden oh,*
*The farmer grows potatoes.*

*The farmer pulls the stem,*
*The farmer pulls the stem,*
*Hi-ho, the garden oh,*
*The farmer pulls the stem.*

*The wife pulls the farmer,*
*The wife pulls the farmer,*

*Hi-ho, the garden oh,*
*The wife pulls the farmer.*

*The farm hand pulls the wife.*
*The farm hand pulls the wife.*
*Hi-ho, the garden oh,*
*The farm hand pulls the wife.*

*The milk maid pulls the farm hand,*
*The milk maid pulls the farm hand,*
*Hi-ho, the garden oh,*
*The milk maid pulls the farm hand.*

*Then Maggie pulls the milk maid,*
*Then Maggie pulls the milk maid,*
*Hi-ho, the garden oh,*
*Then Maggie pulls the milk maid.*

*The little dog pulls Maggie,*
*The little dog pulls Maggie,*
*Hi-ho, the garden oh,*
*The little dog pulls Maggie.*

*The cat pulls the little dog,*
*The cat pulls the little dog,*
*Hi-ho, the garden oh,*
*The cat pulls the little dog.*

*The mouse pulls the cat,*
*The mouse pulls the cat,*
*Hi-ho, the garden oh,*
*The mouse pulls the cat.*

*The potato pops out of the ground,*
*The potato pops out of the ground.*
*Hi-ho, cherry-oh, the*
*It's potato scones tonight!*
*It's potato scones tonight!*
*(Raines, 1991).*

**Something to think about—**
Sing the song for several days until the children know it, then have a potato pull, like a tug of war. Place a strip of masking tape on the floor. Tie a handkerchief around the center of a rope and have the children pretend it is a potato. As they sing the song, add characters to each side of the rope. Let them struggle back and forth, and at the end when the potato pops from the ground, they all relax, let go of the rope and fall to the floor. There are no winners or losers, just the fun of physically matching the pulling strength on both sides of the rope.

## For Science And Nature: Potatoes In A Glass

**What the children will learn—**
To observe the growth process of the potato

**Materials you will need—**
Sweet potatoes, toothpicks, clear plastic glasses, water, pitcher, calendar, pencil, optional — patio plant container

**What to do—**

1. Let the children stick toothpicks around the middle of the potato to support it on the rim of the glass.

2. Pour water almost up to the rim of the clear plastic glass.

3. Place one end of the potato in the water with the toothpicks supporting the other end out of the water.

4. Mark the date on the calendar when you placed the potatoes in the water. Draw a small rebus symbol, a picture of the glass with the toothpicks supporting the potato.

5. Observe changes each day and record the changes on a calendar by drawing symbols. For example, when the potato starts to sprout, draw a small thin green sprout.

6. Continue observing the potato and recording changes, such as number of new leaves, until the vine is well developed. If possible, plant the potato in a large patio plant container.

**Something to think about—**
Compare the appearance of different varieties of potatoes, sweet potatoes, red, white, new potatoes and stored potatoes.

# REFERENCES

Berger, Thomas. (1990). Illustrated by Carla Grillis. **THE MOUSE AND THE POTATO.** Edinburgh, Scotland: Floris Books.

Demi. (1990). **THE EMPTY POT.** New York: Henry Holt and Company.

Ehlert, Lois. (1988). **PLANTING A RAINBOW.** San Diego: Harcourt Brace Jovanovich.

Heller, Ruth. (1984). **PLANTS THAT NEVER EVER BLOOM.** New York: Grosset & Dunlap.

Rylant, Cynthia. (1984). **THIS YEAR'S GARDEN.** Illustrated by Mary Szilagyi. New York: Aladdin Books, Macmillan Publishing.

## Additional References For Plants—I Like Growing Things

Briggs, Raymond. (1970). **JIM AND THE BEANSTALK.** New York: Putnam & Grosset Group. *Jim climbs a large beanstalk and finds a giant at the top who does not act like Jim or the readers will expect.*

Caseley, Judith. (1990). **GRANDPA'S GARDEN LUNCH.** New York: Greenwillow. *After helping Grandpa in the garden, Sarah and her grandparents enjoy a lunch made from home-grown vegetables.*

Cherry, Lynne. (1990). **THE GREAT KAPOK TREE.** New York: Harcourt Brace Jovanovich. *In the heart of the Brazilian rain forest, a woodcutter is chopping down a great kapok tree. The heat and effort exhaust him; as he sleeps, the creatures who make their homes in the tree emerge and plead with him not to destroy their world.*

Cooney, Barbara. (1982). **MISS RUMPHIUS.** New York: Viking Penguin. *Once long ago, Miss Rumphius was a little girl named Alice who lived by the sea. When she grew older, she remembered her grandfather's words: "You must do something to make the world more beautiful."*

McCloskey, Robert. (1948). **BLUEBERRIES FOR SAL.** New York: Viking Penguin. *An exciting story about what happens when a little girl wanders away from her mother while picking blueberries.*

# SCIENCE AND NATURE

*Listen to the Rain*
*Where Butterflies Grow*
*The Very Quiet Cricket*
*Bugs*
*A Tree Is Nice*

## LISTEN TO THE RAIN

*By Bill Martin, Jr. and*

*John Archambault*

*Illustrated by James Endicott*

*LISTEN TO THE RAIN is an enchanting poem telling the story of a rainstorm. The sound effects build from the beginning "whisper of the rain" to the steady "singing of the rain" on to the driving force of the "roaring pouring" rain. As the poem proceeds, the rainstorm recedes and the listener is left at the end with the "wet, silent, after-time of rain." The beautifully simple and elegant illustrations, and even the dark blue end paper pages, are a perfect setting for the drama of a rainstorm.*

## Circle Time Presentation

This book is an exhilarating "rainy day" selection. Present it by having the children listen to the sounds of the rain as it is happening. Read LISTEN TO THE RAIN as dramatically as the words imply. As the drama builds, say the words louder, then as the storm recedes let the sound of your voice recede until it is only a whisper at the end.

STORY STRETCHER

## For Art: Water Drop Splash Prints

**What the children will learn** - To use an abstract shape to create an interesting print

**Materials you will need—** A variety of scraps of colored posterboard, paper towels, plastic bowl of water, ball point pens, scissors

**What to do—**

1. A day before the art project is to begin, place a sheet of posterboard onto a table and purposefully drop some water drops onto it. Allow the water drops to dry and they will bleach out the color in the posterboard, leaving the shape of the drops of water.

2. Show the children what happened to the sheet of posterboard and discuss how it happened.

3. Let them make their own "water drop splash prints." Cut the posterboard into strips.

4. Before letting the children make their splashes, demonstrate how to just drop the water without wetting the whole board.

5. Leave the strips of posterboard overnight to dry.

6. The next day, have the children use ball point pens and draw around the water drops to emphasize their shapes.

7. Display the "Water Drop Splash Prints" on a bulletin board along with the book jacket from LISTEN TO THE RAIN and a copy of the poem.

**Something to think about—** For younger children, do not be concerned if they lack the dexterity to draw around the shapes exactly. Let them simply make large circles around the water drop shapes. Older children may enjoy adding legs, paws, beaks or tails to create animals from the water drops.

ANOTHER STORY STRETCHER

## For Art: Rainstorm Pastels

**What the children will learn—** To experiment with shading pastel chalks

**Materials you will need—** Pastel chalks, colored and white construction paper, plastic bowls, water, paper towels, optional — colored pencils

**What to do—**

1. Working with a small group of children at the art center, look through James Endicott's illustrations in LISTEN TO THE RAIN. Point out that the backgrounds for his paintings look like pastels.

2. Demonstrate how to use pastel chalks: the sides make wide soft marks, points make darker, sharper marks, using wet paper versus dry paper and blotting dry chalk with wet paper towels.

3. Let the children experiment making different textures.

4. After they have explored the possibilities, let them use whole sheets of different colored construction paper and create pastel prints. They can add drawings of

rainstorms if they like using colored pencils.

**Something to think about—**
As with all art activities, what the child chooses to draw or paint should be an individual decision. Many teachers are hesitant to even demonstrate art techniques because they fear hampering the child's creativity; however, children become more creative when they know many possible ways to use the art materials.

## For Library Corner: Listening To The Rain

**What the children will learn—**
To hear the changing sound effects of the rainstorm

**Materials you will need—**
Cassette tape, recorder, stapler, posterboard or chart tablet, markers

**What to do—**
1.   If possible, record a real rainstorm. Sometimes recordings can be made from a television program. If this is not possible, make the tape of the poem without the sound effects.

2.   Record yourself reading LISTEN TO THE RAIN. Make a softclick as the sound for the page-turning signal. The clicking of a stapler works well.

3.   In addition to providing a copy of the book, print a large copy of the poem on posterboard or a chart tablet to display in the library. Let the children decorate the edges with symbols which remind them of the rain, as clouds, umbrellas, raindrops, boots.

**Something to think about—**
Older children can think of sound effects which they can make to add to the tape for it to sound like a rainstorm.

## For Music And Movement: Splashing Our Way To School

**What the children will learn—**
To put on rain gear and to enjoy a puddle

**Materials you will need—**
Boots, rain slickers, rain hats, umbrellas, optional — large sheet of plastic, tubs of water

**What to do—**
1.   If it is a rainy warm day, let a few children at a time dress in the rain gear and go outside with an aide or volunteer to splash in the puddles on the playground.

2.   If it is not raining, create some puddles by placing a large sheet of plastic in a low place on the playground, fill it with water, and let the children enjoy splashing.

3.   Another alternative is to pretend walking in the rain. Let several children dress in rain hats and coats, and hold umbrellas. Make up a story of children walking to school. Use many movement words, such as tiptoeing through the edge of a puddle, jumping over, splashing through and drying off for the children to pretend.

4.   After one group finishes, have another group dress in the gear and tell a slightly different story.

**Something to think about—**
If you have a recording of the song "Singing in the Rain," play the song and teach the children the words. Ask parents to send in rubber boats, umbrellas, and slickers which can be left at school for a variety of play activities.

## For Science And Nature: Where Do The Animals And Insects Go When It Rains?

**What the children will learn—**
To think about what happens to birds, insects, plants and shells when it rains

**Materials you will need—**
Models or pictures of animals, insects and objects from the book, such as a butterfly, sea shell, cocoon, fish, grasshopper, bird, twig, dandelion, leaf

**What to do—**
1.   Let a few children help you set up the science table. Begin by looking through the book again for possible display items.

2.   Brainstorm where these objects or pictures of them might be found. For example, bring a twig and some leaves in from the playground, look outside for a grasshopper, find a picture of a butterfly in a book, have someone bring a sea shell from home. If an object cannot be found, draw a picture or model one from playdough.

3.   After the objects are collected, let the children arrange them in the same order they appear in the book.

4.   End the session by conducting a circle time for all the children around the science and nature display. Let the children who helped construct the display tell what happens to each animal, insect, shell or plant when it rains.

**Something to think about—**
Science and nature displays can always be mathematics activities when you emphasize sequencing as in this activity.

# WHERE BUTTERFLIES GROW

*By Joanne Ryder*

*Illustrated by Lynne Cherry*

*In this magnificently illustrated book, the facts of science and the wonder of nature merge with the reader's own imagination. The story of the metamorphosis of the black swallowtail butterfly begins with the invitation to imagine being small and hidden in a tiny egg. In a poetic voice, we are invited to imagine the growth from egg to creeper to cocoon to swallowtail. We see a lovely meadow of plants, a few small animals and birds in the full-page illustrations, beautiful in nature's colors. On a few pages, enlargements show the details of the caterpillar's changes. At the end of the book, the teacher is given directions for growing a butterfly garden and keeping a caterpillar in a terrarium.*

## Circle Time Presentation

Have the children look at the cover of WHERE THE BUTTERFLIES GROW and count the number of butterflies they see on the cover. Have a child who is sitting near you tell the other children what the border of the picture contains — caterpillars. Have the children close their eyes and imagine that they are very tiny and living in a dark little place, then the egg cracks and they see bright sunshine. Have them open their eyes and begin reading WHERE BUTTERFLIES GROW. Read in a slow, almost whisper voice at the suspenseful parts, then build to a crescendo when the caterpillar puffs up his orange horns and sprays a strong scent to keep from being eaten by the bird. Let your voice fall again and read with suspense, building again to a peak when the butterfly begins to soar above the meadow.

STORY STRETCHER

## For Art: Caterpillars In The Meadow

**What the children will learn—**
To make full-page illustrations

**Materials you will need—**
White construction paper, typing paper or manilla paper, tape, crayons or chalks, pencils, fine line black markers or pens

**What to do—**

1. Show the children the full-page illustrations in WHERE BUTTERFLIES GROW. Call attention to the ways the artist stretched her work across two pages.

2. Provide long paper, such as manilla paper, or tape two sheets of typing paper together.

3. Also point out to the children the way Lynne Cherry illustrated this book by both drawing and painting. Look closely at the rocks and grasses to see the way she created texture.

4. Let the children experiment with texture on small scraps of paper.

5. Encourage the children to draw their pictures with pencils first, use chalk or markers to color it, then add texture with sides of pencils, black fine-line markers, or rough crayon edges.

**Something to think about—**
For very young children just using more than one drawing instruments, crayons and pens, will be experimenting. For older children, each art technique adds to their repertoire, and as they explore the possibilities of that medium, they become more creative.

STORY STRETCHER

## For Creative Dramatics: From Egg To Caterpillar To Pupa To Butterfly

**What the children will learn—**
To think of motions which express how each stage of the butterfly's life feels

**Materials you will need—**
None needed

**What to do—**

1. Set the tone of the creative drama by having the children curl up and make themselves as tiny as they can be. Darken the room slightly and begin to read the book in almost a whisper.

2. Switch the lights on when the creeper bursts from the egg into the sunlight.

3. Have the children imagine how it feels as a creeper, balancing

on tiny leaves with two rows of feet.

4. Ask the children to take a deep breath, puff out their cheeks, arch their backs and pretend to shed a layer of skin.

5. In a whisper, tell the children to stay very still, not moving a muscle while avoiding the beak of a hungry bird.

6. Then dramatically, have them take a deep breath and blow it out, pretending to spray a strong smell so the bird goes away.

7. Let the children rest quietly, curled up slightly, then stretch one arm out and pretend to form a "silken sling" to attach themselves to a branch.

8. Have them rest in this position for what seems like a long time, then gradually start to move .

9. Ask them to begin gently moving their arms until they are ready to fly, slowly at first, then to soar and fly around landing at will.

10. Have them land on a flower, perch on all fours, put their heads down and pretend to drink sweet nectar before darting off to another flower, and then to soar again.

**Something to think about—**

Plan this creative dramatics experience more than once during the week so that children have a chance to improvise more movements.

STORY STRETCHER

## For Library Corner: Our Science Report On "Where Butterflies Grow"

**What the children will learn—**
To recall facts

**Materials you will need—**
Chart tablet or posterboard, markers, WHERE BUTTERFLIES GROW and THE VERY HUNGRY CATERPILLAR by Eric Carle

**What to do—**

1. Show the children two books about butterflies, one fact and one fiction. WHERE BUTTERFLIES GROW is fact, and THE VERY HUNGRY CATERPILLAR is fiction because caterpillars do not eat people food.

2. Look through the illustrations of WHERE BUTTERFLIES GROW and have the children recall a list of important information they want to recall about butterflies and where they grow.

3. Write key words on a chart tablet or posterboard as the children tell their important facts.

4. After everyone in the group has contributed, read the key word chart and after each word is said, let a child tell a fact, something that is true about caterpillars and butterflies.

**Something to think about—**
Older children can keep a learning log, a journal of what they learn. It can be written or drawn, depending on the age and abilities of the children.

STORY STRETCHER

## For Science And Nature: Sequencing Growth Cards

**What the children will learn—**
To sequence the growth process from the egg to caterpillar to pupa to butterfly

**Materials you will need—**
Pictures of caterpillar egg, caterpillar in variety of stages, pupa, butterfly

**What to do—**

1. Using copies of prints found in the book or from other nature resources, make a set of sequence cards showing the growth process from egg to butterfly.

2. Place the book and the sequence cards on the science and nature display table. The children will naturally begin to sort them by order of growth based on their information gained from hearing you read WHERE BUTTERFLIES GROW and from examining the book on their own.

**Something to think about—**
Add additional sequence cards for older children with short sentences describing the stage pictured on the card. For younger children, let them sequence by matching the pictures and the cards exactly.

ANOTHER STORY STRETCHER

## For Science And Nature: Habitat For Butterflies To Grow

**What the children will learn—**
To observe caterpillars in their habitat

**Materials you will need—**
Terrarium, moss, twig with leaves, grasses, hand-held magnifying glasses, caterpillars

**What to do—**

1. Construct a terrarium following the directions in the back of WHERE BUTTERFLIES GROW.

2. Place the magnifying glasses near the terrarium for the children to observe the changes in the caterpillars.

**Something to think about—**
If possible, visit a butterfly garden in your community. Check with the science education departments in conservation agencies or with county extension agents.

# SCIENCE AND NATURE

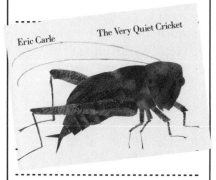

## THE VERY QUIET CRICKET

*By Eric Carle*

*From the day little cricket is born he wants to chirp, so he rubs his wings together but nothing happens. And so the pattern is set. Cricket meets and tries to greet other insects but nothing happens. A locust, a praying mantis, a worm, a spittlebug, a cicada, a bumblebee, a dragonfly, mosquitoes, a luna moth greet cricket, but he cannot return their sounds with his sound because he is the very quiet cricket. Quiet until he meets a female cricket, and then when he rubs his wings together he hears a beautiful sound. In marvelous bold Carle style, the reader is treated to wonderfully textured collages while made to feel badly that poor cricket has no sound.*

## Circle Time Presentation

This unit could be subtitled insects and the sounds of nature. Tiptoe over to the circle time area, sit very still and whisper to the children. Ask if they have ever known someone who has laryngitis, someone who has "lost their voice." Talk like someone who can barely speak and tell about a time when you had laryngitis from a cold and how frustrating it was when you tried to talk and no sounds came out of your throat. In a whispering but expressive voice read THE VERY QUIET CRICKET.

STORY STRETCHER

## For Art: Textured Wings

**What the children will learn—**
To add texture to crayon and collage artwork

**Materials you will need—**
White construction paper, variety of colored tissue paper or scraps of construction paper, crayons, scissors, glue, sandpaper scraps, leaves, small comb

**What to do—**

1. Demonstrate for the children who come to the art center during free play how to add texture to paper.

2. Place the sandpaper under a scrap of construction paper or colored tissue paper. Peel the paper from the sides of crayons and place them on their sides. Rub them over the paper and watch the pebbly imprint of the sandpaper come through on the top of the paper.

3. Continue the process by having the children make several pieces of paper with different textures by rubbing crayons over the sandpaper, leaves and a small comb.

4. Look with the children at Eric Carle's illustrations in THE VERY QUIET CRICKET and see if any of their paper is similar to Carle's.

5. Leave the children to create whatever pictures they like. Some will use their textured paper to create insects with beautiful wings.

**Something to think about—**
Younger children will continue experimenting with the process of texturing while older children will begin to see the many possibilities for insect art.

(Idea adapted from Cheryl Brashear.)

STORY STRETCHER

## For Library Corner: Children Tell Cricket's Story

**What the children will learn—**
To repeat the recurring phrases in the story

**Materials you will need—**
Tape recorder, cassette tape, listening station, headphones

**What to do—**

1. With the group who choose the library corner during free play, read again THE VERY QUIET CRICKET, pausing for the children to read the recurring phrases, "But nothing happened. Not a sound."

2. Practice the various tasks each group member is to perform on the tape. For example, one child might introduce the book by saying, "This is the story of THE VERY QUIET CRICKET by Eric Carle. The cover of the book is a picture of a large gray-black cricket with big red eyes."

3. The children can join you in reading the book by repeating the recurring phrases on cue.

4. After the practice session, record the tape. Let the recorders be

the first children to hear the tape at the listening station.

**Something to think about—**
This activity is a good one to do after you lead the children in the movement activity listed below.

STORY STRETCHER

## For Music And Movement: Insects' Dance

**What the children will learn—**
To associate specific movements with insects

**Materials you will need—**
None needed

**What to do—**
1. At a second group time of the day, read again THE VERY QUIET CRICKET, stopping at each page for a volunteer to improvise the movements of the insects and of the worm, who pops out of an apple to greet Cricket.

2. After the children think of ways to move which illustrate the various insects and the worm, read the story again and let all the children do the movements at once. They should be free to move around the room and add any sound effects they like.

3. Have the children return to the circle time area and have them show the way Cricket must have "felt" each time he could not make a sound. Let them show Cricket's feelings to the person sitting next to them by using facial expressions.

**Something to think about—**
This Story S-t-r-e-t-c-h-e-r is both a movement activity and a creative dramatics one. To make the activity a musical one, ask a music teacher for some suggestions of classical violin recordings which could be used as a background.

STORY STRETCHER

## For Science And Nature: Cricket Habitats

**What the children will learn—**
To state what crickets need to survive

**Materials you will need—**
Crickets, small pitcher of water, cotton balls, margarine tubs with lids, plastic wrap, grass, twigs, leaves, reference book on insects

**What to do—**
1. Find a source for crickets from a science school supply store, or if you live in an area where there are many crickets, the families of the children can bring them in.

2. Talk about what crickets need to live — air, water and shelter.

3. Have the children construct a cricket habitat in a terrarium or a large glass container with plastic wrap spread over it with small holes in the top.

4. Let the children pour water from the pitcher into the margarine tubs.

5. Show them how to drop the cotton balls into the water, squeeze out the excess water and then place the cotton balls on the lids of the margarine tubs. Place the lids inside the terrarium.

6. Explain that the crickets drink from the cotton.

7. Add a bit of grass, leaves and twigs to the terrarium.

**Something to think about—**
Discuss the difference between real crickets and Eric Carle's THE VERY QUIET CRICKET.

(Idea adapted from Pam von Bredow.)

ANOTHER STORY STRETCHER

## For Science And Nature: What Do You Hear?

**What the children will learn—**
To discriminate between sounds of nature and people-made sounds

**Materials you will need—**
Tape recorder, cassette tape, listening station, headphones

**What to do—**
1. If possible, find a "free from traffic sounds place," and make a taperecording of the sounds of nature and of the sounds of people.

2. To focus on the sounds people make, taperecord your family. Someone can cough, laugh, cry, sigh, breath heavily as after exercising, sing. If you have a baby in your family or a friend's family, try recording babbling, cooing, jabbering.

3. With the small group of children who select the science and nature center during free play, make a recording of the classroom sounds.

4. Go to a wooded area with a small group of children. Sit quietly and listen to the sounds of nature.

5. Record the sounds near the earth and in the trees.

6. Have a parent or friend help edit the tape.

7. Back in the classroom, decide on instructions for the tape. Tell the children to listen to the tape, turn it off whenever directed and decide with others listening to the tape whether the sounds heard are the sounds of nature or of people.

**Something to think about—**
Whenever possible, use a tape recorder which has a separate microphone.

# SCIENCE AND NATURE

## BUGS

*By Nancy Winslow Parker*

*and Joan Richards Wright*

*Illustrated by Nancy Winslow*

*Parker*

*In an unusual combination of rhymes, scientific facts and illustrations, the authors invite young readers to enjoy the book from many different levels. On the left side of the open pages, a rhyme about a person and a bug is printed with clear, simple, colorful illustrations. On the right side of the open pages, Parker provides a scientific drawing of the bug and the authors discuss facts about the insects. The book ends with a picture glossary of growth stages of bugs, a phylum chart and a bibliography of other resources. Cleverly conceived and well-executed, the book interests children on an everyday occurrence level, yet introduces them to the fascinating world of fifteen common insects and one slug.*

## Circle Time Presentation

Have the children recall the insects THE VERY QUIET CRICKET met, and discuss that Cricket's story was an imaginary one, and that insects do not talk in human voices to each other. Ask the children what insects they have seen or felt. Elicit some discussion about biting insects as mosquitoes and fleas, and begin reading the first page where Thelma is bitten on the thigh by a housefly. Read only the rhyming pages of the book. When you finish reading, ask the children if they noticed anything special about your reading. Read again the first page and have them notice how short your reading was. Then read the right hand side of the page where a horsefly is described. Look through the other pages of the book and read at least two others the children request. Tell the children there is a special tape of this book in the library corner. On one side of the tape is the short version of the book and on the other side is the long version.

STORY STRETCHER

## For Art: My Close Encounter With A Bug Or A Slug

**What the children will learn—**
To recall and illustrate an experience they had with a bug

**Materials you will need—**
Choice of art media, easel, paints and brushes, crayons, colored pencils, chalks, markers, large sheet of paper

**What to do—**
**1.** With the children who come to the art center during free play, discuss some of your encounters with bugs, a bee sting, a mosquito bite.

**2.** Just as the children in the book encounter bugs, have the children in the classroom volunteer their own stories of close encounters with bugs or slugs.

**3.** Fold the large sheet of art paper down the middle. Ask the children to draw or paint on the left side of the paper.

**4.** When the drawings or paintings are completed, ask the children to dictate or write on their own a sentence or two about the bug or slug encounters.

**Something to think about—**
These illustrations could be bound into a class book. See the appendix for binding instructions. They can also be used for a class creative dramatics session with the class role playing what happened in their close encounters with a bug or a slug.

STORY STRETCHER

## For Creative Dramatics: People And Bugs And Slugs

**What the children will learn—**
To role play characters' reactions to bugs and slugs

**Materials you will need—**
None needed

**What to do—**
**1.** Let the children discuss how some people are afraid of bugs and slugs. Talk about how some run away, others go for the bug spray or fly swatter and some jump on chairs.

**2.** Look at the illustrations of the people and their reactions to bugs and slugs in the book BUGS.

**3.** Have children volunteer to be the different characters: Thelma, Ada, Grant, first Nick, boy holding cat, baby Doug, Sam, Ben, Rita, Grandma, second Nick, father, nurse and three children, girls catching fireflies.

4. Let each child who is supposed to act out the illustrations look at her or his picture one more time.

5. Then read BUGS again and let the children act out the scenes.

**Something to think about—**
Cue younger children for their scenes by saying, "Tina, get ready," or "Michael, get ready."

S T O R Y   S T R E T C H E R

## For Library Corner: Long And Short Versions Of Bugs

**What the children will learn—**
To listen to two different types of information

**Materials you will need—**
Tape recorder, cassette tape, two readers

**What to do—**
1. Ask a friend or family member to make a tape with you.

2. Rehearse the reading of BUGS.

3. Record the short version, only the rhyming pages on one side of the tape and place a small drawing of Thelma on that side of the tape label.

4. Record the longer version with both the rhyming pages and the scientific pages. Have the friend or family member record the scientific information.

5. Draw a horsefly on the label for the second side of the cassette tape to help the children distinguish between the two versions.

6. Place the cassette tape, listening station and headphones on a table in the library corner.

**Something to think about—**
Collect books on insects and place them in the library area on a dis-

play table. If possible, have men and women speak on the tapes, as well as people from different age groups and speakers with a variety of dialects.

S T O R Y   S T R E T C H E R

## For Mathematics And Manipulatives: Symbols For Size

**What the children will learn—**
To identify symbols which relate to the actual lengths of insects

**Materials you will need—**
Paper, marker, basket containing a variety of objects from around the classroom such as crayon box, pieces of chalk, crayon, paper clips, small toy cars

**What to do—**
1. Have the children select some objects from the basket and draw them.

2. Then ask the children to take the object and draw around it creating an outline.

3. Discuss that this is the actual size of the object.

4. Look at the illustrations in BUGS. Have the children notice that in the pictures of the children and the bugs and slug, the insects are drawn larger than they really are.

5. Have the children decide if the insects in the scientific drawings are really that large.

6. Call attention to the line on the right hand side of each of the scientific drawings. That line indicates the actual size of the insect or slug.

7. Let the children discuss why the illustrators drew the bugs and the slug so large.

8. Have the children draw a line beside their first drawings to indicate the length the object from the basket really is.

**Something to think about—**
For older children, notice other symbols used in the scientific drawings. The parts of the insect or slug are numbered, then a key is provided. In addition, the scientific signs for male and female are used.

S T O R Y   S T R E T C H E R

## For Science And Nature: Young Entomologists

**What the children will learn—**
To appreciate the contributions that insects make to our world

**Materials you will need—**
Dead insect specimens, white tray or plate, magnifying glasses, blunt end tweezers, popsicle sticks

**What to do—**
1. Talk with the children about how some scientists only study insects; they are called entomologists.

2. Discuss that although the scientists study live insects, you do not have the equipment to study live insects to protect the children from getting bitten or stung, so the class will look closely at some dead specimens.

3. Have the children watch you as you place an insect onto the white tray or plate with the tweezers. Then use the end of the popsicle stick and move it gently.

4. Ask the children to tell you what they noticed about how you were handling the insect.

5. Let the children examine each insect under the magnifying glasses and look closely at the insect's body parts.

**Something to think about—**
Young children enjoy big words. Help them learn how to pronounce "entomologists."

## A TREE IS NICE

*By Janice May Udry*

*Illustrated by Marc Simont*

*Published in 1956, A TREE IS NICE is a Caldecott Medal book. In an almost poetic voice, the text and the illustrations help the young child see the value of a tree. Udry describes trees and their beauty in landscapes, as well as what they do for us. She ends with planting a tree and taking pride in watching it grow. Simont illustrates the book with chalks, charcoals and pen and ink sketches. He alternates color prints and black and white prints. In these days of ecological concerns, Udry's book with Simont's lovely illustrations is a timely addition to the early childhood curriculum.*

## Circle Time Presentation

Ask the children to tell what they see on the cover of the book. When someone mentions the Caldecott Medal, explain that the medal is given to illustrators whose pictures are judged as the most distinguished for a book published in a particular year. Tell the children that this book was made in 1956, when some of their parents were children. Emphasize that you like this book because of the words and the pictures; the words remind you of beautiful trees and playing in and around trees. Call attention to the little girl watering a small tree and ask the children to look closely at the illustrations and see if they can find that little girl again. Read A TREE IS NICE.

STORY STRETCHER

## For Art: Chalk Sketches

**What the children will learn—**
To use two media together to make a print

**Materials you will need—**
Manilla paper or construction paper, scissors, ink pens, chalks, margarine tubs with water, sponges

**What to do—**
1. With the children who come to the art center during free play or center time, look again at Marc Simont's illustrations in A TREE IS NICE. Call attention to the way he made dark lines and colors.

2. Let the children propose ways they can make their sketches and use the chalks to fill in with color.

3. Assist the children in folding their papers twice, making three tall sections.

4. Let the children cut their papers into three sections or leave it the original width if they like.

5. Demonstrate how to wet the paper with the sponges and rub the chalk over the damp paper.

6. Leave the children to use the pens and chalks on their own.

**Something to think about—**
Often teachers complain that the children tire of drawing and painting. Using a variety of art media and simple techniques of cutting the paper into different shapes will entice the children back into art activities.

STORY STRETCHER

## For Library Corner: Writing About Planting A Tree

**What the children will learn—**
To recall an experience and to see their spoken words become written words

**Materials you will need—**
Chart tablet, poster, markers, crayons, 3 x 5 index cards, glue or large Post-it notes

**What to do—**
1. Recall with the children their experience of planting a tree. (See the Story S-t-r-e-t-c-h-e-r for Science and Nature listed below.)

2. After they have discussed the experience, tell them that you have arranged for each child to have a small tree, a seedling, to take home with them, but you want to write some special instructions so they and their parents will know how to care for the tree.

3. Draw a wide margin, three to five inches, along the left side of the chart tablet or posterboard.

4. Have the children dictate sentences giving the step by step instructions they recall for planting a tree. Print their sentences on the chart tablet or posterboard, leaving the left margin blank.

**5.** After they have completed their list of instructions, tell them that many instructions also have simple pictures to help the readers remember the steps.

**6.** Let the children brainstorm some simple pictures which would help them remember what to do. For example, someone could draw a picture of the seedling, or the shovel, or a hand packing the soil.

**7.** Ask the children to volunteer which simple pictures they will draw and color with crayons or markers.

**8.** Give the children a small index card or Post-it note and let them draw and color their symbol or picture for that step.

**9.** Attach the drawings along the left margin of the chart tablet.

**10.** Make a smaller version of the planting chart and print it to send home with the seedling.

**Something to think about—**
Young children need to see writing in a meaningful, functional form to help people recall information, as well as to help them remember a special experience.

STORY STRETCHER

## For Mathematics And Manipulatives: Measuring Our Tree's Growth

**What the children will learn—**
To measure and compare changes in growth of a tree

**Materials you will need—**
Twine or yarn, scissors, envelopes, tape

**What to do—**
**1.** Cut a strip of twine or yarn longer than the tree the class planted is tall.

**2.** Hold the twine up alongside the tree and cut it the length of the tree.

**3.** Take the length of twine inside and tape it vertically in place on a blank wall.

**4.** Every two weeks, cut another length of twine, tape the length to the wall to make a graph so the children can see how much the tree has grown.

**5.** Let each child measure the tree, cut a length of twine, place it in an envelope and send it home. Do not send home a written explanation.

**6.** Have the child give the envelope to the parent and tell what it means. The twine is a symbol of the growth of the tree which the children can explain.

**Something to think about—**
If you have the children plant their seedlings and let them grow in the classroom for a while, then they can cut shorter lengths of twine to measure their little trees. Place both lengths in the envelopes, one representing the outside tree and one representing the inside tree.

STORY STRETCHER

## For Music And Movement: Swaying In The Breeze And Enjoying The Trees

**What the children will learn—**
To move like trees in the wind and to pantomime activities which take place related to trees

**Materials you will need—**
None needed

**What to do—**
**1.** On a windy day have the children observe how the trees sway back and forth.

**2.** Inside the classroom, collect the children in the circle time area and begin to sway back and forth in a gently rocking motion.

**3.** Start swaying your arms gently, rocking your body from foot to foot and tell the children that you are pretending to be a tree and the wind is picking up.

**4.** Move faster and talk about how the birds are hovered next to your trunk and around your feet as the wind blows stronger and stronger.

**5.** Talk about the rain coming and now as you sway, the leaves are beginning to shake. Shake your body as you continue to move faster.

**6.** Begin to slow down; tell the children the storm is passing.

**7.** Move your hands to look like birds. Tell the children the birds are shaking their wings, stretching them, and now are beginning to fly. Place your thumbs together, move your fingers and let your bird fly away.

**8.** Abruptly stop, stand very still without saying a word, with your arms extended and your hands hanging down. When you have everyone's attention, say, "The wind and rainstorm have stopped."

**Something to think about—**
Do the movement activity on more than one day. Children enjoy repeating experiences.

STORY STRETCHER

## For Science And Nature: Planting A Tree

**What the children will learn—**
To plant a tree and care for it until it takes root

**Materials you will need—**
Small tree, shovel, compost material, watering can

**What to do—**
**1.** Discuss with the center director or school principal that your class would like to plant a tree and decide on the best location. If it is not possible to plant a tree outside,

plant one in a large indoor container.

2.  Plan a tree planting ceremony with parent or community volunteers.

3.  Purchase the tree, ask for a donated tree from a community nursery, or replant a small tree from a wooded area.

4.  Have the tree in the classroom for a day or two for the children to examine closely.

5.  On the special occasion, have a parent start digging the hole and let each child participate in each step — digging the hole, mixing the compost and soil, placing the tree in the hole, unwrapping the roots, refilling the hole, stamping the soil down tightly and watering the tree.

6.  Observe the tree as often as possible, helping the children notice changes.

**Something to think about—**
Call the agricultural extension agent in your county and find out which government agencies, organizations and private industries in your community provide seedlings. Give each child a seedling and send simple, printed instructions home to parents about how to plant and care for their tree. (See the Story S-t-r-e-t-c-h-e-r for Library Corner for instructions.) (Sources for seedlings suggested by Henry Bindel.)

# REFERENCES

Carle, Eric. (1990). **THE VERY QUIET CRICKET**. New York: Philomel Books.

Martin, Jr., Bill, & Archambault, John. (1988). Illustrated by James Endicott. **LISTEN TO THE RAIN**. New York: Henry Holt and Company.

Parker, Nancy Winslow, & Wright, Joan Richards. (1987). Illustrated by Nancy Winslow Parker. **BUGS**. New York: Mulberry Books.

Ryder, Joanne. (1989). Illustrated by Lynne Cherry. **WHERE BUTTERFLIES GROW**. New York: Lodestar Books.

Udry, Janice May. (1956). Illustrated by Marc Simont. **A TREE IS NICE**. New York: Harper & Row.

## Additional References For Science and Nature

Cowcher, Helen. (1988). **RAIN FOREST**. New York: Farrar, Straus and Giroux. *The creatures of the rain forest are frightened by a machine and wonder how long they will have a home.*

Hines, Anna Grossnickle. (1989). **SKY ALL AROUND**. New York: Clarion Books. *A father and daughter share a special time when they go out on a clear night to watch the stars.*

Koss, Amy Goldman. (1987). **WHERE FISH GO IN THE WINTER AND ANSWERS TO OTHER GREAT MYSTERIES**. Los Angeles: Price Stern Sloan, Inc. *Brief, illustrated verses provide answers to a variety of questions about nature, including why some animals shed their skins and why leaves change colors.*

Thornhill, Jan. (1989). **THE WILD LIFE 1-2-3: A NATURE COUNTING BOOK**. New York: Simon and Schuster Books for Young Readers. *Illustrations of animals from around the world accompany the numbers one to twenty, then skip to twenty-five, fifty, one hundred and one thousand.*

Tresselt, Alvin. (1990, first published in 1946). Illustrated by Leonard Weisgard. **RAIN DROP SPLASH**. New York: Mulberry Books. *In poetry form, the story of how a rain drop grows to become a puddle, a pond, a lake, a river and the sea.*

# SEASONS: FOCUS ON FALL

*Gilberto and the Wind*
*Apples and Pumpkins*
*Arthur's Thanksgiving*
*Over the River and Through the Wood*
*Squirrels*

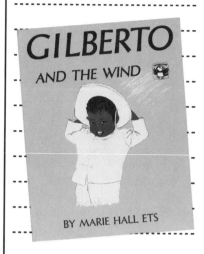

GILBERTO

AND THE WIND

BY MARIE HALL ETS

## GILBERTO AND THE WIND
*By Marie Hall Ets*

*Children relate to the simplicity of this classic tale of a little child playing with the wind. The text is rich in descriptive words but simple in story structure. On each set of pages, Gilberto has a different experience with his friend, the wind. In the beginning, the wind whispers and Gilberto goes out to play. Near the end, the wind howls and Gilberto hides inside. The story is told with sparse line drawings, highlighted with white chalk on tan paper.*

## Circle Time Presentation

Ask the children to look outside the classroom window and decide if the wind is blowing. What do they see that lets them know the wind is blowing? Is it brisk or calm? Would it sound like a whisper in our ears or a howl? Show the children the cover of GILBERTO AND THE WIND and ask whether or not they think the wind is blowing. Read the book through once without pausing to discuss Gilberto's fun with the wind. Read it a second time and pause several times in the book for children to talk about similar experiences.

STORY STRETCHER

## For Art: White Chalk On Colored Paper

**What the children will learn—**
To use chalk for highlighting

**Materials you will need—**
Construction paper, pencils, chalk, clothesline, clothespins

**What to do—**
1. With the children who select the art center during free play or center time, look again at the illustrations in GILBERTO AND THE WIND. Help the children see that Marie Hall Ets showed the wind by using white chalk for shading and by showing the clothes blowing to one side.

2. Ask the children to make pictures with the wind blowing.

3. Title the children's prints using their names as, "Damien and the Wind," "Teresa and the Wind."

4. Stretch a length of clothesline across the classroom.

5. Display the pictures on a clothesline by pinning them in place with clothespins.

**Something to think about—**
Wet chalk drawings on gray or brown construction paper would also be a good art activity to accompany GILBERTO AND THE WIND.

STORY STRETCHER

## For Creative Dramatics: Pretending To Be Gilberto And The Wind

**What the children will learn—**
To pantomime Gilberto's experiences with the wind

**Materials you will need—**
Chart tablet or posterboard, marker

**What to do—**
1. Look through the book and let the children decide on a key word or phrase which captures the essence of each scene in the book. Write the word or phrase on the chart tablet. For example, "door" would go with Gilberto peeking around the door to hear the wind whispering as he opened it. "Balloon" would remind the children of the second scene, and so on.

2. Read back through the list and pause for children to volunteer what each key word means.

3. After a thorough discussion, ask the children to improvise motions which would tell the scene, such as pretending to open a door and peaking around it.

4. At random, select children to pantomime the scenes. Whisper in their ears which scenes they are to do.

5. Have the pantomime actors do their motions and let the audience decide which scene is being dramatized.

6. Refer the children back to the chart after each scene and see if they can guess what was being pantomimed.

**Something to think about—**
Younger children will need visual cues, as well as word cues from the chart. With simple drawings, the chart can be turned into a rebus chart for retelling the story. See the appendix for an example of a rebus chart which combines words and drawings.

## For Science And Nature: Blowing Soap Bubbles

**What the children will learn—**
To blow bubbles

**Materials you will need—**
Large baby food jars, dish pan, warm water, liquid soap, bubble wands, straws, strainers, spools

**What to do—**
1. If possible, do this activity outside.

2. Mix liquid soap with warm water in baby food jars. Experiment with the proportions, but usually one-half to a teaspoon of liquid soap per jar is sufficient.

3. Using bubble wands from commercial bubble sets, let the children blow bubbles.

4. Then experiment with a variety of other "bubble makers." Fill a small plastic dish pan with the warm water and liquid soap mixture. Place a tea strainer in the mixture and let the children whirl it through the air to create a lot of tiny bubbles.

5. Experiment with spools by letting the children dip one end of a spool into water then into the liquid soap. Then they blow through the other end and it makes a bubble.

**Something to think about—**
Older children can manipulate the scientific variables by experimenting with different consistencies of soap and water, using different bubble makers, as a slotted spoon or spatula, even bending a coat hanger for a giant bubble wand.

## For Water Table: Enough Wind To Sail A Boat

**What the children will learn—**
To compare the effects of a variety of sources of wind current

**Materials you will need—**
Water table, water, sailboats made at the woodworking and carpentry bench, cardboard

**What to do—**
1. Fill the water table with water.

2. Allow the children to play on their own with the sailboats before starting the experiment.

3. Have the children try to make their sailboats move. Let them experiment with a variety of sources of wind without providing suggestions. For example, first they will blow with their own breaths. Then, two or three children will get together and blow. Others may improvise fanning with a piece of cardboard.

4. On another day, take the water table outside and let the children sail their boats where the real wind can blow the sails. The water table will need to be very full of water for the wind to reach the sails and have the boats skim along the water.

**Something to think about—**
Also experiment with toy plastic sailboats which have plastic sails in place. See which types of crafts catch the wind.

## For Woodworking And Carpentry: Making Gilberto's Sailboat

**What the children will learn—**
To construct a simple sailboat

**Materials you will need—**
Wood scraps, saw, vice, tacks, tack hammer, pencils, plastic straws, paper or fabric, glue, scissors

**What to do—**
1. Ask for parent or volunteer assistance.

2. Use wood scraps or pieces of wood which have been cut for the sailboats.

3. Thread a pencil into a plastic straw.

4. Bend the tip of the straw and tack it into the wooden base to form the mast.

5. Cut a piece of paper or a scrap of fabric to form the sail. If fabric is used, place a bead of glue around all the edges to stiffen them. The size of the sail will depend on the size of the scrap of wood. Usually the width of the boat plus an inch and the length of the mast plus an inch or two is sufficient.

6. Cut two small holes in the fabric or the paper, one about a half inch from the top of the sail and one about a half inch from the bottom of the sail.

7. Thread the sail onto the mast made from a straw and a pencil.

8. Secure the bottom and the top of the sail by tacking it to the bottom and top of the mast, leaving enough loose paper or fabric for the sail to billow.

9. Use the sailboats for the Science and Nature Story S-t-r-e-t-c-h-e-r listed above.

**Something to think about—**
If possible, allow the children to saw the lengths of wood.

## APPLES AND PUMPKINS

*By Anne Rockwell*

*Illustrated by Lizzy Rockwell*

*In simple text and bright simple illustrations, the story is told of a trip to a farm where there is an apple orchard and a pumpkin patch. Beginning with scenes of the drive through the country, the animals in the farmyard, the orchard and the pumpkin patch, the story follows a natural progression and ends with the little girl taking the pumpkin home to carve a jack-o-lantern. The pictures are bold enough to be seen easily in a group time presentation. While the book is a first for Lizzy Rockwell, it is in the familiar Rockwell family style of illustrating, which children enjoy.*

### Circle Time Presentation

Show them the cover of APPLES AND PUMPKINS and discuss that this is a book about a farm, the Comstock farm, and a little girl who went with her family to the farm and helped with the harvest. Read APPLES AND PUMPKINS, and at the end ask how the little girl helped with the harvest. Let the children tell about farms they have visited, or if they live on farms, have them talk about the crops they harvest. Since the book is a short one, read it a second time, then dismiss the children from the circle by letting them tell which they like to eat, apple pie or pumpkin pie.

STORY STRETCHER

### For Art: Sponge Painting With Fall Colors

**What the children will learn—**
To use a printing technique to show trees with fall colors

**Materials you will need—**
Red, orange, yellow and green tempera paints, scissors, sponges, margarine tubs and lids, construction paper or manilla paper

**What to do—**

**1.** Cut the sponges into small pieces, about two inches.

**2.** Pour each color paint into its own margarine tub.

**3.** Place the lid to the margarine tub beside each tub of paint and place the piece of sponge on the lid.

**4.** Using scraps of paper, let the children experiment with the sponge printing.

**5.** Look again at the illustrations in APPLES AND PUMPKINS, calling particular attention to the scenes where the family is driving through the mountains and we can see the fall foliage on the hills.

**6.** Ask the children to draw a fall scene and to decorate it with their sponge paints.

**Something to think about—**
Encourage the younger children to experiment with overlapping the sponge prints. The older children will think of a variety of ways to use the fall sponge painting, to look like leaves on a tree beside a house, leaves which have fallen onto the ground or fall foliage seen from a distance.

STORY STRETCHER

### For Cooking And Snack Time: Little Pumpkin Pies

**What the children will learn—**
To roll pie crust

**Materials you will need—**
Pie crust dough, premixed or made from scratch, rolling pin, flour, waxed paper, biscuit cutter, muffin tins, shortening or vegetable oil, canned pumpkin pie filling, mixing bowl, large serving spoon, toaster oven, cookie sheet, glasses, milk

**What to do—**

**1.** Demonstrate how to roll the pie crust dough by placing a sheet of waxed paper on the table, lightly flour it and roll flat with the rolling pin.

**2.** Let the children roll the dough and each cut one circle with the biscuit cutter.

**3.** Turn a muffin tin over with the bottom up and lightly grease with shortening or brush with vegetable oil.

**4.** Show the children how to shape their circle of crust over the individual bottoms of the muffin tins.

5. Place in a hot oven, 400 degrees, and brown. It only takes two or three minutes.

6. Let the tiny pie crusts cool and remove from the muffin tins.

7. Precook the pumpkin pie filling so that it has already thickened. Pour into a mixing bowl.

8. Using a large serving spoon, let the children fill their pie crusts.

9. Place the little pumpkin pies on a cookie sheet. Pop them back into the oven or microwave just long enough to warm the filling.

10. Serve at snack time with cold milk.

**Something to think about—**
As an alternative, if you do not have cooking facilities, bake the pie crusts at home and let children fill them with butterscotch pudding the next day.

STORY STRETCHER

## For Music And Movement: "Old McComstock Had A Farm"

**What the children will learn—**
To sing about the animals they saw on the Comstock farm

**Materials you will need—**
None needed

**What to do—**
1. Look through the illustrations of APPLES AND PUMPKINS and find all the animals on Mr. Comstock's farm. There's a cow, hen, baby chicks, rooster, geese and a turkey.

2. Sing "Old McDonald Had a Farm" but change the farmer's name. Since this was the Comstock farm sing, "Old McComstock Had a Farm."

3. Sing about the animals in the order in which they appear in the book.

4. End the song with,

*Old McComstock had some apples
With a crunch crunch here and a crunch crunch there.
Here a' crunch, there a' crunch, everywhere a crunch, crunch.
Old McComstock had some apples.
Yum, yum — yum, yum, yum
(Raines, 1991).*

**Something to think about—**
Write the words to the song on a large chart tablet or posterboard for the class's Big Book of Music.

STORY STRETCHER

## For Science And Nature: Visit A Pumpkin Patch

**What the children will learn—**
To observe how pumpkins grow on vines

**Materials you will need—**
Parent volunteers, field trip permission forms, transportation

**What to do—**
1. Make the arrangements ahead of time with the farm manager.

2. Train the parent volunteers to help the children have a good experience. Talk about the observations you would like the children to make.

3. Assign no more than two children per adult.

4. When visiting the farm, select a pumpkin to bring back to the classroom for carving.

**Something to think about—**
If you do not have a pumpkin farm near you or a gardener who grows pumpkins, visit a nursery which sells pumpkins at Halloween.

ANOTHER STORY STRETCHER

## For Science And Nature: What's Inside A Pumpkin?

**What the children will learn—**
To label the parts of the pumpkin

**Materials you will need—**
Pumpkin, large carving knife, smaller paring knives, large mixing bowl, smaller mixing bowls,

**What to do—**
1. Place the pumpkin on the science and nature display table.

2. Encourage the children to try and lift it to see how heavy it is, but keep it over the table.

3. Touch it and feel how cool it is, how smooth the skin is and how bumpy it is in places.

4. Cut a large circle around the stem and remove the stem.

5. Let the children examine the cap closely, touching the rough end of the stem, the sticky side of the inside of the pumpkin.

6. Lift the seeds and membranes out of the center of the pumpkin and place in the large mixing bowl. Let the children touch the seeds and separate them from the membranes, placing the seeds in smaller mixing bowls.

7. Either carve the pumpkin into a jack-o-lantern or cut large wedges from the pumpkin for the children to look at more closely.

8. Let the children cut off small slivers of pumpkin with the paring knife and taste the raw pumpkin.

**Something to think about—**
This experience is planned as a science activity for the children to learn about pumpkins, but you can also use the pumpkin meat and seeds for cooking as well. Take the meat from the center of the pumpkin and boil it until it is soft, add pumpkin pie seasonings and use for the fillings in the pumpkin pies served for snack. You can also toast the pumpkin seeds. Wash them, then place on a cookie sheet in a hot oven to toast.

## ARTHUR'S THANKSGIVING

*By Marc Brown*

*Marc Brown has succeeded in writing and illustrating another comical Arthur tale that provides a few insights into the problems of "being in charge." Arthur was chosen as the director of the school Thanksgiving play. His buddies, Francine, Muffy, Brain, Buster and Binky Barnes, all want different parts than the ones in which Arthur has cast them; finally, Arthur allows them their choices. His dilemma, however, is finding someone to play the turkey. He approaches his mother, father, sister, D.W., and even the principal, but all refuse. The listeners to this story are delighted to see that even Arthur realizes the show must go on and plays the turkey himself.*

### Circle Time Presentation

Talk with the children about what it means to be a director. Have them discuss any school or church plays they may have attended to see their older brothers and sisters acting. Read ARTHUR'S THANKSGIVING. Discuss the funny costumes and sets.

STORY STRETCHER
### For Art: Delicate Feather Paintings

**What the children will learn—**
To use a different kind of brush

**Materials you will need—**
Feathers, construction paper or manilla paper, water, tempera paint, large plastic containers or meat trays, small plates

**What to do—**
1. Mix paint so that it is about one-half water and one-half paint. Pour small amounts into plastic containers so that it covers the bottom of the container.

2. Use fall paint colors and for each color of paint provide a feather and a plate beside it to rest the feather on when not in use. If the feather is left in the paint, it will absorb too much paint and will not be a good brush.

3. Demonstrate for the children how to float the feather on top of the paint, how to gently lift it over to their paper and how to use the quill end of the feather like a brush handle.

4. Display the children's feather paintings in a fan shape on a bulletin board.

**Something to think about—**
If you do not have access to feathers, make your own by folding a sheet of construction paper lengthwise over and over until it is not more than two-inches wide and se-

cure at the bottom. With scissors, cut the paper into a feather shape and fray one edge. The multiple layers of paper will be feather-like.

(Idea adapted from one by Milissa Earl.)

STORY STRETCHER
### For Cooking And Snack Time: Cranberries

**What the children will learn—**
To recognize the cranberry flavor in many forms

**Materials you will need—**
Ripe or frozen cranberries, bowls, canned cranberry sauce, graham crackers, cranberry juice, spoons, napkins, glasses or cups

**What to do—**
1. Place bowls of ripe cranberries and cranberry sauce in the center of the snack tables.

2. Let the children taste the cranberries and compare the tastes.

3. Read the labels on the cranberry sauce and tell the children that sugar has been added.

4. Serve cranberry juice and graham crackers for the snack foods.

**Something to think about—**
Make a cranberry punch in a crock pot, sweeten it with sugar or apple juice, adding cloves and cinnamon.

STORY STRETCHER
### For Library Corner: Reading And Telling "Arthur's Thanksgiving"

**What the children will learn—**
To create a tape so other children can listen to Arthur's adventure

**Materials you will need—**
Cassette tape recorder, tape

**What to do—**
1. With a small group of children who choose the library corner during free play or center time, plan

to make a tape of ARTHUR'S THANKSGIVING. Decide on a signal to record so that the listeners know when to turn the page, as when you point to the children they should say, "Gobble, gobble." Have everyone say the last line together, "Happy Thanksgiving!"

2. Practice for a few pages and then record the story.

3. After the recording of you reading ARTHUR'S THANKSGIVING, help the children realize that they can tell this story as well by looking at the pictures.

4. Let the children decide which pages they would like to tell. When you get to the page where all his friends tell Arthur which parts they want to play, have different children tell what each character said. Also, select three different children to say what the principal and Arthur's mother and father said.

5. Practice telling the story once. Be certain you tell the story as the narrator and not read the story, so that when it comes time for the children to tell their parts they will tell the story without worrying about exact dialogue.

6. Mark the sides of the tape by drawing a small book on the side which is read and a smile on the side which is the story telling.

**Something to think about—**
With younger children, record the book reading on one day and the storytelling on another day. Older children can add sound effects and tell what the characters said, using appropriate voice inflection.

ANOTHER STORY STRETCHER

## For Library Corner: Story Sequencing

**What the children will learn—**
To retell a story using props as reminders of the scenes

**Materials you will need—**
Sheet of paper, crayon, lunch box, pancake turner, newspaper, drawing of turkey suit, "calling all turkeys" printed announcement, sunglasses, black hat, Indian head band, white collar, basket, pie pan, turkey feather, paper with math problems, sheet of music, plate, flashlight

**What to do—**
1. Look through the book with the children and decide what props would be needed to symbolize the different scenes. Some possible props are the pie pan for the pumpkin pie, the basket for the cranberries, the sheet of music for when Arthur was playing the piano, etc.

2. Assemble or make the props with the children's help.

3. Have the children sit around the table and divide the props so that each child is responsible for three props. Place those props in front of the child.

4. Discuss again with the children what the props represent.

5. Read the story, and as the scenes are read, the child with the appropriate prop holds it up then places it in the center of the table, forming a line of props.

6. After the story has been read, let the children stand so that they can see the props in a line from left to right and have them take turns telling the parts of the story, using the props as the cue.

**Something to think about—**
While this activity is a part of the library corner because it is story retelling, the teacher could choose to emphasize the concept of order or

sequence. The props could be placed along the table in order on top of number cards and with the numeral, number word and the ordinal word such as, first, second, third, fourth, etc.

STORY STRETCHER

## For Music And Movement: Doing The Turkey Trot

**What the children will learn—**
To move as the lyrics direct them

**Materials you will need—**
None needed

**What to do—**
1. Teach your children to do the "Hokey Pokey."

2. Write new lyrics to the "Hokey Pokey" using the names of the turkey body parts instead of their body parts. For example, when the song says, "Put your right arm in," let the children sing,

*You put your right wing in,*
*You take your right wing out,*
*Put your right wing in*
*And flutter it all about.*
*You do the turkey trot and*
*You turn yourself around.*
*That's what it's all about"*
*(Raines, 1991)*

3. Continue adding verses for the long neck to stretch it all about, spreading tail to strut it all about and beak to gobble it all about.

4. Rehearse the song and sing it and do the motions for another class as your version of Arthur's Thanksgiving Play.

**Something to think about—**
Young children do not do well with scripted plays. If your children are invited to perform for a school function, have them sing or do movement activities which they already know.

## OVER THE RIVER AND THROUGH THE WOOD

*By Lydia Maria Child*

*Illustrated by Iris Van Rynbach*

*The old classic tune for Thanksgiving, "Over the River and Through the Wood," provides the text for the book and illustrations of an old-fashioned village with horse and sleigh, women in long dresses and men in waistcoats help the children to understand another era. The book is an appropriate selection to emphasize the end of fall when the first snowfall comes. The large picture format with pencil drawings and watercolor washes capture the glistening snow and hillside scenes for the trip to grandfather's and grandmother's. The music and lyrics to the song are provided at the end of the book.*

## Circle Time Presentation

Have the children look at the cover of the book and notice the river and the woods, the family in the horse-drawn sleigh and the tiny house far off in the distance. Tell them that this is the story told in song form of the trip to the little house. Open the book and read the title page and then sing the remainder of the book. The children will be delighted and will immediately ask you to sing it again. Instead of singing it, read it and emphasize the phrasing, using appropriate voice inflection, as when saying, "Hurrah for Thanksgiving Day!" Sing the book through again and tell the children that today in the music area, you will be recording some children singing the song so that the book and the song can be placed in the library together.

STORY STRETCHER

## For Art: Washes Over Pencil Drawings

**What the children will learn—**
To use mixed media to illustrate a late fall day

**Materials you will need—**
Pencils, construction paper, watercolors, small brushes, margarine tubs with water, paper towels or old newspaper

**What to do—**
1. Have the children who come to the art center look more closely at Iris Van Rynbach's illustrations in OVER THE RIVER AND THROUGH THE WOOD. Ask the children how they think they need to create that same effect. Let the children experiment if they like.

2. Ask the children to draw a late fall scene, a Thanksgiving scene or an old-fashioned scene.

3. Demonstrate how to use the watercolors. For example, the children need to know how to add more paint to the brush to get a darker color and how to dip the tip of the brush in water for a lighter color. Also show the children how to dry excess water from their brushes by dabbing onto the paper towel or old newspaper.

4. Show the children how to dip the tip of their brush in white paint to add snow to the rooftops.

**Something to think about—**
Older children can mix three media: pencil and crayon drawings and watercolors. Younger children will enjoy experimenting with making lighter and darker watercolors without actually producing a picture.

STORY STRETCHER

## For Blocks: An Old-fashioned Village

**What the children will learn—**
To build a tiny village based on the illustrations in OVER THE RIVER AND THROUGH THE WOOD

**Materials you will need—**
Small and large blocks, cotton batting or white butcher paper, horses, people, sleigh or materials to make a sleigh

**What to do—**
1. Ask the block builders to look through the illustrations in OVER THE RIVER AND THROUGH THE WOOD and tell them that you have set aside a table for their block village.

2. Spread the cotton batting or white butcher paper on the table as the first snow in late fall.

3. Let the children improvise buildings and people. They can

make a sleigh from a box or build one from small connecting blocks.

4. Leave the village up for at least a week and notice how the children become more inventive with adding different decorations.

**Something to think about—**
Younger children may build houses and not plan as much together as older children. However, cooperative tasks should be encouraged and praise given as much for the children working together as for their construction project.

STORY STRETCHER

## For Housekeeping And Dress-up Corner: Dressing In Old-fashioned Clothes

**What the children will learn—**
To fasten buttons and tie ribbons

**Materials you will need—**
Long coats that button, woolen scarves and, if possible, top hat and bonnet, long dresses, ribbons, full-length mirror

**What to do—**
1. Sort through the dress-up clothes and see which ones could look like old-fashioned ones. Store away the zipper and velcro closing garments, as well as the modern fiber-filled synthetic clothes.

2. Invite parents to send other items. Old quilted robes and velveteen items are good ones for the children to use for dress-up.

3. Add brightly colored ribbons to the collection of clothes.

4. Begin the dress-up session with the children, but as they begin to improvise costumes on their own, leave them.

5. Ask several of the dress-up players to leave their costumes on for the second group time of the day. Have the children sing the song while wearing their dress-up clothes.

**Something to think about—**
Adult-sized dresses and coats look old-fashioned because they are long on the children. Frilly women's blouses, long enough for a dress for a child, make lovely old-fashioned dresses when tied around the waist with a brightly colored ribbon.

STORY STRETCHER

## For Music And Movement: Learning The Thanksgiving Song

**What the children will learn—**
To sing a traditional Thanksgiving tune

**Materials you will need—**
Chart tablet or posterboard, marker, cassette recorder, tape

**What to do—**
1. Teach the song to the children who come to the music area during free play or center time.

2. Print the words to the song on chart tablet or posterboard. Let the children see you printing the words and read them as you write so that they can see the relationship between written and spoken language.

3. Sing the song through from beginning to end while running your fingers or a pointer under the words.

4. Break the song into verses and have the children echo sing with you. You sing the verse, pause, and then they sing it again with you.

5. Sing the song through from beginning to end.

6. Taperecord the song and place the tape and the book in the library corner.

7. Add the chart tablet page or the posterboard to the class' Big Book of Music.

**Something to think about—**
For younger children add rebus symbols to the charts as reminders of the verses.

STORY STRETCHER

## For Sand And Water Table: Ice Skating

**What the children will learn—**
To glide miniature skaters along their ponds

**Materials you will need—**
Three plastic dish pans, water, tiny plastic people, index cards, straws, permanent marker, tape

**What to do—**
1. Fill dish pans with water and place in freezer until frozen solid.

2. Place the three dish pans with frozen water, "miniature ice skating ponds," into the water table.

3. Let the children play with their tiny ice skaters and have them skate along the ponds.

4. When the ice begins to crack, add warning signs by printing messages with permanent ink on index cards, tape them to straws and place in the water.

5. Have the children decide when it has thawed too much for the skaters to be on the ponds.

**Something to think about—**
If you live in an area where the ponds usually freeze, take this opportunity to talk about safety. If you live in an area where the ponds sometimes freeze, it is even more important to talk about safety because children will find the frozen water such a novelty.

## 8
## SEASONS: FOCUS ON FALL

### SQUIRRELS

*By Brian Wildsmith*

*A beautifully illustrated multi-media book with everyday and little-known facts about squirrels written in an informative yet interesting manner. Wildsmith tells how easy it is to recognize a squirrel and writes about the squirrels' behaviors in the different seasons, but focuses on how they store nuts in the fall. The illustrations are as bright and colorful as the language. Even adults will learn some new facts about squirrels.*

### Circle Time Presentation

Construct a "K-L" poster by drawing a line down the middle of a sheet of posterboard or a chart tablet. At the top of the first column write "What we *know* about squirrels." Print "What we *learned* about squirrels" on the top of the second column. Talk with the children about squirrels, and after a few minutes, help them summarize what they know, such as, "Squirrels eat acorns." Read Brian Wildsmith's SQUIRRELS, pausing for the children to enjoy the lovely illustrations. After reading the book comment that you learned a great many new facts about squirrels after reading the book, as squirrels' homes are called "dreys." Let a child restate your fact and write it under the column marked "What we *learned* about squirrels." Have the children contribute other new facts they learned while listening to the book. Print their new facts on the chart as well. Reread both columns emphasizing the children's prior knowledge about squirrels before hearing the book, then what they learned.

S T O R Y   S T R E T C H E R
### For Art: Multi-media Prints

**What the children will learn—**
To combine media to create a new artistic treatment

**Materials you will need—**
Manilla paper or construction paper, watercolors, brushes, tempera paints, margarine tubs, old newspaper or paper towels, random small plastic objects

**What to do—**
1. Set up one area of the art table for watercolors with paints, brushes, water in margarine tubs and old newspapers or paper towels for drying excess paint or water on brushes.

2. Set up another area of the art table for tempera painting. Pour tempera paints into margarine tubs. Place paint tubs on old newspaper or paper towels.

3. With the children who come to the art center during free play, look through the illustrations and decide which illustrations are a combination of watercolors and tempera paints.

4. Look at the pictures of the squirrel's nest and let the children see that there are random overlapping shapes.

5. Let the children experiment with how to make the "jumble" of overlapping shapes by pressing small plastic objects, such as small blocks or plastic cookie cutters or even wheels of small trucks and cars into the paints, then pressing them onto the paper.

6. Ask the children to choose any or all of the media to create their fall or squirrel scene.

**Something to think about—**
For younger children, choose only one medium, watercolor, tempera paints or object printing.

S T O R Y   S T R E T C H E R
### For Mathematics And Manipulatives: Estimating Acorns

**What the children will learn—**
To estimate how many acorns can be placed in different containers

**Materials you will need—**
Acorns, large basket, variety of sizes and shapes of containers including baskets and plastics

**What to do—**
1. Fill a large basket with acorns.

**2.** Let the children guess how many acorns each container will hold.

**3.** Then, they prove their "guess-timates" by filling the containers and counting the acorns.

**Something to think about—**
This activity can also be used for equivalent weights. Use a balance and fill a basket with acorns and let the children try to balance the other side by counting how many acorns it takes to balance the weight.

STORY STRETCHER

## For Music And Movement: Scampering Squirrels Finding Acorns

**What the children will learn—**
To search for objects while the music is playing

**Materials you will need—**
Paper bags, crayons, acorns, recording of instrumental music with a fast tempo, tape or record player, large basket

**What to do—**
**1.** Call the children together on the circle time rug to explain how to play the game.

**2.** Distribute the paper bags and crayons.

**3.** Ask the children to draw a symbol of fall on their bags.

**4.** Have the children close their eyes like little sleeping squirrels while the music is playing and you and the teacher's aide or a parent volunteer hide acorns around the room.

**5.** Stop the music, return to the circle time rug and explain to the children that when the music starts again they are to be little squirrels and scamper around the room looking for acorns.

**6.** Start the music and let the squirrels fill their paper bags with as many acorns as they can find.

**7.** Stop the music and let a few children tell where they found acorns.

**8.** Continue this process of starting, stopping, describing where to find acorns.

**9.** At the end of the search, return to the circle time rug and have the children share their acorns by pouring them into a big basket.

**Something to think about—**
Younger children can search until they each find five acorns and then return to the circle to wait for their friends. Older children can play a variation of the game by taking turns and using the cold and hot signals.

ANOTHER STORY STRETCHER

## For Music And Movement: "Five Little Squirrels Went Out To Play"

**What the children will learn—**
To sing new words to a familiar tune

**Materials you will need—**
Chart tablet or posterboard, marker

**What to do—**
**1.** Print the words to "Five Little Squirrels Went Out to Play" on the chart tablet or posterboard

**2.** Sing the fingerplay the children know, "Five Little Ducks Went Out to Play."

**3.** Teach the children the squirrel variation by singing each stanza while running a pointer or one's fingers under the words.

**4.** Sing "Five Little Squirrels Went Out to Play."

*Five little squirrels went out to play,*
*On a skam-pering, win-dy, au-tumn day.*

*But the one little squirrel with a bushy tail,*
*He hid the nuts all along the trail,*
*He hid the nuts all along the trail.*

*Four little squirrels went out to play,*
*But the one little squirrel worked all the day,*
*He hid the nuts with a crack, crack, crack.*
*He hid the nuts saying, "I'll be back,"*
*He hid the nuts saying, "I'll be back!"*
*Three little squirrels went out to play,*
*On a skam-pering, win-dy, au-tumn day.*
*But the one little squirrel with a bushy tail,*
*He hid the nuts all along the trail,*
*He hid the nuts all along the trail.*

*Two little squirrels went out to play,*
*But the one little squirrel worked all the day,*
*He hid the nuts with a crack, crack, crack.*
*He hid the nuts saying, "I'll be back,"*
*He hid the nuts saying, "I'll be back!"*

*One little squirrel went out to play,*
*On a skam-pering, win-dy, au-tumn day.*
*But the one little squirrel with a bushy tail,*
*He hid the nuts all along the trail,*
*He hid the nuts all along the trail.*

*No hungry squirrels went out to play,*
*On a cold and win-dy, win-ter day.*
*But the one little squirrel with a bushy tail,*
*He found the nuts all along the trail,*
*He found the nuts all along the trail.*

*The one little squirrel with a bushy tail,*
*Shared his nuts stored along the trail.*
*And the five little squirrels who went out to play,*
*Said, "We'll hide nuts on autumn days,*
*We'll hide nuts on autumn days."*

*"Yes, we'll hide nuts on autumn days!"*
*(Raines, 1991)*

**Something to think about—**
Include "Five Little Squirrels Went Out to Play" in the class' Big Book of Music. Ask some of the children to decorate the song by adding thumbprint squirrels.

## For Science And Nature: Observing Squirrels

**What the children will learn—**
To observe and tell about squirrels they have seen

**Materials you will need—**
Field trip permission slips, parent volunteers, transportation, posterboard or chart tablet, marker

**What to do—**

1. If you do not have a wooded area near the school or center, arrange for a field trip to a park.

2. Plan for one parent volunteer per two children, if possible.

3. Spend some time instructing the parents in how to help the children become good observers.

4. When observing, have the children stand or sit very still and watch the squirrels without talking.

5. After they have observed the squirrels, let the children tell about what they saw the squirrels doing, where they were, how they moved and if they saw squirrels of different sizes.

6. When you return to the classroom, let the children come to the science and nature area, a few at a time during the next center time and tell about their observations.

7. Print or let the children write at least one sentence from each child on the posterboard or chart tablet.

**Something to think about—**
After all the children have sentences on the squirrel data chart, older children can summarize the information by description, habitat, food supply movements. Younger children can group and count sentences which have similar information.

## REFERENCES

Brown, Marc. (1983). **ARTHUR'S THANKSGIVING.** Boston: Joy Street Books.

Child, Lydia Maria. (1989). Illustrated by Iris Van Rynbach. **OVER THE RIVER AND THROUGH THE WOOD.** Boston: Little, Brown and Company

Ets, Marie Hall. (1988, first published in 1963). **GILBERTO AND THE WIND.** New York: Puffin Books.

Rockwell, Anne. (1989). Illustrated by Lizzy Rockwell. **APPLES AND PUMPKINS.** New York: Macmillan Publishing Company.

Wildsmith, Brian. (1974). **SQUIRRELS.** Oxford: Oxford University Press.

### Additional References For Seasons: Focus On Fall

Lewis, Tracey. (1988). **WHERE DO ALL THE BIRDS GO?** New York: E.P. Dutton. *The book tells where the birds, tortoises, squirrels, mice, fish, horses and people go when it gets cold.*

King, Elizabeth. (1990). **THE PUMPKIN PATCH.** New York: Dutton Children's Books. *Told through photographs, the book shows a commercial pumpkin patch from preparation of the soil, planting of seeds, growing stages of the pumpkins and through to the fall harvest.*

Provensen, Alice, & Provensen, Martin. (1978). **THE YEAR AT MAPLE HILL FARM.** New York: Atheneum. *A description of what happens to animals, plants and people during each season and month by month on the farm.*

Tresselt, Alvin. (1951). Illustrated by Roger Duvoisin. **AUTUMN HARVEST.** New York: Lothrop, Lee and Shepard Books. *Autumn brings the first frost, migrating geese, burning leaves and a fine harvest.*

Wheeler, Cindy. (1982). **MARMALADE'S YELLOW LEAF.** New York: Alfred A. Knopf. *Simple text and illustrations follow a lovely cat the color of orange marmalade as he chases a falling leaf.*

# SEASONS: FOCUS ON WINTER

*The Snowy Day*
*White Snow, Bright Snow*
*Caps, Hats, Socks, and Mittens*
*Owl Moon*
*Keep Looking!*

## THE SNOWY DAY

*By Ezra Jack Keats*

*A Caldecott award book, THE SNOWY DAY is a favorite among young children and their teachers. Peter plays in the snow, making patterns as he walks, building a snowman, making snow angels and ends the day by stuffing some snowballs into his pockets before going home to a warm house. As his mother helps him get undressed, he tells her about his adventures. In bed, he remembers the day, but when he gets up to check on the snowballs in his pocket, he makes another discovery about the snow. That night he dreamed the snow melted, but when he awoke it was still there and his winter fun began again. Keats' marvelously simple illustrations are graphic collages of big shapes textured with prints and chalk shadings to add depth.*

## Circle Time Presentation

Many of the children will already know and love THE SNOWY DAY by Ezra Jack Keats. Have the children recall any surprise snow mornings they can remember. Let them discuss all the snow activities they enjoy. Ask the children to stretch out on the floor and pretend to be making snow angels. Announce the Story S-t-r-e-t-c-h-e-r-s for THE SNOWY DAY, including snow chalk prints, icing cookies and a special taping of the adventures of Peter's Magic Snowman.

STORY STRETCHER

## For Art: Chalk And Paint Object Prints

**What the children will learn—**
To mix media to create special effects

**Materials you will need—**
White construction paper, white and pastel colored chalk, thick tempera paints, margarine tubs of water, sponges, newspaper, small plastic objects

**What to do—**
1. Cover the tables with old newspaper for easy cleanup. Collect supplies for children's experimenting.

2. With the small group of children who choose to come to the art center during free play or choice time, look again at Keats' illustrations for THE SNOWY DAY. Call attention to the fact that Keats' snow scenes all have color in them, as the snow is shaded lightly with pastel colors. The colors are reflections on the snow.

3. Ask the children how they think he might have created the snow pictures. Let the children use the chalks and scraps of construction paper to experiment with shading.

4. Have the children select various small objects from around the room which they can dip into the tempera paints, then press onto their chalked paper to create a print. Some suggestions include small plastic blocks, a thimble, wheels from a small race car, bottle caps.

**Something to think about—**
If you teach older children, add a third medium by letting the children cut bold shapes from construction paper.

STORY STRETCHER

## For Cooking And Snack Time: Icing Snow People Cookies

**What the children will learn—**
To spread icing

**Materials you will need—**
Cookies, icing, waxed paper or paper towels, plastic knives, small plastic bowls of water, optional — raisins, sprinkles and coconut for decorations

**What to do—**
1. Bake or purchase enough snowman cookies for each child to have one.

2. Help the children get started by showing them how to mix the icing or scoop it from a commercially prepared can. It spreads better if the knife is damp.

3. Have the children place the cookie flat on the table, hold it in place with one hand and spread the icing with the other.

4. While the icing is still moist, add decorations.

**Something to think about—**
With the children who select the cooking center during free play, bake cookies from scratch or from

refrigerated cookie dough. Mix powdered sugar and a few drops of water for an inexpensive icing. If the parents of your children can afford to provide "extras" for your classroom, have a sign-up sheet for each week for cooking supplies. Notify the parents one week in advance of the supplies needed for the next week. Cooking is also an excellent activity for parents, grandparents or community volunteers to lead.

STORY STRETCHER

## For Library Corner: Taping A Snowman Story

**What the children will learn—**
To compose a story with several scenes

**Materials you will need—**
Chart tablet, crayons or markers, blue construction paper or manilla paper, cassette tape and recorder

**What to do—**
1.  Set the stage for the children's story by asking them to think what might happen if the snowman Peter made was magic and came to life.

2.  Let them brainstorm some ideas. Write down key words on the chart that reflect the children's ideas.

3.  After the children have expressed a few ideas, fold a sheet of blue construction paper or manilla paper into eighths, using three folds, and ask the children to draw some pictures that show what the snowman did.

4.  When the illustrations are finished, let each child tape record a story of Peter's Magic Snowman.

5.  Label the cassette tapes of each child's story and place them at the listening station in the library corner.

**Something to think about—**
Younger children can draw and write a story with four scenes, while older children may develop a story with other characters.

STORY STRETCHER

## For Music And Movement: Peter's Snowy Day Actions

**What the children will learn—**
To interpret the text by using movements

**Materials you will need—**
None needed

**What to do—**
1.  Read THE SNOWY DAY again, and as you read, interpret the movement. For example, drag your feet as if trudging through the snow, pretend to shake snow from a tree, lie on the floor and make a snow angel, pretend to be undressing, sleeping, waking.

2.  Ask the children to improvise movements that illustrate the text as you read it again.

**Something to think about—**
If your students are experienced at creative dramatics, let them pantomime the motions without your demonstration. Older children can improvise scenes and let their audience guess which scene from the book they are doing.

STORY STRETCHER

## For Science And Nature: How Long Does A Snowball Last?

**What the children will learn—**
To observe the effects of heat on the melting process

**Materials you will need—**
Three snowballs, three plastic containers, note pads, pencils

**What to do—**
1.  Let the children shape snowballs of approximately the same size and density, compacting them about the same amount.

2.  Have the children select various areas of the classroom that they think are cool, warm and hot.

3.  Place a snowball in each bowl in the three spots the children selected.

4.  At various times throughout the morning, have the children check on the snowballs to see which one is melting the fastest.

5.  Have one child become the official observer and write a sentence for each observation or draw what she or he has seen.

**Something to think about—**
If you teach younger children, place a note pad and pencil beside each bowl. Assist in the observation by numbering the pages or recording times when the child is drawing or writing observations. The children can compare the length of time it takes for different size snowballs to melt, or they can compare the melting of unmolded snow with a snowball.

123

## 9

## SEASONS: FOCUS ON WINTER

## WHITE SNOW, BRIGHT SNOW

*By Alvin Tresselt*

*Illustrated by Roger Duvoisin*

*This Caldecott Medal book is a favorite many adults remember from their childhoods. The book begins with a lovely poem about the soft and gentle night when the snow fell. On the next page a story begins with the postman, farmer, policeman and children thinking it might snow, and follows them as they continue their work and play throughout the snow. The reader also sees the effects of the snow falling, freezing and thawing on the human community and on some burrowing rabbits. In the end, they all delight in the return of the warm sunshine. Duvoisin's full page illustrations are typical of an earlier era of picture books, yet they still communicate the story well.*

## Circle Time Presentation

If you knew WHITE SNOW, BRIGHT SNOW as a child, tell the children that this was a book you enjoyed when you were their age. Ask the children to think about it being nighttime and that they are all snug in their warm beds, but outside their houses something is changing. Have the children close their eyes and listen as you read the poem at the beginning of the book. Ask the children why they think the author calls the night, "the secret night." Read the remainder of the book.

STORY STRETCHER

## For Art: Gray Day And Snowy Night Scenes

**What the children will learn—**
To select and use materials that illustrate darkness

**Materials you will need—**
Light gray, dark gray or black construction paper, white tempera paints, small brushes

**What to do—**
1. Set this activity up as a table top activity for all the children to do over the course of a few days.

2. Re-examine Roger Duvoisin's illustrations of the night snow scenes and ask the children how they could go about making this type of scene. Provide the white tempera and dark construction paper for the children to experiment with.

3. Encourage the children to paint their houses in the snow at night or any other nighttime snow scene they choose.

4. Display the nighttime snow scenes in the library corner near the open book shelf where WHITE SNOW, BRIGHT SNOW is kept.

**Something to think about—**
Artwork should be a highly individualized experience where children choose their own media and what they want to paint or draw. However, to encourage art participation, many teachers set up at least one table top activity each morning for art. The children are asked to do this project or one of their own choosing. Encouraging each child to contribute a certain type of picture, as a night scene, helps the children feel a part of a group project while retaining individual expression.

STORY STRETCHER

## For Block Building: Village In "White Snow, Bright Snow"

**What the children will learn—**
To build a model village

**Materials you will need—**
Large hollow blocks or small wooden blocks, transportation toys, wooden or plastic community helper models, cotton batting (large bolt of cotton like that used under Christmas trees), cotton balls, optional — butcher paper, markers

**What to do—**
1. Spread the cotton batting out over the block area, as if snow has just fallen.

2. Invite the block builders to create a village like the one found in WHITE SNOW, BRIGHT SNOW.

3. Have them brainstorm some ideas of how to lay out the town. Call them village planners.

4. Let the builders build on their own, but have one of the leaders recheck the illustrations in the book to determine if they have a complete village. They can stretch cotton balls and place them on the roof tops of their houses and buildings.

5. Leave the village set up throughout the day and refer back to it while rereading WHITE SNOW, BRIGHT SNOW at a second group time.

6. On other days, let more children add to the village by building stores, hospitals, fire stations and other community buildings.

**Something to think about—**
While large hollow blocks do take up a great deal of classroom space, building with the larger blocks requires large muscle use and is a stronger sensory experience.

STORY STRETCHER

## For Creative Dramatics: Guess Who I Am. Guess What I Am Doing.

**What the children will learn—**
To pantomime actions

**Materials you will need—**
Full length mirror, index cards, marker

**What to do—**
1. With a small group of children, rehearse the actions of the postal worker, police officer, farmer, wife, children playing, rabbits. Let the children pretend in front of a mirror.

2. Write the names of each of the characters listed above on separate index cards.

3. When the children are comfortable pantomiming the different characters in WHITE SNOW, BRIGHT SNOW, have one actor draw a card and improvise that character. If the card says "children playing," have the child select several friends to help.

**Something to think about—**
Often teachers think creative dramatics requires entire class participation; however, young children do not need a large audience to enjoy creative dramatics. Members of a small group can dramatize actions for each other.

STORY STRETCHER

## For Library Corner: Cause And Effect Snow Stories

**What the children will learn—**
To write or tell stories emphasizing cause and effect

**Materials you will need—**
Variety of writing papers, pens, pencils

**What to do—**
1. With a small group of children who choose the library corner during free play or choice time, recall a recent snowstorm and what happened to you. Emphasize cause and effect statements. For example, recall that the cold weather caused the car not to start, so you had to get a ride to school with a friend. The snow on the highway caused slow traffic because one lane was closed.

2. Ask the children to tell what the snow caused for them.

3. After each child has remembered at least one thing that happened because of the snow, ask the children to write about their experience.

4. Allow children to write on their own or with a writing partner.

**Something to think about—**
Younger children who are reluctant to write or who may still be in the scribble stage can draw a picture and dictate a caption, or scribble a line. Older children may want to add the effects of the snow on other members of their family, as a brother's gymnastics class was cancelled or Mom's bus was late, causing her to be late for supper.

STORY STRETCHER

## For Science And Nature: Making Burrows To Keep Warm

**What the children will learn—**
To make burrows and tunnels

**Materials you will need—**
Sand, plastic animals, water

**What to do—**
1. Have the children recall that in WHITE SNOW, BRIGHT SNOW the author mentioned that the rabbits crawled into their burrows to keep warm.

2. Show the children how to make a tunnel in the sand by covering one hand with sand and patting moist sand over it until it is hard, then slowly withdraw the covered hand, leaving a tunnel.

3. While the child has a hand in the sand forming the tunnel, call attention to the fact that the hand covered with sand feels warmer. Relate this to the rabbits underground, warm in their burrows.

4. Place small plastic models of animals in the burrows and leave the sand burrows and tunnels on display for a few days.

**Something to think about—**
Older children will be able to form long tunnels and can research other burrowing animals.

# SEASONS: FOCUS ON WINTER

## CAPS, HATS, SOCKS, AND MITTENS

*By Louise Borden*

*Illustrated by Lillian Hoban*

*This book, written as a simple poem, describes each season, but begins and ends with winter. Borden's simple verse, "Winter is caps, hats, socks, and mittens," is illustrated with delightful Hoban drawings of children enjoying each season. The colorful illustrations show indoor and outdoor play and family activities.*

## Circle Time Presentation

Talk about the weather and what we expect of the weather during winter. If you live in an area where winter is not cold, discuss how the weather in your area compares to winter in other sections of the country. Show the pictures of the children getting dressed and ask which season it is. Read the poem for each season. Read the winter poem again and pause for the children to complete the phrases. Announce the Story S-t-r-e-t-c-h-e-r-s for CAPS, HATS, SOCKS, AND MITTENS.

STORY STRETCHER

## For Art: Decorating Windows With Snowflakes

**What the children will learn—**
To fold and cut snowflakes

**Materials you will need—**
Thin typing paper, scissors, tape

**What to do—**
1. Show the children how to fold thin typing paper three times.
2. Demonstrate how to cut in and out at random, cutting notches and curves but leaving some of the edge uncut.
3. Unfold the paper to see the snowflakes.
4. Let the children tape their snowflakes to the windows.

**Something to think about—**
Invite a parent or a grandparent who is an origami expert to come to class and demonstrate folding and cutting paper into animal and decorative shapes.

STORY STRETCHER

## For Cooking And Snack Time: Cinnamon Cider Drink

**What the children will learn—**
To prepare a hot drink

**Materials you will need—**
Apple cider, hot plate or microwave, large saucepan, mugs, teaspoons, cinnamon stick or can of cinnamon

**What to do—**
1. With a small group of children assisting, pour the apple cider into a large saucepan and heat until it is warm. Use a large glass mixing bowl with spout for microwave.
2. Pour the warm cider into mugs, filling about half full.
3. Let the helpers stir the cider with a cinnamon stick or sprinkle a bit of cinnamon into the mug and stir.
4. Ask your assistants to invite the other children over for warm cinnamon cider.

**Something to think about—**
Individual packets of apple cider mix can also be used. The water can be warmed in a coffee maker and the children can each mix their own mug of cider. Many families have extra cups and mugs which they are usually willing to donate. Whenever possible use real cups and mugs which are heavier and easier for young children to handle than styrofoam ones. Real mugs also cut down on the amount of throw-aways and trash generated — a way your class can help with environmental concerns.

## For Library Corner: Writing Our Own Winter Poem, "Winter Is"

**What the children will learn—**
To describe the season

**Materials you will need—**
Chart tablet and marker or chalkboard and chalk

**What to do—**

1.   Read again Louise Borden's description of winter.

2.   Follow the pattern of Borden's poem, but change the specifics. For example, the first phrases are about clothing. Have the children say the names of some winter clothes, such as parkas, sweaters, boots and snowsuits. The next line tells about sledding, but use skating instead. Continue making changes the children suggest.

3.   Look back over the descriptions and write a poem by finishing the phrase, "Winter is." The poem might read,

> *Winter is*
> *parkas, sweaters, boots*
> *and snowsuits.*
>
> *Winter is skating*
> *round the pond*
> *this way then*
> *skating round the pond*
> *that way.*
>
> *Winter is*
> *warm pajamas and*
> *long underwear.*
>
> *Winter is*
> *warm cider or*
> *hot chocolate in*
> *a mug.*
>
> *Winter is sleeping*
> *late, all*
> *nice and snug. (Raines, 1991).*

**Something to think about—**
Older children can write winter poems on their own. Younger children enjoy composing with you or a partner. Do not emphasize

rhyme, but rather complete the thought, "Winter is." Write poems for other seasons.

## For Mathematics And Manipulatives: Sorting Socks

**What the children will learn—**
To match patterns

**Materials you will need—**
A collection of old socks in varying patterns, lengths and colors, basket

**What to do—**

1.   Place the collection of socks on the table in the mathematics and manipulatives center. Begin sorting them into pairs and ask a few children to help you.

2.   Let the children continue the sorting until all the socks are paired. Then count the pairs of socks.

3.   Decide if there are enough pairs of socks for each child to have one pair.

4.   Let the sock sorters distribute the socks to the entire class for a movement activity.

**Something to think about—**
If you have young children, use fewer socks. If you teach older children, include some socks that do not have mates, and complicate the counting process by asking more difficult questions as, "Are there enough pairs of patterned socks for each girl to have a pair?" or "Are there enough white socks for each person to use to make a sock puppet?"

## For Music And Movement: Hand Skating

**What the children will learn—**
To make hand motions that represent skating to music

**Materials you will need—**
Tables, socks, recording of waltz music

**What to do—**

1.   Give each child a sock for one hand, have them put it on and slide it across the surface of the table. Have them pretend the table is a skating rink or frozen pond and that their hand is the skater.

2.   After they have hand skated for a while and are moving their hands fluidly, discuss skating competitions they may have watched on television. Talk about how the skaters move to the music.

3.   Play a recording of some waltz music and have the children pretend to skate with their hands to the music.

**Something to think about—**
After the children have hand skated with their hand socks, let them take off their shoes and waltz around the room to the skating music.

## SEASONS: FOCUS ON WINTER

by Jane Yolen
illustrated by John Schoenherr

## OWL MOON

*By Jane Yolen*

*Illustrated by John Schoenherr*

*This 1988 Caldecott Medal book is the story of a father and his daughter going "owling" on a moonlit winter night. The author and illustrator have captured the pleasure the child feels just being with her father in a quiet, peaceful and natural world. The poetic and warm, yet suspenseful, story is told from the child's point of view. The illustrations, magnificent winter evening scenes in watercolor and ink, will draw the reader back again and again to enjoy the mood. The ending, with the elusive owl's appearance, is a magnificent illustration.*

## Circle Time Presentation

Set the mood for OWL MOON by lowering the lights, talking about how quiet it is in the country when a new snow has fallen, and the excitement of walking at night. Read OWL MOON slowly and with suspense, pausing for the children to see the illustrations, but not to discuss them. After the reading, leaf through the book again and let the children comment on the story and the illustrations.

STORY STRETCHER

## For Art: Crayon Resist Winter Scenes

**What the children will learn—** To follow directions to make a winter night scene

**Materials you will need—** White construction paper or manilla paper, watery black or blue-black tempera paint or watercolors, small brushes, white, black, purple, dark blue and dark green crayons, paper towels or newspapers

**What to do—**
1. With a small group of children at the art center, collect materials for a demonstration of crayon resist. Mix watery black or blue-black tempera paint or provide watercolors.

2. Demonstrate how to make crayon lines on white paper, then wash over them with watery tempera or watercolors. The crayon marks will resist absorbing the paints. Show how to load the brush with paint and dry on the paper towel or newspaper.

3. Look again at Schoenherr's illustrations in OWL MOON. Ask the children how they could use crayon resist to create a snowy night scene. They can use white crayon marks to show the moon shining on the snow and use the black, dark blue and dark green to draw the trees before washing the scene with the paints.

4. Allow the children to experiment on scraps of paper, then encourage them to create a winter night scene.

**Something to think about—** Leave the crayon resist art materials out for several days, which will allow children time to experiment and refine the process.

STORY STRETCHER

## For Creative Dramatics: Imaginary Owling

**What the children will learn—** To re-create the mood of a story by their actions

**Materials you will need—** Flashlight, illustration of owl from book

**What to do—**
1. Ask the aide to open OWL MOON to the two page illustration of the Great Horned Owl and to place the book on a high shelf.

2. Darken the room and ask the children to rise slowly and pretend to be getting dressed very quietly so that they do not wake anyone else in the house.

3. Have them pretend to open the squeaky back door, trying not to make a sound as they follow their father outside.

4. Now outside, ask the children to imagine they are a bit cold, have scarves wrapped around their mouths and are trudging through the snow.

5. Continue on with you pretending to be the father, stop three or four times to call and listen for the owl to return the call.

**6.** Without their knowing it, turn the children in the direction of the owl illustration and call, "Who-o-o-o-who-who-who-o-o." Then turn the flashlight on, shining it on the high shelf to the open illustration in the book, and return the owl's call.

**7.** Turn off the flashlight, describing the owl's wide expanse of wings as it flies away.

**8.** Let the children trudge home again in the snow, following in the father's footsteps.

**Something to think about—**
After the creative dramatics session, let the children tell about how they felt.

STORY STRETCHER

## For Library Corner: Sometimes There's An Owl — Tape

**What the children will learn—**
To verbally cue the page turning signal

**Materials you will need—**
Cassette tape and recorder

**What to do—**
**1.** With a small group of children in the library corner, decide on a good page turning signal for OWL MOON. One possibility is to have the children repeat in whispering voices what the child was thinking throughout the story, "Sometimes there's an owl and sometimes there isn't."

**2.** Let individual children say the phrase at your signal. Practice the whispering when reading the book through once.

**3.** Record the tape and leave the book at the listening station.

**Something to think about—**
If you do not have time in your schedule for making the tapes with the children, ask a parent or grand-parent or older children to make the tapes. Having the children participate in making the tapes for the listening station encourages them to enjoy the books on tape.

ANOTHER STORY STRETCHER

## For Library Corner: Writing A Nighttime Walking Adventure

**What the children will learn—**
To express in writing a real or imaginary walk

**Materials you will need—**
An assortment of writing papers and instruments

**What to do—**
**1.** Discuss with a small group of children who select the writing area how they felt on their imaginary owling walk. Ask the children to recall any nighttime walks they have taken and how they felt, how it was different or alike from the walk in OWL MOON.

**2.** Encourage the children to write an imaginary walk where they are looking for something special or where something surprised them.

**3.** Let the children choose writing partners or write on their own if they so choose.

**Something to think about—**
Writing is a process that takes time. Allow children long writing periods without ringing bells to change activities every fifteen or twenty minutes.

STORY STRETCHER

## For Science And Nature: Researching Great Horned Owls And Other Owls

**What the children will learn—**
To compare factual information about owls

**Materials you will need—**
Reference materials on owls, construction paper, scissors, chart tablet, marker

**What to do—**
**1.** Ahead of time, ask the school or community children's librarian to select some reference materials on owls, including the Great Horned Owl.

**2.** With a small group of children, visit the library and let them help you select some materials to place in the classroom science and nature center.

**3.** Have the children cut feather-shaped book markers and place them in the reference materials where they locate pictures of owls.

**4.** Read about the Great Horned Owl's and other owls' habitats, food, behaviors.

**5.** With all the children together, let the children who selected and learned from the reference materials share with the others what they have found out about the Great Horned Owl.

**6.** On a chart tablet or piece of posterboard, draw a line down the center. On the left side, print key words or phrases that describe the Great Horned Owl. Tell the children that as they learn about other owls, they may write the names of the owls and write or draw a message about the owl on the chart.

**Something to think about—**
Include collections of paintings and drawings, like Audubon bird prints, for the children to compare.

## KEEP LOOKING!

*By Millicent Selsam and*

*Joyce Hunt*

*Illustrated by Normand Chartier*

*This beautifully illustrated book of watercolors depicts an old farm house and winter scenes. At first glance the scenes look empty, but upon closer observation the reader can see birds, squirrels and chipmunks, field mice, rabbits, a woodchuck, a heap of garter snakes, a box turtle, spiders, raccoons, an owl, two skunks, a bat and a family of deer. While the text is inviting, it is the superb watercolors that will draw the young reader back to this book again and again.*

## Circle Time Presentation

Read the title of the book to the children, KEEP LOOKING! Ask them why they think the authors chose that title. After a few comments, have a child sitting near you find the rabbit in the picture. Look closely also for the chickadee in the foreground. Ask the children what season is pictured on the cover. Have the children count all the birds on the third and fourth pages, noticing that some are easily camouflaged by the snow and branches. Read KEEP LOOKING! Ask one of the children who normally shows little interest in books to take the book to the library corner and say that during free play you will come over to look at the book more closely with him or her.

S T O R Y   S T R E T C H E R

## For Art: Hidden Pictures

**What the children will learn—**
To camouflage an animal or bird in a picture

**Materials you will need—**
Paper, crayons, pencils or watercolors and brushes

**What to do—**
**1.** Have the children notice the lovely watercolor illustrations in KEEP LOOKING! Suggest that some of them might like to make watercolor pictures.

**2.** Ask everyone to hide at least one bird or animal in their pictures so that they are not easily seen.

**3.** At a later circle time, let the children share some of their hidden pictures. Display others in the art area.

**Something to think about—**
Collect other winter scenes with animals and display them in the art area, mixing them with the children's winter pictures.

S T O R Y   S T R E T C H E R

## For Library Corner: "Keep Looking!" Listening Station Recording

**What the children will learn—**
To describe the winter scenes

**Materials you will need—**
Cassette tape recorder and tape

**What to do—**
**1.** With a small group of children who choose to come to the library corner, look at Normand Chartier's illustrations and find all the birds and animals in each winter scene.

**2.** Have the children take turns describing the scenes. For example, "This is a close-up view of the bird feeder with chickadees, a blue jay and juncos on the ground."

**3.** After the children have described all the scenes in the book, tell them that now you want to record their descriptions for other children to hear at the listening station.

**4.** Have the children decide on a page turning signal. You record an introduction to the tape with instructions about the page turning sound, then record the children's descriptions.

**5.** Record the text to KEEP LOOKING! on the opposite side of the tape, and place the tape and book at the listening station.

**Something to think about—**
If you have some children in your class who are fluent in another language, pair them with an English speaker and let both children record their descriptions in their first language.

## For Mathematics And Manipulatives: Horizontal Bar Graphs Of Birds At Our Winter Feeder

**What the children will learn—**
To record, count and chart the number of birds they see

**Materials you will need—**
Two note pads, pencils, chart tablet or posterboard, marker, unifix cubes or small blocks of the same size

**What to do—**
1. As a part of your regular classroom job assignments, during this unit select two bird watchers. Have one child go to the window and look for birds at the feeder at the end of circle time each day. Have the second child look for birds at the end of free play or choice time each day. Instruct the assigned bird watchers to make a hash mark (/) for each bird they see.

2. Prepare the note pad for the assigned bird watchers by drawing a line down the center of the pages and writing the date at the top of each page of the note pad. The first bird watcher records hash marks on the left and the second bird watcher records hash marks on the right.

3. Prepare a second note pad for incidental observations the other children in the class may make. Date each page of the note pad and ask the children to write their names or initials, then make a hash mark for each bird they see.

4. At the end of the week, make a large bar graph with unifix cubes or colored blocks to show the number of birds the assigned bird watchers saw and the number the other children observed. Place a sheet of chart tablet or posterboard on the table. Starting at the bottom of the chart on the left side, write the days of the week, leaving enough space for three unifix cubes. Select three different colors of blocks, a color for each of the two assigned bird watchers and a third color to represent the class observations.

5. Let the children look back at each day's record on the note pad and count the number of birds each of the assigned bird watchers saw and place the same number of unifix cubes or blocks on the chart in a horizontal line across from the date. Count the number of birds the other class members noted and place a corresponding number of blocks on the chart.

**Something to think about—**
For younger children prepare a chart representing the class bird watchers. Older children can chart the number of different birds that came to the feeder each day. Older children also can use binoculars to observe the birds.

## For Music And Movement: Fly And Look

**What the children will learn—**
To listen for verbal cues

**Materials you will need—**
Pictures of birds, cassette recording of instrumental music, cassette player

**What to do—**
1. Place pictures of birds at random around the room.

2. Have the children sit on the circle time rug and tell them the directions for the activity. When the music starts, they are to fly around the room like birds, looking for bird pictures. When the music stops, they return to the circle time rug, their nest.

3. Play the music and watch the birds flying. After a few children have spotted some of the bird pictures, stop the music and have the children return to their nest.

4. With all the children in the nest, let one child, "the teller," describe where he saw a chickadee bird picture by telling another child to fly to that area of the classroom. Then the "looker" begins searching for the picture and the birds in the nest say, "keep looking," whenever the child moves away from the picture and say, "looking good," whenever the child gets closer to the picture.

5. Continue by looking for pictures of different birds and reassign the "teller" and "looker" roles.

**Something to think about—**
For younger children, let a child hide one picture at a time and have the little birds close their eyes. When they open their eyes and the music starts, they fly around the room.

## For Science And Nature: Feeding Winter Birds

**What the children will learn—**
To prepare and maintain simple bird feeders

**Materials you will need—**
Fat cut from meat, orange netting, newspaper or butcher paper, large spoons, twine, scissors

**What to do—**
1. Ask the children to bring in plastic netting bags in which oranges and other fruits are packaged. If needed, cut the top off the bag so that it is not too large.

2. Cover the table with newspaper or butcher paper.

**3.** Fill the bags to about the size of a large grapefruit with the meat fat.

**4.** Tie twine around the end of the bag to close it tightly.

**5.** Hang the bird feeder in a tree near a classroom window or one where children can easily observe the birds that feed there.

**Something to think about—**
If this project is too messy for you, there are some already prepared bird feeder balls that look like cheese balls. They are available in some pet stores, large nurseries and even some large supermarkets. Place these feeder balls in the netting and hang outside for the birds. Seed feeders also will attract winter birds. If you ask, parents may donate old wooden bird feeders. If not, check with a naturalist or fish and wildlife employee of state or federal governments for free bird feeders.

## REFERENCES

Borden, Louise. (1989). Illustrated by Lillian Hoban. **CAPS, HATS, SOCKS, AND MITTENS.** New York: Scholastic Inc.

Keats, Ezra Jack. (1962). **THE SNOWY DAY.** New York: Puffin Books.

Selsam, Millicent, & Hunt, Joyce. (1989). Illustrated by Normand Chartier. **KEEP LOOKING!** New York: Macmillan Publishing Company.

Tresselt, Alvin. (1947). Illustrated by Roger Duvoisin. **WHITE SNOW, BRIGHT SNOW.** New York: Lothrop, Lee & Shepard Books.

Yolen, Jane. (1987). Illustrated by John Schoenherr. **OWL MOON.** New York: Philomel Books.

### Additional References for Seasons: Focus On Winter

Hutchins, Hazel. (1989). Illustrated by Ruth Ohi. **NORMAN'S SNOW-BALL.** Toronto, Canada: Annick Press Limited. *A funny tale of a little boy and big sister rolling a huge snowball. In the end the snowball rolls down a hill, catches on the little boy's clothes and pulls them off, except for his mittens that his mother told him to always keep on.*

Krauss, Ruth. (1949). Illustrated by Marc Simont. **THE HAPPY DAY.** New York: Harper & Row. *The story of animals asleep in winter until they sniff a sign of spring, one flower blooming in the snow.*

Neitzel, Shirley. (1989). Illustrated by Nancy Winslow Parker. **THE JACKET I WEAR IN THE SNOW.** New York: Greenwillow Books. *A young girl names all the clothes that she must wear to play in the snow.*

Quinlan, Patricia. (1989). Illustrated by Lindsay Grater. **ANNA'S RED SLED.** Toronto, Canada: Annick Press Limited. *A little girl finds a sled that is old and too little for her. When her mother wants to sell it, the child persuades her to keep it. In the end, mother and child enjoy the old sled.*

Schweiger, Ann. (1990). **WINTERTIME.** New York: Viking. *A dog family experiences the events of winter by observing what happens in winter weather, games children play in winter, how animals and birds behave, how to make a bird feeder, and winter holiday celebrations.*

# SEASONS:
# FOCUS ON SPRING

*Will Spring Be Early? Or Will Spring Be Late?*
*That's What Happens When It's  Spring!*
*My Spring Robin*
*The Story of the Root-Children*
*Wild Wild Sunflower Child Anna*

## WILL SPRING BE EARLY?
## OR WILL SPRING BE LATE?

*By Crockett Johnson*

*Crockett Johnson's groundhog story is appropriate for a unit to make the transition from winter to spring. Groundhog comes out of his burrow on the second morning of February to look for his shadow. He anticipates the excitement the other animals will have when he announces an early spring. However, an unexpected artificial flower fools everyone about spring's early arrival except for grumpy Pig. All the animals were delighting in the arrival of spring until Pig rooted around the flower and discovered it wasn't real. Then, the animals began to feel the cold and blamed the snowstorm on Pig. Johnson's simple illustrations keep the focus on the main actions of the animals.*

## Circle Time Presentation

Pass a red artificial flower around among the children and ask them to describe it. Then, pass a real flower around and ask the children to tell how the artificial flower and the real flower are alike and how they are different. Look at a calendar and point out the day of the week of the second morning in February. Tell the children that Groundhog does something special on this day and that an artificial flower plays an important part in this story. Read WILL SPRING BE EARLY? OR WILL SPRING BE LATE? After the reading, ask the children whether they think they will see their shadows today.

STORY STRETCHER
## For Art: Flower Arranging

**What the children will learn—**
To arrange flowers

**Materials you will need—**
Artificial flowers, vases, index cards, pen

**What to do —**
1. Collect old artificial flowers and vases from parents.

2. Ask the children who come to the art center to arrange some flowers for the snack tables and for the housekeeping and dress-up corner.

3. Bend a small index card in half so it stands up and print the flower arrangers' names on the cards. "Flowers by ____."

**Something to think about—**
Ask a florist or parent with a flower garden to come to class and demonstrate flower arranging. Florist supply houses often have slightly damaged flowers that they will sell or donate to a florist for a school project. Check on this possible resource.

STORY STRETCHER
## For Blocks: Delivering Our Spring Supplies

**What the children will learn—**
To associate the change in season with changes in goods and services

**Materials you will need—**
Toy trucks, vans, wheel toys, boxes, wagons, wheelbarrows, tape, markers, index cards

**What to do —**
1. With the children who choose the block building area, brainstorm changes that need to be made in the classroom because it is spring. For example, spring clothes for dress-up, spring colored paints for the easel, spring flowers and picnic supplies for snack, books on spring for the library, gardening supplies and plants for the science and nature center.

2. Select partners for each task.

3. Let the partners collect the materials, load them in boxes and onto transportation.

4. Print delivery orders on index cards. Also use the children's names as the name of the trucking or delivery company.

5. Have the children in the areas where the materials are being delivered accept the goods and sign the index card receipt.

**Something to think about—**
When classroom supplies are delivered, involve the children in checking your order. If a child's parent works for one of the major delivery companies, request the parent bring the van or truck to school for the children to see.

## For Library Corner: Flannel Board Story Of Groundhog's Announcement

**What the children will learn—**
To retell the story

**Materials you will need—**
Flannel board, felt pieces for Groundhog, truck, flower, Pig, Dormouse, Skunk, Squirrel, Rabbit, Raccoon and Bear

**What to do—**
1. Construct the flannel board pieces.

2. Distribute the pieces to the children and let them place the pieces on the flannel board as you tell the story.

3. Tell the story in your own words as if you were Groundhog.

4. Have the children exchange pieces. Give one child Groundhog and ask him to begin the story again.

**Something to think about—**
For another variation on another day, tell the story from Pig's perspective.

## For Music And Movement: Our Spring Song And Dance

**What the children will learn—**
To follow the melody of a familiar tune while singing a new one and to move as directed in the lyrics

**Materials you will need—**
Chart tablet or posterboard, flower

**What to do—**
1. Print the words on a song chart and keep it with other songs for the class Big Book of Music.

2. Teach the song by singing it through once, then let the children echo sing each verse.

3. Sing the song to the tune of "Here We Go Round the Mulberry Bush."

4. Place a real or artificial flower in the middle of the circle for the children to skip around as they sing.

5. Sing, "Here We Go Round Our Spring Flower."

*Here we go round our spring flower*
*Our spring flower, our spring flower*
*Here we go round our spring flower*
*So early in the morning.*

6. Substitute the following phrases and continue the lyrics,

*Here we go hopping round our spring*
*    flower,*
*Here we go skipping round our spring*
*    flower,*
*Here we go marching two by two,*
*Here we go saying please and thank*
*    you.*

**Something to think about—**
Let the children think of other verses to add.

## For Science And Nature: Measuring Groundhog's Shadow

**What the children will learn—**
To measure lengths of shadows at various times of the day

**Materials you will need—**
Yarn or string, chalk, scissors, envelopes, pencils

**What to do—**
1. Form partners among the children and then go out on the sidewalk and have them look for their shadows.

2. Ask the children to shadow dance, making their shadows move.

3. Demonstrate the measuring process by having one child stand still while the other child draws a chalk line from the feet of the shadow to the head. Both children can work together to cut a length of string or yarn the same length as the child's chalk shadow line.

4. After the partner's shadow is measured, the children place their lengths of yarn in the envelopes and print their names on the outside.

5. Later in the day, repeat the process.

**Something to think about—**
Older children can use standard measuring devices, such as rulers and measuring tapes, to know an exact length and can repeat the process for more comparisons.

THAT'S WHAT HAPPENS
When It's Spring!

by Elaine W. Good
Illustrated by Susie Shenk

## THAT'S WHAT HAPPENS WHEN IT'S SPRING!

*By Elaine W. Good*

*Illustrated by Susie Shenk*

*A young child asks, "When is it spring?" and mother and father answer by showing him nature's signs of spring. The child goes on to discover his own signs: trees budding, wild flowers in a meadow and having more time to play outside. He enjoys helping ready the garden for planting, digging in the soil, fishing, watching the new baby calf and noticing changes in the weather. Shenk's illustrations are brightly colored drawings made with markers, pens and pencil shading. The boldness of colors, detail and child's eye perspective add to the appeal of the book.*

## Circle Time Presentation

Ask the children what happens when it is spring. After a few children have answered, summarize their comments. For example, "The weather changes. We plant gardens. We can play outside more. We see small signs like small buds and small baby animals." Then read THAT'S WHAT HAPPENS WHEN IT'S SPRING! Read the story again, and after each scene pause for the children to think of a word or a phrase that will help them recall that page. Make a chart and list the summarizing words or phrases down the left side under the heading "book."

STORY STRETCHER

## For Art: Pencil And Marker Pictures Of Spring

**What the children will learn—** To combine two drawing instruments

**Materials you will need—** Pencils, variety of colors of markers in small and large sizes, scrap paper, construction or manilla paper

**What to do—**
1.  With a small group of children who come to the art center during choice time, look again at Susie Shenk's illustrations. Have the children talk about how she made them by drawing with a pencil, coloring and overlapping with markers, then shading with a pencil over the markers.

2.  Let the children experiment on scraps of paper by sketching, coloring, overlapping and shading.

3.  Leave the children on their own to finish their renditions of THAT'S WHAT HAPPENS WHEN IT'S SPRING!.

**Something to think about—** Young children's artwork is often a two step process, drawing and coloring, usually with crayons. By calling attention to the overlapping and shading, some children will begin to incorporate these added techniques to their pictures.

STORY STRETCHER

## For Library Corner: Making Our Own Reference Material — Data Retrieval Charts

**What the children will learn—** To summarize with key words and match information from two sources

**Materials you will need—** Chart from circle time, markers, Post-it notes or small index cards, tape, pencils or crayons

**What to do—**
1.  Discuss with the children that libraries contain books, but they also have charts and displays showing information.

2.  After the nature walk (See the Science and Nature Story Stretcher), give each child a Post-it note or a small index card. Ask the children to draw one sign of spring they saw on the nature walk.

3.  Using the chart from circle time where the children listed key words and phrases from the book, let them compare what they saw in the book with what they saw on the nature walk.

4.  Go down the list of key words from the book and have the children tape their drawing or word beside the description of the scene from the book that it matches best.

**Something to think about—** This activity can be continued with small groups over several days or can be started in the library corner during choice time and completed during a later circle time. For older children, this chart can be continued with the "changing signs of spring."

## For Mathematics And Manipulatives: Weather Calendar, Set Of Symbols

**What the children will learn—**
To symbolize the weather

**Materials you will need—**
Large calendar, scraps of construction paper, index cards, scissors, glue, colored pencils, tape

**What to do—**
1. Discuss the different kinds of spring weather.

2. Let the children each design a set of symbols to represent the weather. For example, an umbrella for rain or sunglasses for sunshine. Accept the children's ideas.

3. Post the large weather calendar and count the days with the children. Place a symbol for today's weather on the calendar.

4. Ask the children to predict tomorrow's weather and write or draw their predictions on an index card.

5. The following day, check the children's weather predictions against the actual weather.

6. At the end of the month, group alike symbols and count the number of rainy, sunny and cloudy days. Record the totals for each type of weather on the bottom of the calendar.

**Something to think about—**
The weather calendar is often a routine task in many teachers' opening circle time. However, it can be a good mathematics and science teaching aid if it is seen as a way to organize and recall information.

## For Science And Nature: Spring Nature Walk

**What the children will learn—**
To look for buds, green shoots and sprigs

**Materials you will need—**
Parent volunteers

**What to do—**
1. Scout out an area of the school grounds or neighborhood where the children can see many signs of spring.

2. Assign three or four children per parent. Instruct parents or other volunteers on supervision of the children and how to help the children be good observers.

3. Have the volunteers sit with their children while you read again THAT'S WHAT HAPPENS WHEN IT'S SPRING!

4. Ask the children what signs of spring they expect to see on their walk.

5. Enjoy the nature walk and help the children observe nature's beginning signs of spring.

**Something to think about—**
Return for the same spring walk a week later and periodically over the season to notice and record the changes. In a parent newsletter, suggest "Family Spring Nature Walks" to look for signs of spring.

## For Science And Nature: Mulching Around Plants

**What the children will learn—**
To help plants retain water and warmth they need

**Materials you will need—**
Mulch materials, rakes, water hose or watering can, optional — wagons or wheelbarrows

**What to do—**
1. Talk with the grounds keeper for your school or center about letting the children help by mulching around trees, shrubs or flowers. If possible, ask the grounds keeper to come to class and show the tools he or she uses and to discuss mulching.

2. Recall with the children the scene from THAT'S WHAT HAPPENS WHEN IT'S SPRING! where the father and child removed the straw mulch to expose rhubarb plants.

3. Discuss the purposes of mulch — to keep plants protected from cold winds, like a sweater keeps us warm, to hold water near the soil and to provide food for the roots.

4. Let the children mulch around trees, shrubs, flowers or garden plants, whatever is available, using straw, shredded tree limbs or even grass clippings.

5. Talk with the children about how this is recycling some of nature's materials.

**Something to think about—**
Many cities and counties provide free mulch from tree limbs and lawn materials they shred while maintaining public lands.

## MY SPRING ROBIN

*By Anne Rockwell*

*Illustrated by Harlow Rockwell*

*and Lizzy Rockwell*

*A child recalls that last spring she loved to hear a robin sing. It is spring again and she goes in search of her spring robin. She notices the bees, pretty crocuses, forsythia bushes, magnolia buds, fuzzy fiddleheads, daffodils, violets, frogs and earthworms. Finally at the end of the book, she hears the robin's cheery spring song. The Rockwells' simple, full-color illustrations make the book an excellent choice for circle time presentations.*

## Circle Time Presentation

Ask the children to recall the names of spring flowers and birds. After someone mentions the robin, begin reading MY SPRING ROBIN. After reading the book, ask the children to name more spring flowers that were included in the story. Leaf through the pages and have the children identify the different flowers and shrubs and describe their colors. Look closely at the illustration of the robin and have the children describe the color of its feathers. Mention that the bird is often called "robin red breast." Have the children practice sounding like a robin by saying, "cheer-up, cheerilee!"

### STORY STRETCHER

## For Art: Painting Spring Flowers

**What the children will learn—**
To identify and paint a spring flower

**Materials you will need—**
Pink, purple, yellow tempera paints, easel, brushes, white paper

**What to do—**
1. Look back through the Rockwell book for the illustrations of spring flowers and shrubs. Help the children identify the flowers and shrubs. Also call attention to the colors.

2. Ask the children to include at least one spring flower in their paintings for today.

3. For a variation, on the next day have the children include a bird in their painting. On another day, ask for paintings or drawings of spring activities the children enjoy.

**Something to think about—**
Place an arrangement of spring flowers near the easel and the children will be inspired to paint with the spring colors. If you have violets, place purple, white and green paint on the easel. If you have daffodils, provide yellow and green paints.

### STORY STRETCHER

## For Library Corner: Book Of Our Favorite Spring Flowers And Birds

**What the children will learn—**
To describe, draw and write about their favorite spring flowers and birds

**Materials you will need—**
Heavy white typing paper or construction paper, colored pencils or markers, ruler, pencil

**What to do—**
1. With the small group who choose the library center, begin discussing their favorite spring flowers and birds. Encourage them to use specific colors, as rosy stripes on a white flower.

2. Make a one-inch margin along the left hand side of the paper by drawing a line from the top of the page to the bottom. Ask the children not to draw in the margin because it will be covered when the book is bound.

3. Let the children draw and write about their favorite spring flowers and birds.

4. Bind the children's illustrations and writings into a class book to place in the library corner. (See the appendix for binding instructions.)

**Something to think about—**
Share the children's book at group time and compare the children's fa-

vorite flowers and birds with those found in MY SPRING ROBIN.

## For Mathematics And Manipulatives: Spring Flower Puzzles

**What the children will learn—**
To use fine motor coordination to reassemble photos of flowers

**Materials you will need—**
Magazine, calendar or seed catalog pictures of flowering trees, shrubs and flowers, thin cardboard or posterboard, glue or rubber cement, scissors, masking tape, plastic bags

**What to do—**
1. Let the children at the mathematics and manipulatives center select and cut out pictures of favorite spring plants.

2. Cut pieces of thin cardboard the sizes of the pictures.

3. Rubber cement or glue pictures onto the cardboard. Let dry for a few hours.

4. Draw random puzzle shapes onto the backs of the cardboard.

5. Cut puzzle pieces.

6. Store in large plastic bags. Make a label from masking tape and print the name of the flower or plant on the label.

**Something to think about—**
Ask parents to save cardboard backs from tablets and legal pads. Posterboard and cardboard from gift boxes can also be used.

## For Science And Nature: Visiting A Nursery

**What the children will learn—**
To identify spring plants native to the area

**Materials you will need—**
Parent permission slips, volunteer assistants, transportation

**What to do—**
1. Visit a nursery and talk with the manager about the age of your children and what you want them to observe when they visit the nursery.

2. Plan with volunteers and get parental permissions for the field trip.

3. With the children, identify the flowering plants and shrubs, focusing on the ones that are native to your area.

4. Have the children observe the different jobs of the nursery workers.

**Something to think about—**
If it is not possible to visit a nursery, ask a nursery owner to bring plants to your classroom.

## For Science And Nature: Listening For Birds

**What the children will learn—**
To listen for sounds of birds

**Materials you will need—**
Cassette tape and recorder

**What to do—**
1. Have the children sit quietly on the edge of the playground near some trees and listen for at least three minutes without saying a word. Ask them what they hear — crickets, traffic and birds chirping and singing.

2. Sit quietly again for three to five minutes and have the children concentrate on the bird sounds.

3. Tape record the sounds from your outside quiet time.

4. Whisper an introduction to the tape telling where, when and why the tape was made.

5. Place the finished tape on the display table in the science and nature center.

**Something to think about—**
Take a quiet walk in a nearby woods and listen for more bird sounds. Older children can take turns taking the tape recorder home to record nature sounds near their homes.

## THE STORY OF THE ROOT-CHILDREN

*By Sibylle von Olfers*

*The story is based on a 1906 German tale. In the spring, the root-children awaken, sew their new capes, paint the beetles and bugs and dance in a procession as Mother Earth opens the door into the sunshine. In the woods, they are the beautiful lilies-of-the-valley, flower-bells and violets. They play with butterflies, snails and beetles. They dance in the meadows until Mother Earth calls them to hide again until next spring. von Olfers' charmingly quaint illustrations are full-page with text on the facing page. The margins of most of the illustrations are decorated with flowers and their roots.*

## Circle Time Presentation

Collect all five books from the spring unit and ask the children if these stories are real, could have happened or are imaginary. Tell them that THE STORY OF THE ROOT-CHILDREN is like WILL SPRING BE EARLY? OR WILL SPRING BE LATE? It is an imaginary story. Read THE STORY OF THE ROOT-CHILDREN. Announce the Story S-t-r-e-t-c-h-e-r-s for the day related to the book, spring T-shirts and spring procession.

STORY STRETCHER
### For Art: Spring T-shirts

**What the children will learn—**
To use liquid embroidery to create flower designs

**Materials you will need—**
Old white T-shirts, liquid embroidery, scraps of fabric, straight pins, newspaper

**What to do—**
1. Ask parents to send old white T-shirts to school.

2. Discuss THE STORY OF THE ROOT-CHILDREN and how they sewed their beautiful gowns and capes to dress for the spring procession. Tell the children that instead of gowns and capes, you will decorate spring T-shirts for the parade.

3. Demonstrate how to use the liquid embroidery and let the children practice on scraps of fabric.

4. Fold several thicknesses of newspaper and place inside the T-shirt. Pin the T-shirt in place so the child has a smooth canvas for sketching.

5. Let the children draw spring flowers with the liquid embroidery. Leave the T-shirts pinned in

place until the paint dries thoroughly.

6. Wear the T-shirts for the Music and Movement activity.

**Something to think about—**
If you have a parent who can bring a portable sewing machine to class, make spring capes by cutting a circle from fabric, cutting a neckline, stitching edges and adding ribbon ties.

ANOTHER STORY STRETCHER
### For Art: Botanical Prints

**What the children will learn—**
To make pictures of plants like botanical prints

**Materials you will need—**
Botanical prints, pencils, colored pens and markers, heavy white or manilla paper, construction paper

**What to do—**
1. With a small group of children at the art center, look again at von Olfers' illustrations, noting how the plants are drawn showing the root systems.

2. Show the children the botanical prints, discuss the plants and point out the parts.

3. Suggest that some of the children might choose to make botanical prints for the art display area.

4. Mat some of the prints on contrasting colors of construction paper.

**Something to think about—**
Libraries often have collections of fine art prints to loan. Many wild flower prints also show the root system. Check out the prints from the library and display them around the classroom.

## For Library Corner: Our Version Of The Root-Children

**What the children will learn—**
To retell the story of the root-children

**Materials you will need—**
Tape recorder, cassette tape, stapler, listening station

**What to do—**
1. With the small group who come to the library, ask the children to look at the illustrations in THE STORY OF THE ROOT-CHILDREN without saying a word. Leaf through the book, pausing for the children to examine each illustration.

2. Then, ask the children to take turns retelling the story in their own words.

3. Taperecord the retelling and click a stapler as a page-turning signal.

4. Let the story retellers become the first ones to hear the story at the listening station.

5. Taperecord yourself reading the book on the other side of the tape.

**Something to think about—**
Story retelling helps children internalize the underlying pattern of how stories are told. Taking turns in the retelling emphasizes the importance of listening.

## For Music And Movement: Spring Flowers On Parade

**What the children will learn—**
To march in a procession

**Materials you will need—**
T-shirts, march music, cassette tape player

**What to do—**
1. Discuss how the root-children marched from Mother Earth up to the meadow, then played in the forest and the stream.

2. Let the children pull on their spring T-shirts they decorated for the Art activity.

3. Play the march music and have them form a procession, marching around the room or up and down the hallway.

4. Stop the music periodically for the children to pretend to play in the forest, stream and meadow.

**Something to think about—**
Older children can make large placards of posterboard flowers. A bee can buzz around from flower to flower, and wherever the bee lands when the music stops, that person becomes the next bee.

## For Science And Nature: Root Systems Of Plants

**What the children will learn—**
To recognize the root systems of plants

**Materials you will need—**
Potted plants, potting soil, watering can

**What to do—**
1. Spread newspaper over the science display table or use the sand table.

2. On the table, tap the bottom of a potted plant to loosen the plant. Turn the pot upside down and gently remove the soil from around the roots of the plant.

3. Examine the root system and discuss how nutrients are absorbed through the roots.

4. Help the children repot the plants.

**Something to think about—**
If possible, unpot a variety of sizes of plants to compare the sizes of the root systems. Also, root some plants, like sweet potatoes, in water in a clear container so the children can observe their roots developing.

## WILD WILD SUNFLOWER CHILD ANNA

*Nancy White Carlstrom*

*Illustrated by Jerry Pinkney*

*Carlstrom writes in a lively rhythm about a young girl's love of the outdoors, and Pinkney illustrates in lively realistic spring colors. Anna delights in the "greening of the fields," discovers dandelions, juicy berries, ponds, trees and dreaming in the meadow. Anna frolics as she wanders in sandals and barefoot, exploring and enjoying plants and insects that arrive in the late spring. The illustrations with bright yellows, many shades of green and highlights of flowers in subtle roses and blue will bring the young reader back to the book to savor the beauty of the season.*

## Circle Time Presentation

If possible, dress in a bright yellow blouse or shirt. Place some spring flowers in a vase near you. Give each child a sheet of yellow construction paper. Talk about the fact that you have read books about the beginning of spring, such as WILL SPRING BE EARLY? OR WILL SPRING BE LATE? and MY SPRING ROBIN. Ask the children to listen to the story and decide if this spring book is about the beginning of spring or the end of spring. Also, tell the children that each time they see the color yellow in the illustrations to put their pieces of construction paper in the air and then return them to their laps when you start reading the page. Read WILD WILD SUNFLOWER CHILD ANNA. Discuss the beauty of the illustrations and how the artist, Jerry Pinkney, chose yellow for every page. Let the children decide whether it is early or late spring and tell what they saw in the book that made them think it was late spring.

STORY STRETCHER

## For Art: Wild Wild Sunflower Children

**What the children will learn—**
To use large and small brushes to paint

**Materials you will need—**
Yellow and white construction paper, large and small brushes, yellow, blue, red, pink, green, purple paints, manilla paper, crayons, scissors, glue

**What to do—**
1. Let the children practice making flower prints on small scraps of construction paper with small brushes.

2. Show them Pinkney's illustrations of the flowers. Point out that they are just small brush strokes and swirls of colors with a contrasting color in the middle.

3. Ask the children to paint a meadow of wild flowers on their yellow construction paper.

4. Have the children do a smaller self-portrait on the white sheet. color it, cut it out and place it in the meadow of spring flowers. At the bottom of their spring print, tape a caption that reads, "Wild Wild Sunflower Child _____," and add the child's name.

**Something to think about—**
Consider placing the children's paintings in a large scrapbook or photo album with plastic pages. Place a small photograph of the child beside the caption.

STORY STRETCHER

## For Cooking And Snack Time: Picnic On A Lovely Spring Day

**What the children will learn—**
To plan and prepare their snack to be served outside

**Materials you will need—**
Cheese, crackers, variety of fruits, plastic knives, peanut butter, juice or milk, napkins, tablecloths, picnic basket

**What to do—**
1. Ask the children to plan some simple foods they might prepare for a snack to take on a picnic. Some of the possibilities are listed above.

2. Let the snack helpers pack the picnic snack in a picnic basket.

3. Once outside, let other helpers prepare cheese and crackers, peanut butter and crackers and sliced fruit.

**4.** Ask other children to help with serving by setting up napkins and fruit juice or milk.

**5.** Have a clean-up crew dispose of the paper napkins, fold tablecloths and wash plastic knives for reuse.

**Something to think about—**
Let the children sit on the ground if it is warm and dry. Enjoy their company and conversation in a leisurely manner without rushing on to other activities. Picnics are for lounging around and savoring the beauty of nature.

## For Library Corner: Remembering Our Meadow Observations

**What the children will learn—**
To recall specific descriptions of plants and insects as well as what they enjoyed about their walk

**Materials you will need—**
Writing and drawing paper, pencils, markers, crayons

**What to do—**
**1.** During free play or center time, with the small group of children who select the writing area of the library corner, discuss that when we have an experience sometimes we take pictures to help us remember it. Ask the children some other things they can do to remember, such as drawing a picture or writing a note. Tell the children they can do either or both, drawing and writing to help them remember the class walk in the spring meadow.

**2.** Discuss some of the plants and insects the children expected to see before they went on the walk and some of the ones that surprised them.

**3.** Encourage the use of many descriptive words, as colors, textures, fragrances, locations. For example, one child might say, "I saw the green sticker plant," and you can help the child clarify that this was a cockle-burr, that it is green now but will turn brown later, that it was found at the edge of the stand of trees.

**4.** After the children have discussed what they observed, what they expected to see, what surprised them as well as some specific plants and insects, ask them to write or draw one observation from their walk.

**Something to think about—**
To help children who say they can not write or they do not know how to spell, ask them to use whatever they know how to write. We do not expect children to develop oral language without attempting it many times and making many attempts before moving from saying, "Da, da" to "Daddy." Yet, some teachers expect children to emerge in their writing knowing how to spell and write. We want to encourage them to use whatever they know to write. It may be scribbles that tell us the child knows to move the print from left to right and write in lines. It may be writing where the child takes her first name and rearranges the letters and prints a few "mock" letter forms that have letter shapes but are not real letters. Their writing may be a combination of some sound/letter combinations. Help parents understand children's emerging literacy and attempts at writing as welcomed signs that they are beginning to construct print for themselves. The children will eventually learn to read and write, just as they eventually learned to talk by making many attempts.

## For Music And Movement: Meadow Movements

**What the children will learn—**
To move in the ways mentioned in the story

**Materials you will need—**
None needed

**What to do—**
**1.** Have the children who choose creative dramatics for free play sit on the circle time carpet. Read again WILD WILD SUNFLOWER CHILD ANNA. Pause after each movement description and have a volunteer move in that way.

**2.** Next, show just the illustrations and let the children take turns making the appropriate movements.

**3.** Ask the children to stand and move around the room in any way they choose while you read the book again.

**Something to think about—**
Young children are learning to gain control of their bodies. As they see other children improvise movements, then they are confident to try. Beginning with volunteers taking turns, then everyone moving as a group, will help the reluctant ones feel more confident. If you have several children who do not like the spotlight on them, skip the taking turns with movements to match each page and go on to group movements where they can blend in without all the attention on them. This Music and Movement Story S-t-r-e-t-c-h-e-r also could be a circle time activity for a second circle time of the day.

## For Science And Nature: Take A Walk In A Meadow

**What the children will learn—**
To identify spring flowers and plants

**Materials you will need—**
Name tags

**What to do—**

1. Arrange the field trip by getting parent permissions and making arrangements with the place you will visit.

2. Make name tags and assign parent volunteers for each child so that adults are responsible for specific children.

3. Train the adults in how to encourage the children to observe the plant, insect and animal life in the meadow.

4. Once back in the classroom, ask the children to close their eyes and recall their favorite places.

5. Ask the children to tell their parents about this favorite place and, if possible, arrange to go there as a family.

**Something to think about—**
If you do not live in an area where there are meadows to explore, go to a park, a botanical garden or even a neighborhood nursery and enjoy the beauty of the spring flowers.

## REFERENCES

Carlstrom, Nancy White. (1987). Illustrated by Jerry Pinkney. **WILD WILD SUNFLOWER CHILD ANNA.** New York: Macmillan.

Good, Elaine W. (1987). Illustrated by Susie Shenk. **THAT'S WHAT HAPPENS WHEN IT'S SPRING!** Intercourse, PA: Good Books.

Johnson, Crockett. (1959). **WILL SPRING BE EARLY? OR WILL SPRING BE LATE?** New York: Harper & Row.

Rockwell, Anne. (1989). Illustrated by Harlow Rockwell and Lizzy Rockwell. **MY SPRING ROBIN.** New York: Macmillan.

von Olfers, Sibylle. (1990). **THE STORY OF THE ROOT-CHILDREN.** Edinburgh, Scotland: Floris Books.

### Additional References For Seasons: Focus On Spring

Bunting, Eve. (1986). Illustrated by Jan Brett. **THE MOTHER'S DAY MICE.** New York: Clarion Books. *Biggest Little Mouse, Middle Mouse and Little Mouse search in the woods and meadows for gifts for their mother while avoiding the peril of a cat.*

Carrier, Lark. (1989). **A PERFECT SPRING.** Saxonville, MA: Picture Book Studio. *Beautifully illustrated story of two seabirds' adoption of an egg, leading to an unexpected discovery as one hatchling goes to the sky and the other to the water.*

Gomi, Taro. (1989). **SPRING IS HERE.** San Francisco: Chronicle Books. *Award-winning pictures and text take us through a year of seasons beginning when spring arrives and a calf is born.*

Lobel, Arnold. (1970). "Spring" from **FROG AND TOAD ARE FRIENDS.** New York: Harper and Row. *The "Spring" story is the first one in a collection of five short stories about these two illustrious friends. Frog, on a beginning of spring morning, tries to persuade Toad to end his winter hibernation.*

Wellington, Monica. (1990). **SEASONS OF SWANS.** New York: Dutton Children's Books. *As spring arrives, two graceful swans build their nest, baby cygnets are born and the story continues, following the swan family through the seasons of the year and the swans' growing.*

# TEDDY BEARS AND OTHER BEARS

*A Pocket for Corduroy*

*Lost!*

*My Brown Bear Barney*

*Goldilocks and the Three Bears*

*Little Bear' s Trousers*

## 11

## TEDDY BEARS
## AND OTHER BEARS

## A POCKET FOR
## CORDUROY

*By Don Freeman*

*Corduroy goes along with Lisa and her mother to the laundromat. When Lisa's mother tells her to empty the pockets of her clothes for the wash, Corduroy realizes he has no pocket and goes in search of one. By accident, he gets in an artist's laundry bag and when it is time to leave, Lisa cannot find Corduroy. Spending the night alone in the laundromat is quite an adventure. The next day when the manager comes to unlock the laundromat, Lisa is there to rescue Corduroy. At home, Lisa sews a purple pocket on Corduroy's overalls and puts his name and address inside. Don Freeman's story and illustrations have become childhood favorites. The illustrations are simple yet masterfully executed with bright watercolor washes over strong pen and ink drawings.*

## Circle Time Presentation

Recall the original story of Corduroy and his adventure in a department store before Lisa gave him a home. Show the cover of A POCKET FOR CORDUROY, and ask if any of the children have heard this Corduroy story. No doubt some will already know it, but will enjoy hearing it again. Discuss going to the laundromat, sorting and washing clothes. Read A POCKET FOR CORDUROY. Announce the Corduroy activities for the day or week, pocket pictures in the art area, sorting clothes in the housekeeping and dress-up corner, washing clothes in the water table, writing a "lost teddy bear" announcement in the library corner. Teach the children the "Searching for Corduroy Song — Where, Oh Where Has My Little Bear Gone?" (See the Story Stretcher for Music and Movement listed below.)

### STORY STRETCHER
## For Art: Pocket Pictures

**What the children will learn—**
To use a focal point in their drawings

**Materials you will need—**
Small swatches or pieces of fabric, scissors, white construction paper or manilla paper, glue, colored pencils or crayons

**What to do—**
1. With the children who come to the art center during choice time, discuss that Lisa sewed a pocket on Corduroy's overalls.

2. Ask the children to draw Corduroy or one of their favorite toys and put a pocket on the toy.

3. Help the children cut small swatches of fabric for pockets and glue them onto their pictures.

4. Display the "Pocket Pictures" near the library corner where A POCKET FOR CORDUROY is on the bookshelf.

**Something to think about—**
Encourage the children to draw their toys large enough so that they almost fill the page. Older children can place a pocket at random on the sheet of paper and draw the toy around the pocket.

### STORY STRETCHER
## For Housekeeping And Dress-up Corner: At The Laundromat

**What the children will learn—**
To sort clothes by colors

**Materials you will need—**
Laundry baskets, clothes from dress-up corner

**What to do—**
1. Place the laundry baskets in the area.

2. Take all the clothes from the hangers and drawers and place them on the floor.

3. Demonstrate how to sort the clothes by colors for washing.

**Something to think about—**
Make a washer and dryer by letting the children paint large cardboard boxes to resemble the appliances. Cut the top of the box so it lifts, for children to place the clothes inside.

### STORY STRETCHER
## For Library Corner: Writing Lost Bear Announcements

**What the children will learn—**
To write notices for their lost toys

**Materials you will need—**
Large index cards or half sheets of paper, pencils, markers, crayons, thumbtacks or tape, bulletin board

**What to do—**

1. With the children who choose the library during free play, discuss that a "lost bear" announcement posted in the laundromat could have told the artist where to call Lisa to let her know Corduroy was found.

2. Ask the children what Lisa should write for her "lost bear" announcement.

3. Let the children write or dictate their own announcements, decorate them and post them on the bulletin board with the "pocket pictures" from the Art activity.

**Something to think about—**
The children's announcements can be a combination of drawing and writing. Extend the activity on other days by having the children write announcements of lost and misplaced toys and objects from the classroom. Continue the practice of a lost and found bulletin board so that the children become accustomed to writing and checking the board.

STORY STRETCHER

# For Music And Movement: Lost Corduroy Song — "Where, Oh Where Has My Little Bear Gone"

**What the children will learn—**
To sing the words to a new song with the proper feeling

**Materials you will need—**
Chart tablet or posterboard, marker, ruler or pointer

**What to do—**

1. Print the words to the following song on chart tablet or posterboard to keep as a part of the class's Big Book of Music.

*Where, Oh where has my little bear
    gone?*
*Where, Oh where can he be?*
*With his soft brown fur
and his green overalls,*
*Oh where, Oh where can he be?*

*Where, Oh where has my little bear
    gone?*
*Where, Oh where can he be?*
*With his black button eyes
and his warm little smile,*
*Oh where, Oh where can he be?*

*Where, Oh where has my little bear
    gone?*
*Where, Oh where can he be?*
*I've searched high and low
My mother says go,*
*Oh where, Oh where can he be?*

*There, Oh there is my little lost bear
There, Oh there is where he must be
I've come back to the laundromat
to look once more
There, Oh there is my little lost bear
There, Oh there is my little lost bear!
I knew it's where he must be!*
    *(Raines, 1991)*

2. Sing the song to the tune of "Where, Oh where is my little lost dog?" Sing the song through once, then have the children sing along as you run a pointer along under the words, pausing where the children need to pause.

3. Repeat the song at intervals throughout the day, as coming in from the playground, at the beginning and end of the second circle time and as the children are leaving at the end of the day.

**Something to think about—**
Use the song for a "Hide and Seek Corduroy" game. Let one child hide Corduroy while the others close their eyes and sing. Then they open their eyes and continue singing while they search for Corduroy.

STORY STRETCHER

# For Water Table: Washing Clothes

**What the children will learn—**
To wash clothes by hand

**Materials you will need—**
At least two plastic dishpans, water, mild detergent, clothes from the housekeeping and dress-up corner, mop or sponge, clothes drying rack

**What to do—**

1. Place at least two plastic dishpans in the water table. Fill one with water for washing and one with water for rinsing.

2. Show the children how to add the detergent and how to wash and rinse the clothes.

3. Let the children hang their wash on the drying rack when finished.

4. Since there will be spilled water and drips under the drying rack, help the children use the sponge and mop when needed.

**Something to think about—**
This activity is an excellent one for outdoor play. If your center or school has a washer and dryer, divide the class into three groups and each group can actually wash and dry a load of clothes.

## 11

## TEDDY BEARS AND OTHER BEARS

## LOST!

*By David McPhail*

*While a delivery truck driver is fixing a flat tire, a bear crawls into the back and falls asleep. When he awakens, he is in the city, lost and afraid. A little boy hears him crying and helps the bear find his way back to the forest, but then the little boy is lost and the bear must help the boy find the city. David McPhail's illustrations of city life include skyscrapers, parks and sidewalk scenes of a fruit stand and a hot dog vendor. The pictures inside the library and inside the bus are particularly appealing. The illustrations of the little boy and the huge bear are innocent and expressive. The pencil and chalk drawings are soft, yet rich with color and shadows.*

## Circle Time Presentation

Discuss a time when you got lost and ask a few children to briefly tell about their experiences of being lost. Cover the title of the book and have the children look at the cover and tell what they think the little boy and the big bear are doing. Ask them to predict what the title of the book is. Then uncover the title and read LOST! Read the book and pause to let a child predict what the boy will do when he hears crying. Pause again at several points to ask, "What do you think the little boy will do next?" At the end of the book, pause before the last scene and ask, "What do you think the bear will do next?"

STORY STRETCHER

## For Block Building: City Scenes And Skyscrapers

**What the children will learn—**
To construct tall buildings

**Materials you will need—**
Large hollow blocks, toy trucks, cars and buses

**What to do—**
1. With a small group of block builders, discuss how the city looked in the book LOST! Ask them to talk about how they might go about building some skyscrapers and other city scenes.

2. Leave the block builders to their constructing, but check with them periodically to talk about their progress.

3. If there is a great deal of toppling over of the skyscrapers, show the children how to build a broader solid foundation and gradually narrow the floors as they go up.

**Something to think about—**
Young children sometimes have difficulty telling how to do something and planning a city ahead of time. They will need to just get started and let the city evolve. Older children can draw up a city plan and map out a variety of buildings.

STORY STRETCHER

## For Creative Dramatics: Getting Help When Lost

**What the children will learn—**
To role play ways to ask for help when lost

**Materials you will need—**
None needed

**What to do—**
1. Have the children recall a time when they were lost for a few minutes as in a grocery store or a department store. Ask how they were found.

2. Pretend to be a child lost in a department store and look for the nearest cash register and go there and wait for your mother or father. Let the aide or a child pretend to be the salesperson.

3. Pair children in twos and ask them to decide who will be the lost child and who will be the salesperson. Let them role play the lost and found scene.

**Something to think about—**
Avoid frightening children with stories of strangers snatching youngsters.

STORY STRETCHER

## For Cooking And Snack Time: A Hot Dog Stand

**What the children will learn—**
To prepare hot dogs for snack or lunch

**Materials you will need—**
Hot dogs, tongs, buns, saucepan, hot plate or microwave, tray, card table or picnic table, napkins, posterboard, marker, optional — garnishes

**What to do—**
1. Cook hot dogs in hot water or following microwave directions. Let young children assist you; older children can cook with you nearby for safety.

2. Place the hot dogs on a tray and take them outside for serving.

3. Construct a hot dog stand from a card table or picnic table. Make a sign that reads, "Hot Dogs, Get your hot, hot dogs here!"

4. At snack time or lunch time, have the children come by the stand and pretend to pay the hot dog vendor. After they pay, the children add any garnishes they want and sit together to eat.

**Something to think about—**
Young children can choke on pieces of hot dog, so talk with the children about chewing their food well. If the hot dogs are served as snack food, cut the hot dogs and buns in half. An alternative to the hot dog stand is a fruit seller's stand.

STORY STRETCHER

## For Library Corner: Writing Directions For The Lost Bear's Journey To The City And Back

**What the children will learn—**
To decide important points in writing directions

**Materials you will need—**
Note pads or paper, pencils or pens

**What to do—**
1. Read LOST! again. As you read, write down all the places the bear went and how he got there.

For example, rode in truck to city, walked to fountain, walked to skyscraper, rode elevator to top of skyscraper, rode elevator down, walked across three streets to the park, rode boat on park lake, walked to playground, walked to library, ran to catch bus, rode bus to forest.

2. Ask the children to pretend the lost bear came to see them at this school. Let them give directions to the bear to return to his home.

3. Write the directions and draw maps or pictures of the way for the bear to return home.

**Something to think about—**
Younger children can draw directions for the bear to get to their house from the school or to get to a favorite playground. Older children can research the nearest area where bears might live near the school and plan the actual directions.

ANOTHER STORY STRETCHER

## For Library Corner: Maps, Globes And Children's Guides To Cities

**What the children will learn—**
To associate finding one's way with reading a map, looking at globes and reading a city guide

**Materials you will need—**
Old road map, scissors, name tags, pins, marker, if going to city library — field trip permission forms

**What to do—**
1. Make arrangements with the librarian.

2. Plan transportation, secure parent permissions and instruct parent volunteers about the purposes of the trip, safety and ways to handle any disruptions.

3. Cut up an old road map into name tags. Print children's names with a marker. Attach with pins.

4. Discuss the purpose of the field trip to the library.

5. Let the children explore the maps and globes with the librarian and with the volunteers' assistance.

6. Allow time for the children to check out guidebooks to cities that have been written specifically for children. They usually contain simple maps.

**Something to think about—**
If a field trip is not possible, invite someone such as a librarian to bring maps and globes to the classroom. Younger children may not understand the representations of such distant places because they think mostly about where they are at the moment. However, they are not too young to understand that people find their way by looking at maps. Older children might compose a guide to the neighborhoods where they live.

## MY BROWN BEAR BARNEY

*By Dorothy Butler*

*Illustrated by Elizabeth Fuller*

*A little girl narrates the story of all the places that her brown bear Barney goes with her. They go shopping, to the beach, to grandmother's and to bed. They play with her friend Fred and they garden. Her mother says brown bear Barney cannot go to school. But, there is a surprise at the end. Elizabeth Fuller's brightly colored illustrations are framed with the words printed below the frames. The illustrations depict a warm family feeling.*

## Circle Time Presentation

Show the cover of the book and ask the children to think of all the places this little girl might take her stuffed animal, Barney. Make a list of the places the children named by writing them on a chalk board or a chart tablet. MY BROWN BEAR BARNEY is a good book to use the "verbal cloze" process while reading. Read the book through once, then reread the book and pause for the children to fill in the recurring phrase, "and my brown bear Barney." After the reading, ask the children to recall all the places the little girl took her brown bear Barney. Refer back to the book and to their list of other places she could take Barney.

STORY STRETCHER

## For Art: Framing Story Pictures

**What the children will learn—**
To draw a picture within a frame

**Materials you will need—**
Construction paper or manilla paper, large markers, crayons, newspapers

**What to do—**
1. Place newspapers on the art table. Show the children how to make an edge around their papers by holding a large marker in place with the tip down and pulling their paper under the tip.

2. Point out that the illustrations in MY BROWN BEAR BARNEY are all in frames. Ask the children to draw a frame from the book or a framed picture of where they would like to take their teddy bear.

**Something to think about—**
Let older children cut strips of construction paper and glue a frame around the edge of their paper.

For younger children, you make the frame an inch or so inside the edge of the paper, and let the children draw inside the frame.

STORY STRETCHER

## For Cooking And Snack Time: Brown Bear Barney Apple Snacks

**What the children will learn—**
To prepare healthy fruit snacks

**Materials you will need—**
Red delicious and golden delicious apples (apples are mentioned twice and pictured three times in the book), paring knives, cutting boards

**What to do—**
1. Let each child decide whether he wants a red or yellow apple.

2. Have the children wash the apples thoroughly.

3. Working with a small group of children at a time, show them how to cut their apples into slices by putting the apple down on the cutting board and holding it firmly in place.

4. Encourage the children to cut up the entire apple, then start eating.

**Something to think about—**
While small plastic knives can be used for cutting, they are more difficult to use. If young children are shown how to hold the apples in place and how to use the paring knives, and the adult remains at the table, there is no safety problem. This is also a good time for a safety lesson.

STORY STRETCHER

## For Creative Dramatics: Everywhere My Brown Bear Barney Goes

**What the children will learn—**
To dramatize going shopping, playing with a friend, gardening, a day at the beach, a visit with grandmother, going to bed and a first day at school

**Materials you will need—**
Large paper grocery bag or shopping bag for each of the seven scenes, items that go with each scene as shown in the book, as picnic basket with play food, beach towel and sunglasses for the beach

**What to do—**
1. Ask several children to act as helpers and collect all the items that will be needed for each scene.

2. Give each child a large grocery or shopping bag. Let each child collect the items for her scene. Plastic food, clothes from the dress-up corner and stuffed animals can be collected from around the room.

3. After the collections are made, review the book and let the children decide if they want to bring anything from home to complete their scene. If something is needed, ask the child to draw a picture of the item as a reminder.

4. When all the bags are filled with the items for each scene, line up the actors according to when their scene appears in the book. Have them dress up in the clothing. Then when their scene is read from the book, they step out of the line and pretend to use whatever object is in the bag. For example, digging with the spade for gardening, bouncing the beach ball or eating a snack before bed.

**Something to think about—**
With younger children, you may need to assist more with the collection of items. With older children, do not read the book again, but let the actors dress up, then guess which scene is being depicted as each piece of clothing or item is brought out by the actor.

## For Housekeeping And Dress-up Corner: Packing For Grandmother's

**What the children will learn—**
To plan for a trip and to pack a suitcase

**Materials you will need—**
Suitcase, pajamas, toothbrush, hairbrush, some flowers, some carrots from the little girl's garden, a tidbit for grandmother's cat, Brown Bear Barney

**What to do—**
1. Review the scene in the book where the little girl packs for a trip to grandmother's. Look at all the things she takes and have the children say some other items they would need, as toothbrush, hairbrush, a change of clothes.

2. Leave a small group of children in the housekeeping and dress-up corner to pretend they are going to grandmother's. They will assign roles and play the scene without your assistance.

**Something to think about—**
While we often plan for specific role playing, as in the creative dramatics center, some of the most creative drama and language development happens when the children are left to their own devices. They improvise, extend the storyline and take on the roles without a teacher's direction. However, the addition of a special prop, as the suitcase, may stimulate the play in a new direction.

## For Library Center: Writing More About My Brown Bear Barney

**What the children will learn—**
To use the form of the story to write more scenes

**Materials you will need—**
Paper, pencils, chart tablet, markers

**What to do—**
1. With a small group of children, reread MY BROWN BEAR BARNEY. Recall that when you read the book at circle time that the children thought of some other places the little girl could take her teddy bear.

2. Write the children's list of other places on a small chalk board or a chart tablet.

3. Have the children brainstorm some items that the little girl could take with her to these places. For example, some child will probably list the caregiver's house, and some things that could be taken to the caregiver's are a favorite book, a blanket and some cookies to share.

4. Let the children draw another place they would like to take brown bear Barney and some of the things that could go with them.

5. Encourage the children to write about the place and the things they drew in their pictures.

**Something to think about—**
Young children may scribble or write "mock" letters, shapes that are similar to letters. Older children may write captions for their drawings and will be able to spell many of the words correctly or "invented spellings," ways of spelling that use whatever letters they know or sounds they hear. For example, one five year old wrote, "kak" meaning "cake."

# TEDDY BEARS
# AND OTHER BEARS

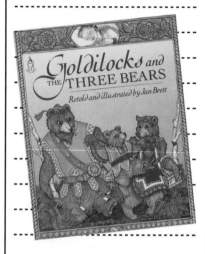

## GOLDILOCKS AND THE THREE BEARS

*Retold and illustrated*

*by Jan Brett*

*The classic folk tale of GOLDILOCKS AND THE THREE BEARS is retold in lovely illustrations, rich in detail, with story borders and exquisite coloring. The house, dishes, furniture and clothing are decorated in elaborate Old World patterns and carvings. The bears' house has a thatched roof and carved doors and pillars. The porridge bowls are richly decorated porcelains. The beds have carved figures of bears on the headboards. Goldilocks' dress and the three bears' vests are edged with braids, tassels and woven trims.*

## Circle Time Presentation

Ask the children to bring in copies they may have at home of GOLDILOCKS AND THE THREE BEARS. Make a display of the books and compare the illustrations. Then read Jan Brett's GOLDILOCKS AND THE THREE BEARS. After reading the book, call the children's attention to the story borders on the picture. Tell the children that all the books will be in the library and they can decide which illustrations they like best. Reread the story and have a child pretend to be Goldilocks. Tell the children that during free play or choice time, you or the aide will stay in the circle time area and any children who want to act out the story may join you.

STORY STRETCHER

## For Art: Story Border Pictures

**What the children will learn—**
To decorate and mat their pictures with story borders

**Materials you will need—**
Construction paper, thick white typing paper, glue, crayons or colored pens

**What to do—**

1. Let the children examine Jan Brett's borders of the illustrations in the book. Tell them these are called story borders and include little pictures about the story.

2. Have the children draw any scene they would like from the story. Use the thick white typing paper.

3. Place the typing paper on the construction paper and a border should appear. Draw around the sheet of typing paper to create the border. Remove the typing paper.

4. Let the children decorate their story borders.

5. Glue the picture into place inside the borders.

6. Display the border pictures near the collection of GOLDILOCKS AND THE THREE BEARS books.

**Something to think about—**
Create a collection of story border pictures for other favorite folk tales.

STORY STRETCHER

## For Creative Dramatics: Our Version Of "Goldilocks And The Three Bears"

**What the children will learn—**
To listen for their cues and to pantomime the actions

**Materials you will need—**
Three bowls, three chairs, three mats or cots

**What to do—**

1. With at least four children, plan the scenes from GOLDILOCKS AND THE THREE BEARS. Let the actors decide what props they need and what their actions might be for the scenes.

2. Rehearse each scene.

3. Read the story again or tell it in your own words.

**Something to think about—**
If you have more than four actors volunteer, have the remaining children become the audience, then do the play again with the audience becoming the actors. Children can also pantomime the actions out of order and let the audience guess which scene is being portrayed.

## For Library Corner: Writing About The Three Bears' Visit To Goldilocks' House

**What the children will learn—**
To retain the story structure while reversing the roles

**Materials you will need—**
Writing paper, pencils and pens

**What to do—**

1.  Ask the children what might happen if the three bears came to Goldilocks' house. Let them brainstorm some ideas.

2.  Have the children work with partners and draw and retell the story as the "Three Bears' Visit to Goldilocks' House."

3.  Later in the day, let the partners read their stories like wordless picture books to the class. Have the artists/authors read their stories while sitting in chairs with signs that read, "Author."

**Something to think about—**
Younger children may work individually and draw one major scene from their stories. Older children who are already writing may want to bind their stories into books and start a collection of "rewritten versions of folktales." (See the steps in binding a book in the appendix.)

## For Mathematics And Manipulatives: Sets Of Threes

**What the children will learn—**
To form sets of threes

**Materials you will need—**
Three teddy bears, three bowls, three chairs, three mats or three cots, large index cards or half sheets of paper, marker or crayon

**What to do—**

1.  Ask the children to tell you which number is in the title of the book. Have them find all the examples of sets of threes that appear in the book.

2.  Let the children make a collection of props that represent the story in sets of threes.

3.  Line up the props in the order they appear in the story.

4.  Let the children retell the story in sequence by looking at the sets of threes.

5.  Write cards to represent each set of three. Print 3 bears, 3 bowls, 3 chairs, 3 beds.

6.  Read the story again and replace the props with the index cards.

**Something to think about—**
Let young children also draw a picture on the card to remember what each word means. Shuffle the cards and let them place them in order. Also, consider making sets of threes throughout the day. Count out straws in sets of three at snack time. Ask a child at the art center for a set of three pieces of construction paper. Read a set of three books in the library corner.

## For Work Bench: Woodworking And Carving

**What the children will learn—**
To shape and carve wood

**Materials you will need—**
Volunteer who knows woodworking, workbench, wood, tools

**What to do—**

1.  Ask a parent or grandparent who knows about woodworking to come to the class and bring some samples of finished and unfinished work, as well as the tools they use.

2.  Have the volunteer demonstrate how she or he carves the wood. Ask the volunteer to emphasize how he or she uses tools safely.

3.  Help the children learn the names of the woods, names of the types of woodworking and the names of the tools.

4.  If possible, have some wood available, and throughout the morning let the volunteer help one child at a time carve some wood.

**Something to think about—**
Often grandparents and older relatives are neglected as sources for volunteers. Also, do not be concerned that the children actually make a finished project. It is important that they see how the wood is carved, experience using the tools and begin to appreciate fine craftsmanship.

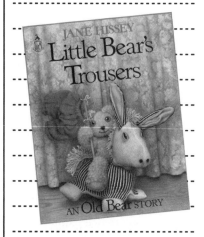

## LITTLE BEAR'S TROUSERS

*By Jane Hissey*

*Little Bear wakes up, changes from his pajamas and starts looking for his trousers. He asks Old Bear who directs him to Camel who wore the trousers briefly for hump warmers then gave them to Toy Sailor who used them for a sail for his boat. Sailor gave them to Dog to keep his two bones in. Dog then gave them to Rabbit who used them for a ski hat for his two ears before giving them to Zebra who tied the legs together and used them to carry building bricks for her house. Zebra then passed the trousers along to Duck who used them for a sand castle flag. Duck gave them to Bramwell Brown who tied the legs, filled them with icing and used them to ice a cake. The toys all decide to celebrate Little Bear finding his trousers by decorating the cake with trousers and having a lost and found trousers party. Little Bear decides to sleep with his trousers under his pillow so he never has to search for them again. Jane Hissey's illustrations make this pretend world of toys coming to life a believable one. The full page illustrations are filled with detail and softly textured, with an almost photographic realism.*

## Circle Time Presentation

Collect many of the stuffed animals and toys from around the classroom. Place a little teddy bear in your lap and begin reading LITTLE BEAR'S TROUSERS. The children will delight in the toys' many "untrouserly" uses for Little Bear's trousers. Pause after each toy sends Little Bear to the next place. Let the children predict how the animal or toy might use the trousers. Continue reading through to the end of the story and compliment the children on their suggestions for using the trousers. The illustrations are so delightful that the children will want you to read it again. Announce to them that you will place the book in the library center and you will be over during center time to read the book again. Give the book to a child who is often not interested in books and ask him to place it on the book shelf. Tell him that you want to read the book to him first.

STORY STRETCHER

## For Blocks: Building Rabbit's Ski Ramp

**What the children will learn—**
To design a ramp

**Materials you will need—**
Large hollow blocks, popsicle sticks, Tinkertoys, yarn or string, stuffed animals

**What to do—**
1. With the group of children who have chosen block building during free play, show the illustration of Rabbit skiing down the banister. Ask if any of the children have been skiing or have seen skiing on television.

2. Have the children decide what they would need to build a hill for skiing, including a ramp like the

one at the beginning of a ski run or a ski jump.

3. When the children begin problem solving and building, withdraw from the activity.

4. Let the children create skis for the stuffed animals by using popsicle sticks, Tinkertoys and yarn or string.

**Something to think about—**
Children who live in areas where skiing takes place may create entire ski resorts with lifts, lodges and restaurants. Others who have little experience may concentrate more on the apparatus for designing a hill and ramp. Older children will sell lift tickets and role play the skiing experience, while younger children probably will focus on the physical experience of having the stuffed animals ski.

STORY STRETCHER

## For Cooking And Snack Time: Decorating Little Bear's Cake

**What the children will learn—**
To decorate a cake

**Materials you will need—**
Cake, icing, decorating equipment, chart tablet, marker, clean-up supplies

**What to do—**
1. If you have a parent or grandparent of one of the children with expertise in cake decorating, invite that person in for a demonstration to make Little Bear's cake.

2. Assign duties for each of the children. A fourth of the children can be bakers, a fourth can be icers, a fourth of the class decorators, and a fourth assemblers and servers. Make a chart with four columns and list all of the children's names.

3. Bake the cake with the first small group.

4. Have the icers complete their part.

5. Ask the decorators to decide whether to have the cake look like Little Bear's cake or another decoration.

6. At snack time, ask the assemblers to call the class members together and serve the cake as if the children were guests at a party.

**Something to think about—**
Older children can work in small groups and each group bake, decorate and serve the cake. Younger children, who are less adept at decorating, can use teddy bear shaped cookies, sprinkles and small candies to decorate the top of the cake.

STORY STRETCHER

## For Housekeeping And Dress-up Corner: Dressing Up The Stuffed Animals

**What the children will learn—**
To dress by seeing front and back, to zip, to button, to retell the story substituting classroom animals

**Materials you will need—**
Stuffed animals or dolls, baby clothes or doll clothes

**What to do—**
1. With the group of children who have chosen this area of the classroom, discuss the book, LITTLE BEAR'S TROUSERS. Ask the children to create a display of all the animals and people in the book. If there is no zebra or camel, let them decide on substitutes. For example, there might be a panda or a giraffe or a tiger stuffed animal.

2. Have the children go through the clothing in the dress-up area and find some that will fit the ani-

mals. Dress the animals for Little Bear's party.

3. After all the animals or their substitutes are dressed, ask the children to line them up in order and leave them on display for the second group time of the day.

4. At a time when all the children are together, reread LITTLE BEAR'S TROUSERS and substitute the classroom animals for those in the story. For example, Panda might substitute for Camel and the children could think of something that Panda might do with Little Bear's trousers, as put them around his shoulders to keep warm.

**Something to think about—**
Younger children may like dressing the animals, but have less interest in creating the display. Older children will enjoy creating their special class display of animals that could have been in the story. They also will enjoy rewriting the story on their own or in small groups with varying amounts of teacher assistance needed, depending on their independent writing abilities.

STORY STRETCHER

## For Music And Movement: Finding Little Bear's Trousers

**What the children will learn—**
To watch for visual clues and to listen for the musical cues

**Materials you will need—**
Instrumental music tape, player, trousers, posterboard or chart tablet for a news board, marker or crayon

**What to do—**
1. At one of the circle times during the day, show the trousers that Little Bear lost. Tell the children that throughout the day, you are going to hide the trousers around

the room and whenever they find the trousers, they should come over to the news board and either draw some trousers or write their names.

2. Check the news board, posterboard or chart tablet and make certain children have a chance to find Little Bear's trousers.

3. At circle time, play a recording of some music and have the children close their eyes while one child, assisted by the aide if needed, hides the trousers.

4. When the music stops, have the children search for the trousers. Restart the music and have the children listen until the music stops, then search again.

5. The finders add their names to the news board.

**Something to think about—**
Make certain that children who are often last and feel less confident find the trousers and have their names on the news board. At the circle time before the musical search, let them tell where they found the trousers.

STORY STRETCHER

## For Sand Table: Building And Decorating Sand Castles

**What the children will learn—**
To use a variety of tools to shape and decorate sand castles

**Materials you will need—**
Sand table, sand, buckets, assorted equipment, as spades, scoops, and improvised tools from cut-ups of plastic bottles, shells or rocks, feathers, construction paper, popsicle sticks, water

**What to do—**
1. Open LITTLE BEAR'S TROUSERS to the terrific illustration of Duck building sand castles

and decorating them with shells, feathers and paper flags.

2. Occasionally, comment on the children's building, and if needed, ask what could help the sand mold better — add a sprinkle of water.

**Something to think about—**
Sand, water, carpentry and construction activities seldom need any teacher assistance. The children enjoy the physical activity while they are internalizing the sensorimotor meanings of weight, volume and capacity and are problem solving by selecting tools for making the shapes they desire.

## REFERENCES

Brett, Jan. (1987). **GOLDILOCKS AND THE THREE BEARS.** New York. Dodd, Mead & Company.

Butler, Dorothy. (1988). Illustrations by Elizabeth Fuller. **MY BROWN BEAR BARNEY.** New York: Greenwillow Books.

Freeman, Don. (1978). **A POCKET FOR CORDUROY.** New York: Puffin Books.

Hissey, Jane. (1987). **LITTLE BEAR'S TROUSERS.** New York: Philomel Books.

McPhail, David. (1990). **LOST!** Boston: Little, Brown and Company.

### Additional References For Teddy Bears And Other Bears

Carlstrom, Nancy White. (1990). Illustrated by Bruce Degen. **IT'S ABOUT TIME, JESSE BEAR AND OTHER RHYMES.** New York: Macmillan. *From early morning to bedtime, Jesse's activities are told in rhyme.*

Goldstein, Bobbye S. (1989). Illustrated by William Pène du Bois. **BEAR IN MIND: A Book Of Bear Poems.** New York: Viking Kestrel. *Bears for all seasons, reasons and rhymes—an illustrated collection of poems, ballads, limericks and rhymes about bears.*

Hissey, Jane. (1986). **OLD BEAR.** New York: Philomel Books. *A group of toy animals tries various ways of rescuing old bear from the attic.*

Nims, Bonnie Larkin. (1989). Illustrated by Madelaine Gill. **WHERE IS THE BEAR AT SCHOOL?** Niles, IL: Albert Whitman & Company. *Rhyming text asks the reader to find, with increasing degrees of difficulty, the hidden bear in each scene.*

Wildsmith, Brian. (1985). **THE LAZY BEAR.** New York: Oxford University Press. *The story of a bear and his adventure rolling down the hill in a wagon.*

# CLASSICS

*Blueberries for Sal*
*Madeline*
*Make Way for Ducklings*
*The Tale of Peter Rabbit*
*Mike Mulligan and His Steam Shovel*

## BLUEBERRIES FOR SAL

### *By Robert McCloskey*

*This Caldecott Honor book, first published in 1948, tells the parallel story of Sal and her mother looking for blueberries on one side of Blueberry Hill, while Little Bear and her mother are out blueberry picking on the other side. Delightfully simple plot with deliciously simple suspense, McCloskey tells a good story that makes the child want to know what is on the next page, whether looking at the illustrations or listening intently during a read-aloud session. The line drawings with no color include realistic landscapes with enough detail to add interest, perspective and contrast.*

## Circle Time Presentation

If some of your children know this book already, ask them to keep the surprise to themselves, then at the end they can talk about the book. Show the cover of the book and point out the Caldecott Honor Medal. Discuss that the medal is given because the illustrations are well done and help to tell the story. Ask the children where they think Sal gets her blueberries. Talk about where they get their blueberries. Read BLUEBERRIES FOR SAL and use a suspenseful voice as the intrigue continues. After completing the book, announce all the Story S-t-r-e-t-c-h-e-r-s for the day. Have the children guess what their snack will be and tell them that they can bake blueberry muffins.

STORY STRETCHER

## For Cooking And Snack Time: Comparing Blueberry Flavors

**What the children will learn—**
To distinguish between the tastes of fresh blueberries, blueberries that have been frozen and canned blueberries

**Materials you will need—**
Fresh, frozen and canned blueberries, large and small bowls, large serving spoons, teaspoons, napkins, cartons or glasses of milk

**What to do—**
1. Ask the cooking and snack helpers for the day to help you prepare the snack.

2. Place fresh blueberries in a bowl on the table.

3. Have the children serve themselves and taste the fresh blueberries.

4. Then place the frozen and canned blueberries on the table.

Have the children compare how the berries look, then taste them.

5. Let the children decide which they prefer.

**Something to think about—**
On another day serve blueberry jam or blueberry pie.

ANOTHER STORY STRETCHER

## For Cooking And Snack Time: Blueberry Muffins

**What the children will learn—**
To read a rebus recipe for making blueberry muffins

**Materials you will need—**
Chart tablet or posterboard, marker, blueberry muffin mix, egg, water, mixing bowl, measuring cup, wooden spoon, muffin tin, oven mit, toaster oven, bread baskets, napkins, cartons of milk, glasses

**What to do—**
1. Print the recipe for blueberry muffins on a chart tablet or posterboard. Use a combination of symbols and words. For example, when the next step is mixing the ingredients, draw a mixing bowl and spoon. (See the appendix for a sample rebus symbol chart.)

2. Divide the class into two groups, as it will probably take two packages of the mix to make enough muffins for everyone.

3. Assign some children to measure, others to mix and some to serve the muffins. Mix and cook the muffins.

4. Place napkins in bread baskets.

5. Empty the muffins into the bread baskets and place on the snack tables.

6. Serve the muffins warm with a cold glass or carton of milk.

**Something to think about—**
If possible, ask a parent or community volunteer to come to the classroom and make the muffins from scratch.

STORY STRETCHER

### For Library Corner: "Blueberries For Sal" Tape

**What the children will learn—**
To listen with anticipation of the next events

**Materials you will need—**
Cassette tape recorder, tape, listening station, headphones

**What to do—**
1. Read BLUEBERRIES FOR SAL with a small group of children listening as you read and record.

2. Let the children introduce the book and give the page turning directions. For example, a child might say, "This is the book we heard in circle time. It is about a little girl and her mother who get a surprise."

3. For the page turning directions, a child might say, "Turn the pages of this book until you see the picture of the car and the little girl holding her mother's hand. When you hear my hands clap, turn the page."

4. Read the story, cuing the children for the hand-claps.

5. At the end of the tape, tell the listeners that if they want to hear more, turn the tape over.

6. Record the children retelling BLUEBERRIES FOR SAL by taking turns looking at the pictures and telling the story.

7. Remember to record the page-turning signals.

**Something to think about—**
For younger children, stop with reading the book. For older children, let them decide on another adventure for Little Bear and Mother Bear when they smell blueberry pies cooking.

STORY STRETCHER

### For Mathematics And Manipulatives: Counting "Kerplinks"

**What the children will learn—**
To associate the sound with another object to be counted

**Materials you will need—**
Fresh blueberries, metal container or mixing bowl, other objects to drop and count

**What to do—**
1. Read the part of the story where Mother knew whether or not Sal was eating blueberries by the sound they made in the bucket.

2. Have the children place their hands over their eyes. Drop fresh blueberries into the metal bowl and listen for the "kerplinks." Tell them to count the "kerplinks" they hear.

3. Let each child drop at least five fresh blueberries in the bowl while the other children hide their eyes. Continue the counting. As the bottom of the metal mixing bowl or container is covered the sound will change.

4. After the children have counted the "kerplinks," then, of course, they get to eat their blueberries.

5. Drop other objects into the metal containers and think of sound words you can count for them. Metal washers might make a "kerscratch," nuts might sound like "kerplunk," apples might sound "kerthud."

**Something to think about—**
Give children interesting objects to count in interesting ways and they will practice making the one-to-one associations necessary for understanding numeration.

STORY STRETCHER

### For Music And Movement: "Here We Go Round The Blueberry Bush"

**What the children will learn—**
To sing new words to a tune they already know

**Materials you will need—**
None needed

**What to do—**
1. At the second group time of the day, sing the song, "Here We Go Round the Mulberry Bush."

2. Tell the children that since you read BLUEBERRIES FOR SAL today that you want to write some new words for the song.

3. Sing, "Here We Go Round the Blueberry Bush."

*Here we go round the blueberry bush,*
*the blueberry bush,*
*the blueberry bush.*
*Here we go round the blueberry bush,*
*so early in the morning.*

4. Ask the children to help you think of other verses that fit the story. Some examples are: "Here we climb up blueberry hill," "Here we go eating the blueberries up," "Here we go running down blueberry hill," "Here we go baking some blueberry muffins," and so on.

**Something to think about—**
Another traditional song that could be used is "Ring Around the Roses."

159

## MADELINE

*By Ludwig Bemelmans*

*MADELINE has been delighting young listeners since 1939. Set in Paris, Madeline lives in a boarding school with Miss Clavel and eleven other girls who do everything together. Until, that is, one night Madeline has to be rushed to the hospital and have her appendix out. When the little girls visit Madeline in the hospital, they notice the toys, candy and doll house from Madeline's papa. That night each girl starts crying to have her appendix out. Bemelmans incorporates famous street scenes of Paris in his black line drawings with a few simple color washes.*

## Circle Time Presentation

Look at the cover of MADELINE and tell the children that this is a drawing of the Eiffel Tower. Count the little girls on the cover. Read MADELINE and let the discussion follow naturally to when children in your classroom were in the hospital. Let them talk about what it was like. If other children have visited in hospitals, ask them to tell about their experiences. Announce that you will need some special helpers during free play to set up a special creative dramatics center, a hospital.

STORY STRETCHER

## For Art: Comparing Paris Scenes

**What the children will learn—**
To match scenes from postcards and photographs to illustrations in MADELINE

**Materials you will need—**
Postcards, photographs or slides of famous Paris scenes

**What to do—**
1. With the children who choose the art center during free play or center time, scatter the cards and photographs out on the art table.

2. Tell the children the names of the places, such as the Eiffel Tower, Notre Dame, Gardens at the Luxembourg, the Tuileries facing the Louvre. If you have visited there, talk about your experiences. If you have not, discuss that this is a place you would like to visit, and tell the children whose cards and photographs these are.

3. With the children, look through Bemelmans' illustrations in MADELINE and try to match the cards and photographs to the pictures in the book.

**Something to think about—**
Ask a librarian to help you select some good picture reference books on Paris and place these in the art center for the children to look at, then move them to the library corner.

ANOTHER STORY STRETCHER

## For Art: Making Get Well Cards

**What the children will learn—**
To design a get well card

**Materials you will need—**
Construction paper, scraps of brightly colored construction paper or scraps of gift wrap, scissors, glue, bits of ribbon, crayons, colored pencils

**What to do—**
1. Talk with the children about when people are sick it makes them feel better to receive a card from a friend.

2. Ask the children to fold their construction paper in half. Let them decide whether they want their card to open horizontally or vertically.

3. On the front of the card, the children can cut and glue pieces of the brightly colored paper in any design they like, or they can draw and illustrate a happy picture.

4. Let the children write their message inside the card. They can write the message on their own, or you write their get well wishes.

**Something to think about—**
If you have a child or staff member who is ill, send the cards to him or her. If not, save the cards for a time when one of the children is ill and send the cards then.

## For Creative Dramatics: Our Friend's In The Hospital

**What the children will learn—**
To role play the medical helpers, family and patient

**Materials you will need—**
Bed, table, telephone, TV, blankets, white coats, stethoscope, tongue depressor, syringe, tissues, note pads, pencils, bag

**What to do—**

**1.** Collect the props from around the classroom and from parents who may be in the medical profession.

**2.** Provide an area for the children to arrange the furniture and the props. Let them improvise with boxes for tables and other pieces.

**3.** When the children have their area arranged, become their first patient and complain of a cold.

**4.** After a few minutes, dismiss yourself from the play and let the players proceed without you.

**Something to think about—**
It is often difficult to assess when an adult should interject himself or herself into the play setting. If you are eager to help a particular child with social skills, do not hesitate to become one of the players. At other times, you may be needed to change the direction of the play or to stimulate some new inventive approach to problem solving.

## For Library Corner: We Miss Madeline

**What the children will learn—**
To retell the story in their own words while looking at the illustrations

**Materials you will need—**
Cassette tape, recorder, listening station, headphones, glass, fork

**What to do—**

**1.** With the children who choose the library corner during center time, read MADELINE again.

**2.** After you have read the book, encourage the children to tell the story in their own words.

**3.** Tape the storytelling and change the title to "We Miss Madeline."

**4.** Remember to plan a page-turning signal for the children who will listen at the listening station. Gently tapping a glass with a fork is a good signal.

**Something to think about—**
Ask a person who is French or someone who can read with a French accent to read MADELINE to the children. Tape record their reading and have it on the other side of the tape.

(Idea adapted from Brenda Dareff-Brown.)

## For Music And Movement: Skating With Madeline And Friends

**What the children will learn—**
To glide across the floor in time with the music

**Materials you will need—**
Tape or record of waltz music, cassette or record player

**What to do—**

**1.** Collect the children together on the circle time rug and have them take off their shoes.

**2.** Start the recording of the waltz music and have the children sit in place and sway their bodies back and forth until they feel the rhythm.

**3.** Then slowly begin to make skating motions across the floor.

**4.** Ask a few children to join you, and then as you skate by, invite a few more until all the children are skating.

**Something to think about—**
If you have some children who are reluctant to join in, encourage them but do not insist.

## 12

## CLASSICS

## MAKE WAY FOR DUCKLINGS

*By Robert McCloskey*

*This Caldecott Award book was first published in 1941 and has become a childhood classic for each new generation of young children. The mallard family, tired from their search for a home, settle in the city where they have a pond and food and are free from other animals that like to trap baby ducks. While their new home in the city has other perils, remarkably, the city adjusts. Clancy, the policeman, even stops traffic for them to cross the street. In sepia chalk drawings with effective shading and shadows, McCloskey succeeds in bringing the mallard family adventure to life on the page even without the advantage of other colors.*

## Circle Time Presentation

Talk with the children about what a classic means, that this book has been enjoyed by boys and girls for a long time. It is a book their mothers and fathers and even some of their grandparents read when they were children. When you show the cover, some of the children will already know the book. Ask them to listen and after the reading, they can talk about their favorite pictures. Read MAKE WAY FOR DUCK-LINGS. Pause on the page where Clancy first spots the mallard family, and let the children predict what will happened next. At the end of the book, ask the children to tell what surprised them, what happened that was unexpected. Remind the children that the book and a special tape will be in the library corner for them to hear the story again.

STORY STRETCHER

## For Art: Ducks In Unexpected Places

**What the children will learn—** To plan and draw a picture with ducks in an unexpected location

**Materials you will need—** Construction paper or manilla paper, choice of media — charcoals, crayons, colored pencils

**What to do—**
1. With the children who come to the art center during free play, talk about how the story of the mallards is really a story of the ducks finding themselves in a place that does not expect to see ducks.

2. Let the children brainstorm some other places we do not expect to see ducks, at school, at home, at church, in department stores, etc.

3. Ask the children to draw any location they would like where ducks are unexpected, but put at least one duck in their picture.

4. Display the "Ducks in Unexpected Places" prints for all the children to enjoy.

**Something to think about—** These prints could be the basis for a series of stories. You could expand the art and story theme by thinking of other animals found in unexpected places.

STORY STRETCHER

## For Library Corner: Stories Of Ducks In Unexpected Places

**What the children will learn—** To compose a story to go with their artistic compositions

**Materials you will need—** Typing paper and pencil or pen or computer and printer

**What to do—**
1. Invite the children who made the drawings of the "Ducks in Unexpected Places" to come individually to the writing center in the library corner to write a story to accompany their pictures.

2. Invite the children to write their own stories. Some can compose their stories using invented spellings. Invite children at all levels of writing to write, even if they are at the scribble stage.

3. When the children have finished their writing, tell the children that you want to remember their stories, even after they have taken them home for their parents to see. To remember the stories, you may want to type them into the computer and then print them.

4. Let the child dictate his or her reading of their writing. Type it and print it. Make two copies so

that the child can take one copy home with the story.

**Something to think about—**
Children need to construct written language and have teachers accept and encourage those constructions. Similarly, they need to see spoken language becoming written language with their teacher modeling writing using pencil, pen, markers and the computer, as well.

## For Library Corner: Clancy Tells Make Way For Ducklings

**What the children will learn—**
To listen to a variation of MAKE WAY FOR DUCKLINGS

**Materials you will need—**
Storyteller, police officer's costume, cassette tape, recorder, listening station, headphones

**What to do—**
1. For the second group time of the day, invite a man to come to the classroom and tell MAKE WAY FOR DUCKLINGS from his perspective.

2. Let the pretend officer dress in a blue uniform, or just a police officer's hat will convey the idea.

3. Tape record "Clancy's" telling of the story as a reverse side of the tape where you read MAKE WAY FOR DUCKLINGS.

4. After "Clancy" tells the story, hopefully with an Irish accent, tell the children that the tape will be in the library corner at the listening station for them to hear again and again.

**Something to think about—**
If you cannot find a "Clancy" storyteller, then don the police officer's hat yourself and become "Clancy."

## For Music And Movement: Duck Family Waddle

**What the children will learn—**
To follow directions in family groups

**Materials you will need—**
None needed

**What to do—**
1. Group the children into duck families. Designate at random who the mother and father ducks are and which children are their baby ducks.

2. Have the baby ducks sit in a circle around mother and father duck.

3. Tell the mother ducks to quack. Then the circle opens up and mother duck lines up her baby ducks, and father duck brings up the rear.

4. Have the children practice their duck waddles by squatting down, tucking their hands under their armpits and then walking.

5. Give the duck families instructions by saying, "Melinda Mallard and your ducks waddle over to the pond."

6. Let the classroom aide be Clancy and stop the traffic for the ducks to pass.

7. Keep each family waddling in different directions, then bring them back to the circle time rug as their safe place on the island.

**Something to think about—**
For younger children have fewer baby ducks in the family. Let older children role play all the people the mallard family met in the city.

## For Science And Nature: Where Do Mallard Ducks Usually Live?

**What the children will learn—**
To describe the habitat where ducks usually live

**Materials you will need—**
Reference books on waterfowl, wheat straw, corn, duck decoy

**What to do—**
1. If possible, visit a wetlands bird sanctuary.

2. Secure reference books on waterfowl with illustrations or photographs.

3. Display the books at the science and nature table and ask the children to help you decide what else could be displayed on the table which would remind them of the habitat that the mallards need.

4. The children will suggest many items, but be certain they talk about places for shelter and a nest, a food source and a water source.

5. Arrange the items the children and you collect. They might include straw and other long grasses, grains of wheat and corn, and a container of water.

6. If some of the parents or grandparents have bird decoys, add those to the displays.

**Something to think about—**
Contact a craft center or senior citizens center and invite someone who paints bird decoys to bring in a mallard for the children to see.

## THE TALE OF PETER RABBIT

*By Beatrix Potter*

*Impetuous Peter Rabbit goes to Mr. McGregor's garden against his mother's command, while Flopsy, Mopsy and Cotton-tail picked blackberries like good little rabbits. Nibbling too much lettuce, carrots, radishes and French beans, Peter began to feel sick and searched for some parsley, but found Mr. McGregor instead. The chase ensued and Peter lost his shoes and his jacket. Peter hid in the tool shed in a watering can where he caught a terrible cold. Peter's family was dreadfully worried when he didn't come home. Finally Peter escaped, lost his way trying to get home and had to return to the garden to find his way through the gate home. A classic tale with classic illustrations, Peter Rabbit is still spell binding after over eighty years in publication.*

## Circle Time Presentation

Invite the children who have copies of THE TALE OF PETER RABBIT to bring their books for other children to see. Read the classic version of the tale and place all the different copies in the library corner, and let the children see how they differ. Before reading THE TALE OF PETER RABBIT, tell the children that this is the story of a rabbit family — the mother, Flopsy, Mopsy, Cottontail and Peter. Tell them that from the title of the story they know that Peter will be the main character. Read the story and let the children tell you the parts of the story where they were afraid for Peter, and the parts when they knew he would be all right. Announce the Peter Rabbit activities for the day.

STORY STRETCHER

## For Art: Little Pictures For Little Books

**What the children will learn—**
To draw on a smaller scale

**Materials you will need—**
Palm-sized copy of THE TALE OF PETER RABBIT, sheets of typing or computer paper, scissors, crayons, colored pencils, stapler, hole-punch, yarn

**What to do—**
1. Show the children the palm-sized edition of THE TALE OF PETER RABBIT, and explain that when the author and illustrator Beatrix Potter wrote the books in 1902, she had them published as little books or palm-sized books which would just fit into a child's hand.

2. Have the children hold the book and see how it fits in their hands.

3. Tell the children that you would like them to make some palm-sized illustrations of a story they would like to write about themselves and their stuffed animal or another adventure for Peter Rabbit.

4. Show the children how to fold the sheet of paper twice so that it has four sections.

5. Have them draw with colored pencils or crayons four pictures for their adventure.

6. Cut the pictures apart by cutting along the folds.

7. Staple the pages together and make a cover, or punch holes in the pages and tie them together by lacing yarn through the holes.

**Something to think about—**
Teach children to bind books in a variety of ways. Encourage older children to write longer stories by using two pages with sets of eight drawings.

STORY STRETCHER

## For Cooking And Snack Time: Peter Rabbit's Salad

**What the children will learn—**
To prepare fresh vegetables for a salad

**Materials you will need—**
Lettuce, carrots, radishes, French beans or green beans, parsley, colander, vegetable peeler, paring knife, paper towels, salad plates or bowls, masking tape, marker, napkins, forks

**What to do—**
1. Let each child prepare his or her own salad.

2. Have the cooking and snack time helpers set up the vegetables, wash the lettuce and place it into the colander to drain.

3. Place the salads in an area where they will be out of the way

until all the children have theirs prepared. Make a label from a strip of masking tape and print the child's name on the label to identify their salads.

4.  Eat Peter Rabbit's Salads at snack time.

**Something to think about—**
If possible, have a few children go with the teacher's aide or the center director or school principal to shop for the vegetables for Peter Rabbit's Salad.

STORY STRETCHER

## For Housekeeping And Dress-up Corner: Dressing The Toy Animals

**What the children will learn—**
To put baby clothes on the toy animals

**Materials you will need—**
Peter Rabbit and other stuffed animals, various baby and toddler clothes

**What to do—**
1.  Place Peter Rabbit with a coat on in the housekeeping and dress-up corner.

2.  Help the children sort through all the dress-up and doll clothes and find clothes that will fit the stuffed animals.

3.  Encourage the children to dress as many animals as they can and share the toys with boys and girls who would like to hold them during the read aloud story time.

**Something to think about—**
Encourage children who seldom go to the housekeeping and dress-up corner to get involved in dressing Peter and his friends. If boys in your class are reluctant to participate, talk with them about how fathers help their children get dressed in the morning.

STORY STRETCHER

## For Library Corner: Taping Peter's Adventure

**What the children will learn—**
To compose phrases that are commentaries on the story

**Materials you will need—**
Tape recorder, cassette tape, listening station, headphones

**What to do—**
1.  Read the story to the children, pause after each page and ask them to say a word or two that pops into their minds. For example, a child might say in response to the first page where Peter and his family are seen in the sandbank under the fir tree, "Oh, they're cute."

2.  Practice for a few pages, letting the children take turns as the commentators.

3.  Compose some directions for the listeners so that they know where the story begins.

4.  Tape record yourself reading the story and the children's comments which are used as the page turning signal.

**Something to think about—**
All of the books in a classic unit should be taped in their original versions as well as these creative variations so that the children can hear the well-loved stories again and again.

STORY STRETCHER

## For Music And Movement: Peter Rabbit, Where Are You?

**What the children will learn—**
To listen for clues for the whereabouts of Peter

**Materials you will need—**
Stuffed toy rabbit, tape or recording of instrumental music, tape or record player

**What to do—**
1.  While the children are outside for play, hide Peter Rabbit but leave his ears sticking out.

2.  Collect the children on the circle time rug and give them the directions for finding Peter.

3.  Tell them that you have hidden Peter in an area of the classroom where Marcy and Danielle and Ti like to play, but they can not go searching for Peter until the music starts, and when the music stops, they must stop. If someone finds Peter, you will stop the music, and they should return to the circle time rug.

4.  Start the music and let the children start their search. Because Peter's ears are visible, someone will find him quickly and bring him to you. Stop the music and have the children return to the rug.

5.  Let the person who found Peter be the one to hide him. Start the music and tell the children to keep their eyes closed until the music stops. When Peter is safely hidden, stop the music and give a clue to Peter's whereabouts. Perhaps he is in a center of the classroom where Phillipe, David and Rebecca like to play. Start the music again and the children can search again.

6.  Continue the process of hiding to the music, giving clues, searching to the music, finding Peter and returning to the circle time rug.

**Something to think about—**
Older children can give their own clues. The classroom aide can help the younger children find good hiding places, leaving the tips of Peter's ears in sight.

## MIKE MULLIGAN AND HIS STEAM SHOVEL

*By Virginia Lee Burton*

*Put out of work by more modern machines in the big city, Mike Mulligan and Mary Anne the steam shovel take on the challenge of digging a new city hall for the little town of Popperville. Mike brags that they can dig as much in a day as a hundred men can dig in a week, and told the man in charge that if they didn't finish the job in a day, the city wouldn't have to pay. Mike and Mary Anne always dig faster when people are watching, so a little boy gathered up all the townspeople to watch. They dug the cellar in just one day, but they had no way out. Mary Anne the steam shovel became Mary Anne the furnace for the new town hall, and Mike Mulligan just took care of Mary Anne. In a comical style, Burton has the reader cheering for Mike and Mary Anne, while giving credit to the little boy who saved the day with his good ideas.*

## Circle Time Presentation

Show the cover of MIKE MULLIGAN AND HIS STEAM SHOVEL. Ask the children what they think the machine on the front of the book can do. Encourage them to brainstorm and accept any answers they provide. Read the story and pause at main action scenes for the children to predict what they think will happen next. At the end of the story, add the word "furnace" to the list of things Mary Anne, the steam shovel, can do.

STORY STRETCHER

## For Blocks: Building The Popperville Town Hall

**What the children will learn—**
To build a sturdy foundation

**Materials you will need—**
Large hollow blocks

**What to do—**

1.   Brainstorm with the children in the block center that the town hall must be one of the sturdiest buildings in town because that's where all the important records and papers are kept.

2.   Ask the children how they can build so that their buildings will not topple over.

3.   Have the children build their structures and decide how to test them.

4.   Help the children to surmise that a sturdy foundation is needed. One way to build a sturdy foundation is to make certain the blocks are lying flat and to line the inside of the foundation row with a second row of blocks that do not break in exactly the same places.

5.   Let the children build their sturdy town hall and, if they are interested, extend the building to all of Popperville.

**Something to think about—**
When young children are asked to brainstorm ideas, many of them will need to show their ideas with actual blocks.  Older children may be able to tell their ideas, but may lack the ability to compare a number of ideas at the same time.

ANOTHER STORY STRETCHER

## For Blocks: Construction Toys

**What the children will learn—**
To use the pulleys and variety of loading and unloading devices

**Materials you will need—**
Construction toys — cement mixers, road graders, dump trucks, flat bed trucks, pick-up trucks and a steam shovel

**What to do—**

1.   Collect the toys from a variety of sources, other classrooms in your building, parents, garage sales.

2.   Bring the construction toys in and place them in the block building area.

3.   Devise ways that children other than the usual block builders play with the construction toys.

4.   After several days of playing with the toys, have the children who played with the vehicles offer to show the other class members how the pulleys, tows and other loading and unloading devices work.

**Something to think about—**
Normally, it is best to allow young children to make their own choices of centers; however, it is often hard for some children who are not assertive to get into the most popular centers.  One means to increase availability is to require that each child visit at least two centers per day, or if you have a long free play period, require three centers per

day. Avoid brief play periods and rotating every fifteen minutes or so because the children do not have time to develop the levels of play needed for vocabulary expansion and for creative improvisations with the equipment and the roles.

## For Library Corner: Puffing Through With Mike And Mary Anne

**What the children will learn—**
To sustain their taping responsibilities for a long story

**Materials you will need—**
Cassette tape and recorder, listening station, headphones

**What to do—**
1. With the children, decide on a page turning signal that would be appropriate for MIKE MULLIGAN AND HIS STEAM SHOVEL. Younger children might simply say "Puff" at your cue; however, they can say each "Puff" with an inflection that is appropriate for the story.

2. In the beginning, have the children say "Puff" in a boastful bragging voice.

3. In the middle of the story where Mary Anne is being replaced by more modern machines, say "Puff" in a sad voice.

4. Near the end, say "Puff, Puff, Puff, Puff, Puff" to indicate how hard and fast Mary Anne is working.

5. At the very end, say "P-u-f-f" in a tired and relieved voice.

6. Without reading the whole story, practice the different voice inflections.

7. Make the tape and signal the cues to the children by your facial expressions, or print the words on large index cards in a way that indicates their inflections. For example, for the boastful, bragging inflection, print "PUFF" in large letters. For the sad inflection, print "puff" in small letters with tear drops dripping down. For the hard and fast working inflection, print "Puff, Puff, Puff, Puff" leaning forward with steam coming out of the line. For the tired and relieved inflection, print "P-u-f-f" with the letters low and spread out and the "f" trailing off.

**Something to think about—**
While most classic children's books are available on commercial tapes, hearing a familiar voice read often brings more listeners to the listening station. If you have a male teacher or staff member in your center or school, ask him to read MIKE MULLIGAN AND HIS STEAM SHOVEL. Also, invite as many fathers to make cassette tapes of books as you do women, so that little boys know that reading is something men enjoy as well.

## For Mathematics And Manipulatives: Comparing Building Materials

**What the children will learn—**
To compare continuous materials by weight

**Materials you will need—**
Large plastic containers or dishpans, balance scales, scoops, gravel, pebbles, sand, crushed stone

**What to do—**
1. Set the materials out in the mathematics and manipulatives area.

2. Pose some thought-provoking questions for the children, such as, "How much of the gravel is needed to equal the same amount of sand?" "How many scoops of pebbles equal half a container of gravel?" "Do dry sand and wet sand weigh the same amount?"

3. The children will think of other interesting questions for themselves. Try to get them to verbalize their equations, even if it is as simple as, "Look, this much sand in here and this much gravel in here makes it even" (meaning balanced or weighing the same).

**Something to think about—**
All ages of children will enjoy getting their hands into the materials and feeling the weights. Encourage them to use their hands and arms as natural balancing scales. Fill one hand with sand and the other with pebbles and decide which is heavier.

## For Sand And Water Table: Digging Like A Steam Shovel

**What the children will learn—**
To operate a toy steam shovel

**Materials you will need—**
Sand table, soil or sand, water, watering can, steam shovel and other construction toys

**What to do—**
1. With the children's assistance, fill the table with soil or sand. This can be an outside or inside activity.

2. Sprinkle the material with water to keep the dust down.

3. Place the steam shovel or some form of earth mover in the sand table.

4. Have the diggers dig a cellar. In the process, they will discover that they need some timbers to keep the wall from caving in. Let them decide how to reinforce the walls of the cellar.

**5.** As the digging progresses, let them add construction toys and trucks to move the dirt that Mary Anne is excavating.

**Something to think about—**
Whenever possible, let the children problem solve for themselves. For example, if the children come to you with the complaint that the walls keep caving in on their cellar, let the children decide several possible solutions. They could wet the soil and tap it into place, use blocks as timbers, use cardboard, or assign someone to hold the soil in place.

## REFERENCES

Bemelmans, Ludwig. (1939). **MADELINE.** New York: Puffin Books.

Burton, Virginia Lee. (1939). **MIKE MULLIGAN AND HIS STEAM SHOVEL.** Boston: Houghton Mifflin Company.

McCloskey, Robert. (1948). **BLUEBERRIES FOR SAL.** New York: Puffin Books.

McCloskey, Robert. (1941). **MAKE WAY FOR DUCKLINGS.** New York: Puffin Books.

Potter, Beatrix. (1902). **THE TALE OF PETER RABBIT.** New York: Frederick Warne & Co., Inc.

### Additional References For Classic Children's Stories

Galdone, Paul. (1973). **THE LITTLE RED HEN.** New York: Clarion. *Little Red Hen invites her friends to help grow wheat but finds she must do everything herself. But when she bakes the bread from the wheat, all of her friends want to eat the bread until Little Red Hen reminds them of who did all the work.*

Minarik, Else. (1957). Illustrated by Maurice Sendak. **LITTLE BEAR.** New York: Harper & Row. *Four delightful stories about Little Bear and his wishes and adventures.*

Steig, William. (1969). **SYLVESTER AND THE MAGIC PEBBLE.** New York: Simon and Schuster Books for Young Readers. *Sylvester, the donkey, found a magic pebble which could grant his wishes. When he meets a scary lion, Sylvester wishes he could become a rock and he does, but now he has no way to hold his magic pebble to return himself to being a donkey.*

Zimmermann, H. Werner. (1989). **HENNY PENNY.** New York: Scholastic. *The classic alarmist tale of Henny Penny and her barnyard friends who met Foxy Loxy on their way to tell the King the sky is falling.*

Young, Ed. (1989). **LON PO PO: A RED-RIDING HOOD STORY FROM CHINA.** New York: Philomel. *Three sisters staying home alone are endangered by a hungry wolf who is disguised as their grandmother.*

# 13

# COUNTING

*The Right Number of Elephants*
*This Old Man*
*One Cow Moo Moo*
*One Hungry Monster*
*Rooster's Off to See the World*

## THE RIGHT NUMBER
## OF ELEPHANTS

*By Jeff Sheppard*

*Illustrated by Felicia Bond*

*A little girl imagines hilarious situations where different numbers of elephants from 10 down to 1 might be helpful. Nine elephants could help to paint the ceiling; eight are enough to provide shade at the beach; five are enough to impress the neighbors with a circus; one is enough for a special friend. Felicia Bond's full-page illustrations are just the right number for this whimsical, imaginative tale.*

## Circle Time Presentation

In addition to the humor of THE RIGHT NUMBER OF ELEPHANTS, the main idea is to count, associate numerals with the quantity they represent, count from ten down to one and to play imaginatively with numbers. Have the children hold up ten fingers and count with you from one to ten, then from ten to one. Tell the children this is a counting story. Show the children the cover of the book and ask them what they think the little girl will count. Read THE RIGHT NUMBER OF ELEPHANTS. Immediately, the children will ask you to read the book again because they want to see the funny pictures. Announce that you will be making a listening tape of the book and that they can hear and see the book in the library corner.

STORY STRETCHER
## For Art: Hidden Parts

**What the children will learn—**
To use humor in their drawings

**Materials you will need—**
Manilla paper, crayons, colored pencils or markers

**What to do—**
1. Have the children look at Felicia Bond's illustrations and notice the body parts of the elephants which are seen in the pictures. For example, in the first scene, there are five elephants' trunks hanging from the tree. In the second scene, just a bit of elephants' ears are seen through the window.

2. Ask the children to draw a picture of themselves doing something they like to do, then add parts of an elephant to their picture.

3. When the children have completed their drawings, ask them to tell you what will happen next.

Write down what they say on a sheet of paper and attach it to the bottom of their picture. End their dictation by printing the directions, "Look on the other side of this picture."

4. Then ask the children to draw what will happen next on the opposite side of their first drawing.

**Something to think about—**
Older children may enjoy working with partners and drawing and writing an entire book together.

STORY STRETCHER
## For Block Building: How Many Are Enough Blocks?

**What the children will learn—**
To estimate the quantity of blocks needed to build a building, then to count them

**Materials you will need—**
Several containers of small building blocks, index cards or scraps of paper, marker

**What to do—**
1. Pour out a container of small building blocks and ask a child to show you how many she or he thinks will be needed to build a small house, a two-story house, a tall building.

2. Ask the children to build the buildings, then after they are built, to come and get you.

3. When the buildings are completed, count the blocks with the children. Leave the buildings intact, and print on an index card or a scrap of paper the numeral that represents the number of blocks used.

4. Display the block buildings for the day and the next day assign different buildings using the same process of asking, "How many blocks are enough?"

**Something to think about—**
Younger children need not know how to count to be able to do this activity. Children in the pre-number stage can show you by putting their hands and arms around a pile of blocks that they think are enough to build their buildings.

S T O R Y   S T R E T C H E R

## For Library Corner: Listening Station — "The Right Number Of Elephants"

**What the children will learn—**
To complete the phrase and use the numerals as page turning signals

**Materials you will need—**
Cassette tape, recorder, headphones

**What to do—**
1. With a small group of children who choose the library corner, make a recording of THE RIGHT NUMBER OF ELEPHANTS.

2. Direct the listeners to turn to the picture of a little boy looking at smoke coming from a tunnel.

3. Practice reading the book with the group, letting the children say the numerals on cue.

4. On the opposite side of the tape, record the story and instead of just having the children say the numeral, record them counting the number of elephants. A child could say, "On this page, I see one, two, three, four, five, six elephants. Six."

**Something to think about—**
Humorous books are excellent choices for the listening station. The children enjoy sharing the funny illustrations.

S T O R Y   S T R E T C H E R

## For Mathematics And Manipulatives: How Many Are Enough?

**What the children will learn—**
To count using one-to-one correspondence

**Materials you will need—**
Chairs, coats, hats, dolls or stuffed animals, crayons or other items from around the classroom

**What to do—**
1. Ask five children to stand. Place five chairs in a row andas you are placing them one at a time ask, "Do we have enough chairs?"

2. Use the same process with coats or hats, then dolls or stuffed animals. Use a variety of items throughout the classroom.

3. Help the children see that to determine if there are enough items we need to match the person to the item and see them one-to-one.

4. Change the number of children and let the other participants go around the room collecting enough items to match the new number of children.

**Something to think about—**
Count throughout the day in this one-to-one correspondence way. Ask, "How many are enough?" Emphasize the quantity, rather than the numeral names.

S T O R Y   S T R E T C H E R

## For Music And Movement: Counting Elephants Backwards

**What the children will learn—**
To count, chant and move on cue

**Materials you will need—**
Posterboard or chart tablet, ten large index cards or sheets of paper, marker

**What to do—**
1. Print the words to the chant on posterboard or chart tablet. Write the numerals on the index cards, one numeral per chart.

2. Read the chant "One Elephant is Enough Fun" through from beginning to end with the children counting with you and you reading the rhyming verses.

*10, 9, 8, 7, 6, 5, 4, 3, 2, 1*
*One, elephant is lots of fun*
*10, 9, 8, 7, 6, 5, 4, 3, 2*
*Two, elephants that might do*
*10, 9, 8, 7, 6, 5, 4, 3,*
*Three, elephants just for me*
*10, 9, 8, 7, 6, 5, 4,*
*Four, elephants bring some more*
*10, 9, 8, 7, 6, 5,*
*Five, elephants too many to hide*
*10, 9, 8, 7, 6,*
*Six, elephants what a fix*
*10, 9, 8, 7,*
*Seven, elephants oh my heavens!*
*10, 9, 8,*
*Eight, elephants the parade can wait*
*10, 9*
*Nine elephants more than fine*
*10*
*Ten elephants, let's begin again.*
*10, 9, 8, 7, 6, 5, 4, 3, 2, 1!*
*One elephant is enough FUN!*
    *(Raines, 1991).*

3. Have ten children stand up to be the elephants and give them the index cards from ten to one.

4. Assist the children in arranging themselves according to the numeral printed on their card in descending order from ten to one.

5. Chant the counting rhyme again and as the number is said in the counting line, the child holds up her number card. As the child's rhyme is said, he sits down. At the end when the counting starts over again, the children stand up.

**Something to think about—**
Younger children can count from one to five. Older children can make up large numbers and rhymes to go with them.

## THIS OLD MAN

### By Carol Jones

*The traditional nursery rhyme is illustrated with modern non-traditional interpretations. A grandfather and a little girl play together, build together, picnic together, and in every scene the grandfather has his drum sticks pounding out the beat of the rhyme. The dog is present in each scene to accompany the phrase, "give a dog a bone." Half dollar-sized circles are cut into facing pages to offer a peek at the part of the illustration that finishes the rhyme.*

## Circle Time Presentation

Show the cover of THIS OLD MAN and ask the children who they think these people are on the cover. Ask the children for some of their grandfathers' names. Read THIS OLD MAN, then read it again substituting a grandfather's name. For example, instead of reading, "This old man," say, "Grandfather Fred." Make a list of ten grandfathers' names, read the book again and this time for each scene use a different grandfather's name.

STORY STRETCHER
### For Art: Circle Pictures

**What the children will learn—**
To layout their illustrations so that a key part is shown in the circle

**Materials you will need—**
Half dollar or item of similar size, pencil, scissors, colored construction paper and manilla paper of the same size, crayons or markers or colored pencils

**What to do—**
1. On a sheet of brightly colored construction paper, let the children draw around a half dollar. Cut out the circle.

2. Show the children the illustrations in THIS OLD MAN, pointing out how Carol Jones showed a key part of the story through the cut-out circle placed on top of the next page.

3. Ask the children to draw a picture that includes either a numeral or a number of objects. For example in THIS OLD MAN, the illustrator used the circle to show the numeral 4 on the door of a playhouse.

4. Demonstrate how to place the construction paper with the circle hole over the drawing paper. En-courage the children to lightly draw around the hole so they do not have to keep repositioning the paper over the hole.

**Something to think about—**
Younger children can draw their pictures, point to a part of the picture they want to emphasize, as their faces, and you can cut a circle to place over that part.

STORY STRETCHER
### For Cooking And Snack Time: Honey For Our Bread

**What the children will learn—**
To spread honey on bread

**Materials you will need—**
Honey, margarine or peanut butter, bread, teaspoons, knives, wet sponges, napkins, glasses, milk

**What to do—**
1. Place several containers of honey on the snack tables.

2. Talk with the children about the illustrations where the grandfather goes to the beehive and the little girl watches at a distance. Also show the picture of grandfather and the little girl eating honey.

3. Show the children how to spread the honey onto the bread. Place one slice of bread down flat on the table. Place a teaspoon or serving of honey in the middle of the bread. Spread with a knife with one hand while holding the bread gently in place with the other.

4. Optional — let the children spread another slice of bread with margarine, butter or peanut butter to make a sandwich.

5. Serve with a glass of cold milk.

**Something to think about—**
Buy coarse bread that does not tear easily. If the honey is very thick, have some warm water in a bowl and place the knives in the warm

water before the children spread the honey. Younger children can squeeze honey from plastic squeeze bottles.

## For Library Corner: Grandfather's Reading

**What the children will learn—**
To enjoy the attention and reading voice of an older adult

**Materials you will need—**
Adult-sized chair, optional — tape recorder and cassette tape

**What to do—**
1. Invite several grandparents to come to your class and read to the children.

2. Ask a grandfather to come to class on the day that THIS OLD MAN is the featured book.

3. Let the children sit with the grandfather two or three at a time and hear the book read. If the grandparent is willing, tape record him reading to the children.

**Something to think about—**
It is important that children have reading role models. Plan for grandparents, parents, older brothers and sisters and staff members from around the center or school, such as custodians, secretaries and cafeteria workers to come to the classroom.

## For Mathematics And Manipulatives: Magnetic Board, Numbers In Rhyme

**What the children will learn—**
To associate number words and numerals

**Materials you will need—**
Magnetic board, magnetized plastic numerals, cassette recorder, tape and player

**What to do—**
1. Tape record yourself reading THIS OLD MAN or tape record a grandfather reading the book. Record directions at the beginning of the tape, which tell the listener to play the tape, look at the book and stop the tape after each number word is read and place that numeral on the magnetic board. Then, turn the tape on again.

2. Place the tape, book, magnetic board and numerals in the mathematics and manipulatives area.

3. Encourage two children to work together. One will be the page turner and the other is the magnetic board worker.

**Something to think about—**
The children will be accustomed to seeing the cassette tape player in the library area and not in the mathematics and manipulatives area. If possible, have two tape recorders so that one can be stationed permanently in the library and the other can circulate between mathematics and manipulatives and other areas of the classroom.

## For Music And Movement: Sing "This Old Man"

**What the children will learn—**
To sing the song and do the motions

**Materials you will need—**
Posterboard or chart tablet, marker

**What to do—**
1. Print the words to "This Old Man" on posterboard or chart tablet to add to the class collection of songs.

2. Say each verse, then sing each verse with the children joining you. Make sure the children know the refrain, "With a nick, nack...."

3. Sing the song and teach the motions as you go.

4. On other days, use the grandfathers' names instead of "This Old Man."

**Something to think about—**
Young children can learn even this long song because it has many repeated lines, includes rhyming words and number words which help them recall what comes next. Sing the song at least twice during the first day and then each day during the counting unit.

## ONE COW MOO MOO

*By David Bennett*

*Illustrated by Andy Cooke*

*A little boy watches as one cow starts a stampede of animals running by and making their noises. The cumulative pattern of adding more animals for each scene heightens the drama of why the animals are running by. The surprise ending sets the boy off running to join the animals. Andy Cooke's cartoon style illustrations match the funny, excitement-building text.*

## Circle Time Presentation

Show the children the cover of ONE COW MOO MOO and ask them if this is a true story or an imaginary one. Have the children count with you from one to ten, then ask them to put up the right number of fingers for the counting rhyme. Read ONE COW MOO MOO and encourage the counting by holding up your fingers as well. The surprise ending of ONE COW MOO MOO is sure to bring some giggles. Read the story again and have the children join in by saying the repeated phrases and rhyming words. At the end have them look at the size of the monster on the last page and compare it to the size of the cow on the cover of the book.

STORY STRETCHER

## For Art: Funny Divided Pictures

**What the children will learn—**
To use a cartooning technique

**Materials you will need—**
Two sheets of paper per child, tape, choice of drawing instruments — pencils, markers, crayons

**What to do—**

1. Look at Andy Cooke's illustrations in ONE COW MOO MOO. Have the children notice that on some pages the head of the animal is showing and on other pages the tail. Show them how it is really a continuing picture.

2. Place two sheets of paper side by side and tape them together on the back.

3. Sketch a simple animal so that it covers both sides of the page.

4. Untape the two sheets of paper so the children can see how illustrators of cartoons make divided animals.

5. Encourage the children to draw their favorite animals from ONE COW MOO MOO or to draw their own pets or zoo animals.

**Something to think about—**
Older children might try illustrating a whole book with divided pictures to show action. Younger children can dictate a sentence that explains what is happening or a sentence to explain how they made the picture. For the mathematical concept, emphasize that this is a whole animal divided into parts.

STORY STRETCHER

## For Library Corner: Flannel Board Counting Story

**What the children will learn—**
To retell the story in order

**Materials you will need—**
Flannel board, flannel board pieces for cow, horse, donkey, pig, hen, goose, sheep, dog, cat, mouse, monster

**What to do—**

1. Construct the flannel board pieces of the animals and numerals by using felt or paper. For paper construction, draw animals on paper, cut them out, cover with contact paper and glue a small piece of sandpaper to the back of the pictures to make them stick to the flannel board. Do not make ten mice, nine cats, etc., but instead make numerals to represent the number of animals.

2. Read ONE COW MOO MOO and place the pieces onto the flannel board.

3. Distribute the animals and numerals at random among the children.

4. Read the story again and let the children add the pieces as their animal is first read and when their numeral is read. At the end where

all the animals are repeated, have the children remove the flannel board pieces, leaving the monster.

**Something to think about—**
Younger children can tell the story using five animals. Older children could make zoo animals or circus animals for a story retelling exercise.

STORY STRETCHER

## For Mathematics And Manipulatives: Number Puzzles

**What the children will learn—**
To match numerals and number words

**Materials you will need—**
Tagboard or posterboard, markers, scissors

**What to do—**
1.   Involve the children in making the puzzles by having them cut tagboard or posterboard into eight pieces.

2.   On the left side of the piece write a numeral. On the right side, write the corresponding number word.

3.   Draw a puzzle shape line down the space between numeral and word and cut in two pieces along the line. Make a different shaped line for each number puzzle.

4.   Have the children reassemble the pieces matching the numerals and words.

**Something to think about—**
For younger children, instead of using the number word, make circles for the numeral. For example, the numeral four would be on one side of the puzzle piece and four large circles or balloons would be on the other side. You might also make a puzzle by drawing the number of animals from ONE

COW MOO MOO instead of just making circles.

STORY STRETCHER

## For Sand Table: Writing Numerals In The Sand

**What the children will learn—**
To practice forming the numerals

**Materials you will need—**
Sand table with sand or large plastic tubs with sand, tongue depressor or wooden stick, watering can

**What to do—**
1.   Show the children how to sprinkle the sand with water so that it is wet enough to write in.

2.   Let the children write their initials and names in the sand.

3.   Have the children practice writing the numerals from one to ten in the wet sand.

4.   Read ONE COW MOO  MOO and as you read ask the children to form the numerals in the sand when they hear the number word read.

**Something to think about—**
The experience of writing in the sand is a strong sensory activity and helps the children retain the numeral form better. For younger children, model writing the numeral and have them copy yours. For older children, write numerals above ten and use the number words printed on paper for them to read and then write the numeral in the sand.

(Adapted from Milissa Earl's classroom.)

STORY STRETCHER

## For Science And Nature: Animal Sounds

**What the children will learn—**
To identify real animal sounds

**Materials you will need—**
Battery operated cassette tape recorder, cassette tape, pictures of real animals, index cards or posterboard, clear contact paper or laminating film

**What to do—**
1.   Contact a naturalist with a park service, or a county agent with the agricultural service, or if you live in a farming community, ask a parent for assistance.

2.   Explain that you want your students to be able to recognize real animal noises.

3.   Have the animal caretaker record many animals making their natural sounds. Record the tape again onto a blank tape, add directions for the children to listen to the animal sounds, then place the animal pictures in order of the sound they hear.

4.   Collect pictures of real animals from calendars and magazines. Cut them out and glue onto large index cards or pieces of posterboard. Cover with clear contact paper or laminating film.

5.   Make a display in the science and nature center of the real life animal pictures, the tape player and tape.

6.   Have the children listen to the tape and place the pictures in the same order as the animal sounds they hear on tape.

7.   On the opposite side of the tape, record the answers.

**Something to think about—**
This is an excellent parent project. One parent might record the animal sounds and another parent who has good recording equipment can re-record the tape, editing the sounds and fitting in your directions.

## ONE HUNGRY MONSTER:
## A Counting Book In Rhyme

*By Susan Heyboer O'Keefe*

*Illustrated by Lynn Munsinger*

*A bewildered little boy has a problem, feeding ten hungry monsters and getting them out of his house. Lynn Munsinger's hairy monsters with horns on their noses work their way through the little boy's house, devouring everything in sight. As the number of monsters increase, their antics get funnier. Finally, the little boy takes control and orders them out of his house, while managing to save an apple-sauce muffin for his midnight snack. The hilarious illustrations and text are wonderfully suited to each other.*

## Circle Time Presentation

Ask the children to tell the times when they are very hungry, as when they wake up in the morning, snack time at school, when they get home, dinner time. Tell the children that sometimes you get very hungry at night when you remember something delicious in the refrigerator. Your stomach starts to "growl" and you feel like a hungry monster. Read ONE HUNGRY MONSTER. This book is so entertaining that the children will ask you to read it again. At the second reading, pause for the children to enjoy several of the hilarious pictures like the spaghetti wigs and monsters hanging from the chandelier.

### STORY STRETCHER
## For Art: Playdough Hungry Monsters

**What the children will learn—**
To shape three-dimensional forms

**Materials you will need—**
Playdough or clay

**What to do—**

**1.** Have the children who choose the art area look again at Lynn Munsinger's funny monsters.

**2.** Ask the children to sculpt some funny monsters of their own.

**3.** Display the funny hungry monsters as centerpieces for the snack table.

**4.** Since the emphasis of this unit is counting, be sure to count the number of hungry monsters on the snack tables.

**Something to think about—**
Often teachers hesitate to show children pictures, as the Munsinger monster's, because they are afraid the children will copy rather than design their own. However, from our experience, the children are inspired by seeing other artists' work. They incorporate some of the features, then branch out on their own.

### STORY STRETCHER
## For Cooking And Snack Time: Applesauce Muffins

**What the children will learn—**
To follow directions in a simple recipe

**Materials you will need—**
Toaster oven or microwave, packaged muffin mix, muffin tin, optional paper liners, mixing bowl, eggs, water, shortening, posterboard or chart tablet, marker, glasses, milk

**What to do—**

**1.** Print the recipe on posterboard or chart tablet which can become a part of the Class Recipe Book. Use rebus symbols for directions. For example, where the recipe on the back of the muffin mix calls for two eggs, draw two eggs and show one breaking open over a mixing bowl. (See a sample rebus chart in the appendix.)

**2.** Have the children who come to the cooking area during choice time prepare the muffins.

**3.** Bake the muffins according to the directions on the package box.

**4.** Serve the muffins warm with a glass of cold milk.

**5.** Count the muffins and emphasize one-to-one correspondence. One muffin per one napkin, one napkin per one glass of milk, one serving per child.

**Something to think about—**
If one package will not serve the entire class, prepare one package ahead of time and warm the muffins in the microwave or oven before serving at snack time. This is also an excellent activity to in-

volve a parent who may prepare muffins from a favorite recipe, rather than the packaged variety.

## For Housekeeping And Dress-up Corner: A Monster Clean-up Job

**What the children will learn—**
To clean and arrange the housekeeping and dress-up area

**Materials you will need—**
Usual appliances, utensils, clothing found in this area

**What to do—**
1.   Discuss with the children that when the hungry monsters left the little boy's house, it was really a mess.  Tell them that while there haven't been monsters in the classroom, the housekeeping and dress-up area needs straightening up because it has been used so much and is out of order.

2.   Let them decide among themselves who will arrange the dishes and utensils in the kitchen, who will straighten up the clothes, who will set the table, who will dust, sweep, mop.

3.   Divide the clean-up into as many people as there are participants.

4.   Stay close by and encourage the cleaners.  Try singing a favorite song which they know so well that they can sing while they work.

**Something to think about—**
This clean-up activity can be used for the entire class instead of just the housekeeping and dress-up area.  For younger children, try playing a tape of a familiar song with the goal that the area will be tidied by the end of the tape.  For older children, have a class meeting and plan some rearrangements that will make the classroom easier to clean.

## For Library Corner: Flannel Board Of Ten Hungry Monsters

**What the children will learn—**
To retell the story in number sequence

**Materials you will need—**
Flannel board, felt pieces of boy, ten monsters, muffin

**What to do—**
1.   Construct the flannel board and pieces of felt.

2.   Give ten children the monster felt pieces and whisper in each child's ear which number her monster is.

3.   Read the story and as the children's monsters are read, they place their monster on the flannel board.

4.   Near the end of the story when the little boy orders the monsters out of the house, have the children remove their monsters by counting backwards.  Monster ten leaves first, followed by monster nine, and so on.

**Something to think about—**
Consider making a tape recording of the book and leave the book, cassette tape and flannel board pieces out and available in the library corner for the entire week.

## For Library Corner: Listening Tape, Monster Rhyme

**What the children will learn—**
To complete the rhyme

**Materials you will need—**
Cassette tape and recorder, glass, fork

**What to do—**
1.   With the children who chose the library corner during free play or choice time, read ONE HUNGRY MONSTER again.

2.   Tell the children that this is such a popular book that you want to make a tape recording of it.  Let one child be the page signal turner by gently tapping a fork against a glass.

3.   Have the other children finish the rhyme whenever you pause in the reading.

4.   Tape record yourself reading, the children saying the rhyming words and the page turning signal of tapping the glass.

5.   Let the children listen to the tape and decide if they want to tape it again.

**Something to think about—**
Try to involve children who show little interest in books in the taping sessions.  They will probably visit the library more often and look at the books they have helped to tape record.

## ROOSTER'S OFF TO SEE THE WORLD

### By Eric Carle

*Eric Carle spins another delightful tale which is as enticing visually as it is dramatically. One rooster in his vibrantly colored plumage decides to take a trip around the world and invites two cats, three frogs, four turtles and five fish to join him. Their adventure ends at nightfall when they are tired and hungry and then in reverse order, the five fish, four turtles, three frogs and two cats leave the one rooster all alone. Young children will enjoy counting the characters in the illustrations and in the small insets at the corners of each set of pages. The bold collage and paint illustrations are distinctively Carle's. In usual Carle fashion, the end paper pages for the inside cover of the book are also decorated. Small black prints of the animal shapes march one after the other in lines down the page.*

## Circle Time Presentation

The large illustrations in ROOSTER'S OFF TO SEE THE WORLD make it a terrific circle time book. Introduce the book by asking the children what time of the day they think it is by looking at the picture of Rooster and the sun. Show them the end paper pages and name the animals they see. Tell them all these characters are in the book, but there are more of some of the animals than of others. Read ROOSTER'S OFF TO SEE THE WORLD. After the reading, have the children tell how many animals joined Rooster and how many left Rooster.

### STORY STRETCHER

## For Art: Torn Paper Collage Animals

**What the children will learn—**
To make collages of scraps of construction paper

**Materials you will need—**
Scraps of brightly colored construction paper and whole sheets of white and blue construction paper, crayons or markers, glue

**What to do—**

1.   Have the children select characters from the story and draw on a sheet of construction paper very large outlines of the one rooster, or the two cats, or the three frogs, or the four turtles or the five fish. If they select the fish, they can draw five large fish on the blue construction paper.

2.   Show the children Eric Carle's illustrations and how they are composed of many little pieces.

3.   Demonstrate how to tear the construction paper scraps and glue them on. Have them fill in their outlines with torn paper to make the collages.

**Something to think about—**
For younger children, pre-cut the shapes, and they can tear the scraps of paper and glue them on. For older children, vary the activity by using colored tissue paper, or have them add dapples of paint onto their finished collages to create more texture, like Carle's illustrations.

### STORY STRETCHER

## For Creative Dramatics: Stick Puppet Play Of Rooster's Trip

**What the children will learn—**
To listen for their cues of when to have their animals appear

**Materials you will need—**
Construction paper, stapler, posterboard, artboard or paper plates, tape, long straws or tongue depressors

**What to do—**

1.   Let the children make their own stick puppets by attaching their art collages onto tongue depressors.

2.   Staple the collage onto a backing of posterboard, tagboard or a paper plate to reinforce it. Place small pieces of tape over the staples to make it more secure when the stick puppet is held up.

3.   Then staple the whole puppet into place on a stick, a tongue depressor or a long straw. Cover the staples on both sides with tape to make it even more secure.

4.   Read the book, ROOSTER'S OFF TO SEE THE WORLD, and let the children have their stick puppets appear on cue and move them when the puppets are speaking.

**Something to think about—**
Create a stage for the puppets by placing a spring action curtain rod across a door opening. Hang a cur-

tain from the rod and the children can use the door opening as their stage. Another easy stage is to turn a table on its side and the puppeteers sit behind the table. Then when their character appears, they use the edge of the table for their stage.

## For Library Center: Flannel Board Story Of Rooster's Trip

**What the children will learn—**
To retell the story in sequence

**Materials you will need—**
Flannel board, felt pieces of sun, moon, rooster, two cats, three frogs, four turtles, five fish

**What to do—**
1. After having read the book at the first circle time of the day, during center time use the flannel board and pieces with a small group of children to tell the story of ROOSTER'S OFF TO SEE THE WORLD.

2. Let the children hold the felt pieces and as their characters are mentioned, add the pieces to the flannel board. Then, when the moon comes out and the animals and fish leave, let the children take the flannel board pieces off the board.

3. Tell the story a second time without reading it from the book and let the children add their pieces.

4. Leave the flannel board, felt pieces and book in the library center for the children to retell the story on their own or with friends.

**Something to think about—**
If you do not have felt, make the flannel board pieces of brightly colored construction paper scraps. Glue the pieces onto posterboard or tagboard to make them sturdier.

Attach a piece of sandpaper to the back of the flannel board characters and they will stick to the flannel better.

## For Mathematics And Manipulatives: Counting Rooster's Travelers

**What the children will learn—**
To practice counting to five forward and backward

**Materials you will need—**
Colored wooden blocks in red, black, green, brown and blue or sheets of construction paper in red, black, green, brown and blue that have been taped around the blocks

**What to do—**
1. Tell the children the blocks represent the characters in ROOSTER'S OFF TO SEE THE WORLD. Have one red block to represent rooster, two black blocks to represent the cats, three green blocks to represent the frogs, four brown blocks to represent the turtles and five blue blocks to represent the fish.

2. Retell the story using the blocks to represent the animals, but instead of saying the number each time, as three green frogs, have the children count, "1-2-3 green frogs."

3. When the animals are leaving, let the children count backward and say, "3-2-1-0 green frogs."

4. Continue the activity by mixing up the blocks on the table so that they are not in any order.

5. Let the children retell the story on their own, counting blocks and sequencing the story.

**Something to think about—**
For younger children, use the flannel board pieces from the library center activity listed above to count and tell the story. Use a sheet of construction paper to cover the felt animal pieces, then uncover one at time for the children to count, "1-2-3-4 brown turtles." Older children may enjoy adding characters as six spotted dogs or seven baby hamsters. Let them think of ways they can decorate the blocks to remember the characters.

## For Music And Movement: Mister Rooster's Chant

**What the children will learn—**
To retell the story in song form

**Materials you will need—**
Chart tablet or posterboard and marker

**What to do—**
1. Print the words listed below on chart tablet or posterboard.

2. Chant the words by alternating clapping your hands and slapping your knees, a beat a syllable. Add an extra beat at the end of each line.

3. Let the children do the clapping and get the beat while you read the chant through from beginning to end.

4. Have the children practice a verse at a time, then put all the verses together for the entire chant.

*Mister Rooster said,*
*"I'm off to see the world,*
*Won't you come with me?"*
*Two cats said, "Yes,*
*We will come with you.*
*We're off to see the world.*
*But Rooster, what will we do?" (long pause)*

*Once upon a time,*
*Mister Rooster said,*
*"I'm off to see the world,*

Won't you come with me?"
Three little frogs said, "Yes,
We will come with you.
We're off to see the world,
But Rooster, what will we do?"
    (long pause)

Once upon a time,
Mister Rooster said,
"I'm off to see the world,
Won't you come with me?"
Four little turtles said, "Yes,
We will come with you.
We're off to see the world,
But Rooster, what will we do?"
    (long pause)

Once upon a time,
Mister Rooster said,
"I'm off to see the world,
Won't you come with me?"
Five little fishes said, "Yes,
We will come with you.
We're off to see the world,
What will we do?"  (long pause)

Then it got dark (speak dramatically in
    a loud whisper)
and all the animals said,
We're off to see our home.
We're sleepy and tired and want to be
    fed.
So the five little fishes
swam away,
and the four little turtles
crawled home,
the three little frogs
jumped away,
and the two cats
ran home too.
So now, what was the Rooster to do?
    (long pause)

He just went back home too.
But when he slept he dreamed
A beautiful dream about
A trip around the world.
A trip, a trip, a trip,
A trip around the world.
A trip, a trip, a trip,
A trip around the world! (clap, clap).
    (Chant written by Raines.)

**Something to think about—**
Teachers who are not musically inclined are often more comfortable
chanting than singing. There is no
right tune for the chants, simply
say them to the beat, and you will
find yourself singing-saying the
words.

# REFERENCES

Bennett, David. (1990). Illustrated by Andy Cooke. **ONE COW MOO MOO.** New York: Henry Holt & Co.

Carle, Eric. (1972). **ROOSTER'S OFF TO SEE THE WORLD.** Saxon-ville, MA: Picture Book Studio.

Jones, Carol. (1990). **THIS OLD MAN.** Boston: Houghton Mifflin Company.

O'Keefe, Susan Heyboer. (1989). Illustrated by Lynn Munsinger. **ONE HUNGRY MONSTER: A Counting Book In Rhyme.** Boston: Little, Brown and Company.

Sheppard, Jeff. (1990). Illustrated by Felicia Bond. **THE RIGHT NUMBER OF ELEPHANTS.** New York: Harper & Row.

## Additional References For Counting

Bucknall, Caroline. (1985). **ONE BEAR ALL ALONE.** New York: Dial Books for Young Readers. *A counting book from one to ten told in rhyme with teddy bears joining each other for a day of fun.*

de Brunhoff, Laurent. (1986). **BABAR'S COUNTING BOOK.** New York: Random House. *Babar's three children go for a walk and count what they see.*

Ehlert, Lois. (1990). **FISH EYES: A Book You Can Count On.** San Diego: Harcourt Brace Jovanovich. *A counting book depicting the colorful fish a child might be if he turned into a fish himself.*

Giganti, Paul, Jr. (1988). Illustrated by Donald Crews. **HOW MANY SNAILS? A Counting Book.** New York: Greenwillow Books. *A young child takes walks to different places and wonders about the number and variety of things seen on the way.*

Scott, Ann Herbert. (1990). Illustrated by Lynn Sweat. **ONE GOOD HORSE.** New York: Greenwillow Books. *While a cowboy and his son check the cattle, they count the things they see.*

# 14

# COLORS

*Color Dance*
*Mouse Paint*
*Alice's Blue Cloth*
*Harold and the Purple Crayon*
*The Mixed-up Chameleon*

## COLOR DANCE

*By Ann Jonas*

*Three girls, each dressed in different colored leotards, red, yellow and blue, dance with large scarves of the same colors. As they dance, their scarves overlap and the secondary colors are formed. At the end of their dance, a boy enters with a large white scarf to make colors pale, a large gray scarf to make the colors dark and a large black scarf to make the colors almost disappear. The color words in the text are also printed in their corresponding colors. A color wheel is included at the end of the book for the teacher's reference. Ann Jonas' beautiful illustrations depict the children's agile movements. The text and illustrations combine as a celebration dance, a ballet of color.*

## Circle Time Presentation

Wear a sweater or shirt of one of the primary colors. Sing the song which begins with, "Mary wore a red dress, red dress, red dress. Mary wore a red dress all day long." Sing a few variations using the children's names and their colors of clothing. Show the cover of COLOR DANCE and ask what words the children would use if they sang about the girls on the cover. Point to the picture of each dancer and sing, "This girl wore a blue leotard, blue leotard, blue leotard. This girl wore a blue leotard all day long." Read the story and let the children savor the pictures throughout. End the circle time presentation by announcing the many color mixing activities planned for the day.

S T O R Y   S T R E T C H E R
### For Art: Tempera Paint Mix

**What the children will learn—**
To mix primary colors to make secondary colors

**Materials you will need—**
Tempera paints of the primary colors, paint containers such as baby food jars, coffee stirrers, paintbrushes, meat trays from the supermarket or plastic or paper plates, white paper

**What to do—**
**1.** Working at the table in the art center, have the children first paint a brush stroke of the two primary colors you have chosen for the day, such as red and blue.

**2.** Allow the children to experiment by mixing two primary colors. Assist by showing them how much paint is needed to notice the subtle changes.

**3.** Have the children continue mixing until they have a color that is close to the one on the color wheel, then paint a brush stroke of the color onto a sheet of white paper.

**4.** Retain their brush stroke papers to use the following day to add more primary and secondary colors.

**Something to think about—**
If possible, display a color wheel from a paint store. Let the children experiment with the color combinations and make their own color wheels.

S T O R Y   S T R E T C H E R
### For Cooking And Snack Time: Decorating With Food Coloring

**What the children will learn—**
To mix food coloring to make a variety of new colors

**Materials you will need—**
Two or three packages of food coloring depending on how many children will be at the snack table at once, small plates or bowls, cake icing, graham crackers, small plastic knives

**What to do—**
**1.** Discuss with the children that the tops of the food coloring bottles indicate the color inside, not the color of the liquid which looks almost black.

**2.** Using only the selected primary colors for the day, as blue and red, demonstrate how to mix the colors a drop at a time into the white cake icing and then stirring.

**3.** Let each child place a small amount of icing into his bowl, then mix the colors.

**4.** Have the children spread a small amount of icing onto their graham crackers for snack time.

**Something to think about—**
Encourage the children's experimentation rather than exact color mixing.

## For Housekeeping And Dress-up Corner: Dressing In Primary Colors

**What the children will learn—**
To sort by shades of primary colors

**Materials you will need—**
Clothing from the dress-up center, three large paper grocery bags, strips of primary colored construction paper, full-length mirror, scissors, stapler

**What to do—**
1.   With two or three children helping, sort through the dress-up center clothing and choose those pieces that are mostly red, yellow or blue.  Place the remainder of the clothing in storage for a few days.

2.   Have the helpers cut a large strip of construction paper about four inches wide.  Let them staple the blue strip around the top of one grocery bag, a yellow strip around the top of the second bag and a red strip around the top of another bag.

3.   Show the helpers how to sort the dress-up clothing by colors.  After they have practiced, replace the clothing back in the housekeeping area and have other children come over and sort through the clothes.

4.   Have three children dress in the primary colors.  Ask one child to put on all red, one all blue, and one all yellow clothes.

5.   After the children dress up in their primary colors, let the three of them go around to other children in the classroom and find colors of toys and blocks that match their clothing.

**Something to think about—**
In addition to the color matching, this activity also provides younger children more practice with buttons, zippers, and ties.  Consider placing baby clothes in the area and letting the children dress their stuffed animals and dolls in the primary colored baby clothes.

## For Mathematics And Manipulatives: Matching Red, Yellow, Blue

**What the children will learn—**
To select objects by their color names or match by colors

**Materials you will need—**
A large plastic mixing bowl, smaller plastic containers of the primary colors, objects of primary colors from around the classroom, as wooden cubes, crayons, toys, puzzle pieces

**What to do—**
1.   With two or three helpers, let the children make a collection of small objects in the primary colors from around the classroom.

2.   In a table in or near the mathematics and manipulatives materials, place the objects the children collected in a large mixing bowl.  Then let the helpers sort the objects by color into the appropriate smaller containers. (If you do not have plastic containers in the primary colors, tape blue, red and yellow construction paper around the base of any colored container.)

3.   Continue the process by having two or three other children come to the area, and as you tell them a color name, have them find objects to place in the bowl of the same color.

**Something to think about—**
Teachers often do too much for children.  For example, the teacher in this activity may be tempted to go around the classroom and collect the objects without the children assisting; however, getting the children involved in setting up an activity is a valuable learning experience.

## For Music And Movement: Color Dancing With Scarves

**What the children will learn—**
To observe colors as their scarves overlap and to move in time with the music

**Materials you will need—**
Recording of a waltz, tape or record player, large colored scarves in the primary colors

**What to do—**
1.   Have the children sit around the edge of the circle time rug.

2.   Begin the tape or record of the music and let the children move their bodies back and forth in a swaying motion until they get a sense of the tempo.

3.   Bring out the large scarves and let three children dance with them around the room, while the other children continue moving by swaying their bodies in a standing position.

4.   Change the dancers often.

5.   After the dancing is finished, overlap the scarves on the floor and let the children see the changes in the colors.

**Something to think about—**
Younger  children will need a smaller group.  Older children may enjoy forming partnerships and seeing how they can move to make a variety of colors by overlapping the scarves as they move.

## MOUSE PAINT

### By Ellen Stoll Walsh

*Three delightful white mice climb into three jars of paint, red, yellow and blue. When they climb out, they leave puddles of paint, which when stirred, stepped in and danced through to produce lovely orange, green and purple. After their fun, they rinse off in the cat's bowl of water. They finish the adventure by painting paper in the primary and secondary colors, but they leave a little strip of white so they can hide from the cat with their white fur against the white paper. Ellen Stoll Walsh's cut paper collage illustrations are simple, clever and amusing. Young children will delight in the mice's antics and in their color discoveries.*

## Circle Time Presentation

The illustrations in MOUSE PAINT are bold enough to be seen easily by the whole group and dramatic enough to entice story reading from the pictures alone. Present the story first as a wordless picture book and let the children tell you what they think is happening. Then, read the book to confirm their story telling. Announce the color mixing activities planned for the day, but suggest the children look out for the color mice who might jump into their paints.

STORY STRETCHER

## For Art: Fur Fabric Printing

**What the children will learn—**
To make textured prints

**Materials you will need—**
Primary colors of tempera paints, margarine tubs, paper, swatches of fur fabric or pieces of terry toweling can be used, newspaper

**What to do—**

**1.** Cover the table with newspaper to make clean-up easier and to give children a surface to experiment on before making their prints.

**2.** Let the children assist filling margarine tubs with paints.

**3.** Show the children how to hold the swatch of fur fabric by the backing, load the paint onto the fur and press onto the paper to make a "pebbly textured" print.

**4.** Encourage experimentation with mixing colors.

**5.** Let the children wash out the fabric, just as the mice washed themselves in the cat's bowl.

**Something to think about—**
During the first day of the printing, the children will be enjoy experimenting with color mixing like the mice; however, encourage a variety of different textures by squeezing the fabric into different forms and using various amounts of paint. Also try the reverse — dropping paint onto the paper, then going over it with dry pieces of fabric to pick up some of the paint, leaving still a different texture.

STORY STRETCHER

## For Library Corner: Listening By Color

**What the children will learn—**
To associate color words with color cards

**Materials you will need—**
Cassette tape, tape player, stapler, scissors, red, yellow, blue, green, orange, purple posterboard or construction paper

**What to do—**

**1.** Record a cassette tape of yourself reading MOUSE PAINT.

**2.** Use the stapler as a "clicker" for the signal to turn the page.

**3.** Cut 3" x 5" cards of the different colors of construction paper or posterboard and distribute the color cards among the listeners.

**4.** As the tape is playing have the listeners hold up the matching color card whenever they hear the color word. For example, when the listener hears "yellow feet," if she has the yellow card, she holds it up.

**Something to think about—**
This activity can be done by individual children with some practice or with as many as six children with each child having one color card. Younger children can also use the book and match the color cards to the pictures of the mice in the book.

## For Mathematics And Manipulatives: How Many Objects Fit On The Paper?

**What the children will learn—**
To arrange objects by the amount of space and to match colors

**Materials you will need—**
Primary and secondary colors of construction paper, an assortment of objects from around the classroom of the same colors

**What to do—**
1. Make a collection of items from around the classroom that are of the primary or secondary colors. For example, puzzle pieces, unifix cubes, wooden counting blocks, toys.

2. Place the items in the center of the table in the mathematics and manipulatives area.

3. Have each child at the table select a sheet of construction paper, then place objects on the paper that match the color of the paper.

4. After each child's paper is filled, have him count the number of items on his paper.

**Something to think about—**
For young children who do not yet know how to count or who can not count as high as the number of objects on the paper, count with them as they remove each item from the paper to the table. Have older children compare whether there are more or fewer objects of each color. For example, are there more or fewer purple items than red ones?

## For Music And Movement: Hiding From The Cat

**What the children will learn—**
To listen for musical cues

**Materials you will need—**
Recording and record or cassette player

**What to do—**
1. Tell the children that they are the little mice who can dance around in their pretend paint puddles while the music is playing, but when they hear the music stop, that is their cue to hide from the cat.

2. Let the children dance long enough to enjoy the music before stopping it.

3. Repeat the process at least five times. Make it a rule that the children must hide in a different place each time.

**Something to think about—**
Let young children say some of the places they will hide when the music stops. For older children, add clues about where the cat is in the room, as on the windowsill, in the teacher's chair or peeking out from under the snack table. Then, in addition to finding a hiding place, they must avoid these areas.

## For Sand Table: Digging For Colors

**Materials you will need—**
Sand table filled with sand or rice, string, tape, six plastic straws, one wooden block of each of these colors, red, yellow, blue, green, orange and purple (or any small objects of these colors), scraps of construction paper in the same colors, small shovels or spades

**What to do—**
1. Have three children assist you. Place two strings across the sand table vertically and one string horizontally, forming six squares.

2. Let the children make construction paper flags by cutting strips of construction paper and taping them to straws.

3. Have one child dig in each "square" of sand and hide one object, one color per square.

4. Ask the "hiders" to have a friend come over and dig for the hidden color treasure. When they find the color, let them stake out the square by placing the colored flag in the sand. They continue digging until all the colored wooden blocks are found.

5. The diggers can now rearrange the color squares by hiding the wooden cubes in different squares of sand. Then they invite other children over.

**Something to think about—**
You may use fewer colors for younger children, and to complicate the task for older children, as many as three objects may be hidden in each square.

## ALICE'S BLUE CLOTH

*By Deborah van der Beek*

*Alice helps her mother bake a cake, but when she lets Tom Tiddler, the cat, get up on the table, her mother sends them both out of the kitchen. Alice entertains herself with a long blue cloth, pretending to be a queen and a knight, then by building a house with the cloth as the roof. She scatters her toys throughout her blue cloth house before she and Tom fall asleep. When they awaken, the blue cloth is gone. It now covers the table on which Alice's mother has placed the cake and the decorations for a birthday party. The illustrations are painted in warm soft colors and Alice's antics with Tom and the blue cloth are delightfully expressive.*

### Circle Time Presentation

If available, have a large bolt of blue cloth or a tablecloth near your chair while reading ALICE'S BLUE CLOTH. Tell the children you are going to pretend to be doing things with the cloth and ask them to guess what your pantomimes are. Wrap the cloth around your shoulders and pretend it is a royal cape, then rub it against your cheek as if it were a cuddly blanket and you were falling asleep, and finally spread it out like a picnic blanket and have some of the children sit around the edges to keep it in place. Have the children guess all the things the little girl on the cover of the book might do with the blue cloth. Then read ALICE'S BLUE CLOTH. After the reading, ask the children to share some other ideas for using the blue cloth. Some of the suggestions might include a cloth for the seashell table, a tent in the library corner for reading under or a curtain for the puppet stage.

STORY STRETCHER
### For Art: Our Blue Creations

**What the children will learn—**
To construct mixed media pictures or sculptures

**Materials you will need—**
Swatches of blue fabric and all available blue art supplies, such as blue tempera paint, blue construction paper, blue watercolor paint, blue poster board, blue playdough, blue markers, crayons, chalk and colored pencils, scissors, glue

**What to do—**
1. With the small group of children who have chosen the art center during free play, collect as many blue art supplies as you can find.

2. Place the collection on a table or a shelf in the art center.

3. Ask the children to cut a small swatch of "Alice's blue cloth" and to make a picture using the piece of cloth and at least three things from the blue art materials collection.

4. Exhibit the blue mixed media designs on bulletin boards and as centerpieces for the snack tables.

**Something to think about—**
It has been said that creative people take the ordinary and use it in extraordinary ways. Mixed media creations allow ordinary materials to be used in extraordinary ways.

STORY STRETCHER
### For Blocks: Houses And Blue Tents

**What the children will learn—**
To build using materials found around the room

**What to do—**
1. With the small group of children who choose the block area, review the way Alice built her pretend house using chairs, cushions, books, toys and her large blue cloth.

2. Ask the children to look around the room and think of materials they could use to construct their blue house.

3. Let the children work without your assistance. Their trial and error attempts are really good thinking, good problem solving.

**Something to think about—**
Creativity is really problem solving by getting an idea, trying it out and making changes that are needed to make the idea work. When parents ask about why you are allowing the children to play

so much, tell them you are working on their problem solving abilities. Building a tent from a blue cloth requires physical reasoning and balance (physics), equivalencies and sense of area (mathematics), cooperation (social problem solving) and even a sense of aesthetics (art).

## For Cooking And Snack Time: Rebus Cake Recipe

**What the children will learn—**
To follow recipe directions

**Materials you will need—**
Chart tablet or posterboard, marker, mixing bowls, measuring cups and spoons, wooden mixing spoon, spatula, cake pans, hand mixer, cake mix and ingredients required as two eggs, milk or water, shortening, icing, toaster oven or microwave

**What to do—**
1. Have small group of children look at the back of the box of the cake mix and find the directions for making the cake.

2. With the children's help, reprint the directions onto chart tablet or posterboard. Let the children draw symbols for the ingredients and some of the actions. For example, two eggs, measuring cup, mixing bowl, cake pan, oven.

3. Follow the directions for baking the cake and let the children take turns with each step. It may take several turns of stirring to mix the ingredients.

4. After the children have seen how difficult it is to mix with the wooden spoons, let them use the hand mixer.

5. Bake the cake.

6. Let other children ice the cake and have another group serve it during snack time.

**Something to think about—**
Try a sprinkling of powdered sugar instead of the very sweet commercially prepared icings which many children do not like.

## For Creative Dramatics: Alice's Blue Fantasies

**What the children will learn—**
To improvise actions with a prop

**Materials you will need—**
Large blue cloth or tablecloth

**What to do—**
1. Recall with a small group of children all the things Alice did with her blue cloth in the story.

2. Brainstorm some other ideas for using the cloth.

3. Let each child have a turn pantomiming with the cloth and the other children can guess what is being acted.

4. After each person has had a turn, let the children who want to remain with the activity continue on their own.

**Something to think about—**
Children who are not yet good at pantomiming for an audience may eagerly play with the prop in the housekeeping and dress-up center. This spontaneous play which occurs when they lose themselves in the roles is often more elaborate and creative than pantomime.

## For Music And Movement: Alice's Exercises

**What the children will learn—**
To gain control of their large leg muscles

**Materials you will need—**
Optional — recording of music with a steady beat, cassette player

**What to do—**
1. Show the children the picture of Alice lying on her back, holding her legs up in the air and walking her feet up the drawers of the kitchen cabinet.

2. Have the children stretch out on the circle time rug, place their legs up in the air and pretend to walk them up the wall.

3. Demonstrate how to do other leg exercises, such as riding a bicycle and scissors movements.

**Something to think about—**
Young children may not have enough control of their large muscles to walk up a pretend wall, so have them place their feet against a real wall and walk their feet up. Older children who are playing soccer can demonstrate leg exercises which they do to strengthen their muscles. Have a good time without forcing children into strenuous exercises. An active curriculum with plenty of time for inside and outside play is the best exercise program.

## HAROLD AND THE PURPLE CRAYON

*By Crockett Johnson*

*In this classic tale first published in 1955, Harold takes his crayon with him on a walk where he proceeds to draw adventures, supplying everything he needs. When he needs more light, he draws a moon to shine on his path. When he wants a walk in a forest, he draws a tree. But occasionally, Harold's drawing has some unexpected results, as the dragon he drew to protect the apples frightens him so that he shakes his crayon and draws a sea. In the end, Harold's purple crayon comes to the rescue and we find him safely tucked in bed.*

## Circle Time Presentation

If possible, wear something purple for this day. Use your name and sing the familiar song, "Mary wore her red dress, red dress, red dress, Mary wore her red dress all day long," but instead sing your name and say you wore your "purple sweater, purple sweater, purple sweater" all day long. Sing the song using any of the children's names who have on purple clothing. Read HAROLD AND THE PURPLE CRAYON. Pause at several intervals where Harold is in trouble and let the children predict what he will draw to escape his peril. For example, pause after he has drawn the "terribly frightening dragon" and let the children predict what he will do next. End the circle time by briefly announcing all the centers that have special color activities for the day.

S T O R Y   S T R E T C H E R

## For Art: Harold's Purple Crayon Mural

**What the children will learn—**
To cooperate in designing a mural to tell another Harold adventure

**Materials you will need—**
Long length of butcher paper, tape, purple crayons

**What to do—**
1. Tape a long sheet of butcher paper in place on a table.

2. Have the children recall the many different scenes in HAROLD AND THE PURPLE CRAYON.

3. Ask them to imagine and then draw what might happen if Harold came to their house.

4. Request that they first draw the scene in purple crayon and then they can add other colors later.

**Something to think about—**
Consider having other purple art days when children can make a variety of purple creations. Spread as many purple art supplies as possible out on the art table in the center. Provide purple construction paper, paint, crayons, playdough, food coloring, markers and ask the children to make something purple in Harold's honor.

A N O T H E R   S T O R Y
S T R E T C H E R

## For Art: Harold The Purple Expert Meets The Mice In Mouse Paint

**What the children will learn—**
To mix blue and red to make purple

**Materials you will need—**
Powdered or liquid tempera paints, white margarine tubs for mixing, popsicle sticks or plastic straws, easel, brushes, paper

**What to do—**
1. Recall with the children what happened in MOUSE PAINT.

2. Ask a child to find the pictures in the book that illustrate how the color purple is made by mixing red and blue.

3. Let the children experiment with their paints without indicating to them that they need more blue than red.

4. As the children mix the paints, discuss with them which color they have more of in their mixtures.

5. After the children have discovered that quantities make a difference, ask them to pretend that they are Harold and that he is the expert on purple. Have them tell the little mice what they need to remember when mixing purple — to use a

little bit of red and a lot of blue to make purple.

6. Let the children use their purple paints to paint at the easel.

**Something to think about—**
Use premixed paints with younger children. Older children can experiment by measuring with a teaspoon and writing a more exact equation, as four teaspoons blue to one teaspoon red.

### For Cooking And Snack Time: Harold's Purple Fruits

**What the children will learn—**
To associate purple with a color that appears in natural foods

**Materials you will need—**
Plums, seedless prunes, purple seedless grapes for eating, prunes and grapes with seeds for demonstration, knife, scissors, purple construction paper, napkins

**What to do—**
1. Place the seedless grapes, seedless prunes and plums in a nice arrangement on the snack tables.

2. Let the children use the scissors to snip off a little bunch of grapes.

3. Call attention to the fact that the purple grapes are seedless.

4. Ask the children to guess whether or not there are seeds in the plums and prunes.

5. Have them eat a plum and leave the seed on their napkin.

6. Ask them to guess whether or not there is a seed in the prune, then eat the prune to decide.

7. Cut open a seedless grape and a grape with seeds and show them the difference.

8. Cut open a seedless prune and a prune with seeds and show them the difference.

9. Discuss that prunes are dried plums.

**Something to think about—**
Whenever possible, emphasize healthy natural snacks. Also, do not force any child to eat something she or he does not want.

### For Creative Dramatics: Role Playing Harold's Adventure

**What the children will learn—**
To improvise movements to tell a story

**Materials you will need—**
None needed

**What to do—**
1. Give a small group of children purple crayons and ask them to pretend to be Harold and draw in the air what they think Harold would draw and act the way they think Harold would act.

2. Read aloud HAROLD AND THE PURPLE CRAYON.

3. Pause waiting expectantly for them to act out and draw the first scene of Harold going for a walk.

4. Continue reading and heighten the drama by reading dramatically and expressively.

5. When the role-players have finished, ask them to act out their favorite scene without saying a word and see if the audience can guess which scene it is.

**Something to think about—**
If you have a video camera, consider video-taping the role-players and let them watch themselves on tape.

### For Library Corner: Writing Our Harold Adventures

**What the children will learn—**
To describe their scenes from the Art activity

**Materials you will need—**
Mural from art center, purple markers and crayons

**What to do—**
1. With the small group of children who select the writing area of the library corner during free play, let each child discuss Harold's coming to his or her house.

2. After the children have improvised their stories, ask them to think of a good sentence or caption for their stories which could be printed right on the mural. For example, Harold finds the refrigerator empty and draws my favorite snacks or Harold finds all my toys on the floor and draws a toy box.

3. Have the children watch you as you print the caption they dictate. Then reread their sentences in a very fluent manner.

**Something to think about—**
Encourage children to write their own sentences, even if they are at the scribble stage. Talk about how we can all tell the differences between writing and drawing and that they should write whatever and however they know to write. Some children will scribble. Others will use letter names or beginning letter and sound associations. Accept whatever level of writing the child brings to the task, just as we accept whatever level of drawing they bring to their artwork.

## 14
## COLORS

## THE MIXED-UP
## CHAMELEON

*By Eric Carle*

*In recognizable Eric Carle style, THE MIXED-UP CHAMELEON is both a literary and artistically appealing story. We selected the book for a colors unit, but it could be used for a unit on positive self-concepts. When he finds himself in a zoo, Chameleon envies all the beautiful colors the animals have and wishes he could be those colors, then he begins to wish he could be like the animals in other ways, such as big like a polar bear, swim like a fish, run like a deer. Each time he wishes, Chameleon magically receives a part of the animal, the deer's antlers, the fish's gills, the flamingo's wings. Growing more absurd looking with each wish, finally Chameleon sees a fly, becomes hungry and wishes he could be himself again. Magically, he becomes Chameleon and is mixed-up no more.*

## Circle Time Presentation

Send home a newsletter telling the parents that Friday is "Favorite Color Day." Ask them to let their children wear their favorite colors to school that day. At the beginning of circle time on "Favorite Color Day," let the children say what they are wearing in their favorite color. If you have some children and parents who forget, have swatches of construction paper in primary and secondary colors ready and pin that swatch to the child's clothing. Discuss with the children that there are little animals called chameleons that camouflage themselves by taking on whatever color they need to hide. Mention that these are real animals, but that this story is about a chameleon who has some magical things happen to him so he is not real. Read THE MIXED-UP CHAMELEON and pause on the page that shows all the zoo animals and let the children describe them by color and prominent features, as the elephant's long trunk, the deer's antlers, the turtle's shell. Because the book is a humorous one, be prepared for children to want you to read the book again. Also call attention to the fact that the book will be available in the library corner and that there is a tape and flannel board story to go with it.

STORY STRETCHER

## For Art: Painted Paper Collage

**What the children will learn—**
To construct a collage in a two-step process

**Materials you will need—**
Fingerpaint paper, primary and secondary colored paints, scissors, white paper, glue

**What to do—**
1.  Have the children who choose the art center during free play look again at Eric Carle's illustrations. Call attention to how the different colors have subtle patterns in them, shading or lines.

2.  Ask the children to select one color of fingerpaint and paint an entire page this color, add a subtle pattern and let the fingerpaint dry.

3.  The next day, ask the children to share their fingerpaint paper and cut different shapes from it to glue onto the white paper and make colorful collages. They can make the funny, mixed-up Chameleon, or they may choose to make zoo animals or other scenes that interest them.

**Something to think about—**
Many of the activities in MORE STORY S-T-R-E-T-C-H-E-R-S: MORE ACTIVITIES TO EXPAND CHILDREN'S FAVORITE BOOKS are written for minimal teacher explanation. Even this two-day art project will need little explanation. Of course, if it is the first time the children have fingerpainted, then more explanation is needed. However, after they have become accustomed to the art routines as where the supplies are stored, how to cleanup and what to do with their work when finished, then few directions are needed. This art activity could be set up for free play or center time or it could be a table-top activity for as soon as the children arrive. The first arrivals will complete theirs and then during center time other children will make their fingerpaint papers one day and cut and paste collages on the next.

## For Housekeeping And Dress-up Corner: Favorite Color Day

**What the children will learn—**
To sort clothing by colors

**Materials you will need—**
Full length mirror, dress-up clothes, paper bags, construction paper, stapler

**What to do—**
1. Staple sheets of construction paper in the primary and secondary colors to paper grocery bags.

2. Let the children who select this center during free play sort the clothing by color by placing the garments into the appropriate paper bag.

3. During clean-up time, leave the clothes in the bags and the next day, have the children sort them by other characteristics as those with snaps, zippers and buttons or adult, children and baby clothes, or blouses, shirts, pants and dresses.

**Something to think about—**
This Story S-t-r-e-t-c-h-e-r, which takes place in the housekeeping and dress-up area, is also a mathematics activity. Many good activities for young children have the potential for a variety of learnings. Younger children may need to sort by fewer colors and older children may be able to sort by two simple attributes as color and whether the garment is adult, child or baby clothing.

## For Library Corner: Mixing Up The Mixed-up Chameleon Flannel Board

**What the children will learn—**
To retell the story by adding features to Chameleon

**Materials you will need—**
Flannel board, felt pieces, large plastic bag

**What to do—**
1. Construct a large gray Chameleon and felt pieces to attach to him. Make pink flamingo wings and webbed feet, a bushy fox tail, orange fish fins, brown deer antlers, a long yellow giraffe neck, green turtle shell, blue-gray elephant's trunk, black seal's flippers, and a hat and umbrella.

2. Leave the flannel board, felt pieces and book out on a table in the library corner. The children will naturally turn through the book and retell the story.

3. Store the flannel board pieces in a large plastic freezer bag so they are easy to use.

**Something to think about—**
Flannel board stories are an excellent form of cooperative learning. One child can retell the story by looking at the illustrations in the book while a second child places the felt pieces on the flannel at the storyteller's cue. Also, tape record this book and a child can work alone, listening to the tape and placing the pieces on the flannel board as the story is heard.

(Adapted from an idea by Diana Hankinson.)

## For Mathematics And Manipulatives: What's Your Favorite Color?

**What the children will learn—**
To read a simple data retrieval chart

**Materials you will need—**
Box of crayons with primary and secondary colors, easel, paper, tape

**What to do—**
1. Tape a large sheet of paper to the easel and place in the mathematics and manipulatives area.

2. Print the names of the primary and secondary colors on the paper using the matching crayon. Print red with the red crayon.

3. During free play or center time, ask the children to visit the center at some time and select the color that is their favorite and make a hash mark on the chart.

4. Count the number of hash marks and write at the bottom of the chart the numeral for each color. Print the numeral and the number word in the corresponding color. For example, if six children like purple, write the numeral 6 and the word "six" in purple crayon.

5. Report on the results of your data collection during the second circle time of the day.

**Something to think about—**
This activity can be done as a part of circle time to prepare to read THE MIXED-UP CHAMELEON.

## For Science And Nature: Distinguishing Features

**What the children will learn—**
To describe distinctive features of zoo animals

**Materials you will need—**
Pictures of zoo animals, tape recorder, cassette tape

**What to do—**
1. Make a display of pictures or books with illustrations of zoo animals.

2. With the small group of children who choose science and

nature during center time or free play, discuss the zoo animals and how Chameleon envied them. Help them recall the animals Chameleon wanted to be like and what the distinguishing features of these animals were, as giraffe's long neck, turtle's shell, fish's fins.

3. Look at the pictures or book illustrations of the zoo animals and decide what their distinguishing features are, as panda's black and white fur, leopard's spots, tiger's stripes.

4. Let the children take turns looking at a picture and describing the animal by saying, "I'm looking at a picture of a zoo animal. It runs fast, lives in the woods, and has antlers. Which animal is it?" At least one of the descriptions must be a distinguishing characteristic, as antlers.

5. Other children can listen to the tape and hear the clues and sort the animal pictures into the same sequence as the descriptions on the tape.

**Something to think about—** Older children can find photographs of a number of animals with similar characteristics, as deer, elk, moose, and the children will tape more information for their listeners to decide among the possibilities. Younger children need not sequence the pictures but can turn the tape off after each description and search for the animal, then turn it back on to hear more descriptions and find more pictures.

## REFERENCES

Carle, Eric. (1975). **THE MIXED-UP CHAMELEON.** New York: Harper & Row.

Johnson, Crockett. (1955). **HAROLD AND THE PURPLE CRAYON.** New York: Harper & Row.

Jonas, Ann. (1989). **COLOR DANCE.** New York: Greenwillow Books.

van der Beek, Deborah. (1989). **ALICE'S BLUE CLOTH.** New York: G. P. Putnam's Sons.

Walsh, Ellen Stoll. (1989). **MOUSE PAINT.** San Diego: Harcourt Brace Jovanovich.

### Additional References For Colors

Beskow, Elsa. (1987). **PETER IN BLUEBERRY LAND.** Edinburgh, Scotland: Floris Books. *Peter, who searches for red cranberries and blueberries as a birthday present for his mother, meets a tiny elf king who takes him on quite an adventure as well as helping him find the berries.*

Ehlert, Lois. (1989). **COLOR ZOO.** New York: J.B. Lippincott. *Introduces colors and shapes with illustrations of shapes that form animal faces when overlaid on top of each other.*

Hoban, Tana. (1989). **OF COLORS AND THINGS.** New York: Greenwillow. *Collection of photographs, four to a page, of toys, foods and everyday objects grouped by color.*

McMillan, Bruce. (1988). **GROWING COLORS.** New York: Lothrop, Lee & Shepard Books. *Photographs of green peas, yellow corn, red potatoes, purple beans and other fruits and vegetables illustrate the many colors of nature.*

Tafuri, Nancy. (1988). **JUNGLEWALK.** New York: Greenwillow. *Here is a wordless adventure story for even the youngest child. Bright, bold and enchanting illustrations bring the world of toucans and zebras right outside your window.*

# CATS, DOGS AND OTHER PETS

*Charlie Anderson*

*Annie and the Wild Animals*

*Herbie Hamster, Where Are You?*

*Clifford's Birthday Party*

*Carl Goes Shopping*

## CHARLIE ANDERSON

*By Barbara Abercrombie*

*Illustrated by Mark Graham*

*Two girls, Elizabeth and Sarah, take in a stray cat which they name Charlie. Every morning when they leave for school, Charlie leaves for a walk and doesn't return until that night when he sleeps on the foot of Elizabeth's bed. One stormy night Charlie does not come home and the two girls go searching for him. They continue their search the next day and find him at the house of another family which calls him by the name of "Anderson." Charlie Anderson, the cat, has two homes, a daytime home and a nighttime home with Elizabeth and Sarah, who also have two homes. One with their mother during the week and one with their father on the weekends. Graham's beautiful pastel drawings convey the tenderness and affection the two families feel for their shared pet.*

## Circle Time Presentation

Let the children look at the picture of the cat on the cover of the book and have children who have cats for pets describe their cats. If you have a toy cat that is gray, place it on your lap while you are reading. Tell the children that this book is filled with beautiful pictures and that you will read the story first, and then look more closely at the illustrations and how the artist shaded the pictures to show nighttime. Read the book and pause after the scene of the girls waiting on the deck for Charlie and let the children predict what might have happened to the cat. At the end of the book talk about sharing families and that, like Elizabeth and Sarah, many of us have more than one family.

STORY STRETCHER

## For Art: Pastel Night Scenes

**What the children will learn—**
To draw and shade with pastel chalks

**Materials you will need—**
Scraps of construction paper, sheets of construction paper in blue, gray, purple, damp sponges, pastel chalks, hair spray

**What to do—**
1. Demonstrate for the children how to dampen their construction paper with the wet sponge. Also demonstrate how to make marks with the pastel chalk and how to hold it on its side and rub to make shading.

2. Let the children experiment on scraps of construction paper.

3. Look again at the illustrations in CHARLIE ANDERSON, then let the children choose the colors they want to use for their night scenes.

4. The children can work on their own and finish the pastel drawings.

5. Spray their pastel prints with hair spray so that the chalk will not flake off.

**Something to think about—**
Use beautiful illustrations in children's literature to inspire children's artwork, not to provide a model for the children to copy.

STORY STRETCHER

## For Cooking And Snack Time: Chocolate Chip Cookies To Celebrate Charlie's Return

**What the children will learn—**
To bake chocolate chip cookies

**Materials you will need—**
Refrigerator cookie dough, cookie sheet, knife, bowl of warm water, toaster oven, spatula, plates, napkins, glasses, milk

**What to do—**
1. Follow the directions for preparing the cookies. Read the directions aloud to the cooking and snack helpers.

2. Let the children slice the cookie dough in one-inch circles. Dip the knife in warm water and it will slice the cookie dough more easily.

3. Then slice each round into quarters.

4. Place onto cookie sheet and bake at the temperature and length of time recommended on the package.

5. Serve hot from the oven with glasses or cartons of cold milk.

6. During snack time mention that Elizabeth and Sarah's neighbor had made chocolate chip cookies for them when they were searching for their lost cat.

**Something to think about—**
Invite a parent or grandparent who enjoys baking to help the children make chocolate chip cookies from scratch.

STORY STRETCHER

## For Library Corner: Writing And Drawing About Our Pets

**What the children will learn—**
To recall and share their experiences with pets

**Materials you will need—**
Drawing paper, colored pencils, crayons, markers

**What to do—**
1.   Talk with the small group of children who come to the writing center about their pets. Ask what kind of pets they have, where they got them, what they like doing most with their pets, what responsibilities they have for caring for their pets, and so forth.

2.   After the children have talked for a while, ask them to write about or draw a picture about their pets.

3.   Let the children share their work with each other and decide whether to leave their work as a "work in progress" piece and return to it tomorrow or whether it is completed.

4.   When you have collected several pieces of writing and drawings, decide whether or not the collection would make a good class book on pets.

**Something to think about—**
Children should be free during center time or free play to choose the activities in which they want to participate. The discussion could be about pets or could revolve around the positive feelings and emotions about having two fami-

lies to love, just as Charlie Anderson had two families.

ANOTHER STORY STRETCHER

## For Library Corner: Composing Lost Pet Notices

**What the children will learn—**
To include needed information to locate and return their lost pet

**Materials you will need—**
Typing paper, markers, newspaper, tape

**What to do—**
1.   Discuss with the children that Elizabeth and Sarah went from door to door searching for their cat, Charlie. Mention that sometimes in the newspaper or in the grocery store window you see notices about lost pets. If available, read some of the lost pet notices from the newspaper.

2.   Have the children pretend that Charlie Anderson, the cat, belongs to them, and discuss the information they would write in their notice.

3.   Compose the "lost pet" notice with the children and post copies around the classroom.

4.   Have the toy cat disappear from the classroom and send notices to the other classrooms. Arrange for someone to find it.

**Something to think about—**
Take the opportunity when toys or coats or hats are lost to compose "lost" notices. These real opportunities help young children see functional needs for reading and writing and help them feel a part of the solution to problems.

STORY STRETCHER

## For Music And Movement: Where Are You, Charlie Anderson?

**What the children will learn—**
To search the classroom while the music is playing

**Materials you will need—**
Stuffed toy cat, tape player or record player and recording of instrumental music

**What to do—**
1.   Collect the children on the circle time rug and explain how to play "Where are you, Charlie Anderson?"

2.   Tell the children you have hidden the gray striped toy cat you had on your lap while you were reading the book during circle time. They are to search for it while the music is playing and as they look they are to call, "Charlie Anderson."

3.   Start the music and encourage the "searchers" to look for the toy cat.

4.   Stop the music and if no one has found the cat yet, give clues, such as Charlie Anderson likes a soft blanket to sleep on. Then the children will think to look in the doll bed.

5.   When a child finds Charlie Anderson, let her become the next person to hide Charlie. Have the other children close their eyes and let the "hider" find a special place for Charlie.

6.   After Charlie is hidden, start the music again for the children to search.

7.   Repeat the process for several hiding, searching, clue-giving and finding turns.

**Something to think about—**
Older children can provide their own clues for where Charlie Anderson is hiding. With younger children, hide several toy cats around the room so that the children are more likely to find them.

# CATS, DOGS AND OTHER PETS

## ANNIE AND THE WILD ANIMALS

*By Jan Brett*

*Annie, who lives in a remote forest, enjoyed the company of her cat, Tabby, especially during the long winter. But then Tabby disappeared. Annie was very lonely and decided to tame a wild animal to be her pet. She left corn cakes at the edge of the forest and went there each day to greet the animals, but the moose was too big, the bear and the wildcat too grumpy, and the stag and the wolf were not soft like Tabby. Finally, when spring came, Tabby returned bringing three baby kittens with her. With Jan Brett's signature borders, the full-color illustrations are richly detailed with Eastern European or Ukrainian patterns in the clothing and furniture of Annie's little cottage.*

## Circle Time Presentation

Look at the title page and the illustration of the little girl holding her cat. Read the first pages about the snowy winter days and that Annie did not have any other children to play with, but she had Tabby. Pause after the scene where Annie is longing for a new friend and ask the children for suggestions about what she might do. Continue reading past the part where Annie meets the moose and let the children talk about what the problems would be having a moose for a pet. Read on and discuss each wild animal. Let the children predict what Annie will do when she has no corn meal left to make food for the animals. Pause before the last page of Tabby and her three baby kittens and let the children guess how the story will end.

STORY STRETCHER

## For Art: Patterned Borders

**What the children will learn—**
To decorate the borders of their artwork

**Materials you will need—**
Paper, ruler, fine tip markers

**What to do—**
1. With a group of children who select the art center during free play or center time, look again at Jan Brett's illustrations in ANNIE AND THE WILD ANIMALS.

2. Let the children examine the borders closely and admire the many different details that Brett added.

3. Help the children draw a border around their papers by placing the ruler parallel with the edge of the paper and drawing a straight line on the inside edge.

4. Ask the children to draw about the story or about themselves and a pet they own or would like to own. Then encourage them to decorate the borders.

**Something to think about—**
Young children who already have difficulty with drawing will not be able to draw small designs for the borders, but they can draw slanted lines or rows of lines with felt markers to create borders.

STORY STRETCHER

## For Housekeeping And Dress-up Corner: Ethnic Costumes

**What the children will learn—**
To dress in unfamiliar clothing

**Materials you will need—**
Costumes from different cultures, if possible, Eastern European or Ukrainian sweaters, vests, decorative blouses with embroidery

**What to do—**
1. Write the parents a message in the newsletter asking for ethnic costumes.

2. Have a parent from a culture like Annie's wear an ethnic costume, and if possible, bring a recording of some music used for folk dancing.

3. If possible, let the children try on the clothing and leave some pieces for pretend play and dress-up.

**Something to think about—**
Invite grandparents with different cultural heritages to come to the classroom and tell about games they played as children.

STORY STRETCHER

## For Library Corner: Telling Border Pictures

**What the children will learn—**
To retell the story of ANNIE AND THE WILD ANIMALS

**Materials you will need—**
None needed

**What to do—**

1. With the children who select the library corner during center time, look through Jan Brett's illustrations of ANNIE AND THE WILD ANIMALS and let the children retell the story. Each child can take a turn telling a page.

2. Have the children examine the borders of the pictures more closely. Let them describe what they see the animals doing. The borders are the story of the animals when Annie doesn't see them.

**Something to think about—**
Story retelling is an excellent means for young children to develop how stories are constructed. The repeated actions of Annie returning to the woods each day to leave a corn cake and finding a different animal makes the steps of the story predictable.

STORY STRETCHER

## For Mathematics And Manipulatives: How Many Days Did Annie Feed The Animals?

**What the children will learn—**
To count the animals and mark the days on the calendar

**Materials you will need—**
Calendar

**What to do—**

1. With the group of children who select the mathematics and manipulatives center during free play, read ANNIE AND THE WILD ANIMALS.

2. Place a large calendar on the table and each time Annie leaves a corn cake at the edge of the wood, mark a day on the calendar.

3. Count the number of marks.

4. In the story, Tabby came home in the spring. Look through the calendar and find out how long from today's date until spring.

**Something to think about—**
Young children do not have a well-developed sense of time. What is important is that they begin to develop the sense of the calendar as a symbol for time.

STORY STRETCHER

## For Science And Nature: Baby Kittens

**What the children will learn—**
To handle baby kittens carefully

**Materials you will need—**
Baby kittens, basket or box, blanket

**What to do—**

1. When one of the children's cats has kittens, invite the family to bring the kittens to school.

2. Let the child tell about the kittens — when they were born, how they looked, how the mother acted, what their names are.

3. Place the kittens on a blanket in the middle of the circle time rug.

4. Show the children how to hold a kitten gently.

5. Ask the parent and the classroom aide to assist in helping the children hold the kittens.

6. Put the kittens back on the blanket and let the children watch them for a while.

**Something to think about—**
If a kitten seems to be in distress, is crying or clawing too much, return the kitten to the box or basket.

# 15
# CATS, DOGS AND OTHER PETS

## HERBIE HAMSTER, WHERE ARE YOU?

*By Terence Blacker*

*Illustrated by Pippa Unwin*

*Every hamster owner can identify with Danny who discovers that Herbie is not in his cage. The search begins with Danny going from house to house looking for Herbie and, in the process, observing the neighborhood activities and the neighborhood eccentrics. Danny looks for Herbie and seems to be just a step behind him, until he hears Miss Peachum scream that she sees a rat in her bathroom and runs into the street wrapped in a towel. The illustrations are chock full of interesting details in every house, and the reader is invited to try to spot Herbie Hamster among them.*

## Circle Time Presentation

Find out if any of the children own hamsters. Let one or two children share their experiences if they have lost their pets. Read HERBIE HAMSTER, WHERE ARE YOU? Because the book is a funny one, the children will request that you read it again. Read it a second time, then mention that when they look at the book in the class library they can try to find Herbie in each picture.

STORY STRETCHER
## For Art: Hide Your Pet

**What the children will learn—**
To draw a picture and hide their pet in it

**Materials you will need—**
Choice of art media, papers, paints, crayons, chalks, markers, colored pencils

**What to do—**
1. With a few children at the art table, look through the illustrations in HERBIE HAMSTER, WHERE ARE YOU?

2. Let the children search for Herbie in the pictures. Help them see the clues the illustrator has given by looking at the end paper pages where there are larger pictures of Herbie and where he was hiding.

3. Ask the children to draw any picture they like but to hide their pet in it. If they do not have a pet, they can hide Herbie in their picture.

4. Display the pictures along a chalk rail or low bulletin board so the children can have the fun of looking for each other's pets in their pictures.

**Something to think about—**
Younger children often choose to draw Herbie, since he is so easy to draw. Older children often compose elaborately detailed pictures and even the teacher has difficulty spotting their pets.

ANOTHER STORY STRETCHER
## For Art: Painting To The Music

**What the children will learn—**
To interpret what they hear with lines on a paper

**Materials you will need—**
Butcher paper or manilla paper, tempera paints, brushes, easels, tables, recording of piano music, tape or record player

**What to do—**
1. Since this will be a popular activity, provide extra painting space on table tops.

2. When the children are ready with their painting supplies, begin the music.

3. First, have the children take their brushes and move them through the air in response to the music, as if they were directing an orchestra.

4. Then, have them lightly touch the tip of their brushes in paint and move the brush along their paper in response to the music.

5. Have the children stay very quiet and simply listen to the music as they paint whatever lines feel right to them. Tell them they may just paint lines or they may paint a picture.

**Something to think about—**
On other days, try recordings of different instruments and a variety of types of music from classical to rock and roll. Be prepared on the rock and roll day for a messy cleanup.

## For Blocks: Building Herbie's Street

**What the children will learn—**
To build ornate two-story row houses

**Materials you will need—**
Variety of sizes of shoe boxes, blocks, tape, construction paper, scissors, glue, staples, markers or crayons

**What to do—**

1. Let each block builder have a shoe box.

2. Place a heavy block inside.

3. Tape the lid shut.

4. Look at the pictures of the elaborately decorated houses on the cover of Danny's and Herbie Hamster's street. Tell the children to look at these houses for inspiration. You would like them to create row houses that look different from these but that are beautifully decorated.

5. Have the children brainstorm ways they could turn these shoe boxes into ornately decorated houses.

6. Turn the shoe boxes on end so that they stand up like two-story houses. The heavy block inside will help the shoe box stand without toppling over easily.

7. Allow the children to cut and paste, staple and glue, improvising with whatever materials they choose.

8. Display the houses for a week for the children to enjoy and for other builders to add to the collection.

**Something to think about—**
For younger children, assist with covering the boxes with construction paper and let them cut and paste the ornamentation.

## For Music And Movement: Musically Seeking Herbie

**What the children will learn—**
To look for Herbie and to follow the musical directions

**Materials you will need—**
Stuffed animal, rhythm instruments — drum, tambourine, triangle

**What to do—**

1. With all the children seated on the circle time rug, explain that this stuffed toy animal is Herbie.

2. Tell the children that they are to close their eyes and the classroom aide will hide Herbie. No peeking.

3. Explain that when Herbie is hidden, you will begin playing one of the rhythm instruments and that will be a clue to where Herbie can be found. If they hear a low drum beat that means to look low in the classroom, either on the floor or near the floor. If they hear the tambourine, they should look higher, on tables or inside shelves. If they hear the high sounding triangle, they should look high, on top of coat racks, on high shelves in closets.

4. Play each instrument and let several children give examples of places they would look.

5. Let the aide hide Herbie, the children search, and randomly play the instruments, giving clues until Herbie is found.

6. When Herbie is found, the finder can whisper to the aide where to hide Herbie next.

**Something to think about—**
For older children, use more instruments, but let them classify the sounds of the instruments as low, medium and high before they are played.

## For Science And Nature: Taking Care Of The Class Hamster

**What the children will learn—**
That pets need shelter, food, water, exercise and careful handling

**Materials you will need—**
If possible a hamster and cage complete with water supply, tiny tray for food, reference book on hamsters, notebook, pen or pencil

**What to do—**

1. Before purchasing the hamster or allowing a child's pet hamster to visit the classroom for a while, read to the children from a reference book what hamsters need.

2. Plan for the hamster's arrival by selecting a good space for the cage.

3. If the hamster is a class pet, let the children name it. If the hamster has been brought by a child, have the owner tell the pet's name and why it was given that name.

4. Instruct the children on how to handle the pet and on care and feeding.

5. Observe the pet daily, and write questions the children ask in the notebook, as well as their comments.

6. During a circle time later in the week, read some of the questions and comments. If you do not know the answers to the questions and cannot find them in a reference book, consult a veterinarian.

**Something to think about—**
Help the children enjoy the pet as a pet, but also help them to see that they are thinking like scientists when they ask questions and seek answers.

## 15

## CATS, DOGS AND OTHER PETS

## CLIFFORD'S BIRTHDAY PARTY

*By Norman Bridwell*

*Clifford, the big red dog, has become a favorite among young children. Clifford's size is both his delight and his dilemma. When Emily Elizabeth, Clifford's owner, has a birthday party for him, some hilarious events follow. Clifford blows up a huge beach ball for the children to play with, bursts a piñata with doggy treats and is given a sweater for his nose among other gifts. After each gift is given, there is a funny thing that happens to the gift. The story ends with Clifford's family arriving, hidden in a huge birthday cake on the back of a truck. In almost comic book style, Norman Bridwell has succeeded in illustrating a book that young children will want read to them often.*

## Circle Time Presentation

Show the children the cover of the book without reading the title. Often simply showing the cover of a Clifford book brings applause from the audience collected on the circle time rug. Ask the children how old Clifford is and they will know by the one candle on the birthday cake. Read CLIFFORD'S BIRTHDAY PARTY and pause after each present is given for the children to predict what Clifford will do with this present. At the end of the reading, the children will request that you read it a second time. End circle time by announcing the Clifford activities for the day.

STORY STRETCHER

## For Art: Presents For Clifford

**What the children will learn—**
To extend the story with a different present for Clifford

**Materials you will need—**
Construction paper or manilla paper, gift-wrap ribbons, thumbtacks or tape, choice of media — crayons, markers, chalks, paints, colored pens

**What to do—**
1.   Make a bulletin board background of huge, enormous Clifford, the Big Red Dog.

2.   Ask the children to draw or paint a picture of a present they would like to give Clifford.

3.   When the pictures are completed, roll them up like a scroll and tie a gift-wrap ribbon around them. Thumbtack or tape the ribbons to the background of Clifford, the Big Red Dog.

4.   Later during the birthday party open the pictures to see what the presents are.

**Something to think about—**
The Clifford background for the bulletin board could also be made by the children. You can cut a huge Clifford from two pieces of butcher paper taped together and the children can take turns painting him red. Then cut him out and staple him to the bulletin board.

ANOTHER STORY STRETCHER

## For Art: Making Party Hats

**What the children will learn—**
To construct and decorate a party hat

**Materials you will need—**
Sheets of construction paper, scissors, scraps of gift-wrap paper and construction paper, stapler, gluesticks, tape, ribbons

**What to do—**
1.   Show the children how to roll a sheet of construction paper into a cone shape.

2.   Staple it in place and round off the edge that will be on top of the head.

3.   Bring out collage materials, such as scraps of brightly colored construction paper, gift-wrap paper and bits of ribbon.

4.   Let the children decorate their party hats by gluing on bits of brightly colored paper and ribbons.

5.   Cut ribbons long enough to tie under the children's chins.

6.   Staple the ribbons onto the hats and cover the staple with tape so that the paper is reinforced and the ribbon doesn't pull loose from the paper.

7.   Put the hats away until it is time for "Clifford's Birthday Party."

**Something to think about—**
Younger children will have difficulty waiting to wear their hats.

Let them wear them as soon as they are made.

## For Cooking And Snack Time: Clifford's Birthday Party

**What the children will learn—**
To decorate a cake

**Materials you will need—**
Cake or cakes, frosting, spatulas, bowl of warm water, cans of different colored cake decorating icing, plates, napkins, glasses, forks, milk

**What to do—**
1.  Bake the cake or cakes ahead of time.

2.  Have some children frost the cake using a spatula. Dipping the spatula in warm water helps the frosting spread more easily.

3.  Let other children decorate the cake by using the cans of colored icing which spreads when they push on the nozzles.

4.  Serve the cake at snack time with glasses or cartons of cold milk.

5.  Sing "Happy Birthday" to Clifford.

6.  Stack Clifford's picture presents on each table and let the children take turns telling about their presents for Clifford.

**Something to think about—**
Younger children find it easier to decorate long flat sheet cakes. Older children can help bake the cakes one day and decorate them on another. If you have parents or grandparents who decorate cakes for a hobby, ask them to come to class and show the children some of their special tricks and the special tools they use.

## For Housekeeping And Dress-up Corner: Pet Supply Store

**What the children will learn—**
That caring for animals requires many different supplies

**Materials you will need—**
Leashes, bowls, empty dog food and cat food cans, flea collars, chewy toys, traveling cages, blankets, baskets

**What to do—**
1.  Turn the housekeeping and dress-up area into a creative dramatics center and call it the "Clifford and Friends Pet Supply Store."

2.  Invite parents to send in pet supplies, being careful that they have been thoroughly cleaned.

3.  With the children, improvise display areas and materials from around the classroom.

4.  Add a cash register, note pads, order blanks, pens and pencils and other supplies for the check-out stand.

5.  Leave the pet supply store up for at least a week and the children will add props and invent roles.

**Something to think about—**
Add reference materials on different pets and their needs so that the children role play reading to find information and directing their customers to books about pets.

## For Music And Movement: Party Piñata

**What the children will learn—**
How to play with a piñata as a part of birthday celebrations

**Materials you will need—**
Piñata, scarf, yardsticks, blindfolds

**What to do—**
1.  Show the children the part of CLIFFORD'S BIRTHDAY PARTY where he is blindfolded and hits the piñata until it breaks.

2.  Uncover the piñata from where you have it hidden under a scarf.

3.  Hang the piñata in a place where it is safe for the children to hit at it.

4.  Let the children take turns hitting the piñata with the yardsticks until it bursts, spreading its contents on the floor.

5.  Then the children can enjoy scrambling for the treats, candies or little toys that were inside. Ask the children to take only one treat.

**Something to think about—**
This activity is a good one to do outside by tying the piñata from a tree limb. For young children do not use a blindfold. Older children can make a piñata as an art project.

## CARL GOES SHOPPING

*By Alexandra Day*

*A wordless picture book except for the first and last pages, CARL GOES SHOPPING has numerous possibilities for children to tell their own stories. Carl's owner tells him to watch the baby in the carriage, but the baby hops on Carl's back and explores the department store. The baby plays with the toys, looks at a book titled "Rottweilers I Have Known," tries on women's hats, visits the electronics department, rolls on the oriental rugs, samples foods, opens all the cages in the pet department before rushing back through the store for Carl to put the baby back in the carriage. The baby's mother returns, pats Carl on the head and says, "Good dog, Carl." One of a series of Carl adventures, Alexandra Day's realistic paintings have just enough mystical shading to let the child know this is just pretend.*

## Circle Time Presentation

Wear a hat like one in the book when you read the story of this wordless picture book. Teachers often hesitate to share wordless books because they do not want to impose their stories on the children, but with a bit of encouragement the children can tell their own versions. Explain to the children that this book is called a wordless picture book because most of the pages have no words on them. Have the children look at the cover and tell them that Carl is a Rottweiler dog who is a family pet. Read the words on the first page where the mother tells Carl to watch the baby carriage. Let the children predict what might happen. Then read/tell the remainder of the story in story form without pausing to point out the pictures. Explain to the children that when you come to the library corner today that you would like to hear them read CARL GOES SHOPPING. Give the book to a child to place in the library.

STORY STRETCHER

## For Art: Department Compartments In A Picture

**What the children will learn—**
To illustrate a sequence of scenes

**Materials you will need—**
Large sheets of manilla paper or butcher paper, choice of art materials, markers, crayons, chalks, colored pencils, catalogs, scissors, glue

**What to do—**
1. Have the children fold their papers three times to make eight compartments. The first fold is halves, the second fold makes fourths and the third fold makes eight compartments.

2. Talk about the different departments in a department store.

3. Ask the children to pretend that each compartment on their paper represents a different department in the store.

4. Have the children draw or cut and paste items from each department, or draw themselves and their pet or Carl and the baby in the different departments.

**Something to think about—**
Let the younger children fold their papers twice to make four compartments and have them cut and paste catalog pictures to make a collage. Older children can take their artwork and let it be a plan for a story board for a piece they can write in the writing center.

STORY STRETCHER

## For Housekeeping And Dress-up Corner: Silly Hats, Beautiful Hats, Colorful Hats, Hats And More Hats

**What the children will learn—**
To role play whatever the hats remind them of

**Materials you will need—**
Variety of hats and scarves, full-length mirror

**What to do—**
1. Ask parents to send in many different kinds of women's hats and scarves.

2. Try on a hat or two yourself, model it using exaggerated motions and laugh at yourself.

3. Assist the children in trying on the hats and admire how they look.

4. Place the full-length mirror where the children can see themselves model their hats.

**Something to think about—**
On another day, have a variety of men's hats. Let both boys and girls try on the different hats.

## For Library Corner: A Story To Go With Department Store Pictures

**What the children will learn—**
Composing a story is like composing a picture

**Materials you will need—**
Strips of typing paper, pens, pencils, stapler, tape, cassette tapes and recorder, listening station, headphones

**What to do—**

1. Ask the children to compose a story using their pictures from the art activity, telling what happened in each department. Tell them that you want to tape what they are telling.

2. Give them a little time to think about what they would like to say and to decide if they are pretending that Carl is their pet or if they are pretending that they have their own pet in the department store.

3. At the beginning of each child's story, tape a message, as "This is Michelle's story."

4. Have the children number the compartments of their department store pictures so that when they tell the story they might say, "In picture number one, my dog Randy is going up the escalator with me. In picture two, we find a lady at the candy counter who gives us chocolate and peanut candy."

5. After the children have tape recorded their stories, ask them to decide on a title.

6. Print the title on a strip of paper and tape it to the bottom of the picture.

7. Group the pictures together by fives. Staple the five pictures together and place the tape of those children's stories with the pictures.

8. Set up the listening station for the children to hear themselves on tape while looking at the pictures.

**Something to think about—**
For young children, record one story on one side of the tape and a second story on the other side so that they only have two pictures to look at while listening to the tape. They also can match the names on the pictures with the names you print on the labels for the cassette tapes.

## For Music And Movement: Following The Paw Prints

**What the children will learn—**
To step in rhythm with the clapping

**Materials you will need—**
Scraps of construction paper or posterboard, scissors, masking tape

**What to do—**

1. Let the children help you cut paw prints from scraps of construction paper or posterboard. The paw prints do not have to be exact. Have the children look at the last page of CARL GOES SHOPPING for a sample of a paw print.

2. Do not tell the children what the paw prints will be used for, and the next day before the children arrive, tape the paw prints to the floor. Space some close together and others far enough apart that children will have to leap to reach from one to the other.

3. At music and movement time, collect the children on the circle time rug and start to clap several rhythms. Have the children join you in repeating the rhythms with their own clapping.

4. Then stand and sway while clapping.

5. Next, move off the rug and have the children line up behind each other.

6. Then, have each child stand on a paw print. You clap a rhythm, and they echo clap. When you stop clapping they have to move to the next paw print before you start again. Increase the speed and complexity of the rhythms and vary the amount of time they have to get from paw print to paw print.

**Something to think about—**
One variation is to have each child stand on a paw print and play "Simon Says." For example, "Simon says, 'Stand like a flamingo with one leg in the air.'" Or, "Simon says, 'Hop like a kangaroo to the next paw print.'"

## For Science And Nature: Visiting A Pet Store

**What the children will learn—**
How the owner cares for each pet and what the different animals are

**Materials you will need—**
Parent volunteers, transportation, field trip permission slips, identification name tags, index cards, scissors, pins, tape

**What to do—**

1. Secure enough parent or other volunteers that there are no more than two children per adult.

2. Arrange with the pet store owner and clerks how you want them to interact with the children.

3. Check the parent permission slips and prepare the identification name tags with the children's

names, addresses, telephone numbers.

**4.** Print the identification information on pet-shaped cards you have cut from large index cards.

**5.** Pin the cards to the children's clothing and place tape over the straight pins.

**6.** At the pet store, help the children identify each animal and let the owner talk about how important it is to take good care of one's pets. Find out how the owner cares for these pets.

**Something to think about—**
Call a veterinarian for information about which pet stores have good reputations because they take good care of the animals. If the veterinarian does not have a recommendation, call the local humane society. Only visit an animal shelter if you are prepared to explain what happens to all the animals who are not adopted.

## REFERENCES

Abercrombie, Barbara. (1990). Illustrated by Mark Graham. **CHARLIE ANDERSON.** New York: Margaret K. McElderry Books.

Blacker, Terrence. (1990). Illustrated by Pippa Unwin. **HERBIE HAMSTER, WHERE ARE YOU?** New York: Random House.

Brett, Jan. (1985). **ANNIE AND THE WILD ANIMALS.** Boston: Houghton Mifflin Company.

Bridwell, Norman. (1988). **CLIFFORD'S BIRTHDAY PARTY.** New York: Scholastic.

Day, Alexandra. (1989). **CARL GOES SHOPPING.** New York: Farrar Straus Giroux.

### Additional References For Cats, Dogs And Other Pets

Asch, Frank. (1980). **THE LAST PUPPY.** New York: Simon & Schuster Inc. *The last puppy born is eager not to be the last puppy adopted by a family. Just as he assumes no one will want him, he finds himself being placed in the hands of a little boy.*

Carrick, Carol. (1974). Illustrated by Donald Carrick. **LOST IN THE STORM.** New York: Clarion Books. *The suspenseful story of two boys searching for their dog who gets lost in a storm on the beach.*

Cherry, Lynne. (1990). **ARCHIE, FOLLOW ME.** New York: E. P. Dutton. *The adventures of a little girl and her cat Archie as they explore the woods during the day and in the evening.*

Gackenbach, Dick. (1984). **WHAT'S CLAUDE DOING?** New York: Clarion Books. *When Claude's friends gather outside his house to entice him to come out and play with the other neighborhood dogs, he decided to stay inside beside his owner who is home from school because he is sick.*

Turner, Dona. (1980). **MY CAT PEARL.** New York: T. Y. Crowell. *The story of a cat's day told in a warm and comforting way with simple illustrations and text.*

# TRANSPORTATION

*The Wheels on the Bus: An Adaptation of the Traditional Song*
*First Flight*
*How Many Trucks Can a Tow Truck Tow?*
*Dinosaurs Travel: A Guide for Families on the Go*
*Train Song*

## THE WHEELS ON THE BUS

*By Maryann Kovalski*

*The book is an adaptation of the traditional song by the same title. Grandma, Jenny and Joanna went shopping for winter coats and tried on everything on the racks. Finally, after making their purchases, they wait for a long time at the bus stop. To entertain the two girls, Grandma has them sing "The Wheels on the Bus." They become so excited and preoccupied with their singing and doing the motions that they miss the bus and end the day by taking a taxi home. Kovalski's cheerful city-in-the-winter illustrations are chalk drawings with pencil outlines and shadings. Grandma and the girls stand out while the city background is shaded lighter.*

## Circle Time Presentation

Begin singing, "The wheels on the bus go round and round..." and watch which children join you in the singing. Then, discuss whether or not the children like to go shopping. Tell the children that in this story the girls do not go shopping with their parents but with their grandmother to buy new winter coats. Talk about the different types of coats the children in the class have, as blue ones with zippers, red ones with hoods, pink ones with a white stripe, brown ones with a tie string at the waist. Read the book and tell the children that they may join you anytime they think they know what the author will say next. Encourage their singing the song with hand signals. Immediately after reading the book, the children will comment that the author didn't get the words right. Most children and teachers sing that the horn on the bus goes "beep, beep, beep." In the book the horn goes "toot, toot, toot."

STORY STRETCHER

## For Art: The View From The Bus

**What the children will learn—**
To think of themselves as passengers on the bus looking out the window and seeing a different perspective

**Materials you will need—**
Construction paper, scissors, glue stick, chalk, pencils, colored pencils, paper towels or sponges

**What to do—**
1. Cut out outlines of the frame of a bus window.

2. Show the children how the frame sits around the sheet of construction paper.

3. Ask the children what they might see from the bus window.

4. Look at Maryann Kovalski's illustrations and discuss how they were made from colored chalk, colored pencils and pencils. Tell the children that they can draw with the pencils first and add shading with the chalk or just draw with the chalk.

5. Demonstrate for the children how to very lightly dampen their construction paper with a wet paper towel or sponge and then use the chalk to draw.

6. Create a display of bus window pictures near the library area.

**Something to think about—**
If your children ride school buses, make the window frame a golden yellow and shaped like a rectangle. If they ride city buses, make the window frame a color and a shape that are common for the buses in your city.

STORY STRETCHER

## For Blocks: Role Playing Driver And Passengers

**What the children will learn—**
To cooperate in building and playing the scenes from the song

**Materials you will need—**
Steering wheel, large hollow blocks or chairs, tin can with hole in the lid, newspaper, books, earphones, packages

**What to do—**
1. Ask three of the regular block builders to look around the room and ask children who don't usually play in the blocks to come to that area for a special activity.

2. Let the children improvise blocks and chairs for the bus.

3. Give one of the children the steering wheel representing the bus driver. Discuss what the pas-

sengers might be doing, as reading newspaper, books, taking care of baby, holding their packages from shopping, listening to music with earphones.

4. Let the children collect their materials to be passengers.

5. After the children have played for a while on their own, go over and lead them in singing "The Wheels on the Bus."

**Something to think about—**
Encourage participation in the block area by children who do not use the center by planning special activities there.

STORY STRETCHER

## For Housekeeping And Dress-up Corner: Shopping For New Coats

**What the children will learn—**
To role play clerks, cashiers and customers

**Materials you will need—**
Children's coats, construction paper or tagboard, markers, shopping bags, note pads, pens, sales leaflets, cash register

**What to do—**
1. With a small group of children helping, convert the housekeeping and dress-up corner to a department store. Brainstorm ideas and collect items from around the classroom.

2. Begin the play by pretending to be Grandma with her two granddaughters, Joanna and Jenny, trying on coats.

3. After the play is started, ask another child to pretend to be Grandma; leave the children to play on their own.

4. When it is time for free play to be over, announce, "Hurry children, it is almost time for our bus!"

**Something to think about—**
Ask parents for donations to help with the department store appearance. Do not be concerned if you have few materials. One of the advantages of having a classroom where children are free to play is that they create their own representations and symbols. The grocery bag may have "Food Mart" printed on the outside, but the child will pretend it is a department store name. Providing pads and pens for the area leads the children to improvise "literacy play," examples of reading and writing in everyday life.

STORY STRETCHER

## For Mathematics And Manipulatives: Change For The Bus Ride

**What the children will learn—**
To match or recognize quarters, dimes and nickels

**Materials you will need—**
Real quarters, dimes and nickels, file folder, tape, marker, plastic sandwich bag, tin can with hole cut in lid

**What to do—**
1. With the small group of children who choose to come to the mathematics and manipulatives area during free play, talk about how much city bus rides cost.

2. On the inside of a file folder, print, "Bus Rides, _ cents, one way." Tape quarters, dimes and nickels in whatever amount is needed onto the inside of the folder.

3. Have the children match their money to the ones taped onto the folder.

4. After they have the right amount of change, let them drop it into the tin can and sing, "The

money on the bus goes clink, clink, clink..."

**Something to think about—**
Young children who live in the city may be familiar with bus tickets or passes. If so, make tickets to show the amount of the bus ride, and let them use the "clinking can" as the place where they buy the ticket.

STORY STRETCHER

## For Music And Movement: Writing More Lyrics For "The Wheels On The Bus"

**What the children will learn—**
To compose added lyrics by following the pattern from the traditional song

**Materials you will need—**
Copy of the lyrics printed on chart tablet, markers

**What to do—**
1. Have the children recall all the verses to "The Wheels on the Bus." Sing it together if it helps.

2. Ask the children to think of some other verses. Have them recall the noises they hear on the bus.

3. After the children have decided on their additional lyrics, tell them you want to write their new compositions so you can remember them tomorrow.

4. Print the new lyrics on the chart tablet.

**Something to think about—**
During the second group time of the day, bring the chart tablet to the circle area and let the small groups who made up the new lyrics lead the rest of the class in learning them.

First Flight

by David McPhail

# FIRST FLIGHT
## By David McPhail

*In a delightful combination of reality and fantasy, McPhail tells the story of a little boy's first flight traveling alone to see his grandmother. He takes along his teddy bear, and in the process of going through the metal detector, the bear becomes an adult-sized traveling partner. All the little boy's fears are transferred to the big bear who experiences finding his seat, obeying the pilot's safety reminders about seat belts, going to the bathroom, being scared during turbulence, napping and reading on board, and finally arriving safely to grandmother's waiting arms where the bear returns to teddy bear size. The little boy's and bear's expressions are reminders of many first time and veteran travelers' expressions.*

## Circle Time Presentation

Announce in a very official sounding voice, "Fasten your seat belts please." Tell the children that when you travel in your car, you fasten your seat belt and when you fly to see your relatives, you hear these words, "Fasten your seat belts please." Let children who have flown on airplanes talk about their trips. Ask what they did first, second, and continue the discussion. Discuss that sometimes people are a little frightened when they fly because they do not know what to expect. Read FIRST FLIGHT. When the story is finished, have the children tell you when they noticed that teddy bear had become a big bear.

STORY STRETCHER

## For Art: Sky Backgrounds For Our Planes

**What the children will learn—**
To use watercolors to paint a sky

**Materials you will need—**
Watercolor paints, paper, brushes, margarine tubs of water, paper towels or old newspapers, pencil, white construction paper, crayons, scissors, glue

**What to do—**
1. Demonstrate for the children how to load watercolor paints onto the brush, how to dilute the colors with water and how to dry the brush on paper towels or dabbing onto old newspapers.

2. Have the children paint a sky using any colors they like, blue sky, gray for storm or multicolored for a beautiful sunrise or sunset.

3. Let the children draw, decorate with crayons and cut out an airplane to put in their sky.

**Something to think about—**
One way to exhibit the children's artwork is to hang it with fishing wire from the ceiling. Create mobiles by hanging pictures at different levels. Reinforce the back of the picture by placing a strip of masking tape across the top and the bottom. The pictures will not curl and can be viewed more easily with the taped reinforcements to hold them in place.

STORY STRETCHER

## For Blocks: Building An Airport

**What the children will learn—**
To construct terminals, parking garages, hangars, runways

**Materials you will need—**
Large hollow blocks, toy airplanes, cars, trucks

**What to do—**
1. Have the children look through the illustrations in FIRST FLIGHT and notice all they can about the airport. Call attention to buildings, parking and runways.

2. Ask the children to begin building an airport today and tell them that the construction can continue throughout the week.

3. Let the children who choose block building during center time or free play tell about their construction each day, then ask for any ideas they have for what they would like to add.

4. Encourage the continuing process of examining books you provide on airports and airplanes, then having the children plan and construct.

**Something to think about—**
The long-term building project allows children to experiment with the materials, try a variety of approaches, then create their designs.

Creativity does not happen when children are given only short bursts of time to play.

## For Housekeeping And Dress-up: People Who Help At The Airport

**What the children will learn—**
To role play a variety of airport community helpers

**Materials you will need—**
Uniforms, coveralls, chalk board, chalk, paper bags, marker

**What to do—**

1. Invite parents to donate old uniforms and hats.

2. With a small group of children who select the housekeeping and dress-up corner during free play, look through the illustrations in FIRST FLIGHT and ask the children to tell the occupations of the people who help operate airports and airplanes.

3. Write what the "helpers" are called on the chalk board, as sky-cap, baggage handler, ticket agent, flight attendant, pilot.

4. With the children, sort through the uniforms and decide what pieces of clothing each person might wear.

5. Write the occupation on the outside of a paper grocery bag and place that helper's clothing in the bag.

6. Ask one child to be the little boy who is taking his first flight. Let the children decide among themselves who will play the other roles.

7. Leave them to improvise their own play.

**Something to think about—**
Pretending is an excellent preparation for a travel adventure. In a parent newsletter, discuss your transportation unit and suggest several ways parents can help prepare their children for traveling on a plane for the first time.

## For Mathematics And Manipulatives: How Much Will Our Suitcase Hold?

**What the children will learn—**
To judge capacity

**Materials you will need—**
Variety of suitcases, duffel bags, backpacks, clothes from the housekeeping and dress-up corner, paper, pencil or pen

**What to do—**

1. Talk about when you pack to go on a trip, it is difficult for you to decide what to take and what to leave at home, so you look at your suitcase and try to think of all you would like to take.

2. Bring out a suitcase that has clothes hanging out of it and will not close.

3. Take the pieces of clothing out one at a time, and make a list of everything that is in the bag.

4. Bring out a small suitcase and ask the children to guess how much of the clothing from the big bag will fit into the little bag.

5. Let a child or two gather up in their arms the amount of clothing they think will fit and have them pack it into the bag.

6. Continue letting children use different suitcases, duffel bags and backpacks.

**Something to think about—**
For younger children, simply give them each a suitcase or bag and have them pack it full of clothes, then bring it to you and let them count what they packed. For older children, let them plan what they would need for a trip to different places, then decide which bag fits their needs.

## For Science And Nature: What Is Turbulence?

**What the children will learn—**
To associate turbulence with the wind

**Materials you will need—**
Coats, swings

**What to do—**

1. On a windy day, take the children outside and let them feel the wind against their faces. If it is the season for wearing coats, have them open their coats and face the wind.

2. Let the children observe that the wind makes their coats move around.

3. Ask the children to notice the swings and see how they move in the wind.

4. Have the children sit in the swings and pull their legs up so they are not holding the swing in place. If they feel the wind move them, say this is "turbulence." If there is not enough wind to move the child in the swing, push the swing and say you are the wind moving the swing and the swing is an airplane.

**Something to think about—**
Create a mock turbulence experiment by attaching a small paper or toy airplane to a string that is attached to a yardstick. Place the yardstick in a clay pot with rocks around the base to hold the yardstick in place. Let the children create "turbulence" by blowing on the plane, fanning it to create a turbulent wind or directing an electric fan to blow on the plane. Have the children observe what happens.

### HOW MANY TRUCKS CAN A TOW TRUCK TOW ?

*By Charlotte Pomerantz*

*Illustrated by R. W. Alley*

*This story told in rhyme is a tongue twister to read but a delight to hear. The children will cheer the little tow truck when each new turn adds another tow truck to be towed, and the littlest truck is the hero of the day. Charlotte Pomerantz's book is another of the "I think I can" variety. One can almost hear the little tow truck saying the same words as the little engine, "I think I can, I think I can, I think I can." The illustrations are brightly colored animations of tow trucks with personalities. The children will enjoy finding the surprised little dog in each illustration, expressing some of the same reactions as the listener when the little tow truck perseveres to the cheers of all the other tow trucks in the garage.*

## Circle Time Presentation

Begin the circle time by discussing what tow trucks do. If there is a toy tow truck in the classroom, bring it to circle and have someone tell how tow trucks help motorists. Read the story through from beginning to end without stopping, then read it again and let the children fill in the recurring phrase, "With my red lights turning and my blue lights winking and my headlights burning and my green lights blinking." On another day when the children want you to read the story, pause for them to fill in the rhyming words. Show the cover of the book and ask the children if the story is about a real tow truck or an imaginary one. Have them notice the headlight eyes and the bumper smile. Discuss how much fun imaginary stories can be and that we can look at the pictures in books and tell if they are imaginary or not.

### STORY STRETCHER
## For Art: Tire Track Pattern Art

**What the children will learn—**
To print a variety of patterns using the wheels of toy cars and trucks

**Materials you will need—**
Construction paper or manilla paper, tempera paints, toy cars and trucks, meat trays or other longer flat containers for paints, larger dishpan with soapy water, paper towels or newspaper for dripping toys

**What to do—**
1. Place one toy car or truck in each tray of paint.

2. Demonstrate how to roll the toy cars and trucks in paints, then onto the paper, making tire tracks.

3. Encourage the children to make a variety of designs.

4. Use the terms horizontal, vertical and diagonal to describe the directions of the patterns.

5. Have the children clean up the toys by washing in soapy water and then leaving the toys to drip dry on newspaper or paper towels.

**Something to think about—**
Younger children might use the large wheels from a Tinkertoy set or larger wooden spools and roll them across large sheets of butcher paper or surplus computer paper. Older children might enjoy making large collages by pasting magazine cutouts of different cars and trucks onto the "Tire Track Art" background.

### STORY STRETCHER
## For Blocks: Towing Tow Trucks

**What the children will learn—**
To experiment with a pulley on a tow truck

**Materials you will need—**
Toy tow truck, variety of smaller vehicles, cars, trucks, vans, and if possible, more toy tow trucks

**What to do—**
1. After reading the book, the sight of the tow truck and other vehicles will inspire some rescues by the tow truck crews in the block area.

2. Leave the players to their imaginary rescue scenes.

3. After the players have experienced hooking up the cars and towing them, ask one or two of the children to demonstrate how a tow truck works. Encourage the children to use the word, "pulley."

**Something to think about—**
Younger children may enjoy the mechanics of hooking up the cars to the trucks and driving them around in tow. Older children will

role play scenes where motorists are in distress. Emphasize that the tow truck driver, the motorists, and the police officers work cooperatively to keep the traffic moving.

STORY STRETCHER

## For Mathematics And Manipulatives: A Transportation Count

**What the children will learn—**
To count the number of cars, trucks, vans and buses in a parking lot

**Materials you will need—**
Chart tablet paper or posterboard, crayons or markers

**What to do—**
1. Prepare a simple graph by drawing three columns on chart tablet paper or posterboard.

2. Cut out a picture of a car, a truck and a van, or draw an outline of each and place at the top of each column.

3. Take the children out to the parking lot in small groups.

4. Count with them the number of cars, trucks and vans.

5. Record the number under each column.

6. Bring the second group out and let them count the vehicles, record their number in a different colored marker or crayon.

7. Discuss with the children that the reason the number of vehicles changes is that people are driving in and out of the parking lot.

**Something to think about—**
Add school buses to the chart if they are a parked on the lot. For younger children, count the number of cars or trucks in one row. For older children, count and see how many more cars than there

are trucks, or vans than there are trucks.

STORY STRETCHER

## For Science And Nature: How A Pulley Works In A Tow Truck

**What the children will learn—**
To observe how a tow truck operates by using a pulley to lift a heavy object

**Materials you will need—**
Real tow truck or a pulley mechanism

**What to do—**
1. Survey the parents of your class or school and see if someone owns or has access to a tow truck.

2. Invite the tow truck driver to the school to demonstrate how the pulley works to lift the front wheels of the car.

3. With the ignition off, let small groups of children sit in the driver's seat and look out the back window at the pulley mechanism.

4. Have the driver turn on the lights, and tell the children that this is a signal to the other motorists that the truck needs to get through the traffic to help someone.

**Something to think about—**
In addition to seeing the mechanism of the pulley and how it works to lift the car, the children can see how the tow truck driver is also a community helper. Community helpers are not just the doctors, teachers, firefighters, and police officers we usually include in units. The delivery people, cashiers, mechanics, plumbers, office workers, and tow truck drivers are also community helpers. Inviting parents in the service industries to the classroom helps the children, but it also lets the parents

know that their work is appreciated.

STORY STRETCHER

## For Work Bench: Tools And Wrenches

**What the children will learn—**
To manipulate wrenches to loosen and tighten nuts and bolts

**Materials you will need—**
Set of small wrenches that can loosen nuts from bolts, block of wood or vise from work bench, washers, drill, strong household glue

**What to do—**
1. If possible, drill holes to match size of bolts into a rectangular block of wood for bolts to go through.

2. Place strong glue into the hole and put the bolts through the hole, leaving a long exposed end of the bolt onto which the child can thread the nut.

3. After the glue is set, place a washer on the exposed end of the bolt, then attach a nut.

4. Teach the children to first start the nut by threading it with their fingers, then tightening it with the wrench that matches the size of the nut.

**Something to think about—**
For younger children, place the bolt into the vise on the work bench and let them practice threading the nut onto the end of the bolt. For older children, vary the experience by adding a crescent wrench, which can be adjusted to the sizes of the nuts. Also add a variety of sizes of nuts and bolts. Older children may enjoy helping you construct the nuts and bolts set or assisting a parent or grandparent in the construction.

## DINOSAURS TRAVEL:
## A Guide For Families
## On The Go

*By Laura Krasny Brown*

*and Marc Brown*

*While the main characters are dinosaurs, they are personified, and the book is more a guide to family travel than a story of dinosaurs. From preparing for the trip to the return home, the authors speak directly to the child. Modes of travel included are foot, skateboard, bike, car, subway, bus, train, boat, airplane. Visiting a new place, eating away from home, sleeping away from home, and traveling alone are reassuring sections. Each page of the book contains three or four scenes, but the pictures are large enough to share at group time.*

## Circle Time Presentation

Have the children think of all the ways they came to school this morning—by car, bus, pickup truck, van, subway. Make a list on a chalk board or chart tablet. Continue by discussing how some older children get to school. Walking, skateboarding, bicycling. Then discuss how they would travel if they were going to visit a relative who lives far away. Add train, boat, and plane to the list. Read DINOSAURS TRAVEL: A GUIDE FOR FAMILIES ON THE GO. As each mode of transportation is mentioned in the story, let a child place a check mark beside each. After the book has been read, go back through the illustrations and add specific names to the forms of transportation, as limousine, taxi, helicopter, sailboat, tour bus, bicycle built for two, ferryboat, cruise ship, kayak, jet plane, canoe, surfboard, camel, tugboat.

STORY STRETCHER

## For Art: A Place Different Than Home

**What the children will learn—**
To sculpt modes of transportation

**Materials you will need—**
Playdough or clay, popsicle sticks or plastic knives, index cards, marker

**What to do—**
1. With the children who choose the art center during free play or center time, look through DINOSAURS TRAVEL: A GUIDE FOR FAMILIES ON THE GO and examine the different modes of transportation.

2. Ask the children to choose any means of transportation they would like and make a sculpture for the art display table.

3. Print the sculptors' names on a small index card and place it with their sculpture on the table.

**Something to think about—**
Older children may group their sculpture by whether the means of transportation is for land, sea or sky. Younger children may enjoy concentrating on making land transportation one day, sea and sky transportation on other days.

STORY STRETCHER

## For Housekeeping And Dress-up Corner: Packing For Our Visit

**What the children will learn—**
To pack clothes, toys and books

**Materials you will need—**
Suitcases, duffel bags, backpacks, clothing, telephone, toys, books

**What to do—**
1. Place the suitcases, bags and backpacks in the housekeeping corner and observe the children's interactions.

2. Stimulate the play by calling the children on the telephone and pretending you are their grandmother. Invite them for a visit. Remind them to bring some toys and books, as well as clothes that fit the weather. Pretend you live far away.

3. When the children pretend that they arrive at your house, help them unpack, and discuss why they brought these particular clothes, toys and books.

**Something to think about—**
For younger children, pretend to be the mother or father helping the children get ready for a trip. For older children, stimulate play by posing the problem of what other travel preparations are needed for the family to leave home, as finding a kennel for the family pet, get-

ting someone to water the plants and stopping the paper delivery.

## For Library Corner: Writing About Our Travel Adventures

**What the children will learn—**
To recall traveling with family and to see their spoken words becoming written words

**Materials you will need—**
Chart tablet or posterboard, marker

**What to do—**
1. Ask the children to recall some times when their families traveled together. Discuss their trips for a few minutes.

2. Tell the children that you want to remember what they have told you so you are going to write it down.

3. Have each child tell at least one sentence about a time when their family traveled together for a vacation or even a trip across town.

4. As you print their sentences on the chart tablet or posterboard, repeat what the child has said so that the children can observe spoken language becoming written language.

5. After each child's sentence is printed, reread the sentence in a fluent way and run your fingers or a pointer under the words.

6. When the chart is finished, re-read their traveling together statements.

**Something to think about—**
In some communities where families have little money for traveling, emphasize the many different forms of transportation they see in their city or town.

## For Mathematics And Manipulatives: Vehicles to Count

**What the children will learn—**
To construct and count transportation vehicles

**Materials you will need—**
Bristle blocks, Tinkertoys, Legos, Duplo or other any connecting blocks, index cards, marker

**What to do—**
1. With the children who choose the mathematics and manipulatives area during free play or center time, discuss the different forms of transportation they saw in DINOSAURS TRAVEL: A GUIDE FOR FAMILIES ON THE GO.

2. Ask the children to build as many different kinds of transportation as they can from the blocks.

3. As each form of transportation is finished, place the item on a display table.

4. Make a card with the block builder's name on it and the name of the form of transportation. If Danny built the bus, label it Danny's Bus Service.

**Something to think about—**
Young children often take the same blocks they used to build an airplane and reconfigure them to build a boat. Be sure you explain to the children that you want them to leave their creations intact, then use other blocks to construct the next forms. For younger children accept many of the same forms of transportation. For example, three children may want to build airplanes. Ask older children to each build different forms.

## For Work Bench: Building Airplanes, Boats And Cars

**What the children will learn—**
To safely saw, hammer, and construct a transportation vehicle

**Materials you will need—**
Work bench, vise, safety glasses, saw, hammer, scraps of lumber, nails, glue

**What to do—**
1. Before the woodworking session, cut the scraps of lumber into sizes that will fit into the vise and are not too cumbersome for small children to use.

2. Have the child who is sawing or hammering put on the safety glasses.

3. Secure the wood in the vise.

4. Discuss with the child whether she wants to build an airplane, boat or car.

5. Start the cut for the child to saw through a piece of wood. Assist with the sawing by placing your hands over the child's hands.

6. When the wood is cut in two or three pieces, assist the child in deciding how to attach the pieces together.

7. In addition to nailing the pieces together, glue them so that they hold in place without turning around on the nail head.

8. Display the wooden models alongside the block ones.

**Something to think about—**
If you are inexperienced in even simple woodworking, ask a parent, grandparent or community volunteer to supervise the work. Add a piece of block attached to a plastic straw to create a sailboat. Add wheels from Tinkertoys to make a car.

## TRAIN SONG

*By Diane Siebert*

*Illustrated by Mike Wimmer*

*The cadence of Siebert's train poem sings across the pages. Her "clickety-clack, clickety-clack" beginning sets the pace and the feel of the moving trains. The poet takes the reader to stations in different geographic areas and includes the freight trains with boxcars, auto haulers and hopper cars, as well as passenger trains with sleepers, diners and observation cars. There are pictures of locomotives and cabooses, too. Mike Wimmer's illustrations are realistic oil paintings with just the right mood cast in shadow and sky.*

## Circle Time Presentation

"Clickety-clack, clickety-clack," start the rhythm of the poem and have the children join you saying their "clickety-clacks" for a minute or two. Then have them stop clicking and read TRAIN SONG. After the first reading, let the children tell about any train trips they have taken or any trains that go near their neighborhoods. Have the children join you again in their "clickety-clacks" and for the second reading, let them continue clicking as you read the poem again. Call attention to the illustrations and announce the TRAIN SONG activities for the day. Place the book in the library corner in a "featured book" spot because many children will want to examine the illustrations more closely.

STORY STRETCHER

## For Art: Locomotive Shape

**What the children will learn—**
To paint a real or imagined experience with trains

**Materials you will need—**
Tempera paints, brushes, manilla or gray construction paper, easel

**What to do—**

1.  Cut a large sheet of paper in the shape of a locomotive.

2.  Place brown, gray, red, black and primary colors in the paint tray of the easel.

3.  Encourage the children to paint scenes from their real experiences or imagined ones with trains.

4.  Display their train pictures on a bulletin board.

**Something to think about—**
Add captions to the bulletin board by letting children dictate a few lines. Print their sentences on an index card. For younger children, place the card captions underneath their pictures. For older children, use large index cards. Place their card captions together on a metal ring, let them draw a smaller version of their bulletin board picture on an index card and write their captions on another card. Hang the ring book on the bulletin board. Read the ring book at a second circle time.

STORY STRETCHER

## For Blocks: Train Set, Railroad Tracks, Train Station

**What the children will learn—**
To construct railroad tracks and station

**Materials you will need—**
Train set, hollow blocks, play-dough, popsicle sticks, construction paper

**What to do—**

1.  In the parent newsletter, ask for a volunteer to bring in a train set and set it up in the classroom.

2.  Let the children help the volunteer set up the train set in or near the block area on a low table.

3.  Get specific instructions about operating the train.

4.  After the volunteer has left, ask the children to construct rails, train station, ticket booth, loading dock for a bigger train.

5.  Allow the children to work on their own, and instead of clearing away their blocks at cleanup time, leave the railroad buildings up until the next day.

6.  The next day, introduce the idea of signals. Look at Mike Wimmer's illustration of signal lights and discuss the meaning of the green, yellow and red lights.

7.  Ask the children how they could construct signals for their railroad area. Let them make

signals at every point where they think they might be needed.

**Something to think about—**
Teachers often do too much of the thinking for children. From learning process research, we know that children who problem solve and construct their own solutions retain the information; it is in long-term memory. Block building is an excellent problem solving activity, and as we let them construct their own signals, even deciding what materials to use, they will recall the meaning of the signals long after their play is over.

S T O R Y   S T R E T C H E R

## For Cooking And Snack Time: Eating In The Dining Car

**What the children will learn—**
To associate dining and good manners

**Materials you will need—**
Tablecloths, food for snacks, if possible — cloth napkins, real silverware, dishes and glasses

**What to do—**
1.  Have the children look at Wimmer's illustration of the family eating in the dining car.

2.  Ask the children who would be sitting with them if they were taking a trip on a train.

3.  Seat the children and let each table pretend to be a family eating together on the train.

4.  Encourage them to talk about their trip.

5.  Place a napkin over your arm and tell the children you are their waiter or server.

6.  Give each child some silverware and a napkin and help them to set their own place setting.

7.  Serve each child's snack on a plate and pour juice or milk into glasses.

8.  Have the mothers, fathers and grandparents at each table encourage their children to use their napkins.

**Something to think about—**
In these days of plastic utensils in fast-food restaurants, at schools and in child-care centers, as well as dining in front of the television at home, many children know little about handling real silverware, dishes and glasses. Try a whole week of snack service in this manner with the children exchanging roles as different members of the family.

S T O R Y   S T R E T C H E R

## For Library Corner: Listening Station

**What the children will learn—**
To listen and turn pages at the appropriate signal

**Materials you will need—**
Cassette tape recorder, tape, stapler

**What to do—**
1.  Record an instruction message at the beginning of the tape. For example, "Children, this tape is a recording of TRAIN SONG by Diane Siebert. When you hear the sound of the stapler clicking, turn the page. The person who painted the pictures for this book is Mike Wimmer. Begin by turning to the picture of the dog behind the screen door, then listen while I read."

2.  Place the stapler near the microphone to pick up a louder clicking sound.

3.  At the end of the tape, record your own message about the illustrations. One possible message, "Children, I really enjoyed reading TRAIN SONG. I could hear the 'clickety-clack' rhythm in my head while I was reading to you. If you want to hear the book again,

rewind the tape, and this time say, 'clickety-clack, clickety-clack' while I read. Say your 'clickety-clacks' in a soft voice or you will not be able to hear the 'click' of the stapler which means to turn the page."

**Something to think about—**
For younger children, omit the message to have them repeat the "clickety-clack" rhythm while they listen to the tape again. When you are in the library corner with a small group of children, you might try "clickety-clacking" with the tape. Older children will enjoy helping you make the recording. Have several staplers and let them all make the page-turning signal on cue. Record yourself reading TRAIN SONG on one side of the tape and let the children speak the "clickety-clack, clickety-clack" rhythm as the background while you read the book on the other side of the tape.

S T O R Y   S T R E T C H E R

## For Sand And Water Table: Making Our Own Freight Car

**What the children will learn—**
To improvise freight cars and their functions

**Materials you will need—**
Sand table, plastic food storage bags, twist ties, sand or popcorn or rice, scoop, rectangular box for a model boxcar

**What to do—**
1.  Fill the sand table with sand.

2.  Ask the children to fill their plastic bags with sand and tie them closed.

3.  After a child has filled one bag, have the children who come to the sand table during free play "guesstimate" how many bags it will take to fill the rectangular box.

**4.** Continue until the box is filled. Count the number of bags.

**5.** Then have the children try to pick up their loaded freight car or boxcar.

**6.** Noting it is too heavy, ask how they could get it moved over to the block area. Accept their suggestions and try their solutions. Eventually, someone will suggest using the wagon or wheelbarrow, and you can help the children realize that adding the wheels makes it roll and carry the load.

**Something to think about—**
For a different experience, substitute water for sand and use small round shampoo bottles and a large round container from the school cafeteria or a large pitcher, letting the children "guesstimate" the number of bottles needed to fill their model of a hopper car for liquids.

# REFERENCES

Brown, Laura Krasny, & Brown, Marc. (1988). **DINOSAURS TRAVEL: A GUIDE FOR FAMILIES ON THE GO.** Boston: Little, Brown and Company.

Kovalski, Maryann. (1987). **THE WHEELS ON THE BUS: An Adaptation Of The Traditional Song.** Boston: Little, Brown and Company.

McPhail, David. (1987). **FIRST FLIGHT.** Boston: Little, Brown and Company.

Pomerantz, Charlotte. (1987). Illustrated by R. W. Alley. **HOW MANY TRUCKS CAN A TOW TRUCK TOW?** New York: Random House.

Siebert, Diane. (1990). Illustrated by Mike Wimmer. **TRAIN SONG.** New York: Thomas Y. Crowell.

## Additional References For Transportation

Baer, Edith. (1990). Illustrated by Steve Bjorkman. **THIS IS THE WAY WE GO TO SCHOOL: A Book About Children Around The World.** *New York: Scholastic. Describes in text and watercolor and ink illustrations the many different modes of transportation children all over the world used to get to school.*

Burningham, John. (1973). **MR. GUMPY'S MOTOR CAR.** New York: Thomas Y. Crowell. *Mr. Gumpy's human and animal friends crowd into his old car and go for a drive. They enjoy the trip until it starts to rain.*

Crews, Donald. (1985) **SCHOOL BUS.** New York: Puffin Books. *The story follows school buses from the beginning of the day when the buses are empty to their rounds of picking up children, obeying traffic signals, delivering them to school and bringing them home again.*

Gibbons, Gail. (1987). **TRAINS.** New York: Holiday House. *In unusual boldly colored realistic illustrations, the reader is introduced to many different trains and the various types of cars and cargos.*

Morris, Ann. (1990). **ON THE GO.** Photographs by Ken Heyman. New York: Lothrop, Lee & Shepard Books. *Photographs show people from around the world as they transport themselves, their children and items for trade. From babies on their mothers' backs to spaceships, the photographs illustrate the vastness of the world of transportation.*

# POEMS, CHANTS, RHYTHMS AND RHYMES

*We're Going on a Bear Hunt*
*The Napping House*
*Jump, Frog, Jump!*
*Chicka Chicka Boom! Boom!*
*The Cat's Midsummer Jamboree*

# POEMS, CHANTS, RHYTHMS AND RHYMES

## WE'RE GOING ON A BEAR HUNT

*Retold by Michael Rosen*

*Illustrated by Helen Oxenbury*

*The action chant, "We're Going on a Bear Hunt," has long been a favorite among early childhood teachers. The tale of the bear hunt is told with the teacher leading the chant and the children repeating phrases. It is popular because it involves large muscle movements, action words and sound effects, with the suspense building at the end as the family enters a cave and finds a BEAR! Then, they have to reverse all the actions to arrive safely home. Now, the tale is told in book form with Helen Oxenbury's delightful drawings of a father, baby, older brother and two sisters. Their trek through the tall grasses, the cold river, the oozy mud, the dark forest, even a snowstorm before entering the gloomy cave is told in charcoal drawings, and on alternating pages where the sound effect words are printed, the illustrations are marvelous watercolors.*

## Circle Time Presentation

If the children do not know the chant, "We're Going on a Bear Hunt," perform it for them once, then read the book and ask if it sounds the same. Say the chant again and teach the motions, as "tiptoeing into the cave." Other motions are suggested on the book jacket. After the children have learned the motions, have them think of ways to remember the sequence. For example, use a flannel board cut out of grass for the first scene, then a blue wave for the river, a muddy shoe or footprint for the oozy mud, a tree for the dark forest, a snowflake or a dark storm cloud for the snowstorm, an outline of a cave and then a piece of furry fabric for the bear. Read the book or do the chant again and have children put the flannel board pieces in place.

STORY STRETCHER

## For Art: Charcoal Drawings And Watercolors Of Favorite Scenes

**What the children will learn—**
To express themselves with two different art media

**Materials you will need—**
Manilla paper or white construction paper, charcoals, watercolor paper, brushes, watercolor paints, paper towels

**What to do—**
1. Set up the art table with charcoals one day and watercolors the next.

2. Show the children how Helen Oxenbury drew some pictures in charcoals; the scene following was painted with watercolors.

3. Tell the children that this will be a two-day project and they may choose which to use first, the charcoals or the watercolors.

4. Demonstrate a basic technique with each media. For example, show the children how to draw with the edge of the charcoal and then smudge it with their fingers to fill in the drawing. With the watercolor, show them how to dapple their brush on paper towels to remove the excess water.

**Something to think about—**
If the children are not familiar with charcoals or watercolors, be sure to allow several days for them to explore the possibilities of media before expecting them to create pictures. This time of exploration is needed before they will be able to control the charcoals and watercolors well enough to use them creatively.

STORY STRETCHER

## For Creative Dramatics: Role Playing "We're Going On A Bear Hunt"

**What the children will learn—**
To pantomime the family members in the book

**Materials you will need—**
None needed

**What to do—**
1. Select five students who are good at improvising for the father and four children roles.

2. Tell the actors that they will pretend to be the family in the story, but they will not say the words. They will pretend to do what the family did in the book.

3. Help the father, who is the leader, know where to start in the room, and discuss with the actors where they might stop around the room to play each scene.

4. Ask the father to take the baby by the hand and the older sister to

take the younger sister by the hand. Read the book and have the actors role play.

5. Let the other children, who are watching the drama from the circle time rug, participate by saying the chant with the teacher as the book is read.

**Something to think about—**
Role play WE'RE GOING ON A BEAR HUNT for several days and each day let different children play the roles. If some of the children are reluctant to role play, do not force them, but compliment them on participating in the chant.

STORY STRETCHER

## For Library Corner: Listening Station — "We're Going On A Bear Hunt"

**What the children will learn—**
To repeat the recurring phrases in the chant

**Materials you will need—**
Cassette tape and record, jacks and headsets for listening station

**What to do—**
1. After the children know the chant well, record the class reading the book along with you.

2. Since the phrase, "We've got to go through it!" is repeated at the end of each page, there is no need to add a sound effect to tell the listeners to turn the page.

3. Demonstrate to the children how to use the listening station. Select three or four children to train, and assign them as helpers until the class becomes familiar with how to set up the jacks and headphones. The helpers can be in charge of the volume control and holding the book for the listeners to see.

**Something to think about—**
During the recording, young children can simply repeat the recurring phrase, "We can't go over it. We can't go under it. Oh, no! We've got to go through it!" With the older children, record the entire book being read together. Children also enjoy making up their own scenes and sound effects, as going through a fence, over a bridge or climbing a mountain.

STORY STRETCHER

## For Mathematics And Manipulatives: What Animal Am I?

**What the children will learn—**
To classify by touch

**Materials you will need—**
Paper grocery bag, a variety of small stuffed animals

**What to do—**
1. Place a collection of small stuffed animals into a large paper grocery bag and close the top of the bag.

2. With a small group of children at the mathematics and manipulatives center, play this suspenseful game. Have one child at a time to reach into the bag, feel a stuffed animal and guess what the animal is.

3. Remove the animals one at a time until they have all been guessed. If a child guesses incorrectly, have him describe the animal after it is removed from the bag and he has felt its distinguishing features, as the long ears of a stuffed rabbit.

4. After the guessing is completed, count the animals or group them by color or type, such as stuffed animals that represent pets and those that are wild animals.

**Something to think about—**
For younger children, let them hold the stuffed animals, describe them and discuss their distinguishing features before placing them in the bag. For older more verbal students, consider letting each child feel the stuffed animal in the bag, then describe it for the other children to guess which one it is.

STORY STRETCHER

## For Music And Movement: "We're Going On A Bear Hunt"

**What the children will learn—**
To match movements and sound effects to the words of the chant

**Materials you will need—**
None needed

**What to do—**
1. Reread the book to the class and let them echo chant the recurring phrase. To echo chant, the teacher says a phrase and the children repeat or echo the phrase.

2. After reading the book, repeat the chant. While seated, start the rhythm by alternating clapping hands and patting knees with a one-two beat.

3. Let the children echo chant until they know it well enough to say it with you.

**Something to think about—**
Print the words to "We're Going on a Bear Hunt" on a large chart tablet and use rebus symbols, simple drawings of the long grass, a tree for the forest, a muddy foot print for the oozy mud, etc. See the appendix for a sample of a rebus chart. The chart gives the children sequence reminders and becomes like a Big Book for a shared reading experience.

# POEMS, CHANTS, RHYTHMS AND RHYMES

## THE NAPPING HOUSE

*By Audrey Wood*

*Illustrated by Don Wood*

*An incredibly funny cumulative tale of everyone who gets in bed with Granny to take a nap. First the child, then the dog, next the cat, followed by the mouse and finally, a flea who with one tiny bite awakens the whole bedfull. Don Wood's illustrations for THE NAPPING HOUSE received the New York Times Best Illustrated Children's Book Award. Children enjoy the pictures and delight in remembering the rhyme from the first snooze to the breaking of the bed.*

## Circle Time Presentation

THE NAPPING HOUSE is a wonderful read-aloud selection for group reading because the repeated rhyme encourages the children to "read with" the teacher and the large format makes the pictures easy to see. Ask the children what they like to do when it is raining. You can tell the children that you like to sleep in or take a nap when there is a slow, gentle rain. Show the first page of the text and ask the children what they think is happening inside the house when there is a slow, gentle rain outside. Read THE NAPPING HOUSE. At the second reading, ask the children to join you in the repeated phrase, "where everyone is sleeping."

STORY STRETCHER

## For Art: White Paint On A Blue Canvas

**What the children will learn—**
To highlight with white paint

**Materials you will need—**
Light blue construction paper, pencils, easel, brushes, dark blue and white paint

**What to do—**
1. With the children who choose the art center during free play or choice time, look again at Don Wood's illustrations. Ask the children to describe the colors and the feelings conveyed in the pictures.

2. Demonstrate how to highlight with white paint by drawing something on a sheet of light blue construction paper, then painting the top of the object with white.

3. Let the children experiment on some scrap paper by drawing and highlighting.

4. Allow the children to paint as usual at the easel, but provide blue construction paper as the canvas and white paint for highlighting.

**Something to think about—**
Read the section of the book on the information page, which tells that the original paintings for THE NAPPING HOUSE were done in oils on pressed board. Ask an artist who paints with oils to bring them to class and let the children see her work. Also, ask the artist to bring different types of canvases, boards, paints and brushes.

STORY STRETCHER

## For Housekeeping And Dress-up Corner: Putting The Dolls To Bed

**What the children will learn—**
To dress and undress the dolls

**Materials you will need—**
Dolls, clothing, stuffed animals, doll beds, covers

**What to do—**
1. Ask the parents to provide some baby clothing that is no longer needed in their families.

2. Place the baby clothing and doll clothing out in the housekeeping and dress-up corner and have the children select some pajamas and sleepers that will fit the dolls and the stuffed animals.

3. Let the children play on their own, and you will notice that after getting the dolls ready for bed, they begin role playing parents and children in the "getting ready" for bed routines from their families.

**Something to think about—**
Young children who have difficulty taking a nap should be encouraged to get the dolls and stuffed animals ready for bed. Improvise a play episode by asking what the parent should do if the child doesn't want to take a nap.

## For Library Corner: "The Napping House" Flannel Board Story

**What the children will learn—**
To sequence the characters in the story

**Materials you will need—**
Flannel board, felt pieces for bed, grandmother, child, dog, cat, mouse and flea, light blue construction paper, scissors, marker, large plastic storage bag

**What to do—**
1. Distribute the pieces to individual children.
2. Read THE NAPPING HOUSE and as each character is called have the children place their felt pieces on the board.
3. Cut light blue construction paper the same size as a large plastic food storage bag.
4. Print THE NAPPING HOUSE on the construction paper and place it inside the plastic bag.
5. Store the flannel board pieces in the large plastic bag with the name of the story showing through.

**Something to think about—**
Leave the flannel board out in the library area all the time and arrange the class collection of flannel board stories so that they are easily used and returned by the children.

## For Mathematics And Manipulatives: How Many Are Too Many?

**What the children will learn—**
To associate quantity and load capacity

**Materials you will need—**
Hollow blocks or wooden blocks, cardboard

**What to do—**
1. Have the block builders pretend that the sheet of cardboard is a bed and that the wooden blocks are climbing into bed. Ask how many they think the bed will hold.
2. After their guesses, have them try it out by placing two blocks on the floor like the headboard and footboard of a bed. Then place the cardboard on top like the mattress. Begin piling on blocks and see how many it will hold before the cardboard sinks down in the middle and finally goes to the floor.
3. Try different weights and types of blocks.

**Something to think about—**
This activity could be labeled a science activity because it involves a concept from physics, "load." Also do the activity with fabric and with wood to see what the capacities of these materials are.

## For Music And Movement: Lullaby And Good-night

**What the children will learn—**
To sing a lullaby

**Materials you will need—**
Songbook of lullabies or cassette recording of lullabies, blue posterboard or chart tablet, marker

**What to do—**
1. Print the words to the lullaby on blue posterboard or chart tablet to add to the class's Big Music Book.
2. Sing the lullaby through once without pointing to the words.
3. Teach the lullaby by breaking it down into verses. Sing each verse and run your hands under the words on the chart in a fluid motion which goes with the tune of the lullaby.
4. Have the children sing the song at rest time and stretch out for a nap.

**Something to think about—**
If you have children from different cultures in your classroom, ask their parents to come to the classroom and sing a lullaby from their culture. If they are not able to come to the center or school, ask them to record themselves singing the lullaby and to send you the words printed in their language. Print a lullaby in another language on a chart and teach it to the children.

# POEMS, CHANTS, RHYTHMS AND RHYMES

## JUMP, FROG, JUMP!

*By Robert Kalan*

*Illustrated by Byron Barton*

*Kalan writes a sequence chant of the tale of fly, frog, fish, snake, turtle and boys all chasing each other, but frog escapes. The repeated characters and actions, as well as the large bold colors and recurring phrases, make the book an excellent read aloud selection. Barton's illustrations are vivid with few lines, yet expressive motions. The book is also available in Big Book format.*

## Circle Time Presentation

Cover the title of the book and ask the children to name all the animals and insects shown on the cover. Ask which one they think will be the main character, mentioned the most in the story. Uncover the title and read it, then ask the children to predict what they think will happen in the story. Invite the children to join in reading the story with you whenever they know what the next phrases might be. Read JUMP, FROG, JUMP!, pausing for the children to predict which animal will come next in the story. Read the story again without stopping, while motioning with your hands for the children to join you whenever the characters and phrases are repeated.

STORY STRETCHER

## For Art: Underwater And Over Water Scenes

**What the children will learn—**
To create split horizon scenes

**Materials you will need—**
Blue and green construction paper, tape, scraps of construction paper, scissors, glue, pencils, markers or crayons

**What to do—**
1. Have the children look at the way Byron Barton shows the frog half in the water and half out of the water with the fish below the water.

2. Ask the children how they could put the sheets of blue and green construction paper together to show underwater and over water scenes. Let them improvise and solve the problem. They will usually overlap one sheet of paper onto the other.

3. When they decide how to place the sheet of blue and green

construction paper together to make the underwater and over water background, place tape on the backs of the paper to hold them in place.

4. Tell the children they can add to their underwater and over water scene by cutting animals from scraps of paper and gluing them on or drawing with pencils, markers or crayons.

5. Leave the children on their own to finish their pictures.

**Something to think about—**
Consider creating a bulletin board of life at the pond. Use a split blue and green horizon and let the children add animals and insects made from scraps of construction paper.

STORY STRETCHER

## For Library Corner: Big Book Version Of Frog's Escape

**What the children will learn—**
To read together the recurring phrases

**Materials you will need—**
Big Book version of the story or chart tablet, marker, pointer

**What to do—**
1. If a Big Book version is available, read it with the children. If not, improvise by writing the words to JUMP, FROG, JUMP! on a chart tablet. Print large enough that the children can see the words easily.

2. Read the book or chart through once without using a pointer.

3. Read the book or chart again and have the children join you in repeating the "Jump, Frog, jump!" and in repeating the names and actions of the characters.

4. Let the boys read together, "How did the frog get away?" Let

the girls read together, "Jump, Frog, jump!"

**Something to think about—**
Seeing the words as they are said helps the children associate language and reading. Avoid pointing to one word at a time and reading word-to-word. Instead encourage fluent reading by having the children read phrases which go together.

## For Library Corner: Flannel Board Of Frog's Escapes

**What the children will learn—**
To sequence life at the pond and frog's narrow escapes

**Materials needed—**
Flannel board, felt pieces for fly, frog, fish, snake, turtle, net, basket

**What to do—**
1.   Read the story using the flannel board story and the felt pieces.

2.   Distribute the felt pieces to the children and have them place the pieces on the board in the sequence in which they appear in the story.

3.   Read the story again and reverse the roles from the previous Story S-t-r-e-t-c-h-e-r and have the girls say, "How did the frog get away?" Let the boys say, "Jump, frog, jump!"

**Something to think about—**
Ask the children to make the flannel board pieces from scraps of construction paper, then laminate the characters, glue a piece of old emery board on the back and use them for the story.

## For Music And Movement: Jumping Frogs

**What the children will learn—**
To use hand motions to accompany the story

**Materials you will need—**
None needed

**What to do—**
1.   With a small group of children, think of hand motions that could be used to tell the story. For instance, one finger in the air for the fly, place palms of hands together and make swimming motions for the fish, one hand jumping for the frog, hand and arm slithering for the snake, two hands together palms down for the turtle, throwing motion for the net, chasing around for boys, hands together on the floor for frog caught in basket.

2.   Read the story and have the children practice the motions to teach to the rest of the class.

3.   At a second circle time of the day, have the small group stand in front of their friends and as you read, they can do the motions.

4.   Have the performers join their friends in the audience and do the actions together.

**Something to think about—**
Young children are less self-conscious when they perform in a group. If your school requires that each class perform at parent night, instead of teaching the children new songs, have them do some of the ones they have already learned as a part of the curriculum. Let different groups of children be the leaders.

## For Science And Nature: Frogs In A Terrarium

**What the children will learn—**
To observe the behavior of frogs

**Materials you will need—**
Old aquarium, plants, rocks, small frogs, small glass jar, magnifying glasses

**What to do—**
1.   Get a frog from a science and nature center, or if you live in an area where ponds and frogs are easily found, ask a parent to bring a frog to school.

2.   Build a large terrarium from an aquarium.

3.   Allow the children to look through the sides of the terrarium and observe where the frogs like to hide, what they do, when they eat and when they jump.

4.   Take one small frog from the terrarium and place it in a small glass jar where the children can look at it from all sides.

5.   Keep the frogs for only a few days. Provide water and food, flies and insects.

6.   Return the frogs to the area where they were caught or ask the naturalist or school supplier where the frogs should be let go.

**Something to think about—**
Some school supply houses have tadpoles and frogs at certain times of the year. One of the best experiences for the children is to have a field trip to a pond and observe the varieties of plant and animal life. Ask for and train the volunteers before the field trip so that they can provide good information.

## 17

# POEMS, CHANTS, RHYTHMS AND RHYMES

by Bill Martin, Jr.
and John Archambault
illustrated by Lois Ehlert

## CHICKA CHICKA BOOM! BOOM!

*By Bill Martin, Jr.*

*and John Archambault*

*Illustrated by Lois Ehlert*

*This ABC book tells an unusual tale in usual Lois Ehlert bright, bold graphics. Martin and Archambault have teamed up to create a read-aloud chant. With the opening line of the cheer and the reader is caught up in cheering the letters up the trunk of a coconut tree. The book will become a read-aloud favorite.*

## Circle Time Presentation

Practice reading CHICKA CHICKA BOOM! BOOM! several times before presenting it to the class. Have the children practice saying with you, "Chicka Chicka Boom! Boom!" A natural rhythm will emerge as you read and the children will delight in saying their lines. Pause just before all the letters fall out of the tree, and tell the children to get ready. When you turn the page they should say their lines, "Chicka Chicka Boom! Boom!" At the end of circle time mention that the children should look closely at the way the illustrator changed the borders using bright citrus colors, and how each letter changed when it fell from the coconut tree.

STORY STRETCHER

## For Art: Bright Citrus Borders

**What the children will learn—**
To decorate the borders of their pictures by layering paper

**Materials you will need—**
Bright orange, yellow and pink construction paper, pencil, ruler, hole puncher, glue or stapler, white paper, markers, scraps of construction paper

**What to do—**
1. Draw a one-inch border around the bright orange, yellow, pink construction paper.

2. Let the children punch holes at random between the margin lines and the edge of the paper.

3. Place a contrasting color of construction paper behind the paper with the holes and secure in place with glue or staple sheets together.

4. Ask the children to make a tropical scene by drawing on the white paper with pencils or markers. Some children may want to make a collage picture of a tropical scene by gluing on scraps of brightly colored construction paper.

5. Glue the tropical scene in the center of the construction paper leaving the exposed hole-punched margins as a frame.

**Something to think about—**
Younger children will spend a great deal of their time just punching the holes. Older children can experiment more with creating bold graphics like Lois Ehlert's.

STORY STRETCHER

## For Cooking And Snack Time: Coconut Tasting Party

**What the children will learn—**
To taste coconut in a variety of forms

**Materials you will need—**
Coconut in shell, newspaper, hammer, teaspoons, knife, grater, bowls, cookie sheet, toaster oven, napkins, glasses, milk

**What to do—**
1. Purchase a coconut in the shell.

2. Have the children hold it, feel how heavy it is, how rough the outside is and have them shake it to hear the milk inside.

3. Wrap the coconut in newspaper, then hit it with the hammer so that it breaks open.

4. Pour the milk from the coconut and let the children taste it. Dip the teaspoons in the milk to coat them for a taste.

5. Slice off a small bit of the coconut meat for the children to taste.

6. Peel the coconut and let the children help grate it into bowls. Remind them of how to hold the piece of coconut meat so that they do not grate their knuckles or fingers.

7. Toast the coconut on a cookie sheet in the oven.

8. Let the children taste the toasted coconut.

9. Serve coconut macaroon cookies with glasses of cold milk.

**Something to think about—**
If possible, invite a parent to make coconut macaroons from the coconut the children grated.

## For Library Corner: Recording Chicka Chicka Boom! Boom!

**What the children will learn—**
To say their lines on cue

**Materials you will need—**
Cassette tape and recorder

**What to do—**
1. Practice reading CHICKA CHICKA BOOM! BOOM! with the children so that they know when you want them to say their lines. Have the children repeat the "Chicka Chicka Boom! Boom!" and "I'll meet you at the top of the coconut tree."

2. Record the group reading, and let them critique their performance and decide if they want to do it again.

3. Record the back side of the tape, and for this reading, have the children join in whenever they know the words rather than waiting for the repeated phrases.

4. Let the children critique this recording also, and decide whether or not they want to do it again.

**Something to think about—**
There are some books that are absolutely necessary to have a tape recording of and CHICKA CHICKA BOOM! BOOM! is one of them.

## For Mathematics And Manipulatives: Counting And Sequencing Letters

**What the children will learn—**
To count and sequence the letters of the alphabet

**Materials you will need—**
Magnetic alphabet letters or alphabet blocks or wooden alphabet letters

**What to do—**
1. Ask the children who come to the mathematics and manipulative area during free play or choice time to find as many sets of the alphabet as they can around the room, magnetic letters, wooden puzzle pieces, alphabet blocks.

2. Ask the children to bring the alphabet items to the table in the mathematics and manipulatives area.

3. Have the children arrange their alphabet letters in order.

4. Ask one child to say the letters of the alphabet while touching the letters, but pause after each letter. When the child pauses, the children count. For example, child says, "A" and the group says, "1."

5. Repeat the exercise with all the alphabet sets.

6. Let the children make their names from the alphabet letters, and as they say the letters of their names, the group will count.

**Something to think about—**
Older children can take the phrases found in CHICKA CHICKA BOOM! BOOM! and see how many words they can make from manipulating the letters.

## For Music And Movement: Chicka Chicka Boom! Boom! Up Our Coconut Tree

**What the children will learn—**
To move in sequence while keeping the rhythm of the chant

**Materials you will need—**
Masking tape, optional— long sheet of butcher paper, markers

**What to do—**
1. Place a long, slightly sloping line of masking tape across the floor or make a long coconut tree by drawing a brown trunk on a sheet of butcher paper and taping it to the floor.

2. Assign each child a letter. When you reach Q R S and U V W and X Y Z, assign each set to a child.

3. Tell the children that as you read you want them to move up the trunk of the coconut tree, keeping the rhythm of the chant. Then fall down. As you read their letters they should do the motions that go with the story, but do them keeping the rhythm.

4. Practice once and help any children who need to think of ways to show what their letters did.

5. Begin by having everyone get the beat of the chant by saying, "Chicka Chicka Boom! Boom!"

6. Do the movement activity several times and be prepared for giggles and laughter. Enjoy the fun with the children.

**Something to think about—**
This chant also can be done like the bunny hop with children attaching themselves to the line as they hop along. Have one adult lead the line while the other reads the book.

**225**

# POEMS, CHANTS, RHYTHMS AND RHYMES

BY DAVID KHERDIAN AND NONNY HOGROGIAN

## THE CAT'S MIDSUMMER JAMBOREE

*By David Kherdian*

*and Nonny Hogrogian*

*A delightful cumulative tale about a cat who loved to sing and play the mandolin and how he convinced other animal musicians to join him for a midsummer jamboree. While not a poem or chant or a rhyme, the book is about rhythms and making music. The artists used pencil and watercolor to create a lovely green meadow and forest with wildflowers, ferns, woodland animals and insects camouflaged among the plants.*

## Circle Time Presentation

Ask the children if they know what a "jamboree" is. Some may have heard of a Boy Scouts' or Girl Scouts' Jamboree. It is a time and a place where a lot of people gather to participate in some event. Tell the children that in this story the jamboree is like a concert where music is played. Read THE CAT'S MIDSUMMER JAMBOREE. Read the book again and ask the children to figure out what these words mean — duet, trio, quartet, quintet and sextet. After reading the story, turn back to the picture of the cat with the mandolin and the toad with the harmonica and ask who made up the duet and how many animals there were. Continue showing pictures and identifying the members of the trio, quartet, quintet and sextet.

STORY STRETCHER

## For Art: Midsummer Meadow In Pencil Shading And Watercolor Washes

**What the children will learn—**
To use more than one medium to make a picture

**Materials you will need—**
Construction paper or watercolor paper, scraps of paper, pencils, watercolors, small brushes, margarine tubs, newspaper, paper towels or sponges

**What to do—**
1. Ask the children to draw a meadow or forest scene.

2. Demonstrate on some scrap paper how to add shading and texturing by using the side of the pencil lead.

3. Encourage the children to add some texturing or shading to their pictures.

4. Show them how to use a little watercolor paint on a small brush, and if they have too much water or paint, to lightly dab their brush onto newspaper or paper towels or a sponge.

5. Let the children experiment on smaller scraps of paper and then add the watercolors to their pictures.

**Something to think about—**
Emphasize that watercolor artists let the paint run together to create a background of color.

STORY STRETCHER

## For Library Corner: Flannel Board Story Of Cat's Band

**What the children will learn—**
To retell a story using visual cues

**Materials you will need—**
Flannel board, felt pieces for the cat, mandolin, toad, harmonica, fox, flute, badger, drum, skunk, violin, goose, bassoon

**What to do—**
1. Arrange the animals in order down the left hand side of the flannel board and place musical instruments at random along the right side.

2. Retell the story in your own words, and as each animal is introduced, move the felt piece to the bottom of the flannel board.

3. Have a child come up and select the instrument that goes with the animal and place it in the animal's hands.

4. At the end of the story, put the animals around in a circle and say, "Cat's playing the ___," and pause for the children to say the name of the instrument. Continue naming all the animals and their instruments.

5. End the retelling session by having all the children say to-

gether, "And that's the story of the Cat's midsummer jamboree."

**Something to think about—**
Older children can retell the story and mix up the animals and instruments or add more animals and instruments.

## For Mathematics And Manipulatives: Scavenger Hunt For Sets From Duet To Sextet

**What the children will learn—**
To associate the words and the numerals they represent

**Materials you will need—**
Small paper bag

**What to do—**
1. Tell the children that these number words — duet, trio, quartet, quintet and sextet — are most often used to describe musical groups, but they can be used to describe the number in a set of objects.

2. Give each child a small paper bag to go around in the room and collect small objects. For the first scavenger hunt have them find two objects that go together.

3. Then have the children bring the objects back to the mathematics and manipulatives table, place them on the table and say, "I have a duet of chalk — two pieces of chalk."

4. Continue the scavenger hunt for sets of objects, and have the children return and describe what they have.

**Something to think about—**
Older children may be able to read and write the words and what they represent when they return to the table. Avoid a drill-type lesson and instead concentrate on the children's creating these sets and hearing the new mathematical terms.

## For Music And Movement: Musical Instruments

**What the children will learn—**
To identify the instruments and their sounds

**Materials you will need—**
As many as possible of the following instruments and musicians who play them — mandolin, harmonica, flute, drum, violin, accordion, cassette tapes and recorder

**What to do—**
1. Invite adults or older children who can play these instruments to come to class and to bring their instruments with them. Invite one musician per day, and when all the musicians have visited, ask them to come together on one day and play together.

2. Have the musician play a song he likes and then play a song the children might know, such as "Twinkle, Twinkle, Little Star." Record the songs on cassette tape.

3. After the musicians have played, let the children hold and play the instruments, following the instructions the musician gives.

**Something to think about—**
Contact a music teacher or a band leader and ask to have older children bring their band instruments and play for the class.

## For Music And Movement: Rhythm Band Jamboree

**What the children will learn—**
To form duets, trios, quartets, quintets and sextets

**Materials you will need—**
Rhythm band instruments, recording of some march music and tape or record player

**What to do—**
1. Tell the children that they are going to have a jamboree.

2. Have the children listen to a recording of some march music. Let them clap their hands and slap their knees to get the beat of the music.

3. Allow the children to march around the room following your lead and continue the beat of the music.

4. Have the children sit on the circle time rug and distribute the rhythm band instruments at random among them.

5. Tell the children to put their instruments down on the floor in front of them. Then have two children stand in front of the group and play together while listening to the tape recording. Emphasize the word "duet."

6. Continue adding musicians to the group and letting them play together until you have a "sextet" playing.

7. End by letting all the musicians "jam" together for a "jamboree."

**Something to think about—**
In early rhythm band sessions, demonstrate how to play each instrument.

# REFERENCES

Kalan, Robert. (1981). Illustrated by Byron Barton. **JUMP, FROG, JUMP!** New York: Scholastic.

Kherdian, David, & Hogrogian, Nonny. (1990). **THE CAT'S MIDSUMMER JAMBOREE.** New York: Philomel Books.

Martin, Jr., Bill, & Archambault, John. (1989). Illustrated by Lois Ehlert. **CHICKA CHICKA BOOM! BOOM!** New York: Simon and Schuster Books for Young Readers.

Rosen, Michael. (1989). Illustrated by Helen Oxenbury. **WE'RE GOING ON A BEAR HUNT.** New York: Margaret K. McElderry Books.

Wood, Audrey. (1984). Illustrated by Don Wood. **THE NAPPING HOUSE.** San Diego: Harcourt Brace Jovanovich.

## Additional References For Poems, Chants, Rhythms And Rhymes

Ahlberg, Janet, & Ahlberg, Allan. (1978). **EACH PEACH PEAR PLUM.** New York: Puffin Books. *A pictorial I-spy book with nursery rhyme and storybook characters.*

Hague, Kathleen. (1989). Illustrated by Michael Hague. **BEAR HUGS.** New York: Henry Holt & Company. *A collection of poems about teddy bears and the things they do, including providing comfort at bedtime and playing hide-and-seek.*

Hoberman, Mary Ann. (1978). Illustrated by Betty Fraser. **A HOUSE IS A HOUSE FOR ME.** New York: The Viking Press. *A hill, a hive, a hole are all houses. A wonderfully illustrated poem about houses for insects and animals and people.*

Pearson, Tracey Campbell. (1984). **OLD MACDONALD HAD A FARM.** New York: Dial. *The familiar song illustrated with bright and energetic visual appeal.*

Westcott, Nadine B. (1980). **I KNOW AN OLD LADY WHO SWALLOWED A FLY.** Boston: Little, Brown. *A cumulative song of an old lady who swallows a fly, a spider, a bird and so on through a horse, and she's dead of course.*

# TALL AND FUNNY TALES

*"Stand Back," Said the Elephant, "I'm Going to Sneeze!"*
*Are You My Mother?*
*A Dark Dark Tale*
*The Little Mouse, The Red Ripe Strawberry, and the Big Hungry Bear*
*Here Comes the Cat!*

## 18

# TALL AND FUNNY TALES

# "STAND BACK," SAID THE ELEPHANT, "I'M GOING TO SNEEZE!"

*By Patricia Thomas*

*Illustrated by Wallace Tripp*

*When elephant announces he is about to sneeze, all the animals implore him to hold it. They recall his last powerful sneeze when the water buffalo was bumped along a trail, the monkeys were sneezed right out of the trees, the parrots lost their feathers, the bees their stings, the bear his hair, the crocodile's nose turned inside out, fish lost their gills and the zebra his stripes. The leopard and hippopotamus told elephant he must stop his sneeze. The elephant was about to sneeze when suddenly a little mouse said, "Boo," and the sneeze went away only to be replaced by a tickle. The laugh had the same effect on all the animals, including the zebra losing his stripes. Wallace Tripp's illustrations are just as humorous as the cleverly crafted verse between elephant and the animals.*

## Circle Time Presentation

Ask the children to recall when they felt a sneeze coming on, how they wrinkled and rubbed their noses, and just as it felt it might go away, they sneezed. Have them cover their noses and mouths, pretend to sneeze and then repeat, "Excuse me please for my sneeze." Turn to the title page and show the picture of elephant holding his trunk, trying not to sneeze. Then read "STAND BACK," SAID THE ELEPHANT, "I'M GOING TO SNEEZE!" The children will giggle, laugh and roar at the side-splitting text and illustrations. The book is definitely of the "read it again" variety. For the second reading, pause for the children to provide the phrase, "But please, don't sneeze!"

STORY STRETCHER

## For Art: Funny Moving Animal Pictures

**What the children will learn—**
To construct pictures with moving parts

**Materials you will need—**
Construction paper, crayons, markers or colored pencils, brads, masking tape, scissors

**What to do—**
**1.** Ask the children to look at and talk about the animals' movements and expressions.

**2.** Request that each child select an animal from the book and draw a large picture of it, almost as large as the whole sheet of construction paper.

**3.** Have the children cut out their animals.

**4.** Demonstrate how to cut the animal's head or tail from the body and re-attach it with a brad so that the body part moves. After

the head or tail is cut off, place a little piece of masking tape on the back and on the back of the body to reinforce it. Place the brad through the body, and then through the head or tail.

**5.** When the animals are finished, re-enact their moving as the elephant starts to sneeze, then when he laughs.

**Something to think about—**
After the children have made their first set of "moving animals," let them design other sets, such as all barnyard or circus animals, sets of birds or fish.

STORY STRETCHER

## For Creative Dramatics: Elephant's Sneeze

**What the children will learn—**
To dramatize the animals' actions and expressions

**Materials you will need—**
Chart tablet, marker, or chalk board and chalk

**What to do—**
**1.** With a small group of children in the library corner or on the circle time rug, reread the book.

**2.** As each animal is mentioned, write the name on the chart tablet.

**3.** Have the children notice how the illustrator shows all the animals wide-eyed as they anticipate elephant's sneeze and running away as they experience his laughter.

**4.** Ask the children to dramatize the animals' action and feelings while you read the dialogue.

**5.** Have all the children chant the phrase, "But please, don't sneeze."

**Something to think about—**
Encourage the children who do not volunteer to act out the animal parts to help dramatize elephant's actions. They also can become the

chorus which says, "But please, don't sneeze."

## For Library Corner: Listening Station — "Please, Don't Sneeze" Tape

**What the children will learn—**
To repeat the recurring phrase on cue

**Materials you will need—**
Cassette tape, recorder, listening station, earphones

**What to do—**
1. Practice reading the book with the children saying the phrase, "But please, don't sneeze," when you pause and signal them.

2. Position the tape recorder near you, and snap your fingers for the page turning signal.

3. At the beginning of the tape, record a message for the listeners stating the name of the book, the author's and illustrator's names, instructions to turn to the picture of the elephant standing on hind legs with his mouth open. Also, tell them when they hear you snap your fingers to turn the page.

4. After the tape is made, place it at the listening station in the library corner. Let the children who made the tape become the first set of listeners.

5. Have a child who has shown less interest in books become the page turner for the group.

**Something to think about—**
Humorous books, predictable books that have recurring phrases or add a new character for each scene, as well as folktales, are good selections for the group listening station.

## For Library Corner: Writing A New Tale — Elephant Sneezes At The Circus

**What the children will learn—**
To use the frame of one story to write another one with different characters

**Materials you will need—**
Chart tablet, markers, tape recorder, cassette tape

**What to do—**
1. Ask the children to pretend that the elephant in the story is a circus animal.

2. Turn the tape recorder on for the brainstorming of the changes for each animal and scene.

3. Reread the story and pause at the name of each animal and insert the name of a circus animal. For instance, when the elephant meets a water buffalo, there are no water buffaloes in the circus, so substitute a lion. Next, elephant meets the monkeys, who might be in a circus, but instead of having them sitting in trees, say they are swinging on swings.

4. Rewrite the story as you continue changing animals and settings as the circus theme requires.

**Something to think about—**
For younger children who may not be able to pay attention for a long session, tape record the changes, then print the new versions onto a chart tablet at a later time. Older children can compose different versions, as the whale who is about to sneeze in the ocean or the bull who is about to sneeze in the barnyard.

## For Mathematics And Manipulatives: Elephant's Friends In A Row

**What the children will learn—**
To sequence animals, birds and fish as they appear in the story

**Materials you will need—**
Animals constructed in the art center

**What to do—**
1. Ask the children to line up the animals as they appeared in the book. Reread the story and place each animal along the edge of the table located in the mathematics and manipulatives area.

2. After the animals are lined up from the buffalo to the mouse, take them away in the order they ran away from elephant.

**Something to think about—**
For older children, place an index card on the table with each animal's name on it in the slot where the animal was. For younger children, try colored squares of construction paper that correspond to the color of the animal. The children can help you decide. Add spots for the leopard and black stripes on white for the zebra. Whenever there are two colors that are the same, let the children decide which distinguishing feature should be added so they tell the gray of the water buffalo from the gray for the hippo.

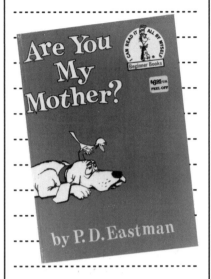

## ARE YOU MY MOTHER?

*By P. D. Eastman*

*This familiar children's book is the story of a little bird who goes in search of his mother and asks different animals and machines, "Are you my mother?" In desperation, the little bird is about to give up when a big machine, the bird calls "Snort," picks the bird up and places him in his nest as his mother is returning with his first worm. Eastman's cartoon-like drawings accompany a simple text filled with repeated phrases that young children enjoy reading with their teacher.*

## Circle Time Presentation

Show the cover of ARE YOU MY MOTHER? and ask the children if this story is real or imaginary and how they know. Ask if any children have heard this story before. If so, ask the children to let you read it through in its entirety and then they can tell what they like about the story. Read ARE YOU MY MOTHER? and use the verbal cloze process which means pausing for the children to complete a line or to repeat a phrase that often appears in the text. Ask the children to suggest some other animals (or farm animals or other machines) the little bird would meet if he went to the zoo looking for his mother.

STORY STRETCHER

## For Art: Mural Of "Are You My Mother?"

**What the children will learn—**
To recall the beginning, middle and end of the story

**Materials you will need—**
Long sheet of butcher paper or long sheet of continuous sheet computer paper, crayons or markers

**What to do—**

1. In the center of the paper at the top of the page, print ARE YOU MY MOTHER?

2. Divide the paper into three sections, for the beginning, middle and end of the story.

3. Talk with the children about the fact that a mural tells a story.

4. Have the children remember what happened at the beginning of the story until Little Bird met the kitten. Ask the children to draw about the beginning of the story on the first long section of paper.

5. Encourage the children to talk about their pictures.

6. On the second day, have the children recall what happened in the middle of the story. When they remember all the animals and machines that Little Bird met, ask who will draw which animals.

7. On the third day, ask the children to recall what happened at the end of the story, from the time Little Bird first met Snort. Have them draw pictures about Little Bird and Snort.

**Something to think about—**
Display the mural on a chalk rail or down at eye level for the children to see. At a circle time later in the week, have three children retell the story by talking about the pictures. Let one child tell about the beginning of the story, one about the middle and one about the ending of the story.

ANOTHER STORY STRETCHER

## For Art: Eggshell Collage

**What the children will learn—**
To dye eggs and to use shells in their artwork

**Materials you will need—**
Boiled eggs, egg dyeing kit, large tablespoons, crayons, small baskets, construction paper, glue sticks, liquid glue

**What to do—**

1. Follow the directions on the egg dyeing kit to decorate and color the eggs.

2. Place the dyed eggs in baskets and display them on the cooking and snack tables as centerpieces.

3. The next day, serve the eggs as a snack. Let the children take the egg they dyed and with the back of a large tablespoon tap on the shell and crack it. Peel the

eggs and eat them. Save the egg-shells.

4. Let the children collect their eggshells and glue parts of the shells onto brightly colored construction paper to create an eggshell collage.

**Something to think about—**
Picking up the small pieces of eggshell and putting glue on them may be too challenging for some young children. They can spread liquid glue over an area they want to cover, then sprinkle the eggshell pieces over the area.

STORY STRETCHER

## For Creative Dramatics: Little Bird's Search

**What the children will learn—**
To pretend the motions of Little Bird

**Materials you will need—**
None needed

**What to do—**

1. Show the beginning of ARE YOU MY MOTHER? and discuss the hatching process.

2. Have the children pretend to be inside the egg all warm and safe, then they begin to feel like jumping, and they kick their arms and legs out and stretch to get free of their shell.

3. Pretend that the circle time rug is the nest. Little Bird stands on the edge of his nest, but he is afraid to fly.

4. Then have five children pretend to be Little Bird and let each Little Bird wander around the room asking the other children if they are his mother. Let the children pretend to be any of the animals they would like.

5. Have each Little Bird go to the different machines and ask if they are his mother. Let the other

children pretend to be the car, boat or airplane.

6. Call the Little Birds to you. Pretend to be Snort and lift the children up one at a time and put them back in the nest on the circle time rug.

**Something to think about—**
Older children can pantomime the action of the entire story and assign roles.

STORY STRETCHER

## For Library Corner: Composing A New Little Bird Adventure

**What the children will learn—**
To predict what might happen next

**Materials you will need—**
Variety of writing and drawing papers, pens, pencils, crayons

**What to do—**

1. With the children who choose the library writing area during free play, read again ARE YOU MY MOTHER?

2. Ask the children what they think will happen next, now that Little Bird has found his mother. For example, Little Bird could go back and introduce his mother to all the animals he met. They could both go looking for his father. A follow-up adventure might be Little Bird's adventure when learning to fly.

3. After the brainstorming, have the children write or draw what they think will happen next.

**Something to think about—**
For younger children, after they have drawn their pictures, ask them to dictate a sentence or two that they would like to go with their pictures. Older children can write on their own using invented spellings. Accept whatever level of writing the children bring to the

task, from scribbling to standard spelling. Just as children gradually refine their skills in art, puzzles, mathematical understandings, they also will refine their skills in constructing words.

STORY STRETCHER

## For Sand Table: Snort And Other Machines That Move The Earth

**What the children will learn—**
To operate mechanical toys with shovels, scoops, pulleys, dumping beds

**Materials you will need—**
Sand table, sand or soil, mechanical toys

**What to do—**

1. Show the illustrations of Snort in ARE YOU MY MOTHER?

2. Talk with the children about all the big machines needed to build roads and dig foundations for buildings.

3. Have the children who brought these toys to school demonstrate how they work.

4. Discuss that these toys will go home with the children who brought them, but that for this week they are sharing with the whole class. Let the children who brought the toys share among themselves first.

**Something to think about—**
Ask the parents to allow the children to bring these toys to school if you do not have them in your classroom.

# 18
## TALL AND FUNNY TALES

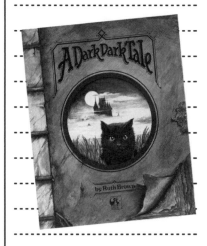

## A DARK DARK TALE

*By Ruth Brown*

*On a dark moor, in a dark house, the tale continues until the sound that is heard in the dark is — surprise, a tiny little mouse. Ruth Brown's dark illustrations lead the reader suspiciously through the house. The mood and suspense are heightened by the shadows, cobwebs and absence of anyone, except the cat.*

## Circle Time Presentation

Darken the room and read the book by shining a flashlight on the pictures. Just before the end of the book turn off the flashlight and pause for a few seconds, then flash it back on again to show the picture of the little mouse cozy in his little bed in the wooden box at the back of the closet. Turn on the lights and leaf through the pictures, pausing for the children to tell you how the illustrator created a suspenseful and surprising story through the use of darkness, shadows and shading. Ask the children when they began to think of this as a scary story. If the children want, read the story again by flashlight. Place the flashlight and the book in the library area for the children to explore on their own.

STORY STRETCHER

## For Art: Crayon Etching A Dark Print

**What the children will learn—**
To make an etching

**Materials you will need—**
Easel, brushes, watercolor or slick sided paper, brightly colored crayons, dark blue, brown and black tempera paints, liquid soap, plastic knives

**What to do—**

1.  Prepare a sample of crayon etching ahead of time. Demonstrate for the children how to cover a sheet of paper with crayons. Have the children write their names or initials on the back of their papers.

2.  Mix dark tempera paints with liquid soap. The soap makes the paint adhere to the crayons. Place two or three teaspoons in a pint of paint, depending on the thickness of the soap. Measurements do not have to be exact.

3.  Have the children completely cover their crayon colored sheet with the paint and let it dry overnight.

4.  The next day, show the children how to etch out a picture by scratching lines with the point of the plastic knife.

**Something to think about—**
Older children can plan to do several scenes for a rewritten version of A DARK DARK TALE. Younger children will just enjoy the process and will not be as concerned about the way to use the technique to create a certain type of illustration.

STORY STRETCHER

## For Block Building: What Fits In A Box This Size?

**What the children will learn—**
To estimate the capacity of a box

**Materials you will need—**
Variety of sizes and shapes of boxes, large hollow blocks, smaller building blocks, index card, pencil, tape

**What to do—**

1.  Look at the last picture in A DARK DARK TALE and discuss all the things the little mouse had inside his box, which was his house.

2.  Bring out a small wooden box and ask what could fit inside. Six plastic connector blocks, ten axles and wheels, five wooden counting blocks?

3.  Bring out a large cardboard carton and ask how many hollow blocks would fit inside.

4.  Place all the boxes in a row and let the children select a box they want to fill with blocks.

5.  After the boxes are filled, have the children count the quantities of different blocks that are inside.

6. Write the list of contents on a large index card and tape to the box.

**Something to think about—**
This activity could have been labeled a Mathematics And Manipulatives Story S-t-r-e-t-c-h-e-r as appropriately as one for block building. Blocks by their very nature are mathematical materials.

## For Library Corner: Another Dark Dark Tale

**What the children will learn—**
To write from another perspective

**Materials you will need—**
Manilla paper, pencil, crayons, variety of writing papers

**What to do—**
1. Read A DARK DARK TALE again. Then ask what the story would be if it were the mouse who was the main character. Look back through the entire book at all the illustrations and have the children imagine what the little mouse might be thinking as he moved from the moor to the house, up the stairs, opened the toy cupboard and found the wooden box.

2. Ask the children to draw and write another dark dark tale and compose the story from the mouse's perspective.

3. Have the children take a large sheet of manilla paper and fold it twice, making four sections.

4. Ask them to draw four scenes of the mouse from the moor to the cupboard and then to tell or write a story that goes with their drawings.

**Something to think about—**
Younger children may just draw the beginning or the end of the story with the little mouse in the picture somewhere. Older children can make eight section stories

and then tell their stories into a tape recorder or write the stories with more detail.

## For Music And Movement: Seeking The Hiding Place

**What the children will learn—**
To find a hiding place by listening to directions

**Materials you will need—**
Small wooden box, tape recording of suspenseful music or instrumental music, cassette player

**What to do—**
1. Read A DARK DARK TALE again with the lights lowered.

2. Tell the children that you have hidden a small wooden box somewhere in the classroom. When the music starts, they are to tiptoe around the room without talking, looking for the box. When the music stops, they freeze.

3. Play the music and let the children tiptoe around the room. Stop the music and then tell the children who are near the wooden box that they are "hot." Tell the children who are far away from the hiding place that they are "cold."

4. Start and stop the music three or four times using the hot and cold signals.

5. When the box is found, stop the music and flip on the lights.

**Something to think about—**
With younger children, hide the box in a more obvious place. With older children, write clues and read them instead of using the hot and cold signals. For instance, one clue might read, "If you like to paint and draw, then the answer is clear, you are getting near."

## For Work Bench: Building A Box

**What the children will learn—**
To use hammer, saw, nails, hinges, vise

**Materials you will need—**
Tools, safety glasses, wood, nails, carpenter's glue, sandpaper, stain, brush, work bench, volunteer woodworker

**What to do—**
1. Ask a parent who likes woodworking to come to class and build a small box like the one in A DARK DARK TALE.

2. Have a group of woodworkers chosen as assistants to hammer, saw, nail and sand the box. Rotate the assistants throughout the day or as long as the volunteer has time for the project.

3. Construct the box, sand and finish it.

4. Decide with the children where the box is to be kept. Some suggestions might include in the writing area for pencils or in the housekeeping corner for decorations.

**Something to think about—**
If you do not have a volunteer and your skills are not adequate for the task, bring a special wooden box to class, have the children look at it closely and appreciate the workmanship that went into its construction. If your volunteer woodworker does not have much time, have the pieces of the box precut. Also continue the woodworking activities by using scraps of wood. If possible, take a field trip to the volunteer woodworker's shop and see all the tools and wood used in building projects.

# 18

# TALL AND FUNNY TALES

# THE LITTLE MOUSE, THE RED RIPE STRAWBERRY, AND THE BIG HUNGRY BEAR

*By Don and Audrey Wood*

*Illustrated by Don Wood*

*The tale of how a little mouse is tricked into sharing his strawberry before the big hungry bear can find it. The full page illustrations, drawn large from a mouse's perspective, never show the narrator who is speaking to the mouse. Witty and marvelously executed illustrations presented in a large format suitable for a group of children to enjoy.*

## Circle Time Presentation

Ask the children to look at the cover of THE LITTLE MOUSE, THE RED RIPE STRAW-BERRY, AND THE BIG HUN-GRY BEAR. Have them decide what the mouse is doing and what he is intends to do with the big red ripe strawberry. Then read the title of the book and ask the children to predict what they think the little mouse is thinking and what he is planning to do. Read the book and pause at least three times for the children to predict the mouse's actions. After the story, ask the children which illustrations were their favorites. Invariably, they like the picture of the little mouse and the strawberry with disguises of glasses, a fake nose and a moustache.

STORY STRETCHER

## For Art: Making Disguises

**What the children will learn—**
To make paper bag masks

**Materials you will need—**
Brown paper grocery bags, scissors, crayons

**What to do—**

1. Let the children decorate the grocery bag masks. Ask them to make a disguise that would keep the hungry bear away.

2. Assist the children in cutting holes for the eyes and mouth.

3. Cut the sides of the paper bag mask so that it can open up on the shoulders.

4. Let the children wear their disguises to the snack table and have the snack helpers try to guess who is inside.

**Something to think about—**
Add yarn and scraps of construction paper for the children to continue refining their disguises during the week.

STORY STRETCHER

## For Cooking And Snack Time: Fresh Strawberries

**What the children will learn—**
To cap, wash and serve fresh strawberries

**Materials you will need—**
A quart of strawberries, teaspoons, colander

**What to do—**

1. Demonstrate how to wash the strawberries under a gentle flow of tap water, then place them in a colander to drain.

2. Show the cooking and snack helpers how to remove the caps from the strawberries by using the edge of a teaspoon.

3. Let the helpers serve the strawberries to their classmates during snack time.

**Something to think about—**
Serve the fresh strawberries, then taste frozen ones and strawberry jam and preserves.

STORY STRETCHER

## For Creative Dramatics: Mouse's Story And Our Disguises

**What the children will learn—**
To act like mouse might have acted

**Materials you will need—**
Disguises from the Art activity

**What to do—**

1. Have the children seated on the circle time rug with their disguises made in Art in front of them on the rug.

2. Decide on a signal for starting and stopping the acting of each scene. You might clap your hands.

3. Ask the children to pretend to be little mouse. In the first scene

where he is carrying a ladder, have them stand up and pretend to carry a ladder.

**4.** Continue with improvised actions for each scene. When it comes to the scene of the mouse in disguise, have the children put on their disguises and say to them, "The big hungry bear can find a red ripe strawberry and a little mouse, no matter how they are disguised." Touch each child's head as a signal to take off the disguises.

**5.** Continue improvising mouse's expressions and actions through the end of the story.

**Something to think about—**
Young children can work in pairs and look at each other's expressions for ideas of how to show mouse's feelings and actions. Older children can pantomime parts of the story and the audience can guess which scenes they are performing.

S T O R Y   S T R E T C H E R

## For Library Corner: Tape Recording Mouse's Treat

**What the children will learn—**
To use their voices to create a mood

**Materials you will need—**
Cassette tape and recorder

**What to do—**
**1.** Read THE LITTLE MOUSE, THE RED RIPE STRAWBERRY, AND THE BIG HUNGRY BEAR.

**2.** Tell the children that you like stories filled with suspense and surprise. Ask a child where in the story he started to worry about the big hungry bear. Have the child turn to that page.

**3.** Ask another child what picture in the story was a surprise to her. Let her turn to that illustration.

**4.** Have the children answer questions throughout the story. Look through the book and find all the questions. Decide who will answer each question. For instance, when the narrator says, "What are you doing?" let one child tell what the little mouse is doing. Continue the process throughout the book.

**5.** Practice reading the book with the children answering the questions.

**6.** Have one child provide the page turning signal by saying, "Uh-oh," in a suspenseful voice when it is time to turn the page.

**7.** Record the story, with the answers to the questions and reading the text.

**8.** Let the recorders be first to hear the tape for the listening station.

**Something to think about—**
Omit answering the questions for young children and have the entire group say the "Uh-oh" page turning signal.

S T O R Y   S T R E T C H E R

## For Music And Movement: Mouse's March

**What the children will learn—**
To march like mouse guarding the strawberry

**Materials you will need—**
Cassette or record recording of march music, player

**What to do—**
**1.** Show the children the illustration of mouse marching with the key on his shoulder that unlocks the lock on the red, ripe strawberry.

**2.** Demonstrate how guards march back and forth in front of something they are protecting.

**3.** Have the children pretend to put a big key on their shoulders like mouse did. Tell them to pre-tend that your story time chair is the red, ripe strawberry.

**4.** Turn on the march music, and have the children march back and forth in front of the red, ripe strawberry.

**5.** Let the marchers go single file marching round the room, then stop the music and have them march as partners two by two, then by threes.

**Something to think about—**
Older children can improvise marching, skipping and galloping. Younger children can practice simply staying in step with the music.

# TALL AND FUNNY TALES

## HERE COMES THE CAT!

*By Vladimir Vagin and*

*Frank Asch*

*An historical undertaking, HERE COMES THE CAT! was the first children's book to be designed and illustrated cooperatively between a Russian and an American artist. The book contains only one phrase of dialogue, "Here comes the cat!" which is printed in both Russian and English. A mouse, the rodent Paul Revere, alerts all that the cat is coming. He rides on a bicycle, swims in a lake, flies in a hot air balloon and sounds the alarm. The surprise ending to this brightly colored book is that there is no cause for alarm; the cat arrives pulling a wagon of cheese.*

## Circle Time Presentation

On the inside cover of the book, the reader is told how to pronounce, "Here comes the cat!" in Russian. Practice saying the phrase until you are comfortable with it before you read to the children. Read the book through the first time and have the children join you in saying in English, "Here comes the cat!" Teach the children how to say, "Here comes the cat!" in Russian and read the book again. After the reading, ask the children to recall some of the illustrations they like and why. Call attention to the street scene where the signs on buildings and street signs are in both Russian and English.

STORY STRETCHER

## For Art: Cooperative Picture Making

**What the children will learn—**
To communicate in planning, drawing and describing their pictures

**Materials you will need—**
Manilla paper, crayons, markers

**What to do—**

1. Draw the head of a cat on a large sheet of paper and have the aide or a volunteer draw the tail of the cat on another. Put the two pieces together and show the children you have one picture. Tell the children that first you and your partner had to talk about what you would draw, decide who would draw each part, then make the drawing.

2. Show the book jacket photographs of Vladimir Vagin and Frank Asch and their head and tail pictures on their easels. Read the paragraphs on the book jacket and discuss that they were not in the same room but in different countries when they cooperated to finish their pictures.

3. Pair children into cooperation partnerships.

4. Ask the children to decide on a real or imaginary animal they would like to draw together, and then one draws the head and the other draws the tale.

5. After the drawing is completed, ask the children to finish coloring and decorating their drawings.

6. Draw a cartoon balloon and announce, "Here comes the _____!" and write in the name of the real or imaginary animal the children drew together.

7. Display their cooperative pictures near the library area where HERE COMES THE CAT! is on the book shelves.

**Something to think about—**
Younger children can use one large sheet of paper, rather than two sheets, and make a picture together. Older children can think of a usual enemy for their animals and draw another cooperative picture showing there was nothing to fear.

STORY STRETCHER

## For Block Building: A Mouse Village

**What the children will learn—**
To plan and build the houses and buildings of a little village

**Materials you will need—**
Variety of small building blocks, index cards, scissors, markers, tape

**What to do—**

1. With the children who often choose block building activities, discuss what materials are in the room that could be used to build a mouse village similar to the one in HERE COMES THE CAT!

2. Let the block builders collect their set of blocks from around the room.

3. If possible, designate a table for the mouse village or an area of the classroom where the project can continue for several days.

4. Let the builders build the mouse village and after much of it is finished, ask them to make signs for the buildings.

5. When the building reaches a plateau of activity, brainstorm with them about other buildings that might be included. Look back at the illustrations in HERE COMES THE CAT! for inspiration.

**Something to think about—**
Older children can make village buildings from painted milk cartons and boxes of various sizes.

STORY STRETCHER

## For Cooking And Snack Time: Cheese And Crackers

**What the children will learn—**
To use a cheese slicer

**Materials you will need—**
Variety of mild cheeses in rounds and blocks, crackers, pitcher, juice, plates, napkins

**What to do—**
1. Demonstrate how to use a cheese slicer.

2. Tell the children about the names of the cheeses you have selected.

3. Let the children slice their samples of the different cheeses. Serve with their crackers and their favorite juice.

4. During snack time, ask the children to tell which cheese they prefer.

**Something to think about—**
Also consider serving cheese logs and a cheese spread. Let the chil-

dren cut and spread the cheese preparations. If your state has a cheese product, be sure to serve a local cheese as well.

STORY STRETCHER

## For Library Corner: Writing A New Adventure For Mouse And Cat

**What the children will learn—**
To predict actions based on what is already known

**Materials you will need—**
Variety of sizes of lined and unlined paper, writing instruments — pens, pencils, markers

**What to do—**
1. With the children who come to the writing area during choice time, read again HERE COMES THE CAT!

2. Ask the children what they think might have happened if the writers had written more pages at the end of the book. What would happen next? Let the children brainstorm more possibilities than there are writers in the area.

3. Give the children a choice of writing papers and writing instruments and encourage them to write about one of the ideas mentioned or another one they may think of for the cat and the mouse.

4. While the children are writing or drawing the next scenes, interact with them when they appear to be "stuck" and can't decide what to say or draw next.

**Something to think about—**
Writing is a noisy activity. Young children write and talk in a writing session, just as they need to talk and draw in an art session. Encourage writing even if it is scribbling. If you have scribblers who insist they do not know how to write, ask them to make marks that

look like writing. If you have children who know some letters but who do not know what sounds and letters match, encourage them to write using whatever letters they know. If you have children who know letter names and sound-symbol relationships who insist they do not know how to spell a word, tell them to write it the way they think it is spelled. The important point to remember is to have children write using whatever they know at this time, just as they draw using whatever abilities they have at the time.

STORY STRETCHER

## For Music And Movement: The Pink Panther Theme For "Here Comes The Cat!"

**What the children will learn—**
To move in response to the music

**Materials you will need—**
Recording of "The Pink Panther Theme Song" by Henry Mancini, cassette or record player, record or cassette cover showing Pink Panther

**What to do—**
1. At a second circle time of the day, tell the children that you have a record about a cat, but it is not a cat bringing cheese. However, when people hear this music they know a cat is coming.

2. Ask the children to just listen at first. Play the first few bars of "The Pink Panther." You will know immediately which children recognize the theme music. Ask one of these children what color this cat is.

3. Show them the cover of the record or the cassette tape and discuss that they might have heard this music on television.

4. Play the entire theme song while the children are seated but move your shoulders, hands and arms, swaying in time to the music.

5. With about five children at a time, dance to the music while the others continue the swaying in time. Then stop the music and invite five other children to join you. Continue until all the children have been asked.

**Something to think about—**
If you have children who do not want to dance, let them continue swaying in the audience. On other days when the children have a better sense of the entire piece, let them dance around the room.

# REFERENCES

Brown, Ruth. (1981). **A DARK DARK TALE.** New York: Dial Books for Young Readers.

Eastman, P. D. (1960). **ARE YOU MY MOTHER?** New York: Beginner Books, Random House.

Thomas, Patricia. (1971). Illustrated by Wallace Tripp. **"STAND BACK," SAID THE ELEPHANT, "I'M GOING TO SNEEZE!"** New York: Lothrop, Lee & Shepard Books.

Vagin, Vladimir, & Asch, Frank. (1989). **HERE COMES THE CAT!** New York: Scholastic.

Wood, Don, & Wood, Audrey. (1989). Illustrated by Don Wood. **THE LITTLE MOUSE, THE RED RIPE STRAWBERRY, AND THE BIG HUNGRY BEAR.** London: Child's Play.

## Additional References For Tall And Funny Tales

Holabird, Katharine. (1988). Illustrated by Helen Craig. **ALEXANDER AND THE DRAGON.** New York: Clarkson N. Potter, Inc. *A very small boy is afraid of the dark, especially when the shadow under his head becomes a fierce dragon. He soon learns, however, that even dragons have their gentle side.*

McKee, Craig, B., & Holland, Margaret. (1985). **A PEACOCK ATE MY LUNCH.** Worthington, OH: Willowisp Press. *A little girl has many imaginary animals who do things with her throughout the day until she finds a friend. Now she and her new friends share their imaginary animals.*

Orama, Hiawyn. (1984). Illustrated by Satoshi Kitamura. **IN THE ATTIC.** New York: Henry Holt. *A child imagines many interesting things to do in the attic.*

Ross, Tony. (1984). **I'M COMING TO GET YOU.** New York: Dial Books for Young Readers. *Somewhere in an unknown galaxy, a hairy howling creature is out to get little Tommy Brown, but there is a surprise ending about the creature's size.*

Steig, William. (1982). **DOCTOR DESOTO.** New York: Scholastic. *A Newbery Honor Book, a classic wit versus strength tale about a mouse dentist who outfoxes the fox who wants to eat him.*

# APPENDIX

# Steps in Binding a Book

 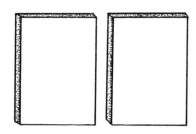 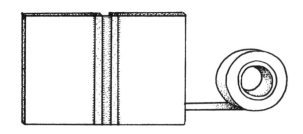

**1.** Cut two pieces of heavy cardboard slightly larger than the pages of the book.

**2.** With wide masking tape, tape the two pieces of cardboard together with ½-inch space between.

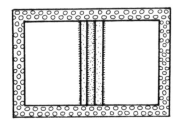  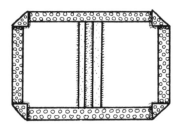

**3.** Cut outside cover 1½ inches larger than the cardboard and stick to cardboard (use thinned white glue if cover material is not self-adhesive.)

**4.** Fold corners over first, then the sides.

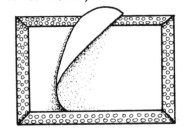 

**5.** Measure and cut inside cover material and apply as shown.

**6.** Place stapled pages of the book in the center of the cover. Secure with two strips of inside cover material, one at the front of the book and the other at the back.

242

# Directions for Making Muffins

1. Preheat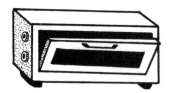

2. Place  in

3. Empty  into

4. Add 1  and ½  water

5. Stir

6. Pour into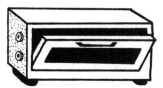

7. Bake in

8. Serve and

# BASIC ART DOUGH

*the best and easiest uncooked dough*

**MATERIALS:**
4 cups flour
1 cup iodized salt
1¾ cups warm water
bowl

**PROCESS:**
1. mix all ingredients in bowl
2. knead 10 minutes
3. model as with any clay
4. bake 300° until hard
5. or air dry for a few days

# INDEX

## Authors and Illustrators

# Titles

This * indicates titles of the books used as the foundation for the STORY S-T-R-E-T-C-H-E-R-S. If only one name is listed, the author is also the illustrator.

## Centers or Activities

### Art Activities

# More Story S-t-r-e-t-c-h-e-r-s® Title Information

| PUBLISHER | TITLE | AUTHOR | ISBN |
|---|---|---|---|
| Black Moss Press | Feelings | Joanne Brisson Murphy | 0-88753-129-6 |
| Child's Play | Quick as a Cricket | Audrey Wood | 0-85953-306-9 |
| | The Little Mouse,...and the Big Hungry Bear | Don and Audrey Wood | 0-85953-182-1 |
| Curtis Brown Ltd. | Owl Moon | Jane Yolen | 0-399-21457-7 |
| Farrar Straus & Giroux | Carl Goes Shopping | Alexandra Day | 0-374-31110-2 |
| Floris | The Mouse and the Potato | Thomas Berger and Carla Grillis | 0-86315-103-5 |
| | The Story of the Root Children | Sibylle Olfers | 0-86315-106-X |
| Good Books | That's What Happens When It's Spring | Elaine W. Good | 0-934672-53-9 |
| Harcourt Brace Jovanovich | Mouse Paint | Ellen Stoll Walsh | 0-15-256025-4 |
| | Planting a Rainbow | Lois Ehlert | 0-15-262609-3 |
| | The Napping House | Audrey Wood | 0-15-256708-9 |
| Harper Collins | A Tree Is Nice | Janice May Udry | 0-06-026155-2 |
| | Big Red Barn | Margaret Wise Brown | 0-06-020748-5 |
| | Harold and the Purple Crayon | Crockett Johnson | 0-06-443022-7 |
| | The Mixed-up Chameleon | Eric Carle | 0-06-443162-2 |
| | The Right Number of Elephants | Jeff Sheppard | 0-06-025615-X |
| | Train Song | Diane Siebert | 0-690-04726-6 |
| | Will Spring Be Early or Late? | Crockett Johnson | 0-06-443224-6 |
| Henry Holt | Listen to the Rain | Bill Martin Jr. & John Archambault | 0-8050-0682-6 |
| | One Cow Moo Moo | David Bennett | 0-8050-1416-0 |
| | The Empty Pot | Demi | 0-8050-1217-6 |
| Houghton-Mifflin | Annie and the Wild Animals | Jan Brett | 0-395-51006-6 |
| | Daddy Makes the Best Spaghetti | Anna Grossnickle Hines | 0-89919-794-9 |
| | Ira Sleeps Over | Bernard Waber | 0-395-20503-4 |
| | Mike Mulligan and His Steam Shovel | Virginia Lee Burton | 0-395-25939-8 |
| | Tacky the Penguin | Helen Lester | 0-395-45536-7 |
| | This Old Man | Carol Jones | 0-395-54699-0 |
| Little Brown | Arthur's Baby | Marc Brown | 0-316-11007-8 |
| | Arthur's Thanksgiving | Marc Brown | 0-316-11060-4 |
| | Dinosaurs Travel: A Guide for Families on the Go | Laurene K. Brown | 0-316-11076-0 |
| | First Flight | David McPhail | 0-316-56323-4 |
| | Lost! | David McPhail | 0-316-56329-3 |
| | One Hungry Monster: A Counting Book in Rhyme | Susan Heyboer O'Keefe | 0-316-63385-2 |
| | Over the River and Through the Woods | Lydia Maria Child | 0-316-13873-8 |
| | Wheels on the Bus | Maryann Kovalski | 0-316-50256-1 |
| Macmillan | A Home | Nola Langer Malone | 0-02-751440-4 |
| | Aaron's Shirt | Deborah Gould | 0-02-736351-1 |
| | Apples and Pumpkins | Anne Rockwell | 0-02-777270-5 |
| | Charlie Anderson | Barbara Abercrombie | 0-689-50486-1 |
| | Keep Looking | Joyce Hunt and Millicent Selsam | 0-02-781840-3 |
| | My Spring Robin | Anne Rockwell | 0-02-777611-5 |
| | Silly Fred | Karen Wagner | 0-02-792280-4 |
| | This Year's Garden | Cynthia Rylant | 0-689-71122-0 |

| PUBLISHER | TITLE | AUTHOR | ISBN |
|---|---|---|---|
| | We're Going on a Bear Hunt | Michael Rosen | 0-689-50476-4 |
| | Wild Wild Sunflower Child, Anna | Nancy White Carlstrom | 0-02-717360-7 |
| Oxford University Press | Squirrels | Brian Wildsmith | 0-19-272105-4 |
| Penguin USA | A Dark Dark Tale | Ruth Brown | 0-8037-0093-8 |
| | A Pocket for Corduroy | Don Freeman | 0-14-050352-8 |
| | Blueberries for Sal | Robert McCloskey | 0-14-050169-X |
| | Gilberto and the Wind | Marie Hall Ets | 0-14-050276-9 |
| | I Like Me | Nancy Carlson | 0-670-82062-8 |
| | Madeline | Ludwig Bemelmans | 0-670-44580-0 |
| | Make Way for Ducklings | Robert McCloskey | 0-670-45149-5 |
| | Pretend You're a Cat | Jean Marzollo | 0-8037-0773-8 |
| | Sloppy Kisses | Elizabeth Winthrop | 0-14-050433-8 |
| | Something to Crow About | Megan Halsey Lane | 0-8037-0697-9 |
| | The Snowy Day | Ezra Jack Keats | 0-670-65400-0 |
| | The Temper Tantrum Book | Edna Preston Mitchell | 0-14-050181-9 |
| | There's a Nightmare in My Closet | Mercer Mayer | 0-8037-8682-4 |
| | Where Butterflies Grow | Joanne Ryder | 0-525-67284-2 |
| Picture Book Studio | Rooster's Off to See the World | Eric Carle | 0-88708-042-1 |
| Putnam | A Walk in the Rain | Ursel Scheffler | 0-399-21267-1 |
| | Alice's Blue Cloth | Deborah van der Beek | 0-399-21622-7 |
| | Animals Born Alive and Well | Ruth Heller | 0-488-01822-5 |
| | Goldilocks and the Three Bears | Jan Brett | 0-399-22004-6 |
| | Little Bear's Trousers | Jane Hissey | 0-399-22016-X |
| | My Great Grandpa | Martin Waddell | 0-399-22155-7 |
| | Plants That Never Ever Bloom | Ruth Heller | 0-488-18964-X |
| | The Cat's Midsummer Jamboree | David Kherdian | 0-399-22222-7 |
| | The Very Quiet Cricket | Eric Carle | 0-399-21885-8 |
| Random House | Are You My Mother? | P. D. Eastman | 0-394-80018-4 |
| | Baby Animals | Margaret Wise Brown | 0-394-92040-6 |
| | Herbie Hamster, Where Are You? | Terence Blacker | 0-679-80838-8 |
| | How Many Trucks Can a Tow Truck Tow? | Charlotte Pomerantz | 0-394-88775-1 |
| Scholastic | Caps, Hats, Socks, and Mittens | Louise Borden | 0-590-41257-4 |
| | Clifford's Birthday Party | Norman Bridwell | 0-590-41258-2 |
| | Here Comes the Cat! | Vladimir Vagin & Frank Asch | 0-590-41859-9 |
| | Is Your Mama a Llama? | Deborah Guarino | 0-590-41387-2 |
| | Jump Frog Jump! | Robert Kalan | 0-590-40063-0 |
| Simon and Schuster | Chicka Chicka Boom Boom | Bill Martin, Jr & John Archambault | 0-671-67949-X |
| Warne | Tale of Peter Rabbit | Beatrix Potter | 0-7232-3460-4 |
| William Morrow | "Stand Back," said the Elephant,"I'm Going to Sneeze" | Patricia Thomas | 0-688-09338-8 |
| | Bugs | Nancy Winslow Parker | 0-688-06623-2 |
| | Color Dance | Ann Jonas | 0-688-05990-2 |
| | Jessica | Kevin Henkes | 0-688-07829-X |
| | Loving | Ann Morris | 0-688-06340-3 |
| | My Brown Bear Barney | Dorothy Butler | 0-688-08567-9 |
| | My Friend Leslie | Maxine Rosenberg | 0-688-01690-1 |
| | We Are Best Friends | Aliki | 0-688-07037-X |
| | White Snow, Bright Snow | Alvin Tresselt | 0-688-41164-4 |